D1223193

GLOBALIZATION THRUST: DRIVING NATIONS COMPETITIVE

GLOBALIZATION THRUST: DRIVING NATIONS COMPETITIVE

RAJAGOPAL

Nova Science Publishers, Inc.
New York

Copyright © 2009 by Nova Science Publishers, Inc.

All rights reserved. No part of this book may be reproduced, stored in a retrieval system or transmitted in any form or by any means: electronic, electrostatic, magnetic, tape, mechanical photocopying, recording or otherwise without the written permission of the Publisher.

For permission to use material from this book please contact us:
Telephone 631-231-7269; Fax 631-231-8175
Web Site: http://www.novapublishers.com

NOTICE TO THE READER

The Publisher has taken reasonable care in the preparation of this book, but makes no expressed or implied warranty of any kind and assumes no responsibility for any errors or omissions. No liability is assumed for incidental or consequential damages in connection with or arising out of information contained in this book. The Publisher shall not be liable for any special, consequential, or exemplary damages resulting, in whole or in part, from the readers' use of, or reliance upon, this material. Any parts of this book based on government reports are so indicated and copyright is claimed for those parts to the extent applicable to compilations of such works.

Independent verification should be sought for any data, advice or recommendations contained in this book. In addition, no responsibility is assumed by the publisher for any injury and/or damage to persons or property arising from any methods, products, instructions, ideas or otherwise contained in this publication.

This publication is designed to provide accurate and authoritative information with regard to the subject matter covered herein. It is sold with the clear understanding that the Publisher is not engaged in rendering legal or any other professional services. If legal or any other expert assistance is required, the services of a competent person should be sought. FROM A DECLARATION OF PARTICIPANTS JOINTLY ADOPTED BY A COMMITTEE OF THE AMERICAN BAR ASSOCIATION AND A COMMITTEE OF PUBLISHERS.

LIBRARY OF CONGRESS CATALOGING-IN-PUBLICATION DATA

Rajagopal, 1957-
> Globalization thrust : driving nations competitive / Rajagopal.
>   p. cm.
> ISBN 978-1-60456-712-0 (hardcover)
> 1. Competition, International. 2. International trade.
> 3. International economic relations. 4. Globalization. I. Title.
> HF1414.R34 2008
> 337--dc22
>   2008023431

HF1414
.R34
2009

0231946856

Published by Nova Science Publishers, Inc. ✛ New York

CONTENTS

PREFACE

The world is rapidly changing today in reference to business, technology and innovation. The human needs are uniformly spreading across the countries which demand greater negotiations and free movement of goods and services. While people continue to live in local realities in the developing countries, these realities are increasingly being challenged and integrated into larger global networks of relationships[1]. The span of expansion of multinational companies across the developing countries towards the manufacturing and services activities endorse the concerns of globalization. The international business thus encompasses a wide range of activities involved in conducting business transactions across the countries, and international marketing functions specifically deal with the strategies associated with the marketing of products and services therein. However, the globalization has created a great deal of debate in economic, policy and grassroots circles the world over. The increasing complexity of globalization may be seen in various dimensions such as economic, political, cultural, legal and technology management, which necessitate a new paradigm for learning and teaching. International marketing is one of the strongest offshoots of globalization in managing business activities across national boundaries conceptualizing one world.

Globalization can be described as the combined influences of trade liberalization, market integration, international finance and investment, technological change, the increasing distribution of production across national boundaries and the emergence of new structures of global governance. The global market place equipped with the application of global communications has become the focus of the global business arena that makes the world markets remain open and involved in the fair competitive practices. Supporters of the globalization concept also argue that allowing free trade and capital movement would also encourage workers to move from one country to another, partly to find better employment opportunities. New growth-trade theories have emphasized the contribution of international trade to economic growth through its effect on capital accumulation. Free trade leads to specialization, contributes to the total factor productivity and offers comparative advantages for the other countries. Trade openness also expands potential markets that allow the domestic companies to take advantage of economies of scale and to diffuse technology, innovation and managerial practices through close alliances with the foreign firms. However, free trade generates neck-to-neck competition among countries for economic sustainability and for the

---

[1] Rajagopal (2007), International Marketing: Global Environment, Corporate Strategy and Case Studies, Vokas Publishing House, New Delhi, pp vii-ix.

ability to essentially for compete against the best in the world. In this adaptation from *Race for the World*, globalization explores the economic benefits of free trade and looks at how the changing landscape will force many companies to reevaluate their strengths and weaknesses.

During the early stage of economic transition, it was presumed that the newly liberalized economies in Central and Eastern Europe would experience high rates of sustained economic growth, with rapid convergence towards trade and economy of the major industrialized economies in the West. A key factor of the transition process is the structural change consisting in the reallocation of resources on the basis of market incentives. Variability in the production and consumption behavior is therefore a potentially useful concept in analyzing the structural changes that have actually occurred in Eastern European transition economies. Among the Central and Eastern European countries, the Polish transition can be viewed as the most successful one in terms of growth levels. Overall impact of political and economic disintegration on trade among the former constituent republics of three demised federations in central and Eastern Europe, the Soviet Union, Yugoslavia, and Czechoslovakia has been followed by a sharp fall in trade intensity, although the legacy of a common past remains strong. However, the process of integration into the world economy has not been uniform across transition countries. After long inward-looking trade policies and import-substituting industrialization, several Latin American countries undertook comprehensive trade liberalization and macroeconomic adjustment in the 1980s and the experience of these countries has been relevant for the economies in Eastern Europe and the former Soviet Union in transition from socialism to market economies.

Globalization in economic reference may be explained as a historical process which has emerged, as the result of continuous development of civilization, human needs, innovation and technological progress. It endorses integration of various types of economies around the world—developed, developing and transitional—particularly through the flow of trade and financial operations. As far as the efficient generation and use of public resources are concerned, much has been done to make the value-added tax system efficient and to privatize public enterprises. In response to the liberalization of economies, there has been significant increase in the imports, primarily due to lower inflation, lesser government intervention, and fewer trade barriers. Globalization aimed at offering extensive opportunities with outward-oriented policies which were designed to bring dynamism and greater prosperity to reach developing countries. Its effects became visual as the time advanced, which has been evidenced by East Asia, transforming it from one of the poorest areas of the world. The living standards in the east-Asian region rose and it became possible to make progress on democracy and economic issues such as the environment and work standards.

In the arena of global trade, coalitions have been traditionally formed within countries, and occasionally, among countries, in order to protect the domestic production of particular goods, services, or sectors of the economy[2]. However, oil and interest rate shocks in the world economy during the 1980s, coupled with debt crises and the rise of a more market oriented economic philosophy, brought about a dismantling of organized protectionism in many countries, eroding the coalitions which had so tightly resisted trade liberalization[3]. Alongside regionalism, the world trading order, the last decade has been marked by increased

---

[2] Rogowski R: *Commerce and Coalitions*, Princeton University Press, Princeton, NJ, 1989.
[3] Goldstine J: International Institutions and Domestic Politics: GATT, WTO and the Liberalization of International Trade, in Krueger A (Ed.) *The WTO as an International Organization*, University of Chicago Press, Chicago, Illinois, 1998.

Institutionalization. This has opened up a new, wider set of issues and interests around which future coalitions of countries may well form. Prior to the Uruguay round, and during the pre-negotiations of that round, developing countries had formed a coalition of 'the South'. The Group of Ten (G-10), led by a 'Big Five' comprising Argentina, Brazil, Egypt, India and Yugoslavia, formed as soon as the US began its push to launch a new round of trade negotiations. The coalition of developing countries successfully blocked some aspects of the US initiatives. However, the G-10 soon found itself split in trying to formulate negotiating positions on the various aspects of trade[4].

The pursuit of industrial success or export competitiveness has become a principal policy goal for governments and industries in the advanced countries. The concept of competitiveness raises concerns amongst the neo-classical economists because it implies the need to capture market share in industries that will result in expanding domestic incomes in the form of higher wages and profits. It goes beyond the need to achieve efficiency or productivity in industries in which a nation has a natural advantage. The discussion in the book analyzes this. After decades of slow growth in many developing countries, international trade has shown optimistic results in recent years following the international trade agreements. The export competitiveness of a country is also significantly driven by the resources availability in the country and by harnessing them. These resources may broadly be classified as natural, monetary, research and development, production and market infrastructure and human resources.

There is an increasing interest among the students to pursue courses related to international relations, international economics and international trade in the undergraduate and graduate programs offered by the universities all over the world. In addition, international trade and economy have become an integral part of management education. There is not enough work done on convergence of international trade and economy from the perspective of management instruction.

Discussions in this book address the impact of globalization among the developing countries towards enhancing international trade and working out effective economic reforms to stimulate overall growth in the country. The role of international institutions like World Trade Organization and various preferential trade agreements among the developed and developing countries has also been analytically discussed in the book. The discussions delineate economic and political factors along with the technological perspectives thereof towards the export growth and competitiveness among developing countries and analyze trade competitiveness in view of the economic reforms and trade liberalization. The roles of a country's specific policies to assure the success of trade liberalization, organizational backing and international concerns have also been analyzed in the book. The readers will find global trade and economic developments illustrated in each chapter of the book amidst the conceptual discussion. The pedagogy of the book includes:

- Short and contemporary illustration in the chapters between the texts to provide readers with contextual examples from the real business houses
- Strategy focus placed in boxes in appropriate chapters illustrating various marketing situations to enhance the contextual knowledge and interest in the subject

---

[4] Kumar R: Developing Country Coalitions in International Trade Negotiations, in Tussie D and Glover D (Eds) *The Developing Countries in World Trade*, Lynne Rienner, Boulder Colorado, 1995.

- Short cases at the end of the book to comprehend the applied perspectives of knowledge on the subject

The new concepts on international trade dynamics, economic shifts and international relations among the developing and developed amidst growing competitive pressures are also strategically focused upon in various chapters in the book. In all, this book contributes to the existing literature and serves as a learning post to the students and a think tank for students, researchers and diplomats. One of the extended objectives of this book is to help readers understand the subject comprehensively and keep them informed about the global shifts in trade and economy across nations in an increasingly competitive environment.

The writing of this book has run into a long span of three years which consumed considerable time on reviewing the literature in the discussions of various topics. The development of comprehensive cases tagged to each chapter of the book has also been a mounting task. I express my thanks to my daughter Ananya for being instrumental in drawing the Tables and charts in this book. My son Amritanshu always stood by with me in the hectic times of revising the draft which helped me in de-stressing and regaining the energy back to work. Finally, I express my deep gratitude to my wife Arati Rajagopal who copy-edited the first draft of the manuscript and stayed in touch till the final proofs were cross checked. She has been the light of the spirit in carrying this comprehensive work.

Chapter 1

UNDERSTANDING GLOBALIZATION

Open trade, competitiveness and emergence of global markets for standardized consumer products are the new commercial reality which has driven the developing nations with a high magnitude of change in the economy and consumer culture. Technology, by accelerating communication, transport and travel, drives the world toward a converging commonality. Well-managed companies have moved from emphasis on customizing items to offering globally standardized products that are advanced, functional, reliable, and low priced. They benefit from enormous economies of scale in production, distribution, marketing, and management. Such dynamism in the business and related activities portrays the functional concepts of globalization. While sometimes globalization is endorsed as primarily a synonym for global business, it is much more than that. The same forces that allow businesses to operate as if national borders do not exist also allow social activists, labor organizers, journalists, academics, and many others to work on a global stage. Today we live in a world which is very different from the one that existed half a century before—a multi-polar world of multiple interests bound together by trade, investment and technology as never before. But it is also a world whose security and equilibrium is no less dependent on a strong transatlantic partnership where not only interests but also values and visions are shared[1]. The contemporary economies of many countries are operating at the leading edge of economic integration, and the accelerating pace of globalization gives work an importance which reaches well beyond the regional dynamics. More and more small and medium size companies are developing alliances with corporate giants in striving to exploit international growth markets and inducing the global economy to work locally by capitalizing on the resources that distinguish one place from another[2].

THE DEBATE – FOR AND AGAINST GLOBALIZATION

Globalization can be described as the combined influences of trade liberalization, market integration, international finance and investment, technological change, the increasing distribution of production across national boundaries and the emergence of new structures

---

[1] Renato Ruggiero: Regional initiatives, global impact: cooperation and the multilateral system, Speech of former Director General, WTO, 07 November 1997, WTO News.
[2] Kanter, R M (1995), Thriving Locally in the Global Economy, *Harvard Business Review* 73 (5), 151-160.

global governance. The global market place equipped with the application of global of communications has become the focus of the global business arena that makes the world markets remain open and involved in the fair competitive practices. At the same time the anti-globalization moves also exist in the process of development that protest against the hazards of suppressive strategies of the global companies affecting the regional trade entities. The efficient multinational companies from the leading countries enter the secured country markets and drain out the regional players from the benefit market segments. However, many Japanese companies have not lived to the anticipated success against the international competition. Consequently, the Japanese markets that were long protected under various tariff and non-tariff barriers were removed by the government nodding to the global business trends of liberalizations. The prominent business moves of the multi-national companies include Japanese electronics and automobile companies, Germany's BMW, Ciba –Geigy, Nestlé, Proctor and Gamble etc. Operating in the global environment requires mastered skills to penetrate into the host countries particularly during conditions when the trade barriers and government protections have been removed and business policies have been restructured. The phenomenon of the global customer is growing in importance every day and so too is the global-customer-centric organization. Yet many companies, especially those designed according to function, country and business unit, are having difficulty re-designing and aligning their structure with the needs of the global customer. The reasons for the globalization of business have been revealed in many ways, of these the significant variables include:

- market saturation in home country
- trade deficit and long disequilibrium in the balance of trade
- increasing foreign competition
- emergence of new markets
- globalization and free trade zones
- opportunities via foreign aid programs

Globalization and its impacts have profound implications for a broad range of issues important to the funding community. These issues range from the sustainable use of the worlds' resources and the protection and preservation of the environment, to the need to improve living standards, safeguard human rights, promote and protect cultures, and ensure democratic and responsive global governance. While the idea of globalization has only recently captured public attention, "globalization" has been occurring for centuries.

Globalization of market opportunities were observed as the outgrowth of the above factors and the scope of such marketing opportunities has increased with the continued deregulation of the significant functional sectors like financial services, leisure industry, information technology etc.

The globalization of labor has benefited advanced economies: it has expanded export opportunities considerably and, by lowering input costs and improving production efficiencies, has boosted productivity and output[3]. The largest and powerful multinational business houses prefer to be aggressive to dominate over the most demanding and emerging

---

[3] Florence Jaumotte and Irina Tytell (2007), Labor globalization: Bane or boon, *IMF Survey Magazine*, IMF Research Department, April.

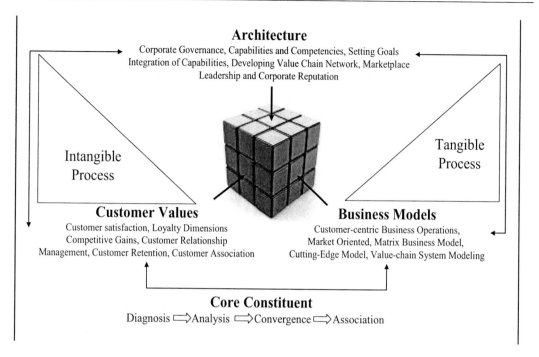

Architecture
Corporate Governance, Capabilities and Competencies, Setting Goals
Integration of Capabilities, Developing Value Chain Network, Marketplace
Leadership and Corporate Reputation

Intangible
Process

Tangible
Process

Customer Values
Customer satisfaction, Loyalty Dimensions
Competitive Gains, Customer Relationship
Management, Customer Retention, Customer Association

Business Models
Customer-centric Business Operations,
Market Oriented, Matrix Business Model,
Cutting-Edge Model, Value-chain System Modeling

Core Constituent
Diagnosis ⇒ Analysis ⇒ Convergence ⇒ Association

Figure 1.1. Global Business Architecture Process.

sectors. General Motors for example is offering credit cards and supermarket groups routinely now offer gasoline, banking, pensions and saving plans apart from the manufacturing and marketing of automobiles. The privatization of the state and public sector ventures like energy, transport and communication led to industry restructuring and further allowed the multinational companies to compete in these countries. The entry to the liberalized state and public sector industries brought more professional rules and guidelines for implementing the quality standards like ISO. But there has been a backlash against liberalism. The traditional calls for intervention to "save" jobs or redistribute wealth still strike a chord. Moreover, many people dislike the fact that seemingly impersonal market forces hold sway over their lives, even though markets in fact reflect the combined preferences of millions of ordinary people. And there is a widespread distrust of the profit motive, as if making losses was preferable.

Globalization is not new, but it is more pervasive than before. A century ago, for instance, there was more cross-border migration than there is now. Throughout the past century, new technologies have continuously caused upheaval. But now in the media age, people are constantly confronted with change that they would otherwise not be aware of. There has been a strong social and political reaction in the initial phase of building the concept of globalization across the countries. The global business process stood by the customers and many firms are engaged in developing customer-centric marketing strategies. The convergence of customer and corporate strategies are one of the core constitutes of global business policies. Such business policy convergence has been explained in Figure 1.1. The anti-globalization arguments were cropped up in reference to economic integration, social integration, and political integration. A study using panel data for 123 countries in 1970-2000 analyses empirically the effects of the overall index of globalization as well as sub-indexes constructed by measuring the single dimensions on economic growth. The results show that globalization promotes growth–but not to an extent necessary to reduce poverty on a large scale. The dimensions most robustly related with growth refer to actual economic flows and restrictions in developed countries. Although less robustly, information flows also promote growth whereas political integration has no effect[4]. The globalization of capital and product markets has many implications for economic welfare. Countries can specialize in the production of goods for which they have comparative advantages, and capital is allocated more efficiently. However, one potentially adverse effect of globalization is the possibility that business cycle volatility might increase. Rapid and badly coordinated capital account liberalization has been blamed for enhancing the vulnerability of emerging markets to unstable international capital flows. At the same time, business cycle volatility in OECD countries seems to have been on a decline in the past decades.

There has been substantial thinking blown in favor of the globalization. Economists, management experts and statisticians were of the strong notion that big demographic and social lifestyle shifts will impact business in this new decade, century, and millennium: fickle fashions, ageing but wealthy populations, retired people inheriting trillions of dollars, an aggressive war for top talent, female consumer influence, human cloning, medical breakthroughs, and a host of other factors, including the huge untapped challenge of mega-city markets in emerging economies. The education system in India continued to be based on the colonial legacy of bureaucratic administration even after fifty years of independence. But, under globalization and liberalization policies of the government, engineering higher education has acquired a new interpretation of increasing *credential* value, where the degree per se is more important for securing a high-paying job, primarily in the software and information technology sector, than for acquiring specific knowledge and skills. This is reflected in the employment pattern of the graduates with a core engineering background[5]. These changes are fundamental to the shape of business because they will alter the way people think and feel.

Globalization and migration intensify relations of interdependence between individuals all over the world and lead to complex forms of social and cultural diversity both within and across societies. The changing structure of family patterns and processes of individualization also contribute to growing diversity[6]. Fears that globalization is imposing a deadening cultural uniformity are as ubiquitous as Coca-Cola, McDonald's, and Mickey Mouse. Many people dread that local cultures and national identities are dissolving into a cross-regional consumerism. That cultural imperialism is said to impose American values as well as products, promote the commercial at the expense of the authentic, and substitute shallow gratification for deeper satisfaction. The core issues woven around globalization are that it can free people from the tyranny of geography. Just because someone was born in France does not mean they can only aspire to speak French, eat French food, read French books, and so on. That we are increasingly free to choose our cultural experiences enriches our lives immeasurably. We could not always enjoy the best the world has to offer. Technology is reshaping culture: Just think of the Internet. Individual choice is fragmenting the imposed

[4] Axel Dreher (2003): Does Globalization Affect Growth?, Working Paper, University of Mannheim, Germany, 1-33.
[5] Arun Kumar Duru (2008), Impact of Globalization on Core Engineering Education in India, *Perspectives on Global Development and Technology*, 7 (1), 55-68.
[6] Vinz Dagmar and Dören Martina (2007), Diversity policies and practices - a new perspective for health care, *Journal of Public Health*, 15 (5), 369-376.

uniformity of national cultures. New hybrid cultures are emerging, and regional ones re-emerging. National identity is not disappearing, but the bonds of nationality are loosening. Some of the questions that have strong hold in the debate of globalization seem to be more lashing against the western influence on pushing global trade.

The Russian confectionery market is proving much more dynamic than those of Western Europe, witnessing constant value growth of more than 3 percent between 2006 and 2007. It is also the largest market in Eastern Europe, with a value approaching US$8.4 billion at fixed exchange rates. Moreover, retail value sales are forecast to grow at a compound annual growth rate of more than 5 percent in constant value terms over 2007-2012, with chocolate confectionery realizing the strongest compound annual growth rate of nearly 7 percent This strong performance is due to the growth of premium chocolate confectionery, which has been supported by the rising disposable incomes of Russian consumers. The Russian confectionery market is characterized by the strong position of local producers offering a wide variety of products. Russian consumers are extremely loyal to local brands, as they are considered to be less "artificial", fresher and using recipes that appeal to the domestic consumers. The Russian confectionery market is likely to face further consolidation, led by Nestlé, Wrigley and Kraft. 2007 proved very eventful in terms of acquisitions and the opening of new production facilities by multinational corporations. Wrigley hit a premium chocolate confectionery jackpot by buying Odintsovskaya KF OOO, with its A Korkunov brand, in January 2007. A Korkunov is a very popular chocolate confectionery brand in Russia. With this acquisition, Wrigley indicated its intention of becoming a significant player in Russia's chocolate confectionery market[7].

Cultural diversity has multiple meanings. Diversity within a society refers to the richness of choice within that society. Globalization focuses on diversity across societies, that is, whether societies are becoming more similar. Cross-cultural exchange tends to favor diversity within a society but not across societies. Trade tends to increase diversity over time by accelerating the pace of change and bringing new cultural goods with each era or generation. Cultural similarities tend to come together over time across the regions. That is, although chain restaurants take an increasing percentage of restaurant sales, growth in dining out has led to an expansion of specialty food opportunities. While cross-cultural exchange alters and disrupts each society it touches, it also supports innovation and creative human energies. The author's views are definitely positive on the benefits of cross-cultural exchange. The *creative destruction* of the market creates a plethora of innovative and high-quality creations in many different genres, styles, and media cross-cultural exchange expands the menu of choice, at least provided that trade and markets are allowed to flourish[8]. Since globalization gathered pace in the 1980s, world inequality has also increased. The strong arguments against the globalization move argue that while some developing countries were able to take advantage of trade to improve their standard of living, many fell further behind as they depended on a single commodity. Rich countries invested erratically and selectively in developing countries and continued to protect their own markets. The anti-globalization movement argues that the world trading system is unfair, undemocratic and unsustainable.

---

[7] Irina Kazanchuk (2008), Strategic Acquisitions in Russian Confectionary, Euromonitor Archive, January 07 http://www.euromonitor.com

[8] Tyler Cowen (2002): Creative Destruction: How Globalization Is Changing the World's Cultures. Princeton, NJ: Princeton University Press. P 65.

Few subjects polarize public opinion as much as the role of globalization in developing countries. Foreign direct investment boosts their economic performance by endowing them with new skills, new technologies, and new jobs—all of which increase their standard of living. In reality, global corporations and the developing countries where they invest have symbiotic objectives. Globalization brings broadly positive economic benefits to developing economies, which in turn represent the best hope for the future of global companies. Both sides should recalibrate their approach. The advantages of the globalization may be viewed as it gives ambitious companies access to the best capital, talent, markets, and resources that the world has to offer. On the contrary it generates neck-to-neck competition for survival for some companies, at least—in that every organization is essentially competing against the best in the world. In this adaptation from *Race for the World*, globalization explores the economic benefits of free trade and looks at how the changing landscape will force many companies to reevaluate their strengths and weaknesses. Globalization is both irreversible and, in its present form, unsustainable. What will come after it is far from determined. It could be a war of all against all, world domination by a single superpower, a tyrannical alliance of global elites, global ecological catastrophe, or some combination thereof[9]. Hence at the positive end globalization gets mixed reviews. However, increasing interconnectivity among the world's people seems to promise a *global village* in which the destructive antagonisms of the past can be left behind, replaced by global cooperation and enriching diversity.

DETERMINANTS OF GLOBAL TRADE

The concept of globalization is characterized by a variety of contradictions prominently pertaining to standardization and simultaneously catering to the local needs. Over the period of global thinking it has been encapsulated that the true nature of globalization should reflect in the attributes "think global, act local". The major determinants of the globalization are as below:

- Market access
- Market opportunities
- Industry standards
- Technology, research and development
- Resource management – internal and external
- Products and services
- Customer prerequisites and needs
- Competition
- Business alliances and cooperation
- Distribution and logistics
- Communication
- Strategy implementation and control process

---

[9] Jememy Brecher, Tim Costello, Brendan Smith, Globalization from Below, Southend Press.

Globalization has increased the access to the markets as the remote markets have been reduced following the political and economic changes world-wide. The market access has also been improved by growing trade blocks at the regional level. Such accessibility to the markets is further reinforced by reducing the trade barriers through far-reaching business communication strategies, product and market development programs and customer relations. This situation has given a boost in determining the market opportunities as narrowing the trade barriers helped in deregulating certain sectors of trade such as financial services. The technical operating standards and protocols are being widely adapted to synchronize with the global industry standards. The resources are managed externally to a large extent as the best and lowest cost materials are procured locally by the multinational companies. The benefits of global sourcing for such companies include low cost labor, uniform quality, innovative ideas, access to local markets, economies to scale, lower taxes and duties, lower logistics costs and more consistent supply. However, there are also some risks in global sourcing that might be political, economic, exchange or supplier risks. In globalization, the product life cycles are getting shorter as the new products are penetrating with higher speed in the markets due to technological development and scale of operations. In this process many products are dropped off the product life cycle either at the stage of introduction or growth. There are few products that sustain till the mature stage is passed. The growth of technology and its dynamic synchronization with the industry is converging fast leading towards quick adaptations of global products. The globalization of customer requirements is resulting from the identification of worldwide customer segments of homogeneous preferences across the territorial boundaries. Business-to-consumers and Business-to-business markets are powered by the consumer demands from the global companies as they are perceived more value oriented and of added benefit.

The globalization process reinforces the concept of locality, for a very simple reason: what is traded in a global context must be produced somewhere; global networks must begin and end somewhere. So the emergence of the global dimension in the lives of our societies does not mean the disappearance of locality, but rather, the strengthening of a concept which is at the very source of globalization. Cities are anchorage points for globalization par excellence because few human territories can offer such complex facilities, built up over time, offering so many facets, material and conceptual, inherited and innovative. The process of going global has enabled individuals, corporations and nation-states to influence actions and events around the world faster, deeper and cheaper than ever before and equally to derive benefits for them. Globalization has led to the opening, the vanishing of many barriers and walls, and has the potential for expanding freedom, democracy, innovation, social and cultural exchanges while offering outstanding opportunities for dialogue and understanding[10].

The global competition is observed on both aggressive and defensive dimensions in the market. The companies that are capable of managing appropriate diffusion of technology and the adaptation process among the customer segments are found to be highly successful. Competition among multinationals these days is likely to be a three-dimensional strategic game wherein the moves of an organization in one market are designed to achieve goals in another market in ways that aren't immediately apparent to rivals[11]. There is growing

---

[10] WTO News: Speech excerpt of Director General, Geneva, May 18, 2006 http://www.wto.org/english/news_e/sppl_e/sppl27_e.htm
[11] Ian C. MacMillan, Alexander B. van Putten and Rita Gunther McGrath: Global Competition- What is the First Move, HBS Working Knowledge, Harvard Business School, June 23, 2003.

consensus among international trade negotiators and policymakers that a prime area for future multilateral discussion is competition policy. Competition policy includes antitrust policy (including merger regulation and control) but is often extended to include international trade measures and other policies that affect the structure, conduct, and performance of individual industries. The leading alliances between the major multinational enterprises may be seen in reference to production, finance, and technology and supply chain along with other complementary activities. To compete in the major global markets the multinational companies manage with substantial financial resources. Logistics and the supply chain management is an art of management of flow of materials and products from the source of production to the end user. This system with the multinational companies includes the total flow of material right from the stage of acquisition of raw materials to the delivery of finished products to the customers. The function of distribution is the combination of activities associated with advertising, sales and physical transfer of the goods and services to the retail and wholesale delivery points as is being observed by the global companies in order to establish their competitive strength in the market. The logistics management is an important function handled by such business companies in the marketing process and effective logistics management improve both cost and customer service performance of the company. Globalization of distribution is particularly important for companies using internet for e-commerce as they can operate on economies of scale with wider reach of customers.

The main trading partners of Tanzania are the European Union, Japan, India and Kenya. Its exports are primarily agricultural commodities with coffee, cashew nuts, tobacco and cotton constituting the largest sectors. Tanzania imports mainly machinery, transportation equipment, industrial raw materials, and consumer goods. The decrease in agricultural production during the past few years, attributable to adverse climatic conditions, food and foodstuffs imports have increased sharply. However, the country is actively pursuing a regional integration strategy. It is a signatory of the Common Market for Eastern and Southern Africa (COMESA) - although it has announced its intention to withdraw - and it is a member of the Southern African Development Community (SADC). Tanzania also aims to strengthen the East African Cooperation (EAC) agreement with neighboring Kenya and Uganda. Under the Lomé Convention, Tanzania receives the full range of aide made available to ACP countries by the European Union, the report notes. As a result, many Tanzanian exports to the EU are exempted from import duties. Likewise, Tanzania's goods enjoy non-reciprocal preferential access to the markets of other developed countries through the Generalized System of Preferences. However, due to Tanzania's limited export capacity, the benefits that the country can reap from these preferential arrangements are minimal. Tanzania has been pursuing an aggressive policy of privatization in conjunction with the support it receives from international financial institutions. The intention of the Government is for all *parastatal* entities to be either privatized or liquidated, although no target date for the completion of this process has been announced. Major privatizations are currently under way in the telecommunications and utility sectors as well as in financial services. Tanzania's lack of enforcement mechanisms for intellectual property infringement is currently being addressed and the Government has indicated that enforcement procedures will be strengthened[12].

---

[12] Country information in the cases is based on the report of World Trade Organization: Tanzania-February 2000, Trade Policy Review, Press Release (PRESS/TPRB/128, 21 February 2000).

The rationale of globalization is governed by factors of comparative advantages, sustained product life cycle, production sharing and extent of internalization. The concept of comparative advantages states that even if a country is able to produce all its goods at lower costs than that of another country, the trade still benefits mutually based on the comparative costs. It may be stated that the comparative costs may help in determining the companies to produce goods in the foreign countries that have comparative advantages over the others and decide either to export goods and services or produce therein. The major variables to measure the comparative advantages are land, labor, capital, resources, cost of infrastructure, energy and tax structure. The internalization factor is a prerequisite for a prospecting company to go global. A multinational firm can serve a market across national boundaries either by exporting from a production facility located in the country of the parent company, or from a third country subsidiary, or it can set up production facilities in the market itself. The sourcing policy of the firm is the result of the firm's decisions as to which of its production facilities will service its various final markets. Thus, the firm establishes an international network linking production to markets. The major issues associated with the concepts of internalization of the firms may be observed towards:

- Extension of direct operation of the firm
- Common ownership
- Control the activities of the market
- The companies have the global horizon
- Firms choose the least-cost location for each functional activity
- Benefit-cost equilibrium
- Focuses on motives and decision process

Such a network enables the firm to grow by eliminating external markets in intermediate goods and subsequently by *internalizing* those markets within the firm. When international markets are internalized the transfer of goods and services may take place. The internalization of markets is more significant wherever the research inputs and proprietary technology are an important part of the manufacturing process. The theoretical dimensions of internalization provides an economic rationale for the survival of the multinational companies considering the industry-specific factors (nature and type of product), region-specific product (territorial advantage), country specific factors (SLEPT[13] issues) and company specific factor reflecting on its managerial know-how.

Maquiladora comes from the Spanish word *maquilar* meaning to perform a task for another. In Mexico, the word referred to the portion of grain collected by millers from grinding other farmers' grains. Today, *maquiladora* refers to a Mexican corporation, wholly or predominantly owned by foreigners, which assemble products for export to the U.S. or other foreign country. The *maquila* industry has transformed the border area of Baja California, which includes the cities of Tijuana, Ciudad Juarez and Mexicali from tourist and agricultural areas into thriving industrial centers. The shelter concept divides the operations in the Mexican facility between production functions and administrative functions. The shelter company typically supplies the plant, handles human resources and administrative tasks such

---

[13] SLEPT: Social, legal, economic, political and technological factors.

as accounting, legal issues, permits, tariffs, transportation and customs issues. Under the North American Free Trade Agreement (NAFTA), U.S. businesses are generally encouraged to source more of their raw materials products within North America, and in most cases, only pay customs duties on any non-U.S. portion of their products. For manufacturers, it is a way to remain competitive without moving operations to Asia and face complicated, time consuming, expensive transportation and customs. The close proximity of Mexico allows easy, inexpensive transportation back into the U.S. Plus, the labor force is adult and plentiful. That's why in the more than 30 years since *maquiladoras* were introduced, there are more than 3,500 companies, including Sony, Ford, General Electric, General Motors and Zenith, that have set up *maquila* operations in Mexico[14].

Production sharing is the contemporary global economic trend that is based on the concepts of comparative advantages that offers economic advantages by stages of the production process. The strategy of production sharing has emerged as a solution to an economic problem in developing countries where the absorption of the surplus manpower in industry is a national economic issue. Consequently the developing countries turn to the developed countries as major cost effective labor market in order to share production of labor orient products. Investment in production sharing operations has become an integral part of global efforts to reduce manufacturing costs and has contributed to the accelerated pace of cross-border integration of manufacturing in North America and the Caribbean Basin. Currently, production sharing seems to be a growing practice. This practice offers both the developed and developing countries a scope to share their resources and strengths for the mutual benefits.

GLOBAL TRADE DYNAMICS

Since World War II, international marketing has received increased attention from the governments of developing countries who wish to revamp their economy. Many geo-political changes have taken place in the global marketing scenario because of the external affairs policies of developed nations. Exports have been one of the major determinants to measure the economic growth of a country. Hence international marketing rose into prominence in the global economic order and emerged as a discipline in itself for studying the technical, managerial, socio-cultural and economic processes of a country. Observing the dynamism of the international market was viewed as a major strategy to control a substantial share of the trade of a country in the world market. Such attempts were made by the developing nations in the eighties. Later, in the early nineties, the new GATT proposal and evolution of the WTO opened new horizons in the field of international marketing by pushing the export oriented economy worldwide. Today, the scope of international marketing has grown and includes the manufacturing sector and its services. International marketing broadly includes export and import activities that govern the marketing environment.

The outreach of the global market place has increased manifolds with the emergence of a more open world economy, relaxed trade and tariff barriers, growing customer needs, inter-dependency and inter-communication factors among the countries. The global marketplace consists of population over 6 billion people which is projected to touch the mark of 10 billion

---

[14] *North American Production Sharing Inc.* www.napsmexico.com

people by 2050 according to the estimation of the United Nations. The global market place is becoming economically, culturally and technologically inter-dependent as the convergence of marketing activities has become more effective due to telecommunication and popularity of the electronic commerce. Leading corporations around the world have turned their attention towards expansion of their business activities in order to maintain their competitive edge and retain the customer loyalty. The global business activities of the current period have been described as the second industrial revolution. The organizational reforms are introduced by many multinational companies in view of changing scenarios in the global marketplace and nature of competition. As markets globalize, the need for organizational reforms towards workplace management, operating systems, and work culture emerges. However, the balance between consistency in the changes and adaptation is essential for corporate success[15]. As long as there are not imbalances in the change process, then maybe by introducing the new systems and its rate of adaptation of the change culture, there may not be any threat to the organizational management. The human value system is a synergy of societal values, family values and individual values generated through the influence of culture. The personality traits are largely evolved through the family value and societal values that govern the family value paradigm. Such process may be described as a pyramidal paradigm of personality and values which has a large base of societal culture in the bottom of the pyramid, groomed into the family values and ultimately shaping the personality at the top of the paradigm[16].

Global markets today not only provide multiple goods and services to customers but also expose their behavior to the cross-cultural differences and innovations. The specialization of the production process has also brought such cultural changes by business penetrations in the low production skills regions across the countries. The apparel from Asian countries like Indonesia, Korea and all types of consumer goods from China, electronics from Japan, perfumery from France may be good examples to explain the specialization and cross-cultural sharing of consumer behavior. Conducting business is a creative enterprise and doing it out of one's own country is more demanding. The industry structure varies dramatically across the countries in the world, and for global enterprises to strive against the odds requires strong adaptation behavior. In international business, a company needs to best prepare itself to achieve competitive advantage in the marketplace. The global business has controllable factors that a company needs to adjust within and build its organization within largely uncontrollable marketing environment comprising of SLEPT factors- social, legal, economic, political and technical. Globalization has helped the trade of less developed countries by opening up markets in Europe and the Americas; however a few less developed countries still have to exploit this opportunity to their full potential.

In 2006, Indonesia's real GDP grew 5.5 percent over a year earlier, slightly faster than the average 4.7 percent per year during 2001-2005. While this growth is moderate in comparison to other Asian countries, it has helped improve disposable incomes and accelerate consumer spending. Consumer expenditure reached US$225.9 billion in 2006, up from US$100.5 billion in 2001. This represents real growth of 26.8 percent. The proportion of consumer expenditure on food and non-alcoholic beverages has declined significantly. It decreased from 62.9

---

[15] Trompenaars F and Wooliams P (2003), A new framework for managing change across culture, *Journal of Change Management*, 3 (4), May 361-375.

[16] Rajagopal and Ananya Rajagopal (2006), Trust and Cross-Cultural Dissimilarities in Corporate Environment, *Team Performance Management-An International Journal*, Vol. 12, No. 7-8, 2006, 237-252.

percent of consumer expenditure in 1995 to 47.0 percent in 2006. The decline reflects the fact that disposable income has improved in Indonesia and people are able to spend more on non-food items. During 2001-2006, for example, expenditure on communications grew at a real average annual rate of 11.9 percent Expenditure on education is also growing rapidly, as more people understand the importance of a good education when competition for jobs is fierce. Annual inflation is expected to be 6.3 percent in 2007 and 6.2 percent in 2008 down from 13.1 percent in 2006. This will help raise disposable incomes of consumers, which in turn accelerates consumer spending. Inflation has been high in Indonesia mainly as a result of a sharp lift in administered fuel prices in late 2005. The spending patterns of Indonesian households depend on their household structure, economic status and income. Businesses could select their target markets based on the spending patterns of different household groups[17].

International marketing involves the companies in making one or more marketing –mix decisions across national boundaries in view of the controllable and non-controllable factors of the market environment. The term international business refers to a wide range of activities involved in organizing business transactions across the boundaries. The international marketing involves operating across multiple countries where the non-controllable factors differ significantly among the markets but the controllable factors in the form of cost and price structures, opportunities for advertising and distributive infrastructure also need marginal adjustments. Global marketing is still a larger focus and more complex wherein the companies coordinate, integrate and control a series of marketing programs for sustaining competition and augmenting growth. Hence, international marketing refers to exchanges across national boundaries for the satisfaction of human needs and wants.

The political movement of trade liberalization induced many developing countries in the beginning of the 1970s and has shown acceleration during the 1980s. The world economy has now entered a radical phase of development, typically referred to as a phase of "globalization". Rapid advances in information technologies and communications, together with the systematic reduction of global trade barriers, have allowed global firms to break up the production process and to locate its various components in different markets around the world. The surge in foreign investment flows represents the most unique feature of the globalization phase. Trade is no longer the sole or even the main vehicle for delivering products and services across borders; investment has become an even more powerful force for integration, as transnational corporations extend their global reach by establishing a direct presence in foreign markets. International trade rebounded in 2002 from its contraction in the preceding year, growing at about 2.5 per cent in volume terms, which was faster than the growth of global output. The rebound occurred despite the weakness of the global economic recovery, greatly reduced capital flows, major changes in exchange rates, increased restrictions on international trade transactions to mitigate risks from terrorism, and rising geopolitical tensions.

---

[17] Euromonitor: Indonesian household spending makes way for growth of non-food sector, Euromonitor Archive, January 08, 2008 http://www.euromonitor.com/

Trade

Globalization is a recurring phenomenon and is aimed at increasing mutual efficiency in trade and economic functions between countries. Neo-liberal institutionalism assumes that states are driven by mutual efficiency concerns. In this process each party bargains for the solution that maximizes the "size of the pie" generated by trade and economic cooperation. Multilateral trading has been an important development which emerged from the implementation of liberalized trade policies by many nations and paved the path for globalization. Over long debates on eight successive rounds of multilateral trade negotiations at various forums of the World Trade Organization, substantial trade liberalization was achieved and important trade rules were established. Tariffs in industrial countries are still trade barriers in a few product categories though many developing countries have reduced tariffs remarkably. A number of developing countries that negotiated their accession during the Uruguay Round consolidated all their tariffs at a ceiling level, which introduced a gap between bound and applied rates. Reductions in tariffs over the years have differed by sector, with less progress in labor intensive industrial products and agricultural products. Textiles and clothing, leather and footwear, fish and fish products and agriculture typically face higher tariffs and more tariff peaks than other product categories. While much of the observed reduction in developed country tariff levels has occurred through multilateral bargaining, tariff reductions have significantly resulted from regional integration and preferential schemes favoring developing nations[18]. Global merchandise has shown a continuous trend of increase in terms of value of exports and imports as exhibited in Table 1.1.

Trade growth was strong in Asia and the transition economies, largely reflecting better economic performance in those regions. However trade was stagnant in Western Europe, and contracted in Latin America as a result of economic turmoil in a number of countries in the region. North America's imports recovered in line with stronger domestic demand, while exports continued to decrease in 2002. Many countries seem to be taking the multilateral trading system for granted, while pursuing their commercial interests on a preferential basis in the belief that this will not jeopardize multilateral, non-discriminatory trade relations[19]. The countries of South-East Asia are home to some 500 million people and have a combined GDP of more than $700 billion. Their largely young populations, with large numbers of well-educated and hard-working people, helped to make the region one of the fastest-growing in the world. Until 1997 there was a feeling that the economic order was changing; that the West seemed to be in decline, and that the Asian century was about to dawn. All the lines on the flip-charts about business prospects in South-East Asia pointed one way: upwards. No one believed that the boom could stop. Australia stood out with strong GDP growth in 2002 (both in excess of 3 per cent). In marked contrast to the industrial economies, the recovery in the advanced developing economies in Asia was strong. With the two most populous countries in the world – China and India – growing very rapidly, the gains in output experienced by developing Asia exceeded that of all other regions. In general, world trade has grown twenty-seven fold in volume terms since 1950, three times faster than world output growth. The contribution of trade barrier reductions via the multilateral trading system to this impressive record has been significant although uneven. Moreover, the greater stability and certainty

---

[18] World Trade Organization,: World Trade Report 2007, pp 29-58.
[19] World Trade Organization: World Trade Report 2003, p 22.

imparted by the rules of the system are also likely to have influenced trade growth over the years[20].

Table 1.1. Global Merchandise Trade by Region (2004-2006)
(Billion dollars and percentage)

World Regions	Exports					Imports				
	Value	Annual Percentage change				Value	Annual Percentage change			
	2006	2000-06	2004	2005	2006	2006	2000-06	2004	2005	2006
North America	1675	5	14	12	13	2546	7	17	14	11
South and Central America	426	14	30	25	20	351	9	28	23	18
European Union (25)	4527	11	20	9	13	5218	11	20	10	14
Common Wealth of Independent States (CIS)	422	19	36	28	24	278	23	31	25	29
Russian Federation	305	19	35	33	25	164	24	28	29	31
Africa	361	16	31	30	21	290	14	28	29	31
Middle East	644	16	33	35	19	373	14	31	19	14
Asia	3276	12	25	16	18	3023	12	27	17	16
World	11762	11	22	14	15	12080	11	22	13	14

Source: World Trade Report, 2007.

The severity of the downturn in world trade values was even more pronounced than in volume terms, as dollar prices of internationally traded goods decreased in 2001. Merchandise exports recorded a decrease of 4.5 percent, the steepest decline in more than a decade, contrasting sharply with the 6.5 percent average expansion recorded in the 1990s. Commercial services exports, which expanded at the same rate as merchandise trade between 1990 and 2000, declined marginally in 2001. This was the first decrease in world exports of commercial services since 1983 as exhibited in Table 1. The pattern of world merchandise exports by product category in 2001 reflects the main features of the slowdown in global economic activities in 2001. Firstly, the burst of the IT bubble and the decline in IT expenditure caused an unprecedented shrinkage of international trade in office and telecom equipment of nearly 14%[21]. The decline in crude oil prices by 9% has been the major factor in the 8% decrease of world fuels exports, as the volume of fuels traded remained roughly unchanged during 2002. The textiles recorded an above average export decrease in 2001, confirming a long-term trade pattern where trade growth consistently lags behind global trade expansion. Since 1990, the share of textiles in world merchandise trade fell from 3.1% to 2.5% in 2002. A noteworthy performance was recorded with respect to agricultural products, for which the export decrease in 2001 was small enough to increase its share in world exports for the first time since 1994.

The year 2006 witnessed robust growth in the world economy and vigorous trade expansion. The United States economy maintained its overall expansion as weaker domestic demand was balanced by a reduction in the external deficit, mainly due to a faster export growth. In Japan somewhat faster economic growth was achieved despite weaker domestic

---

[20] World Trade Organization,: World Trade Report 2007, pp 29-58.
[21] World exports of all three major IT product groups, i.e. computers (SITC 75), telecom equipment (SITC 76) and semiconductors, and transistors (SITC 776) fell at double digit rates. Exports of semiconductors and other electronic components shrank by more than one fifth.

demand reflected in a widening of its external surplus. China and India continued to report outstandingly high economic and trade growth. The dynamic growth in global economic activity was the major factor in the vigorous expansion of global trade in 2006. The four regions with the highest share of fuels and other mining products in their merchandise exports (the Middle East, Africa, the Commonwealth of Independent States (CIS) and South and Central America) again recorded the strongest annual export rise in 2006. Real merchandise export growth is provisionally estimated to have grown by 8.0 per cent in 2006 almost two percentage points faster than in 2005, and well above the average expansion trade during 1996-2006. The expansion of real trade exceeded global output growth by more than 4 percent. Trade in less-developed countries grew by about 30%, fuelled by higher prices for petroleum and other primary commodities. They and developing countries as a whole saw their shares of world merchandise trade reach record proportions. And for some of the smaller suppliers, fear of a setback in textiles and clothing in the face of competition from China proved unfounded in 2006. In general, trade expanded in real terms during 2006-07, faster than production by a large margin[22]. The major economic drivers in global trade are observed as:

- Reduction in trade and investment barriers
- Rapid growth and increase in size of the economies of developing countries and their impact on global production capacity
- Innovations in technologies involving transport and communications

The most prominent explanations, often interrelated, for the retardation in the global economic recovery included erosion of trust in institutional pillars such as public and corporate governance, weakening consumer and investor confidence and rising geopolitical risks. The weakness of fixed investment expenditure – particularly pronounced for non-residential investment – contributed significantly to sluggish overall growth in the industrial countries. Investment expenditures play a critical role in the business cycle. There have been problems in sustaining the recovery once inventory levels had been re- established during the recent past. Investment activity generally picks up when prospects for profitable investment opportunities increase and the utilization of existing production capacities reaches a level that calls for a further increase of these capacities. It has been observed that since 2005 the United States of America recorded its best annual merchandise export growth in more than a decade but its trade deficit continued to grow. However, China's trade growth continued to outstrip other major traders. China's merchandise exports grew by 27%. In the second half of 2006, its merchandise exports started to exceed those of the United States, but for the whole year US exports still exceeded those of China. Consumer confidence in the major industrial economies improved only temporarily in the first quarter of 2002 and declined or stagnated thereafter. Marginal employment gains in some countries and rising unemployment rates in others led to only moderate increases in wage incomes and depressed private consumption expenditure. In some countries this led to an increase in precautionary savings.

Real merchandise exports of Asia remained the most encouraging of all regions at 13.5 percent. Asia's imports rose faster than in the preceding year and faster than world trade but continued to lag behind its export growth. Most of the excess of Asia's export over import

---

[22] World Trade Organization: Press Release # 472, 2007.

growth can be attributed to the region's major traders, China and Japan. The expansion of China's exports was somewhat less dynamic in 2006 than in 2005, while Japan, the Republic of Korea and Chinese Taipei recorded a faster growth (between 10-15 percent). Imports into Japan and Chinese Taipei, however, advanced by only 2-3 percent in 2006[23]. Also, merchandise exports in Africa rose by 21 percent again faster than imports, which are estimated to have increased by nearly 16 percent. The share of Africa in world merchandise exports reached its highest level since 1990. The deterioration in the labor markets of industrial economies with rapidly aging populations rendered their already fragile social security systems even more precarious. The general public is increasingly aware that profound adjustments are needed to restore financial sustainability to social security systems and that these adjustments can have a significant impact on future contributions and benefits. The clouded prospects of social security, and in particular pensions systems, contributed to the erosion of consumer confidence and exerted a negative impact on private consumption expenditure. Consumer confidence was also negatively affected by the wealth effect of continuing falls in stock prices, although in some countries (e.g. the United States and the United Kingdom) this was compensated for by rising house prices.

Direct Investment

Economic growth in the transition economies in 2002 was second only to developing Asia and continued to exceed the global average. Nevertheless, there was a deceleration in the region's economic growth, which can be largely attributed to developments in the Russian economy. Economic growth in Africa and the Middle East remained roughly unchanged in 2002, at about 3 per cent. The moderate gains in regional per capita incomes are unlikely to have a significant impact on poverty levels in the region and one should not lose sight of the large variations in the economic performance of individual African countries. Latin America was the weakest part of the global economy in 2002, recording a decline in output and a steep contraction in imports. Unsustainable, large public sector debt, political instability, sizeable external account imbalances and a reduction in private sector net-capital inflows have contributed to severe slumps in output in a number of South American countries. During the course of 2002, the US dollar depreciated against major currencies like the euro and the yen. Total foreign direct investment (FDI) flows fell by about one quarter in 2002, to roughly $500 billion, with both developed and developing regions suffering sharp reductions. Only China and Central /Eastern Europe attracted larger FDI inflows than in the preceding year. Given the strong correlation between FDI flows and current and future trade flows, this development contributed to the weakness in trade growth in regions other than China and Central /Eastern Europe. One factor contributing to this outstanding performance was the high level of FDI inflows driven by the relocation of labor-intensive manufacturing sectors from Japan and other advanced economies in Asia into China's coastal areas.

The more favorable investment climate is also reflected in a sharp rise in global foreign direct investment (FDI) flows in 2006, which approached the record levels of the past. It has been found that the global FDI inflows surged by one-third to $1.23 trillion, the second

---

[23] World Trade Organization: World Trade Report 2007.

highest level ever[24]. The high growth of global FDI flows can be attributed partly to increased mergers and acquisitions activity and higher share prices. A high level of total net private capital flows to emerging markets was reported by the Institute of International Finance[25]. The exchange rates of the Asian economies with large current account surpluses fared differently in 2006. The real effective exchange rates appreciated significantly on an annual average basis, for Republic of Korea and Singapore and moderately in the case of China. However, the Japanese Yen continued to depreciate during 2006[26].

Total FDI flows increased from about $200 billion in the early 1990s to almost $1.2 trillion in 2000. In 2001, the value of these flows collapsed by about 50 per cent, and in 2002, by another 25 per cent, falling back to about $500 billion, a level first reached five years ago. Both developed and developing regions have been affected by the reduction in FDI flows. Only FDI inflows to China and to Central /Eastern Europe continued to increase. China's FDI inflows rose by 19 per cent, to $ 52.7 billion, and those to Central /Eastern Europe increased by 9 per cent, to $30 billion[27]. The sharp decline in nominal terms of global FDI flows can be attributed to the end of the frenzied boom of mergers and acquisitions and the lower market values of corporations listed on global stock markets. Between the end of 2000 and the end of 2002, the valuation of global stock markets decreased by about 40 per cent, which automatically lowered the transaction value of FDI flows for buying corporations listed on equity markets[28].

Marked differences in domestic demand growth between the United States, developing Asia and the transition economies on the one hand, and Japan, Western Europe and Latin America on the other, contributed to major shifts in trade and current account balances. Japan and Western Europe recorded an expansion in net exports. Consequently, the trade and current account surpluses of Japan and the EU widened with increases equivalent to 1 per cent and 0.7 per cent of GDP respectively. Under the impact of sharply lower capital inflows, Latin America had to cut its imports, which led to a trade surplus and reduced the region's current account deficit. The US current account deficit widened to more than $500 billion or 5 per cent of GDP, which was a historic peak in absolute and relative terms. Given that the aggregate deficit for the OECD area remained almost unchanged in relative terms in 2002, this implied that the level of net imports from developing areas also stayed unchanged. Developing Asia again recorded a substantial current account surplus. Japan, the four advanced developing Asian economies (Hong Kong, China; Korea, Rep. of; Singapore; Chinese Taipei) and China reported large current account surpluses, indicating that these economies had become the principal suppliers of capital to the rest of the world[29].

---

[24] UNCTAD, UNCTAD Investment Brief, No.1, 2007.

[25] Institute for International Finance, Capital Flows to Emerging Market Economies, January 18, 2007

[26] World Trade Organization: World Trade Report, 2007.

[27] The Vienna Institute for International Economic Studies, press release, February 2003: FDI in Central and Eastern European Countries in 2002: Record Inflow Concentrated in a Handful of Countries. http://wiiw.ac.at.

[28] Estimates based on the average decrease of four major stock market indices: NYSE-Composite, FTSE 100, Frankfurt DAX and Tokyo Topix. Source: World Federation of Exchanges at http://www.world-exchanges.org.

[29] The foreign exchange reserves of the five Asian developing economies increased by about $50, while Japan's international reserves increased by $30 billion in 2002.

INTERNATIONAL COMPETITION

The emergence of virtual shopping, liberalization of economic policies in the developing countries all over the world, competition has become like a traditional derby in which many companies participate for a neck to neck race. In this business game the rules are subject to change without notice, the prize money may change in short notice, the route and finish line is also likely to change after the race begins, new entrants may join at any time during the race, the racers may form strong alliances, all creative strategies are allowed in the game and the governmental laws may change without notice and sometimes with retrospective effect. Hence to win the race any company should acquire the strategies of outwitting, outmaneuvering and outperforming the competitors. In this process a company must understand thoroughly all the moves of the rival firms from various sources. The locales of the business rivalry have to be spotted to assess their strengths.

The competing firms pay more attention to the sources of factors, quality thereof, cost and management of the factors in order to prove themselves better than the others. The customer, the end user is the ultimate target of competitor for building aggressive and defensive strategies in business. The competing firms try to attract the customers by various means to polarize business and earn confidence in the market place. It is necessary for the successful business companies to look for such a place of business which provides them more location advantage and holds the customers for their goods and services. The business cordoning or securing the trade boundaries is an essential decision to be taken for building competitive strategies to attack rivals across regions. Even the small business company can compete globally with the firms of all sizes through the internet. The distribution channels, franchisees, carrying and forwarding agents, retailers and mailers with value added services represent an increasingly intense business rivalry or competition in all markets or competitive domains. Many firms like Godrej (Diversified Products), Proctor and Gamble (Consumer Goods), Compaq (Computers) reward their managers handsomely for winning the business battles in their channel wars. In succeeding to the market competition, the institutional and political patronage provides long run support to the companies[30]. The winning in product, channel and factor market place in many instances may not last long in building relationships with the customers. Many business firms have found themselves outmaneuvered in various functional aspects of business by the adept actions of rivals in the institutional arena. The cosmetics market in India is largely dominated by the multi-national companies and operates in a close competitive framework. In 1995, Lakmé Limited, a Tata group company and Hindustan Lever Limited formed 50:50 venture as Lakmé Lever to market and distribute Lakmé's cosmetic products and in 1998, Lakmé sold its brands to HLL, renamed itself Trent and entered into the retail business. The HLL has entered into the cosmetics market when there is a gatecrash of MNCs like Revlon, Maybelline and others and has to build strong market place strategies to outwit the competitors. The corporate statement of HLL after acquisition of Lakmé delineates that by taking on the fashion and glamour platform, the company is not just leading the market over other competitors but has also got a virtual ownership of this business platform. It will be very difficult for any other brand to adopt a similar approach. This statement gives a strong prospective signal of its strategies to the new

---

[30] Rajagopal: Marketing Management-Text and Cases, Vikas Publishing House, New Delhi (India), 2000, pp 91-113.

entrants. Lakmé is at the forefront of product innovation and the most preferred brand in cosmetics.

Many organizations feel that in growing competition establishing strategic alliances would better check the competitor's penetration than the own brand or technology driven company. They recognize that alliances and relationships with other companies of repute are fundamental to outwit, outmaneuver and outperform the competitors by ways of better branding, better service and tagging global brands for assuring the quality of goods and services. Alliances and relationships thus transform the concept of competitor. In international marketing many industries face fierce competition leading to price wars. The foreign manufacturers penetrate in the international markets by offering low priced, high – quality products. The Xerox corporation despite this philosophy can not guarantee market leadership. In a crowded field with some 14 competitors from Japan alone, it faces the toughest market in the USA in the copier machines markets. Retail sales of food and drink in Europe's largest markets are at a standstill, leaving European grocery retailers hungry for opportunities to grow. Most leading retailers have already tried e-commerce, with limited success, and expansion abroad, often with more. But almost all have ignored the big, profitable opportunity in their own backyard: the wholesale food and drink trade, which appears to be just the kind of market retailers need. Recently even some of the hi-tech industries have become susceptible to the competition as the competitive situation has forced some of them to shift their consumer electronics manufacturing to the Far-East as it is at the losing edge in the USA. As the retail community shrinks, they put greater emphasis on their suppliers for quality products at a competitive price that enables them to make healthy margins to attract consumers. If one manufacturer cannot supply the necessary ingredients, retailers will look for other alternatives. This environment has provided an opportunity to shake up an otherwise mature and stable industry such as the photographic industry and has paved the way for a viable competitor to Kodak such as Fuji Photo Film U.S.A. The phenomenon has contributed to Fuji making significant inroads into Kodak's once commanding U.S. market share in particular and to its global share in general.

The relationship between Kodak and Fuji had always been adversarial, as competitors naturally are; however, it took a very serious turn in May 1995 when Kodak filed a Section 301 petition under the U.S. trade law. The petition claimed that Kodak's 7-10 percent market share in Japan was not a result of consumer choice and marketing efforts but rather a result of four principle Japanese wholesalers, backed by the Japanese government, that are exclusive Fuji film supporters. The success of Wal-Mart has taught retailers that diversification, scrambled marketing and "one-stop" shopping are important to consumers. As consolidation sweeps the nation in mass merchants, food and drug accounts, retailers realize they must maintain their competitive advantage or close shop. To survive, they are squeezing manufacturers for quality products at competitive prices to capture profit margins for expansion within the industry. This environment has provided an opportunity for Fuji film to prosper in an otherwise stable and mature photographic industry.

Today an all-out war has emerged. While Kodak and Fuji fight for market share, the real winner and benefactor is the consumer. "Retailers and consumers will be the big winners in this struggle for market share among the big players," says one retailer. "We are going to get more incentives to sell merchandise and the consumer is going to see a lot more new products at lower prices[31]." Kodak and Fuji deny they are engaging in a price war, but for each move Fuji makes, Kodak counters with a vengeance. "Smack them until they figure it out," is how Eric L. Steenburgh, Kodak's assistant chief operating officer describes its strategy towards Fuji[32].

OUTGROWTH OF NEW MARKETS

The World Development Report for 2003 states that "Considerable uncertainty clouds trade growth prospects for 2003. The expectations of a war in Iraq caused a sharp increase of oil prices in the first quarter of 2003 and had a detrimental effect on business confidence and global stock markets. Oil prices started to weaken in the second half of April but remained above the preceding year's level. Information on economic activity in the industrial countries in the first months of 2003 has led to a marked downward revision of output growth in 2003, in particular for Western Europe. As Western Europe accounts for more than 40 per cent of world merchandise and commercial services trade, global trade will suffer accordingly[33]." The global scenario is changing very fast in the emergence of the new markets. The new business opportunities developed from the European Community, enhanced by the reunification of Germany and the thriving economies of the Pacific Rim countries during the 90's. The prospective business countries in the following decade are China, Latin America and the emerging market-based economies in the Eastern Europe. However, the growing momentum towards the privatization and liberal policies show further promising markets in the developing countries.

The story of how Schultz & Co. transformed a pedestrian commodity into an upscale consumer accessory has a fairy-tale quality. Starbucks has grown from 17 coffee shops in Seattle 15 years ago to 5,689 outlets in 28 countries. Sales have climbed an average of 20% annually since the company went public 10 years ago, to $2.6 billion in 2001, while profits bounded ahead an average of 30% per year, hitting $181.2 million last year. To duplicate the staggering returns of its first decade, Starbucks has no choice but to export its concept aggressively. Indeed, some analysts give Starbucks only two years at most before it saturates the U.S. market. The chain now operates 1,200 international outlets, from Beijing to Bristol. That leaves plenty of room to grow. Indeed, about 400 of its planned 1,200 new stores this year will be built overseas, representing a 35% increase in its foreign base. Starbucks expects to double the number of its stores worldwide, to 10,000 in three years. During the past 12 months, the chain has opened stores in Vienna, Zurich, Madrid, Berlin, and even in far-off Jakarta. Athens comes next. And within the next year, Starbucks plans to move into Mexico and Puerto Rico. But global expansion poses huge risks for Starbucks. For one thing, it makes less money on each overseas store because most of them are operated with local partners. While that makes it easier to start up on foreign turf, it reduces the company's share of the profits to only 20- 50 percent.

---

[31] *Supermarket Business*, February 1999, p47.
[32] *The Wall Street Journal*, 18 November 1998.
[33] World Trade Organization: World Development Report, 2003, p 5.

The structure of the global textile market is fundamentally changing in response to policy reforms stemming from the 1995 Uruguay Round of the World Trade Organization (WTO), which instituted agreements to reduce tariffs on textile and apparel products to levels closer to those found elsewhere in manufacturing. The Uruguay Round debate among the member nations of WTO also established the Agreement on Textiles and Clothing (ATC), which stipulated elimination of all bilateral import quotas, sanctioned under the 1974 Multi-Fiber Arrangement (MFA) by 2005. The global network of trade in textiles and apparel has shifted significantly during 1990-2005 with many low-income countries benefiting from higher sales[34].The annual expansion rate of textiles and clothing imports from China into Canada, the United States and the EU was roughly halved between 2005 and 2006 in each of these three markets. The combined textiles imports of the three economies from China rose by 41 percent in 2005 and is estimated to have increased by 15 percent in 2006. Competition from low-cost suppliers in developing countries has put considerable pressure on established exporters of textiles and apparel, particularly those in the newly industrialized countries of Asia including Hong Kong, Macau, Singapore, South Korea, and Taiwan. Textile and apparel trade is strongly influenced by established networks and geographical proximity. Among the developed markets Japan's textiles and clothing imports are the most concentrated on China due both to geographic proximity and the absence of import quotas in the recent past. More than three quarters of Japan's textiles and clothing imports originated from China in 2006. The share exceeds 80% for clothing imports[35].

Emerging Markets, in partnership with business leaders, had pursued a variety of initiatives that had cut costs and provided new customer focused products and services. It was not yet clear, however, what new business model would emerge:

> Today's marketplace isn't where clients are at all ready to pay explicitly for anything. But, in time, it is possible our clients will pick and choose. They might get their sales advice from one place and their research from another and they might trade in a third place and clear through a fourth entity— really unbundling the value proposition. So the challenge for us is to try to re-bundle things back together in intelligent ways that continue to add value to clients[36].
> Simon Lack, Managing Director, Chase Manhattan Bank

The companies having an objective of territorial expansion used a three-pronged attack in its strategy to penetrate into the emerging markets: offensive, defensive, and efficiency initiatives. Offensive initiatives were intended to gain market share where the company had not traditionally been a leader, and thus bring new revenues into the bank. Defensive initiatives attempted to preempt competitors' moves into markets where the company had traditionally dominated. Efficiency initiatives delivered cost savings to the bank from customer self-service or from straight-through processing that squeezed costs out of back office processes. The Asian markets for US companies are growing faster than other countries as the European market is declining for US products. It has been found that the European market has declined from 31 to 20 percent for the US products while the share going to Asia has increased from 20 to 30 percent in the same period. Asian markets are very sensitive to

---

[34] Shelton Ruth K and Wachter Kathy (2005), Effects of global sourcing on textiles and apparel, *Journal of Fashion Marketing and Management*, 9 (3), 318-329.
[35] World Trade Organization: World Trade Report, 2007.
[36] Jeanne Ross and Richard Woodham: Chase Global Markets: Defining New Business Models in the Investment Bank Industry, MIT Sloan School of Management, Working Paper 454-01, August 2001, 1-11.

most of the top brands of the western companies. The markets in Asian countries including Japan shoulder one third of luxury goods and fashion business and by 2005 this region will make up to half of the global business of the luxury goods[37]. However, there remains an absence of well-functioning product markets in transition economies as a sufficient condition under which big bang reduces output initially, while a Chinese-style reform increases output. Big bang dismantles central planning or centralized organization of production, permitting monopolistic and vertically interdependent enterprises to pursue their own monopoly profits by restricting output and inter-firm trade to the detriment of the economy as a whole. The Chinese reform, by maintaining central planning but allowing enterprises to produce for the emerging product markets after they have fulfilled their output quotas under planning, gives enterprises incentives to expand output beyond planned targets[38].

DEFINING CONCEPTS OF GLOBAL TRADE

The contemporary global business models explain that the firms tend to structure themselves as one of four organizational types: international, multidomestic, global and transnational. Depending on the type, a company's assets and capabilities are either centralized or decentralized, knowledge is developed and diffused in either one direction or in many, and the importance of the overseas office to the home office varies. International marketing refers to exchanges across national boundaries for the satisfaction of human needs and wants. The various marketing functions coordinated and integrated across the multiple country markets may be referred to as *global marketing*. The process of such integration may involve product standardization, uniform packaging, homogeneity in brand architecture, identical brand names, synchronized product positioning, commonality in communication strategies or well coordinated sales campaigns across the markets of different countries. The term 'global' does not convey the literal meaning of penetration into all countries of the world. However, it needs to be understood in relative sense and even a regionalization or operating in a cluster of countries may also be taken as a global operation in an applied perspective. The regional marketing efforts like trans-Asian or Pan-European marketing operations may also be viewed as examples of global marketing. The suppliers of products ranging from Budweiser beer to BMW cars have been able to keep growing without succumbing to the pricing pressures of an intensely promotional environment. A strong brand also can open the door when growth depends on breaking into new markets. Starbucks Corporation[39], among the fastest-growing brands, recently set up shop in Vienna, one of Europe's cafe capitals, among 400 new stores planned for opening at overseas locations during 2002. The companies succeed in the regional integration across multiple countries markets as they follow the similar strategies and management principals for a cluster of markets. The fourth annual A.T. Kearney/Foreign Policy Magazine Globalization Index[40] in its report on 2004 global trade states "...measures economic, person-to-person, political, and technological integration in 62 countries, accounting for 96 percent of the world's gross

---

[37] Asia's Brand Barons Go Shopping, *The Economist*, March 28, 1998, p 60.
[38] Wei Li: A Tale of Two Reforms, Rand Journal of Economics, 30 (1), 1999, 120-136.
[39] Gerry Khermouch: The best global brands, Business Week Online, August 05, 2002.
[40] Kearney AT *et.al.*: Ireland clings to the top Global, Foreign Policy, February 24, 2004 www.foreignpolicy.com

domestic product (GDP) and 84 percent of the world's population". Using this system, these countries rank as the most global:

- Ireland
- Singapore
- Switzerland
- Netherlands
- Finland

Europe's real merchandise exports recorded their strongest annual growth since 2000, exceeding import growth which is estimated at 7 percent, however, it has been observed trailing behind the global rate of trade expansion. South and Central America's expansion rate of both exports and imports registered a decline during 2004-06 while Mexico has registered stronger export and import growth than its NAFTA partners during the same reference period. Venezuela recorded a marked contraction of her exports and those of Brazil rose by less than 4 percent during 2006. The combined exports of Africa and the Middle East are estimated to have almost stagnated, while imports, despite their deceleration, continued to expand somewhat faster than the global average.

Historically *multinational marketing* refers to the common strategies in the 'multi-domestic' business environment with strong long preferences. In an applied perspective these differences are very narrow and they show the natural progress from one function to another. In order to perform the global management tasks successfully, it is necessary to develop adequate acquaintance with the issues of trade barriers, market environments and SLEPT factors including their possibilities of effective coordination with the corporate as well as the home country policies. The salient product beliefs, attitudes and social norms vary largely among the markets. Customers' decision making across the countries depends to a large extent on the quality attributes associated with the product and attitude of the customers towards foreign brands. There are also variations in the sensitivity preferences like taste, touch, appearance, odor etc. If the European consumers prefer a car with a stick shift and tight cornering, the Japanese consumers like to have a soft touch and easy control of the machine. These preferences are considerably governed by the traditional, cultural, social and transitional factors thereof like fashion. Such differences drive the marketers to wait for product adaptation in the target segments before setting the volume sales operations.

The *multi-domestic markets* may be defined as the product markets that serve the preferences of the local customers and the functional requirements therein may widely differ from other markets. The products and services such as food and beverages, clothing, entertainment, life-style products may be an appropriate example of the multi-domestic markets which tend to vary considerably across the countries wherein consumers prefer to have the local variants. Philips may be cited as a good example of the company that has followed the multi-domestic strategy. This strategy of the company resulted in promoting innovation from the local research and development process, build entrepreneurial spirit, tailor the products to the individual countries and maintain high quality through backward integration. However, the company had to move on to the challenges that emerged due to the implementation of multi-domestic strategy. The challenging issues before the company include high cost of tailored products and growing fear of duplication across the countries, product innovations were more research based than market driven and the time to market was running slow.

After heading towards globalization, Nestlé fairly decentralized its country specific business activities to provide better magnitude and direction to the regional planning and management experts of the company for yielding prolific sale and marketing results. The Swiss headquarters of the company offered the brand names and most of the product concepts and process information prescribed the high quality standards for local managers and maintained a large energetic and business influencing staff. Simultaneously, the individual country organizations of the company took the responsibility and autonomy for optimizing the sales in the local markets. The company has reviewed its business policies to know how the marketing and sales activities could be managed for higher yields and the strategies that were implemented already had resulted in augmenting the growth in these sectors. The sales force structure of the company has one of the largest treasures of human resources and shoulders greater responsibility of moving the products to the market. The case examines the influential role of sales force of Nestlé in Mexico from the point of view of responsive retail sales management. In the new millennium, Nestlé is the undisputed leader in the food industry, with more than 470 factories around the world and sales of more than CHF 81 billion. In July 2000, Nestlé launched a Group-wide initiative called GLOBE (Global Business Excellence), aimed at harmonizing and simplifying business process architecture; enabling Nestlé to realize the advantages of a global leader while minimizing the drawbacks of size[41].

The multi-domestic company allows its subsidiaries to develop and exploit local opportunities, expects them to create a local knowledge and competency base, and decentralizes significant decision-making to the subsidiaries. The path of global trade as defined by a successful company has been exhibited in Figure 1.2. An example of a multidomestic firm is General Motors, whose extensive European units tend to operate as self-contained entities. The multidomestic markets reflect various preferential attributes of the consumer decisions. The companies selling into multidomestic markets require to localize and adapt its products and services across the markets in reference to varied customer needs and buying preferences. The companies following the multidomestic strategy for their geographic expansion of the business across the countries, largely associate with:

- establishing complete set of value-creation activities—including production, marketing, and R&D—in each major national market
- transferring skills and products developed at home to foreign markets
- Extensively customizing both product offering & marketing strategy

However, the multidomestic strategy of the companies develop into the decentralized federation, suffer lack of control, and national subsidiaries of the companies tend to function in an autonomous manner over the period. Often it has been observed that the companies fail to transfer the knowledge to their subsidiaries uniformly to attain the perfect blend of skills and technology to match the local needs. The key differences in the global and multidomestic markets are exhibited in Table 1.2.

---

[41] Rajagopal (2007), International Marketing: Global Environment, Corporate strategy and Case Studies, Vikas Publishing, New Delhi, India.

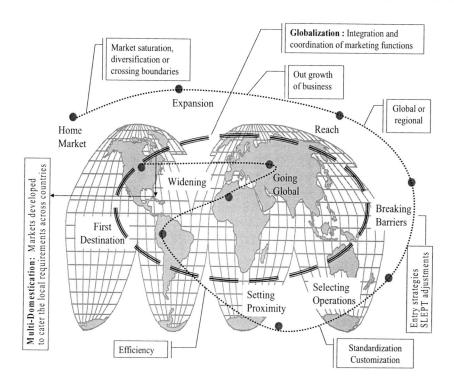

Figure 1.2. Dimensions of Global Trade.

The global products that are standardized in terms of quality, features and packaging do not succeed in the market as they are of low price or consumer psychodynamics but are often preferred by the buyers as such products are value based and offer competitive advantage on the price and non-price factors thereof. In global product markets the company is required to develop technological capabilities to be able to compete by launching new products. An excellent example of an organization which can be precisely characterized as having multidomestic growth strategy may be Unilever which has specialized in the food and cosmetics products catering to the consumer preferences of each country under its business. The company used the multidomestic strategy to gain competitive advantages in its target country markets.

Similarly, another example is Asea Brown Boveri (ABB), the engineering and technology company wherein the key factor of the corporate strategy is encouraging the senior managers to be entrepreneurial in responding to the local needs of the customers, comply with industry standards and coordinate at the different stages of economic development. ABB uses a matrix to organize its activities allowing global optimization of the business and maximize performance in each country. However some companies like ABB get into the internal dilemma while streamlining the growth path as they want to be global as well as local, manage large markets as well as prove their brand value in niches, and radically decentralize the activities or subsidiaries while also looking to centralize the reporting system to demonstrate effective monitoring and control.

Table 1.2. Key Differences in the Multidomestic and Global Markets

Attributes	Market Category	
	Multidomestic	Global
Territorial	Markets are defined within the country borders wherein the customer and competitors are of local origin.	Markets are identified across the country borders. Transactions are held across the borders with the customers and competitors.
Target buyers	Heterogeneous customer targets across the countries that are defined locally.	The segments are territorially cut across the countries with similar customer characteristics from different countries.
Competition	Cost-competition in multi-domestic companies creates greater stress. Local firms pose higher threats and strategies need to be planned on country basis.	Competitors are less in number and exist in major markets. Competition is observed on regional or global platforms.
Operations	Operating in multidomestic markets will have greater difficulty in achieving parent/subsidiary consistency. Strategies are local and coordinating activities among the markets do not benefit significantly.	Higher advantages in coordinating activities within the region or across the countries in the world. Strategies by the global marketing firms can be built on regional or standardized business goals.
Interdependence	Independent operations in local markets. Isolated impact of competition in the market.	Interdependent operations in each country and possess mutual interactions among the markets.

The *transnational companies* have flexible management processes and networks that integrate diverse assets, resources and people into operating units globally. The transnational companies aim at developing the strategic capabilities towards global scaling and competitiveness, national level responsibilities and operational flexibility and cross market capacity to leverage learning on a global basis. In the transnational organizations the ownership of the operations is less clear in terms of manufacturing locations, status of service provider or the manufacturer and marketer of products and services. There is emerging evidence that globalization is beginning to provide new opportunities for global coalitions of advocacy groups to bring market-based pressures to bear upon major transnational firms in a way that promotes higher standards of social and environmental responsibility in production processes and trade relations[42]. The United Nations Conference on Trade and Development in its annual survey of foreign direct investment had constructed an "index of trans-nationality". It works out the ratios of companies' foreign assets to total assets, foreign sales to total sales and foreign employment to total employment; the index is the average of these three

---

[42] Michael E Conroy: Can Advocacy-Led Certification Systems Transform Global Corporate Practices? Evidence, and Some Theory, Political Economy Research Institute, University of Massachusetts at Amherst, Working Paper # 21, 2001, 1-28.

numbers[43]. Transnational organizations require highly flexible coordination process to manage the short term assignments and long-run realignments of basic responsibilities and interactive relationships. Such companies should have the capability of modifying roles and relationships on the basis of each decision on the market situation.

International Business Machines Corporation (IBM) is a good example of transnational business organization as its functional pattern is strategically divided into the principal and subsidiary organizations. The company strives to lead in the creation, development and manufacture of the industry's most advanced information technologies, including computer systems, software, networking systems, storage devices and microelectronics. We translate these advanced technologies into value for our customers through our professional solutions and services businesses worldwide. Currently the company operates in 160 countries. Some of its marketing, operations and research and development activities are centralized and standardized whereas other units operate with substantial degree of independence. The company has a strong corporate identity and some of its promotional themes are uniform across its subsidiaries. It has also formed a strategic alliance with international business partners in the information technology area. The company has 24 manufacturing plants the world over that include North America (10), Europe (6) and Asia-Pacific (8). The research and development of IBM is carried out in 8 countries. The company had 351,889 employees across the countries.

The imperial Chemical Industries (ICI) a multi-product transnational company would be a good reference to be cited as a network corporation. ICI creates, develops and markets products that make the world look brighter, taste fresher, smell sweeter and feel smoother such as paints, foods, fragrances, personal care products, which consumers use every day. Of course, the ICI Group is a huge international business. ICI was formed in 1926 by the merger of four of the largest chemical companies in the UK. In the 70's the inorganic fiber 'Saffil' was launched by the company and is still used in, among other applications, catalytic converters for cars. In 1983, ICI began to abandon its conventional country-by-country organization and established worldwide business units[44]. The laboratories of the company across the countries were given independent roles for developing market driven R&D close to the competitors. The company began its transformation from bulk chemical producer to global specialty products and paints leader with its biggest ever acquisition in 1997. It purchased four businesses from Unilever - National Starch and Chemical, Quest International, Unichem and Crosfield - for $8 billion and added them to its own specialty products and paint businesses. Such strategic shifts created drastic changes in the corporate policies that primarily resulted in narrowing down the human resources and increasing per capita productivity. ICI accelerated its exit from the bulk commodity chemicals market by selling its cyclical bulk chemical businesses for value to new owners who were keen to grow and invest in those sectors. Divestment proceeds, and a rights issue has been used to repay debt and restore the strength of the balance sheet. ICI today is a collection of world class businesses, many of them leaders in their sectors. The company employs more than 35,000 people worldwide. Their product range is 50,000 strong that took the sales in 2003 to £5.8 billion[45].

---

[43] The Economist, 25 September 1997.
[44] Jeremy Main: How to go global-And why, Fortune, August 28, 1989, p.70.
[45] Corporate home page- Group Overview, www.ici.com, 21 May 2004.

DRIVERS OF GLOBALIZATION

There are over 200 countries in the world and it is difficult for the marketer to determine a critical path of success across the countries or regions. Exceptionally, a few companies like Fuji, Kodak and Coca-Cola that have spread their business in over 100 countries developed gradually. The characteristics of the global market place are diverse and international marketing approaches are different. The companies need to adapt a strong rationale for grouping the countries into segments. The multinational and the global corporation are different as the former operates in a number of countries and carries adjustment in the production and marketing practices in each country at a highly relative cost.[46] The global corporation operates with stanch loyalty at relatively low costs with standardization. Coca-Cola and Pepsi-Cola companies have standardized their products globally according to the regional and ethnic preferences of consumers. The most effective world competitors integrate quality and trust attributes into their cost structure. Such companies compete on the basis of appropriate value of price, quality, trust and delivery systems. These values are considered by the companies in reference to the product design, function and changing consumer preferences like fashion. The multi-national corporations know a lot about the business environment in a country, put their efforts on adapting to the given environment, sets up a gradual penetration process in the country. On the contrary, the global corporations recognize the absolute need to be competitive and drive through the lower prices by standardizing its marketing operations. The global corporations treat the world as composed of a few networked and standardized markets rather than many independent and customized markets. Figure 1.3 illustrates the global marketing policy followed by the multi-domestic and transnational and global companies.

There are five major categories of drivers that propel companies towards globalization. These drivers include market, competition, cost, technology and government. Of these, the market driver has been considered as one of the strongest forces that push the process of global marketing.

> "The major driver of change for General Motors today is the same as for most companies; it's globalization. Advances in technology and communication are making the 'small world' a reality, and the world will only get smaller and smaller in coming years…This trend towards global integration should be viewed as an opportunity—not a problem."
>
> -John F. Smith, Jr., CEO of General Motors

The *market drives* comprise the needs of common customers, global customers, global channels and transferable marketing. The common customers needs become a compelling factor for the multinational companies when customers of the different countries have the same needs in a product category. The free trade and unrestricted travel has created homogenous groups of customers across the countries in reference to specific industries. However, some markets that typically deal with the culture bound products like food and beverages, apparel and entertainment strongly resist the shift towards globalization and

---

[46] Theodore Levitt: *The globalization of markets* in International and Global Marketing-Concept and Cases, ed. Meloan W Taylor and Graham L John, Irwin McGraw Hill, Boston, 13-23, 1998.

remain multidomestic serving to the different customer preferences and differentiated products across the countries. On the contrary the global customers need the same products or

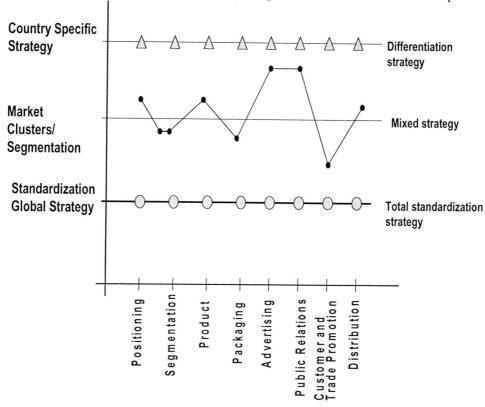

Figure 1.3. Global Marketing Policy Continuum.

services in many countries like in the case of Kodak films or Hilton Hotels. The global channels, distribution and logistics companies offer seamless transport, storage and delivery services. The companies can expand internationally provided the channel infrastructure is met with the distribution needs of the company. Hence their integrated networks thrive to bring the multinational companies close to the global distributors, retail stores like super markets and department stores in order to generate systems effect. Transferable marketing is applied to the same marketing ideas on brand names, packaging, advertising and other components of marketing-mix in the different countries. Nike's campaign anchoring the basketball champion Michael Jordan pulled-up the brand in many countries. This is how the good ideas of multinationals get leveraged world over.

The *competitive drivers* support the companies for matching their strategies appropriately with their moves in the market. The existence of many global competitors indicate that an industry is mature for international business operations. The global competitors operate on cost advantages over the local competitors. The emergence of strong global competitors has served to develop the market infrastructure for the local companies and also help in transfer of technological skills enabling the domestic company to explore the scope of expansion. The competitive efforts put pressure on companies to globalize their marketing activities to derive optimum performance by interpreting appropriately the competitor signals. When Kodak backed out from sponsoring the 1984 Los Angeles Olympics, Fuji Film entered into the sponsorship issue immediately at the prescribed price and was one of the official sponsors of the Olympics. By the time Kodak reconsidered participating in this international event, the time had run out. However, for the Olympics of 1988 and ABC-TV, Kodak became a sports program sponsor[47].

The *cost drivers* are largely based on the scale of economies that involve the cost of production functions in large and complex industries, cost of outsourcing, diffusion and adaptation of technology, tariffs and taxes and costs associated with the basic and advanced marketing functions. The macro economic factors of the neighboring countries also govern the cost drivers. When a new automobile plant is set-up, it aims at designing, manufacturing or assembling and delivering a particular model by penetrating into the neighboring markets to gain the advantages of economies of scale. The Toyota automobile plant in Kentucky manufacture the Camry model for catering to the markets of the NAFTA group of countries. The high market share multidomestic companies derive gains from spreading their production activities across multiple product lines or diversified business lines to achieve advantage through the scope of economies. The manufacturing and marketing activities of Proctor and Gamble, Unilever, Colgate-Palmolive may illustrate this global attribute that is explained by the cost drivers. The other cost drivers include global sourcing advantages, low global communications and automation processes. The location of strategic resources to the production plants, cost differences across the countries and transport costs are also some important considerations of the cost drivers.

The lowering of trade barriers made globalization of markets and production a theoretical possibility, and technological change has made it a tangible reality. Since the end of World War II, the world has seen major advances in communications, information processing, and transportation technology including, most recently, the explosive emergence of the Internet and World Wide Web. The *technology drivers* play a significant role in global business. Global expansion of the multinational companies has been highly stimulated by the technological advancements in the designing, manufacturing and marketing of consumer and industrial products. The services were also improved by many technological breakthroughs. The internet revolution has triggered e-commerce as an open access channel as a strong driving force for global business in the consumer and industry segments. Improved transport and communication now makes it possible to be in continuous contact with producers anywhere in the world. This makes it easier for companies to split production of a single good over any distance. Storage and preservation techniques have revolutionized the food industry for example, so that the idea of seasonal vegetables is no longer relevant today as anything can be exported all year round from anywhere.

In addition, the IT revolution has made the movement of investment capital around the globe an almost immediate process ensuring that financing opportunities across the developed and developing world have both expanded and become more flexible. However, non-economic drivers of global integration, from travel to telephone traffic maintained their forward momentum, making the world more integrated at the end of 2002 than ever before. Technological upgrading, in the form of introduction of new machinery and improvement of

---

[47] Thomas C Finnerty: Kodak Vs. Fuji – The Battle for Global Market Share, Institute of Global Business Strategy, Lubin School of Business, Pace University, New York, 2000, pp 1-23.

technological capabilities, provides a firm with the means to be successful in competition. In the process of introducing better technologies, new lower-cost methods become available, which allow the firm to increase labor productivity, i.e., the efficiency with which it converts resources into value. Firms will adopt these newer methods of production if they are more profitable than the older ones. The ability of a firm to take advantage of technical progress is also enhanced if the firm improves its entrepreneurial and technological capabilities through two competitiveness strategies, namely (i) learning and adaptation, and (ii) innovation. The latter is a process of searching for, finding, developing, imitating, adapting, and adopting new products, new processes, and new organizational arrangements. Because rivals do not stand still, the firm's capacity to develop these capabilities, as well as its ability to compete, depends on the firm's maintaining a steady pace of innovation[48]. Containerization has revolutionized the transportation business, significantly lowering the costs of shipping goods over long distances. Before the advent of containerization, moving goods from one mode of transport to another was very labor intensive, lengthy, and costly. It could take days to unload a ship and reload goods onto trucks and trains. The efficiency gains associated with containerization, transportation costs have plummeted, making it much more economical to ship goods around the world, thereby helping to drive the globalization of markets and production.

The *government drivers* for the globalization include diplomatic trade relations, customs unions or common markets. The government drivers add favorable trade policies, foreign investment regulations, bilateral or regional trade treaties and common market regulations. The introduction of global standard norms like ISO certifications by the respective countries may be one of the effective measures to promote the globalization through uniform quality perspectives. In the past the government barriers to foreign market entry protected the domestic markets and made the global marketing an uphill task. WTO has been instrumental in promoting government drivers for improving trade in the developing countries.

At the Fourth World Trade Organization Ministerial Meeting held in Doha in November 2001, Ministers launched a comprehensive set of multilateral trade negotiations and a work program. This mandate is sometimes referred to as the Doha Development Agenda, reflecting a shared desire to ensure that the trading system is relevant and responsive to the needs of developing countries. Among the areas covered by the negotiations or the work program are market access in manufactures, agriculture and services, certain rules (including anti-dumping, subsidies and countervailing measures, and regional arrangements), trade and environment, trade-related intellectual property rights, the relationship between trade and investment, the interaction between trade and competition policy, transparency in government procurement, trade facilitation, and dispute settlement. Developing countries were particularly instrumental in putting certain issues on the agenda, including trade and technology transfer, trade, debt and finance, small economies, implementation issues (mostly pending from the Uruguay Round) and special and differential treatment. Between 1990 and 2001, South-South trade grew faster than world trade with the share of intra-developing country trade in world merchandise exports rising from 6.5 per cent to 10.6 per cent. Over this period, developing country economies grew much faster than those of the developed and transition countries. The liberalization of the trade and investment regimes of a large number of these countries has played a significant role in this expansion. Much of this expansion in South-South trade took

---

[48] Asian Development Bank: Drivers of Change. Globalization, Technology and Competition, Section III, Competitiveness in Developing Asia, Asian Development Outlook, 2003.

place in developing Asia (which accounts for more than two-thirds of intra-developing country trade). Manufactures, in particular office and telecom equipment, played a leading role in the growth of intra-developing country trade. This strong performance can be attributed in part to open trade and investment policies in the major developing economies of Asia. Trade liberalization in Asia took various forms in the 1990s: some of it was undertaken on a unilateral basis, some arose from multilateral efforts[49].

Integrating a worldwide strategy involves five key dimensions: selecting markets for their global strategic importance; standardizing products; locating value-adding activities in a global network; using uniform marketing techniques; and integrating competitive moves across countries. Industry globalization drivers that are defined as the industry conditions that determine industry globalization potential and organization and management factors largely determine the use of global strategy. Such drivers have the strongest influence in global trade. The application of global strategy in industries with high globalization potential improves business performance. The global companies constantly search for opportunities to achieve the benefits of globalization; take a zero-based view of existing activities; flout conventional wisdom and established practices; systematically analyze industry, strategy, and organizational linkages; and make multiple reinforcing changes in strategy and organization[50]. They assume that strategy should be global unless proven otherwise, and they think globally and act locally.

Besides, the five drivers discussed above there exist other reasons to market products and services globally. The major factors that influence the drivers of globalization may be illustrated as under:

- Market Saturation
- Trade Deficit
- Foreign Competition
- Emergence of New Markets
- Globalization of Markets
- Opportunities via Foreign Aid Programs
- Other Reasons

The most evident reason to drive the companies to go global is the market potential in the developing countries that constitute as major players in the world market. The companies such as *Nintendo, Disney* and the Japanese Motorcycle industries (Honda, Kawasaki, Suzuki etc.) have greatly benefited from exploiting the markets of the developing countries and reassuring their growth in the world market to harness the promising market potential. The emerging scope of spatial diversification has also been one of the drivers for enhancing the global business utilizing the additional production capacity at the economies of scale and low-cost outsourcing. The production sharing can be explained as engines for its heavy duty transport vehicles of Volvo are manufactured in India (Bangalore) as the company gains comparative advantage on factors of production. The thrust of Japanese motorcycle industry in the US markets is aided significantly by its low-cost position. The saturation of the demand

---

[49] World Trade Organization: World Trade Report, Executive Summary, 2003, pp 14-15.
[50] George S Yip and Johnny K Johansson: Global marketing strategies of US and Japanese Business, Marketing Science Institute, Report 93-102, Cambridge, USA.

for the products and services of a company in domestic market may also be an effective driver to globalization wherein the company looks for building the value for its brand across the boundaries. A product which is nearing the end of its life cycle in the domestic market would be beginning to drive its growth abroad. *Dickson Poon's* export of high brand value luxury goods from America to the Far East may be cited as an example of gaining advantage for the general rise in conspicuous consumption that is regarded as a sign of prosperity. Sometimes the cross-culture attributes of overseas markets that become the source of new product ideation, also may be considered as one of the potential drivers for globalization of business and explore the strategic alliances with prominent regional or multinational brands thereof. The tested market entry approaches may be implemented in the emerging markets such as South-East Asia as shown by Revlon in cosmetics though there exists risk of international currency, legal issues and business protocols. However, the most difficult task for the global companies is to develop products with a universal appeal as illustrated by *Gillette* with its fragrances. On the contrary *Lego* is facing hardship in the Far-East markets to popularize its concept of *do it yourself* (DIY) for creative learning against the head-on competition of video games industries attracting the same segment of buyers (age group 5- 14).

ORGANIZING GLOBAL MARKETING

Marketing is an integrated effort of various elements linked with the corporate objective of the organization. The marketing environment is volatile and keeps changing according to the business policy of competing firms, fashion, legal interventions and innovations. Thus, in the modern era, most companies put great efforts into organizing their marketing avenues with response to significant changes in the market. In such a process, it is essential to know consumer orientation at the very beginning. The research and development wing of the company needs to concentrate on new ideas and engineer them to manufacture the products desired by the consumers. Some of the essential determinants on the process are as given below:

- Consumer feedback
- Product improvement
- Distribution and purchase
- Marketing set-up
- Zero defects

In a marketing organization there should be a continuous flow of information from the consumers which will enable the manufacturer to improve the product accordingly. The ideas generated through the feedback of consumers need to be evaluated with the view of accelerating the product improvement process. However, the company should develop a proper match with the supply and distribution system to ensure the availability of the products to the consumers. The marketing department in an organization should consist of a chain of functionaries for managing various marketing operations such as consumer survey, production, research and development. The functionaries should have a horizontal and a vertical network in order to perform their tasks efficiently and to provide feedback to the decision managers. The horizontal networking needs to promote product distribution, sales and promotion at a grassroots level. It is better to spread geographically covering all the sensitive marketing points in the hinterland of the operation of the company.

The networking of a marketing organization can also be built in a pyramidal structure wherein the administration, monitoring and evaluation is done in a synchronized manner. The top management exercises the highest powers while the middle and the lower management are answerable to the personnel of the top management. This is a centralized marketing system where the middle and lower levels of management executives are not given functional autonomy. The service functions have to be coordinated, monitored and evaluated at the middle management level while the planning functions need to be taken care of by the top management of the organization. The service functions include—administration of sales personnel, promotion, marketing research and market surveys. Functions pertaining to strategic planning, product planning, marketing research and decisions about the new projects comprising the planning and program functions rest with the top management. The area functionary in a marketing organization should provide regular feedback to the middle management to enable them to evaluate product performance and modify the marketing strategies as and when required. The product manager's role is to develop product plans and to administer them in the selected market segments. Other important functions such as the job chart of the product manager are stated below:

- Formulation of sustainable and competitive product plans
- Formulating annual operational marketing plans
- Forecasting sales
- Planning sales force
- Developing sales promotion strategies
- Managing the market information system
- Analyzing marketing problems, consumer grievances and working out suitable solutions for them
- Suggesting product improvement

The product manager has to interact with different types of interest groups in order to ensure the smooth functioning of a marketing organization. On the product front, the interactions of the product managers are marked with the personnel of research and development, production, distribution, promotion, media, consumer services, packaging, purchase, sales, fiscal and legal department (to ensure that the product on sale is not violating any regulations stipulated by the government.)

Often, in a vertical organizational network the problem of striking a balance of operational decisions between the apex and the lower level functionaries occurs. The operational decisions consist of marketing and non-marketing functions. The marketing functions consist of planning, program, implementation, monitoring and evaluation while the non-marketing functions comprise research and development and public relations. The balance needs to be struck as what mix of these activities will be attended by apex and grassroots level functionaries. An important point to remember is that along with functional decentralization there remain chances of duplication of efforts. In such circumstances, networking decisions have to be taken on the basis of the extent of the expenditure incurred while performing the tasks. However, there exist advantages and disadvantages of functional centralization and otherwise. Some of the main considerations for organizing marketing are as follows:

Lines of authority and tasks need to be unambiguous and clearly stated to the functionaries at various levels.

- The structure of the global marketing organization must be acceptable, conducive and dynamic to perform the functions on time.
- All the sub-activities should be properly coordinated.
- Information on marketing activities needs to be collected by an efficient department of the organization and the relevant facts must be made available to all the functional units to set their strategies.
- It is essential to maintain integrity among the marketing personnel in an organization.

Environmental control in marketing (with reference to new entrants, buyers and distributors' lobby and the substitutes of products and technology) must be considered while exercising market control approaches. All these areas need to be monitored simultaneously and continuously. It has been observed that new entrants and new technologies work hand in hand and generate latent threats to the existing products. These control operations are termed as strategic control. To achieve such critical control operations successfully, the managers belonging to the strategic level need to look into the following factors:

- Effectively assessing consumerism
- Analyzing the first sight of threats in the market
- Protecting the company's interest in maintaining markets
- Attainment of marketing objectives
- Maintaining the quality of market intelligence
- Keeping the sales level intact.

Operational control in a marketing organization comprises—streamlining of sales, distribution, promotion and product innovation activities. Sales control may be administered by scrutinizing new contracts, competitive sales approaches and new proposals of expanding sales avenues. It is essential to identify brand loyalty among the distributors and encourage exclusive distribution of the product effective monitoring of sales. Promotional control consists of administering effective communication strategies to the distributors and the consumers by way of advertisement, consumer surveys and sales campaigns. Periodical reviews need to be done by the operational control personnel of a company in order to build-up the image of the company and its product thereof in the market. One of the important tasks of operational control is the streamlining of consumer services. This activity can be performed after knowing fully the views of the consumers regarding the services offered by the company through benchmarking. This technique enables one to see at a glance the investment in consumer services providing the value in their perceptions[8]. The marketing manager of a company may prepare a consumer service matrix denoting high, medium and low perceptions of different segments of consumers and thus identify the target area. It is expected of the marketing manager to take clear action if the elements of consumer service fall into certain specific parts of the matrix. The target area emphasizes the importance that needs to be given to the consumers of the "target" segment.

GLOBAL LOCAL MARKETING

The global growth products of multinational companies are mostly centralized in the country of origin and the products that emerge tend to have FABs (features, advantages, benefits) specified by central marketing system of the company. Hence, key technologies and major product introductions cater primarily to customers in that geographical region. Marketing and customers in other regions are relegated to acceptance of custom modifications; or they have the choice to buy from other local suppliers. The product targeting goes beyond the perceived use values of the customers, local preferences and local language. Expectations regarding size, shape, customized items, price and availability vary widely. Hence regional markets tend to be dominated by local companies. Often the companies offer locally engineered or customized products at a differential price to win market share. For growth and success in the new global economy, the guiding principle must be: *Go Global – think Local!* Automation suppliers must become truly global by allowing local development of products for local markets. The best approach is to develop technology (hardware & software) through global alliances – preferably with relatively small, fast-moving local companies. In a global market, there are 3 keys that constitute the winning difference:

- Marketing abilities that assess correctly the local needs in a global arena.
- Proprietary technology and products targeted specifically for local markets.
- High-value-added services offered through effective local service providers.

In the global village of the new economy, automation companies have little choice – they must find more ways and means to expand globally. To do this they need to minimize domination of the central corporate culture, and maximize responsiveness to local customer needs.

Ever since Fujifilm began actively exporting its products throughout the world in the early 1960s, it has been one of Japan's leading companies regarding overseas operations. Besides establishing a world-spanning network of local marketing bases, we were among the first Japanese companies to initiate overseas manufacturing, starting with the 1974 construction of a color photographic paper processing plant in Brazil. Since the 1980s, Fujifilm has arranged for Japanese and local technical staff to cooperatively design and construct overseas manufacturing facilities that make appropriate use of the Company's unique technologies in harmony with local conditions. These efforts have enabled the steady expansion and strengthening of Fujifilm's global production, marketing, and service networks. Having consistently placed strong emphasis on understanding regional characteristics and on respecting and adapting to local cultures, Fujifilm has been highly praised for its localization efforts and contributions to the communities in which it operates. The Company views globalization and localization as two equally crucial elements of its overall business strategy. The localization has been done by the companies to serve the markets in Americas, Europe and Asia-Pacific.

As continued growth in the digitization of diagnostic imaging has also supported rising demand for dry medical imaging film in North America, Fuji Photo Film, Inc., based in Greenwood, South Carolina, in the United States, has been proceeding with the expansion of its medical-use film factory. In March 2003, the company completed that facility and began operating an integrated manufacturing system that performs a full range of manufacturing processes, from coating to processing. Because the range of products manufactured at the facility has been expanded to include dry medical imaging film, Fujifilm has significantly upgraded its systems for efficiently supplying customers throughout North America with our high-quality medical imaging products and related services. Fujifilm's headquarters in Europe, Fuji Photo Film (Europe) GmbH, recently established marketing companies in Poland, the Czech Republic, Slovakia, and Italy. In view of the huge changes under way in Europe - such as the monetary integration in 2002 and the forthcoming enlargement of the European Union in 2004 - Fuji Photo Film (Europe) has been seeking to expand and strengthen its marketing systems so that it can accurately respond to local needs and expeditiously supply products and services. Fujifilm began marketing the DocuCentre Color series of digital color multifunction machines in the Asia-Oceania region during the current fiscal year 2004. The Company also proactively proceeded with measures to expand its manufacturing and marketing systems in the region, particularly in China, which has markets that are expected to grow greatly. Consolidated revenue in this region rose 13.4%, to ¥279.1 billion[51].

The world's most recognized companies and brands, Coca-Cola continues to prosper by innovating and adapting to the local needs of its customers and consumers throughout the world. Despite ferocious competition, significant currency devaluations in key markets, and major acquisition-related write-downs, the company reported first quarter 2002 sales of US$4.08 billion and has predicted long-term growth approaching six percent. Global Marketing helps set global marketing strategies and product positioning, which is then implemented locally and adapted to local marketing needs.

LOOKING BEYOND GLOBAL MARKETING

The continuing debate on global organizations and executives over time still has not found a definitive answer that may be slated to the question of what is really meant by "global." In the dilemma of setting clear objectives of global marketing, some of the corporate leaders feel that they are losing sight of the reality of globalization. However, the companies should pay attention to globalization as the national barriers are quickly coming down. Global companies integrate assets, resources, and diverse people in operating units around the world. The multinational, multi-domestic and transnational companies can build three strategic capabilities: global-scale efficiency and competitiveness; national-level responsiveness and flexibility; and cross-market capacity to leverage learning on a worldwide basis through a flexible management process, in which business, country, and functional managers form a triad of different perspectives that balance one another. In reference to the benefits of the global marketing, it may be firmly stated that the market overseas goes beyond simple and pure marketing considerations as it stands on the trade-off within the array of gains and risks.

---

[51] Fujifilm Corporate Home page: http://home.fujifilm.com/info/profile/operation.html 27 May 2004.

Global marketing under such conditions may determine the following objectives to sail through the distant and somewhat troubled markets across the countries:

- To exploit market potential and growth to the optimum extent
- To set its marketing operations to gain the advantages of economies of scale
- To learn from the leading markets through technology, innovation and competition
- To increase competitive pressure in stronghold markets to make space for survival and sustenance
- To explore the score of diversification of products, services and markets, and
- To gain comprehensive knowledge on doing overseas business successfully

The multinational companies see globalization in general as a matter of replication, spreading a single business model as widely as possible to maximize economies of scale. From this perspective, the key strategic challenge is choosing how much of the model to keep standard and how much to grudgingly adapt to local tastes. Indeed, the scope of generalization or peripheral understanding is as wide as the differences that remain among countries, and those differences continue to be broad and deep with changing customer preferences and competitive moves across the regions. In order to reap the benefits of diplomatic privileges, growing economies and market size a multinational company must properly construct its efforts into its overall organization and perform at the national level but also tailor local strategies, by way of joint ventures, franchising and mitigate risk, in particular the theft of intellectual property.

REFERENCES

Branch, Shelly. "ACNielsen Gives 43 Brands Global Status". *The Wall Street Journal,* October 31, 2001, p.38.

Czinkota, M.R., and I. Ronkainen. *International Marketing.* 5thed. Fort Worth: Dryden, 1998

Dreher Axel; Does Globalization affect Growth, University at Mannheim, Germany *Working Paper*, 2003, pp 1-33.

Elie Ofek: Customer Profitability and life time Value, *Harvard Business School, Press*, Aug. 2002, 1-13.

Frankel Jaffery A: Globalization of the Economy, working paper 7858, *NBER Working Paper Series*, Cambridge, USA, 2000, pp 1-42.

Giddens, Anthony. *Runaway World.* New York:Routledge, 2000.

Graham, Edward M. *Fighting the Wrong Enemy: Antiglobal Activists and Multinational Enterprises.* Washington DC. Institute for International Economics, 2000.

Micklethwait, John and Adrian Woolridge. *A FuturePerfect: The Challenge and Hidden Promise of Globalization.* New York: Crown, 2000.

Rugman, Alan. *The End of Globalization.* New York: Amacom, 2001.

Rust R Zeithaml V and Lemonk: *Driving Customer Equity: How Customer lifetime value is reshaping corporate strate*gy, New York, Free Press, 2000.

Shanklin, William L, and David A Griffith, "Crafting Strategies for Global Marketing in the New Millenium," *Business Horizons,* September-October 1996, p.11-16.

Wind, Jerry, and Vijay Mahajan. *Digital Marketing: Global Strategies from the World's Leading Experts.* New York:Wiley, 2001.

Chapter 2

INTERNATIONAL ECONOMIC ENVIRONMENT

The global economic environment is changing rapidly. Globalization has led to surprising increases in global trade. Trade currently represents 30 percent of world gross domestic product (GDP) and is expected to grow to 50 percent of world GDP by 2020. Greater participation in international trade is a prerequisite for economic growth and sustainable development in today's competitive world economy. In recent years, the international trade environment has changed drastically. World trade in goods and services has grown much faster than production in the post war period, and trade in services has generally grown as fast as trade in goods. World economic growth is projected to accelerate to 4.7%, up from 3.4% in 1999 and 2.6% in 1998. Gains in economic activity are being led by strong expansions in the United States and Asia, robust growth in Europe, and modest improvement in the Japanese economy. Globalization has prompted economic growth of India, China and Russia after 2000 and these three countries have shown extraordinary vigor in pushing their economies at a remarkable competitive level. China's economy gained further momentum, growing by 11.5 percent, while India and Russia continued to grow very strongly. These countries alone have accounted for one-half of global growth over the past year. Robust expansions also continued in other emerging market and developing countries, including low-income countries in Africa. Among the advanced economies, growth in the Euro area and Japan slowed in the second quarter of 2007 after two quarters of strong gains. Overall, the global economy continued to expand vigorously in the first half of 2007, with growth running above 5 percent[1].

MACROECONOMIC ENVIRONMENT

Macroeconomics is the study of the entire economy in terms of the total amount of goods and services produced, total income earned, the level of employment of productive resources, and the general behavior of prices. Macroeconomics can be used to analyze how best to influence policy goals such as economic growth, price stability, full employment and the attainment of a sustainable balance of payments. It considers the performance of the economy of a country as a whole. The principal macroeconomic topics of a country may include

---

[1] International Monetary Fund: World Economic Outlook-2007, Executive Summary.

economic growth; inflation; changes in employment and unemployment, trade performance with other countries as reflected in the balance of payments and the relative success or failure of fiscal and monetary policies. The economy of a country is based on allocation and management resources of its livelihood system. As all economies operate at different levels, it is necessary to have a clear idea of the economic situation of a particular host country in order to make appropriate decisions in international marketing.

Demography and Income Distribution

The world has 6.4 billion inhabitants today. More than 3 billion will potentially be added to our human family over the next 50 years. For decades environmentalists have warned that an ever-rising number of people and their impact on the Earth's finite resources could lead to disaster, not only for wildlife and ecosystems but also for human populations. Besides, the demographic explosion in some countries has led to serious concerns about resource management, consumption levels, income distribution, employment and other macroeconomic factors. These factors, in turn affect the market as people constitute the market. The world today produces and consumes more than ever before. Modern industrial workers now produce in a week what took their 18th century counterparts four years. The growth in the world population is exhibited in Table 2.1. Private consumption expenditures—the amount spent on goods and services at the household level—topped more than $20 trillion in 2000, a four-fold increase over 1960. One quarter of humanity—1.7 billion people worldwide—now belong to the "global consumer class," having adopted the diets, transportation systems, and lifestyles that were once mostly limited to the rich nations of Europe, North America, and Japan. Today, China, India, and other developing countries are home to growing numbers of these consumers. Yet the world is one of contrasts. While the consumer class thrives, great disparities remain[2].

Rapid population growth continues to undermine efforts to reduce poverty in Africa and Asia. Poor economic performance, limited natural resources and high rates of population increase have led to declines in per capita income in some countries. Because of continued increases in numbers, many countries will find themselves "running faster in order to stand still" in their efforts to improve access and quality in health services and education until well into the next century. The pace of population growth inexorably affects markets, capital accumulation, labor availability, employment generation, immigration, migration, health care, retirement benefits, education, and a host of other national considerations. The population of western Asia is projected to more than double by 2050, going from 204 million to 418 million. Though the economic growth and prices are the key drivers of food demand, demographic changes such as urbanization, growth in populations, and changes in the age structure of populations, will likely have more profound long-term implications for the food system of the country. Urban growth rates are expected to be the most rapid in China and Southeast Asia; more moderate in Latin America, North America, and Oceania; and slowest in East Asia. The most rapid rates of growth will occur in Vietnam, Indonesia, Singapore, and

---

[2] Gary Gardner, Erik Assadourian, and Radhika Sarin (2004), State of the World -2004, Chapter 1, Worldwatch Institute, Washington DC.

the Philippines. China's urban population is expected to grow by 300 million people (67 percent) in the next 20 years, a staggering number.

Pacific region is expected to grow by 400 million people, from 2.6 billion in 2000 to 3.0 billion in 2020. However, population growth throughout the Pacific region will not be evenly distributed. By 2020, the largest absolute increase will occur in China (160 million), followed by Indonesia (60 million) and the United States (50 million). In contrast, Japan's population will begin to decline in 2007. Population growth will undoubtedly place demands on the Pacific agri-food system; more people means more food consumption. But the changing rates and distribution of growth will also have significant implications. Japan's declining population implies lower levels of food demand in this affluent nation, a leading importer of food and agricultural products. More rapid population and economic growth in developing and middle-income economies will increase their influence in the Pacific food system, altering production, consumption, and trade patterns. Marketing food products in the Pacific region will increasingly focus on densely populated urban centers, such as the Hong Kong-Shenzen-Pearl River Delta area, Shanghai, Jakarta, Bangkok, Manila, Santiago-Valparaiso, and Lima-Callao. Many of these urban areas are coastal and have modern port facilities, making them easily accessible to foreign suppliers. In some instances, foreign suppliers are more competitive in these coastal urban markets than inland producers who confront inadequate infrastructure and cost-raising policies, like tolls, in getting their products to market. The changing age structure of the region's population affects food demand directly and indirectly. One direct effect is lower food demand. With an aging population, food demand declines, as activity levels and caloric needs decline. A second direct effect is change in dietary composition and the frequency of eating out. According to ERS research[3], older people eat more fresh fruit, fish, and eggs and eat out less frequently than younger people[4].

Table 2.1 World Population Growth

Year	Population	Average annual growth rate (%)
1950	2,555,360,972	1.47
1960	3,039,585,530	1.33
1970	3,707,475,887	2.07
1980	4,452,584,592	1.69
1990	5,281,653,820	1.57
2000	6,079,603,571	1.21
2003	6,299,763,405	1.15
2010	6,815,892,190	1.09
2020	7,541,773,753	0.90
2030	8,175,075,482	0.71
2040	8,722,646,253	0.58
2049	9,147,470,346	0.47

Source: U.S. Bureau of the Census, International Data Base.

---

[3] Economic Research Services: United States Department of Agriculture, http://www.ers.usda.gov
[4] Pacific Economic Cooperation Council: Where Demographics will take the Food System, Pacific Food System Outlook 2003-04, October 2003

In 2002 the world economy grew by 1.9 percent, a slight increase from 1.3 percent in 2001, but below the 2.7 percent annual average in the 1990s. The world's recorded output—and income—grew by more than $1.1 trillion. Lower-middle-income economies saw the fastest growth, followed by low-income economies. Upper-middle-income economies, affected by slowing investment and widespread uncertainty in financial markets, experienced negative growth. High-income economies, accounting for 81 percent of the world's gross domestic product (GDP), almost doubled their growth over 2001, from 0.9 percent to 1.6 percent. Over the past decade economic growth was fastest in East Asia and Pacific (averaging 7.3 percent a year) and South Asia (5.4 percent). Leading this growth were China and India, each accounting for more than 70 percent of its region's output. These two regions even did comparatively well in 2002, with East Asia registering 6.7 percent growth, demonstrating its continuing recovery from the financial crisis in 1998, when annual growth fell to 0.7 percent and a slight decline in the growth over 2001 in South Asia to the extent of 4.3 has been observed[5]. The population growth also affects the pattern of income distribution in a country. The aggregate consuming capacity depends on the total population as well as per capita income. Thus, the advanced countries where growth of population is low, exhibit high propensity to consume the goods and services. It may be observed that the multinational companies from United States of America are actively performing business in the advanced countries of Western Europe, Japan and Canada where per capita income and propensity of consumption are higher. In contrast, Bangladesh and Bhutan as well as other developing countries do not offer a sizeable market potential for the multinational companies.

The growing population has shown various divulging macroeconomic issues in the developing countries towards the incidence of poverty, low rate of employment, inequality in income distribution and the like. However, it must be noted that many developing countries are slowly emerging from poverty in response to the intervention of international community and World Bank. A carefully designed and implemented trade reforms can support growth and can be a "powerful motor" to reduce poverty. However, the mechanisms through which trade reforms affect the population can have varying impacts on the poor versus the rich. The challenge is to identify the appropriate policies that would have a positive impact on growth and a positive impact on the welfare of the poor. Changes in the trade regime affect the population through two main mechanisms. First, the trade regime affects the prices people pay and receive, as well as the demand for and returns to relevant factors of production. Second, the trade regime affects government revenues, and therefore the resources available for the supply of government services. The recent development in the global marketing may be discussed in reference to Western Europe, China and Japan that are becoming more competitive with the United States while the developing countries which have successfully implemented the institutional reforms policies are becoming potential markets. This has already reflected in substantial increase in United States exports to the developing countries since the 90's.

India is central to global stability, peace and economic prosperity, since its development is not just an issue for Indians but for the entire planet. The Government of India's Common Minimum Program showed a country with the vision, resources and capacity to address poverty and the inclusion of the hundreds of millions of rural poor. A recurrent theme is the

---

[5] World Bank: World Development Indicators-2004.

challenge of a "two-speed" model of India where, one in the global fast lane of entrepreneurial talent and technological creativity, a lane where Indian companies were becoming a global presence. In the other lane were the 600,000 villages of rural India where most of India's over 250 million people live at a substantial lower per capita income[6]. Official estimates show a decline in the poverty rate from 36 percent in the early 1990s to 26.1 percent in 1999/2000, but attempts to adjust the household survey underlying the 1999/2000 figures to make it comparable with earlier surveys result in a smaller degree of poverty reduction; how much smaller is a matter of considerable debate, and estimates vary widely. Recent work suggests that poverty has fallen at a somewhat lower rate—from 36 to 29 percent of the population by 1999/2000. Either way, over one quarter of India's population is poor[7]. In parallel with this faster growth, India has made impressive progress towards reducing income poverty, an important element of the Millennium Development Goals (MDGs). Continued progress has also been made on many social indicators, particularly literacy, which rose from 52 percent in 1991 to 65 percent in 2001. These improvements are both real achievements for India—and unquestionably of global significance.

On the contrary in North America over 70 percent of the population lives in the urban area. In the United States and Canada, people are moving away from urban cores to sub-urban habitats. In Mexico the trend of population moves has been found reversed as migration to urban areas remains prevalent. The shifts in the demographic patterns affect the economic activities primarily at the micro level in terms of the use of natural resources, manufacturing and marketing activities. However, in an aggregated manner such micro impacts may be observed at a macroeconomic level in reference to change in per capita income, consumption level, GDP and related indicators. Amidst such demographic shifts and variations in the constituents thereof over the last couple of decades, the world economy has accelerated sharply in 2004, expanding by an estimated 4 percent. The United States and Japan, whose economies grew by more than 4 percent, continued to lead Europe in the recovery. Even stronger growth was experienced by a number of large developing countries, notably China (8.8 percent), Russia (8.0 percent), and India (6.0 percent). Their performance helped power developing countries as a whole to an anticipated 6.1 percent growth rate in 2004, which may be described as an unprecedented expansion over the past 30 years. Across the developing world virtually every region enjoyed substantial growth, and increasing trade volumes thereof played an important role in sustaining the growth in the GDP of these countries.

Structure of Consumption

Demography, society and production resources largely determine the consumption pattern of a region. A system of consumption depends on production and marketing activities in a region. Hence, every country exhibits a specific pattern of consumption potential and structure. The consumption level in a country can be measured in terms of volume and compared with other countries in the region. The structure of consumption in a country may be determined by analyzing the behavioral attributes of the consumers thereof. A country may emphasize producer goods over consumer goods in reference to economic factors; what is

---

[6] Jim Wolfenshon: India – Key to Global Stability and Prosperity, Address of the World Bank President, New Delhi, 17 November 2004 (World Bank New Release No. 2005/164/SAR).
[7] World Bank: India – Country in Brief, September 2004.

considered as necessities in one economy may be luxuries in another. In addition, consumption in most advanced countries is characterized by a higher proportion of expenditures committed to capital goods than in developing countries, where substantially more is spent on consumer goods. The structural differences with regard to expenditures among nations can be explained by a theory propounded by the German statistician Ernst Engel in 1857. The Law of Consumption (Engel's law) states that poorer families and societies spend a greater proportion of their incomes on food than 'well-to-do people'. The Engle's law describes that the people generally spend a smaller share of their budget on food as their income rises. The reason is that food is a necessity, which poor people have to buy. As people get richer they can afford better-quality food, so their food spending may increase, but they can also afford luxuries beyond the budgets of poor people. Hence the share of food in total spending falls as income grows. Developing countries like the Philippines and Sri Lanka spend a larger percentage on food than countries like the United States.

Economic Indicators

The economic indicators are the variables that are used to measure the soundness of a country's economy such as GDP per head, the rate of unemployment or the rate of inflation. Such statistics are often subject to huge revisions in the months and years after they are first published, thus causing difficulties and embarrassment for the economic policymakers who rely on them. The analysis of factors of production is an important consideration in the international marketing to optimize the comparative advantages over natural resources, labor, capital and entrepreneurship. Entrepreneurs thus play an important role in enabling the economy to adapt to changing conditions and to new possibilities for material improvements by creating new production organizations, and even whole new industries. Because of its essential role in initiating the process of production, entrepreneurship is identified by some economists as a "fourth factor of production," alongside land, labor and capital. It may thus be explained that the higher the productivity of a factor of production, the higher may be the income that accrues to its providers. On the other hand, anything that rises above the expected levels of productivity within a society is responsible for increase in the overall prosperity of the society.

Tanzania[8] is one of the most indebted nations in the world and falls in to the category of least-developed country. It is situated on the east coast of Africa; the United Republic of Tanzania is one of the world's least developed countries. Tanzania, which includes the islands of Zanzibar and Pemba, became independent in 1961. The Constitution of the United Republic of Tanzania was adopted in 1977 with amendments passed in 1984 and 1992. The Constitution calls for a parliamentary form of government with a separation of powers among the executive, legislative, and judicial branches of government. The economy of country is essentially dependent on agriculture and has a per capita GNP of US$210. Tanzania's GDP has grown over 3% over the past few years and is forecast to grow at even higher rates through 2001. The country has a large debt burden, which may be an obstacle to its trade and economic development. This large debt burden may be an obstacle to economic development

---

[8] Country information in the cases is based on the report of World Trade Organization: Tanzania-February 2000, Trade Policy Review, Press Release (PRESS/TPRB/128, 21 February 2000).

as costs associated with debt servicing prevent the allocation of resources to activities that could serve to improve economic capacity, competitiveness, and increased investment. Because of Tanzania's program of structural reforms and fiscal restraint, it is in line to receive debt relief under the IMF and World Bank's Heavily Indebted Poor Countries (HIPC) program.

The Tanzanian agricultural sector constitutes over 50% of its national GDP and provides a majority of the country's export earnings, the report says. The sector has been substantially liberalized since the mid 1980s and market forces have been allowed to prevail, the report notes. The Government has withdrawn from direct involvement in production, processing, and marketing activities and has retained only its role in setting policies. The country has in the past few years experienced severe food shortages and varying levels of export earnings due to both droughts and floods. The country has rich natural resources and holds significant strength in the mining industry. Tanzania's mineral sector, focused primarily on gold production, offers one of the best opportunities for growth. With over US$600 million of new investment in this sector likely to be realized in the next 2-3 years, the mineral sector promises to be an increasingly important contributor to GDP and export earnings. However, the viability of Tanzanian gold production is closely tied to international gold prices, which have shown continued volatility. On the other hand, the manufacturing sector of the country is underdeveloped. The sector is dominated by food processing, beverages, agri-business, and light manufacturing, along with some textile and footwear producers. The report says that it has been hampered by high input costs. In particular, the tariff, which provides for high levels of protection for value-added goods, makes it difficult for Tanzanian manufacturers who must source inputs from outside the country. The Tanzania Bureau of Standards (TBS) is charged with the administration of standards issues, which include 572 published standards. TBS is a member of the International Organization for Standards (ISO) and has been notified to the WTO as the contact point for issues related to the Agreement on Technical Barriers. Most Tanzanian standards are voluntary in nature and TBS adopts international standards whenever they exist. The services sector, like the rest of the economy, has undergone significant liberalization in a number of areas, including telecommunications, insurance and financial services. The tourism constitutes the largest component of services GDP and holds promise for continued growth. Tanzania is a net importer of services and intends to underline its commitment to telecommunications liberalization by making specific bindings under the General Agreement on Trade in Services (GATS).

The price indicators in the international markets broadly include export and import price indices, consumer prices, wholesale prices and industrial producer prices. The export and import price indices can be used to determine the impact of exchange rate movements on the prices of exports and imports. International price data have been useful for both multilateral and bilateral trade agreements as often the countries utilize these statistics to negotiate trade agreements for some of the important industrial and consumer products such as construction material, plantation crop products like tea and coffee, cotton textiles, oil, airfreight services etc. A primary reason for measuring import prices is to track the impact they have on domestic inflation. Movement in import prices can often be an indicator of future inflation since some inputs to domestic production, as well as consumption, are imported. Advanced economies of developed countries have also experienced inflation during 2004-2006, but it has increased significantly in many emerging markets and developing countries, reflecting higher energy and food prices. In the United States, core inflation has gradually decreased below 2 percent during 2006-07. However, in the European countries inflation has been observed as constant below 2 percent during 2007, while in Japan, prices have essentially been stagnant. Some emerging markets and developing countries have observed higher inflation pressures, reflecting strong growth and rising food prices in their consumer price indices during 2006-07.

Export and import price indices are essential for assessing the impact of international trade on the domestic economy. Among their most important uses are analyzing developments in the trade balance, measuring foreign prices' contribution to domestic inflation, and deflating nominal values of exports and imports for estimating the volume of gross domestic product[9]. The Producer Price Index (PPI) is a family of indices that measures the average change over time in selling prices received by domestic producers of goods and services. PPIs measure price change from the perspective of the seller. This contrasts with other measures, such as the Consumer Price Index (CPI), that measure price change from the purchaser's perspective. Sellers' and purchasers' prices may differ due to government subsidies, sales and excise taxes, and distribution costs. It is difficult for a marketer to access information about and review all these indicators from each country. However, at any given time, the choice of economic indicators may be identified to determine the entry strategies of a firm. These indicators may reflect on the marketer's domestic operations and the potential business in the host country. The global economy is projected to grow by 5.2 percent in 2007 and 4.8 percent in 2008. The largest downward revisions to growth are in the United States, which is now expected to grow at 1.9 percent in 2008; in countries where spillovers from the United States are likely to be largest; and in countries where the impact of continuing financial market turmoil is likely to be more acute[10].

Financial Indicators

The financial indicators related to international marketing consist of corporate bond yield, factor income, value of local currency with reference to US dollars and money supply. Besides, the extent of foreign direct investment in a country also reveals its financial strength. A foreign investment is classified as a direct investment if the foreign investor holds at least 10 percent of the ordinary shares or voting rights in an enterprise and exerts some influence over its management. The higher yields of the corporate bonds indicate the soundness of the financial conditions in a country. Corporate bond interest rates and associated yield spreads are core topics in financial economics. The factors that affect the level of changes in these variables are important to many financial analysts. An examination of these variables and the relationships between them, as well as possible linkages between yield spreads and stock market behavior, is the focus of major financial analysis. In particular, changes in yield spreads between high and medium quality corporate bonds and Treasury bonds are examined, as are changes in the spread between the differing quality corporate bonds. Variations in the interest rates are given in financial market history and are taken for the financial analysis as the guide posts. Changes in macroeconomic factors such as inflation and the business cycle cause these fluctuations. Investor perception of risk, of course, affects both interest rates and stock market valuations. Interest rates tend to move together due to common influences, such

---

[9] Jemma Dridi and Kimberly Zieschang: Export and Import Price Indices, IMF Staff Working Papers, 51 (1), 2004, pp 1-9.
[10] International Monetary Fund: World Economic Outlook 2007, Executive Summary.

as inflation. Although this is true, the difference between corporate and government bond interest rates, and between corporate bonds rates on different quality bonds is not constant.

Other vital financial indicators include exchange rate, stock trends and long term interest rates. The sensitivity of longer-term interest rates to expectations about future short rates is also operative in a short term. This phenomenon is well illustrated by the rise in Japanese long-term rates during the summer of 1996 when financial markets began to anticipate that monetary policy would be tightened in response to recently published information on growth. Also, the interdependencies among financial markets have certainly increased with globalization; consequently the foreign exchange markets and bond markets abroad collectively have become much more sensitive to changes in financial conditions in partner countries. However, long-term interest rates are not fully protected from the influence of external factors even in the developing countries.

The international investments demand total transparency at both the ends—investor and the host country governance. The Organization for Economic Cooperation and Development (OECD) report "Foreign Direct Investment for Development: Maximizing Benefits, Minimizing Costs" envisages that the host country transparency and the legal protection are among the top concerns of investors[11]. As an example, the case of Tanzania can be cited where red tape in the investment establishment in the country is a prevalent hurdle for investors. Most decisions related to investment are made at the central level; investors interact with local government only during the consultation process and following establishment of the businesses in their area of jurisdiction[12]. Good public governance has two key ingredients: transparency and accountability. Recognizing the importance of improving transparency in the public sector, the economic reform package emphasized the Government's commitment to institutional reforms to generate transparency in a wide front. A main goal of public policy should be to rebuild key public institutions that would strengthen the nation's capacity to implement economic and social policies with popular support, transparency and good governance.

In recent years, economic growth has been driven mainly by consumption, contributing more than 75% of the growth of the country's gross domestic product. Increased investment is one of major factors to allow the country to restore its economic growth rate from 3%-4% levels used over the past couple of years to the pre-crisis levels of 6%-7% and to help create more jobs for millions of the unemployed including new entrants entering the market each year. Investment approvals, however, have been declining since the country was hit by the 1997-98 financial crises. The Table 2.2 exhibits the inflow trend of foreign direct investment in Asian countries.

Over the last twenty years, Mexico has made significant progress in reducing barriers to trade and foreign direct investment (FDI), and this has boosted GDP per capita growth. Nevertheless, Mexico needs to make further progress in reforming its trade policy by further reducing MFN tariff barriers and non-tariff barriers so as to promote efficiency in the economy. Barriers to FDI remain high, particularly in some services and infrastructure sectors, such as telecommunications and domestic land transport. Restrictions to foreign

[11] Organization for Economic Development and Cooperation: Foreign Direct Investment-Maximizing Benefits, Minimizing Costs, OECD, Paris, 2002.
[12] Mathur Rajive D and Chaterjee Sanchita: "Encouraging governance and transparency for investment", Paper presented in the Global Forum on Investment on Encouraging modern governance and transparency for investment, Hosted by Government of South Africa, November 17-18, 2003, Johannesburg.

ownership should be eased to attract higher inflows and thereby improve productivity. To broaden the benefits from FDI, supplier linkages between FDI investors and other firms in Mexico should be enhanced[13].

Table 2.2. Trend of FDI inflows into major Asian emerging market countries
(In US$ million)

	1990-94	1995	1996	1997	1998	1999	2000	2001	2004[a]
China	16,062	35,849	40,180	44,237	43,751	38,753	38,399	44,241	49,308
India	375	2,144	2,246	3,57	2,635	2,169	2,315	3,403	3,449
Indonesia	1,693	4,34	6,194	4,677	-356	-2,745	-4,550	-3,278	-1,513
Malaysia	4,172	4,178	5,078	5,137	2,163	3,895	3,788	554	3,203
Pakistan	322	723	922	716	506	532	308	383	823
Philippines	826	1,478	1,517	1,222	2,287	1,725	1,356	982	1,111
Thailand	1,9448	2,068	2,336	3,895	7,315	6,103	3,366	3,820	969
Vietnam	714	2,336	2,395	2,220	1,671	1,412	1,298	1,300	1,200
Total	26,112	53,122	61,048	65,681	59,972	51,844	46,629	51,405	58,550

a = up to June 30, 2004.
Sources: IMF, UNCETAD and World Bank.

Macroeconomics and Economic Advancement

In the 1990s macroeconomic policies improved in a majority of developing countries, but the growth dividend from such improvement fell short of expectations, and a policy agenda focused on stability turned that out to be associated with a multiplicity of financial crises[14]. The economic advancement of a country may be reviewed in reference to its fiscal, monetary, and exchange rate policies over time, and the effectiveness of the changing policy framework in promoting stability and growth. The contemporary concepts of economic advancement for developed countries include an entire range of governmental functions, including sectoral policy reform, economic integration, privatization, public sector enhancement, labor market competitiveness, investment climate enhancement, e-government, soft infrastructures for developing a knowledge economy, macroeconomic management and effective long-range planning. The weight of the public sector constitutes a serious impediment to more rapid growth for many countries. Importantly the large expenditure burden it requires does not always translate into an efficient and equitable distribution of services. Such performance is reflected by the public sector efficiency and governance in promoting the economic advancement of a country. The challenges of employment generation, economic growth and societal advancement in changing demographic contexts can only be addressed through productive investment and value building. The climate for investment is therefore critical for the countries which need a strategic direction and an economic concentration on value

---

[13] Organization for Economic Co-operation and Development (2007): Maximizing the gains from integration in the world economy, *OECD Economic Surveys*, 18, 93-135.
[14] Luis Servén, and Peter J. Montiel: Macroeconomic Stability in Developing Countries: How Much Is Enough? Working Paper # 3456, World Bank, November 2004.

building rather than value trading, which leads towards the higher degree of economic advancement in a country.

Economic advancement is directly proportional to the educational and training facilities available in the country. Human resources are not only producers of goods and services but also their consumers and also play a multifold role in economic development. Economic advancement is characterized by the following factors:

- Allocation of labor force to agriculture
- Energy available in large amounts at low cost per unit
- High level of GDP and income
- High levels of per capita consumption
- Relatively low rates of population growth
- Complex modern facilities for transportation, communication, and exchange
- Substantial amount of capital for investment
- Urbanization based on production as well as exchange
- Diversified manufacturing that accounts for an important share of   the labor force; and technology that includes ample media and methods for experiment.

These factors may be utilized to examine economic standing of the host country, and analysis of a large variety of information on these variables may help to categorize the countries on an economic development scale. Besides, many historical, geographic, political, and cultural factors are intimately related to the economic well-being of a nation.

Economic System

The economic system of a country is another important factor that a marketer must understand. Traditionally, there are two types of economic systems that exist prominently—state-owned and capitalist. The state-owned, or Marxist, system is pursued in communist countries, where all activities related to production and distribution are controlled by the state. The roots of capitalism in the economy and society have deep penetration. The patterns of economic activity that characterized the period of state capitalism began to change during the great boom of the 1950s and 1960s. The state capitals increasingly traded with each other – and as they did so the basis was laid for a new internationalization of production. World trade grew, on average, at about twice the rate of world output, until 1970s trade in the manufacturing sector was about the same proportion of world output as it had been in 1900 and 1930. Trade did not contract with the recessions of the mid-1970s and early 1980s as it had in the inter-war years. Despite a contraction of world output and world trade in 1982, trade grew faster than output throughout the rest of the 1980s. The concentration of industry through takeovers and mergers, often under the tutelage of the state, had led to the emergence in particular countries of huge firms, able to channel resources into innovation and productive investment on a scale undreamt of before[15]. In motors, the Japanese car firms established production facilities in the US, turning out more vehicles than the third biggest American

---

[15] Chris Herman: State and Capitalism Today, Die Roten Internet Archives, 2002. Extracted on 24 November 2004 (http://www.marxists.de/admin/2002en.htm).

firm, Chrysler; the nationalized French firm Renault began a series of acquisitions in the US, beginning with the small fourth US car firm American Motors; Volvo took over General Motors' heavy truck production in the US; Ford and Volkswagen merged their car production in Brazil; Nissan built an assembly plant in north east England to produce hundreds of thousands of cars a year, while Honda bought a 20 percent stake in Rover.

The living standards of rich and poor countries do not converge at welfare economics standards and most of the gains go to multinationals functioning in the developing countries. Such socio-economic conditions lead towards continuously growing polarization between the rich and the poor countries. The multinational companies are moving to the lowest-cost location implementing their production sharing strategies and emphasize the concept of "knowledge economy" that advocates operations with lesser manpower in order to gain the competitive advantage and streamline their operations[16]. Thus, capitalism in the new global economic order has been characterized largely by private ownership of the means of production and the freedom of transactions in international market governed by the regional trade agreements among the countries with less political interventions. The globalization policies with focus on privatization attempt to overrule the political-economic doctrines that advocate governments to impose political barriers to international trade usually in the form of taxes on imports or quantitative restrictions limiting the volume of legally allowable imports of each particular good in order to "protect" domestic firms manufacturing these same goods from foreign competition and thereby make them more profitable than would otherwise be the case under free competition.

Multiple exchange rates, multiple interest rates, protection of domestic products with licenses, quotas, tariffs in excess of what would have been necessary for infant industries, and a welter of regulations and bureaucratic obstacles to normal business in general have detrimental effects on economic growth. Mainstream economic theory suggests that economic welfare would be maximized when distortions are minimized. The most common pattern of economic reforms in Latin America has been, first, radical liberalization, and second, implementation of prudential norms that moderated the initial liberalization. The policy changes related to the financial system (namely, the removal of interest-rate controls, elimination of mandated credit to "priority" sectors, privatization of state banks, liberalization of the foreign investment regime, and more recently, improvements in the regulatory framework) have improved both the banking system and the stock market[17].

In Central and Eastern European countries, emerging Asian countries and Latin American countries structural reforms have been set off as growth drivers towards macroeconomic activities, international trade, financial markets, generation and use of public resources, governance, and labor markets. The macroeconomic policies adopted during the reforms process in these countries intend to maximize growth curbing rise in inflation and unemployment. Most common form of economic reforms include process of trade liberalization and reducing financial barriers required for investment and production operations to support the international trade movements. Trade liberalization process has also triggered off the opportunities in the countries of Central and Eastern Europe, Asia and Latin America to look for new business partnering countries and expand their international trade

---

[16] Noreena Hertz: The Silent Takeover - Global Capitalism and the Death of Democracy, William Heinemann. London, 2001 pp 22-76.
[17] Rajagopal (2007), Where did Trade Liberalization Drive Latin American Economy: A Cross Sectional Analysis, *Applied Econometrics and International Development*, 6 (2), 89-108.

relations. The paper advocates that such trade relationship should be based on fundamental principles and shared values, which in turn can be translated into clear political messages and a general sustained process of dialogue and cooperation for sustainable trade development among the partnering countries. The negotiations should also be dealt on simplifying the customs rules and procedures and enhancing the coverage of products and services under international trade. New markets, lower production costs and higher profit rates have been the main motivators in investing to the transition countries[18].

Macroeconomic Policies

The macroeconomic policy refers to the top-down strategy developed and implemented in a country by the government and central banks, usually intended to maximize growth while keeping down inflation and unemployment. The growth factors determining the incentives towards investing in human capital for developing new products include government policies. Countries with broadly free-market policies, in particular free trade and the maintenance of secure property rights typically have higher growth rates. By 1990, most developed countries reckoned to have long-term trend growth rates of 2-2.5% a year. However, during the 1990s, growth rates started to rise, especially in the United States. Some economists said this was the result of the birth of a new economy based on a revolution in productivity, largely because of rapid technological innovation but also (perhaps directly stemming from the spread of new technology) due to increases in the value of human capital. In the end of the 20th century, it has been argued that developments in information technology and globalization leading towards free trade through the regional trade agreements, has given birth to a new economy initiated in United States. These developments have shown a higher rate of productivity and growth than the previous economy it replaced. Open economies have grown much faster on average than closed economies. The main instruments of macroeconomic policy are deviations in the interest rates and money supply, taxation and public spending, known as fiscal policy. It has been observed that with the rise of rate of unemployment and inflation, the growth rate of the economy declines and the GDP of the country falls[19]. This may be an evidence of poorly planned macroeconomic policy and implementation thereof. Higher public spending relative to GDP is generally associated with slower growth.

The rise in the rate of inflation is contributed by the high social expenditure and political instability in a country. However, business cycles may simply be an unavoidable fact of economic life that macroeconomic policy, however well conducted, can never be sure of conquering. The long run pattern of growth and recession in the business that may be explained as boom and bust of the economy of a country or a region may be described as business cycle. There are two main versions of the new paradigm that have attracted followers in America lately over the reactions of the previous business cycles[20]. Of these, one version states that the country's long-term growth rate has shifted upwards while the other reveals that the old pattern of boom and bust has disappeared in the light of the free trade and globalization movement by 2000. Strong trade liberalizations in Latin America during the

---

[18] Rajagopal (2007), Dynamics of Growth in Foreign Trade in Transitional Economies: Analysis of European, Latin American and Asian Countries, *Journal of East-West Business*, 13 (4), 37-64.
[19] The Economist: Insecurities, November 11, 2004.
[20] The Economist: Beyond the business Cycles, October 21, 1999.

1980s and the 1990s have introduced a good measure of import competition, but trade policies alone are not sufficient to create a competitive environment in an economy. The presence of non-traded goods, vertical integration, monopolized distribution systems, the limited use of trade policies to foster competition, and sometimes the use of anti-dumping measures, countervailing duties, and safeguards as protective devices have constrained the effectiveness of trade policy as an instrument of competition policy. Competition policies, such as anti-trust, merger controls, and other regulatory means, can prevent the abuse of market power, dominance, exclusionary practices, and complicity among competitors. Domestic competition is further enhanced by foreign ownership and liberalized investment regimes. These latter provisions provide a market presence that enhances competition. A study discusses that trade and competition policies are essential complements and when used together they can lead to higher levels of welfare. There are of course tensions between these two policies that arise from globalization, regional policies, technical barriers, certain forms of industrial policies, and macroeconomic exigencies[21].

Tariff Structures

One of the prime objectives of the World Trade Organization is to negotiate among member countries to reduce tariffs barriers to support free trade conditions. Doha debate among all member countries of the World Trade Organization emphasize efforts to reduce or as appropriate eliminate tariffs, including the reduction or elimination of tariff peaks, high tariffs, and tariff escalation, as well as non-tariff barriers, in particular on products of export interest to developing countries[22]. Tariff cuts of developed countries were introduced in a phased manner, over five years from the beginning of 1995. The result is a 40 percent cut in their tariffs on industrial products, from an average of 6.3-3.8 percent. The value of imported industrial products that receive duty-free treatment in developed countries will jump from 20-44 percent. There will also be fewer products charged high duty rates. The proportion of imports into developed countries from all sources facing tariff rates of more than 15 percent will decline from 7- 5 percent. The proportion of developing country exports facing tariffs above 15 percent in industrial countries will fall from 9-5 percent[23]. It has been observed that uniform percentage reductions in tariff may increase the consumer price in the importing country, whose initial tariff is lower. Thus, importing countries with relatively low tariffs may prefer a bilateral trade agreement to a multilateral one to ensure consumer gains[24]. Erosion of trade preferences currently being enjoyed by the least developed countries and some developing countries remains an important area in the ongoing trade negotiations and is an important issue not only in terms of welfare, but also as it has impacts on incomes for preference-receiving countries[25].

---

[21] Rajapatirana Sarath (1994), The Interface of Trade, Investment and Competition Policies: Issues and Challenges for Latin America, World Bank, Latin America and Caribbean Department, Report # 009.

[22] World Trade Organization: Doha WTO ministerial 2001: Ministerial Declaration, Official Document WT/MIN(01)/DEC/1, 20 November 2001.

[23] World Trade Organization: Understanding WTO www.wto.org

[24] Ishikawa J and Mukunoki H (2008), Effects of Multilateral Trade Liberalization on Prices, *Review of International Economics*, 16 (1), 37-44.

[25] Bchir, M H *et al* (2007), The Doha development round and Africa: partial and general equilibrium analyses of tariff preference erosion, *Agricultural Economics*, 37, Supplement 1, 287-295.

Table 2.3. Tariff Dispersion among Latin American Countries (Standard deviations)

Trade Bloc	Country	1985	1986	1987	1988	1989	1990	1991	1992	1993	1994	1995	1996	1997	1998	1999
Mercosur	Argentina	14.5	20.5	20.5	21.5	21.5	8.6	8.6	7.4	5.0	6.7	7.6	7.0	6.8	6.9	8.3
	Brazil	36.7	30.0	30.0	26.2	17.2	19.8	17.3	14.2	9.5	8.2	6.9	8.5	7.7	7.3	7.8
	Paraguay	-	15.2	15.2	15.2	15.2	13.0	1.4	7.8	6.8	7.7	6.9	7.1	6.7	6.5	7.4
	Uruguay	16.2	18.8	18.8	14.4	14.4	9.7	9.7	5.9	5.9	5.9	7.1	7.3	6.9	7.9	4.3
Prospecting for Mercosur	Chile	3.2	1.7	1.7	1.0	1.0	0.9	0.9	0.7	0.7	0.7	0.7	0.7	0.7	0.7	0.7
	Colombia	28.2	16.8	16.8	17.6	17.6	14.2	8.3	6.3	6.3	6.3	4.9	6.3	6.3	6.2	6.2
	Peru	26.8	25.9	25.9	27.4	27.4	22.6	22.6	4.4	4.4	4.4	4.4	4.4	4.4	2.9	2.5
	Venezuela	28.6	30.2	30.2	31.4	31.4	17.1	17.1	11.3	11.3	11.3	4.8	4.8	6.1	6.1	5.9

Source: Computed on the data available with ECLAC, UNCTAD, WTO and IDB for the referred periods.

The trade among the Latin American and East Asian countries certainly exhibit enormous potential and apart from the trading of physical goods the services trade in terms of consultancy, transfer of technology and managerial training may also be explored bi-regionally. However, there exist differences among both the regions in factor endowment between the generally natural-resource-abundant Latin America and the natural resource-scarce Asia-Pacific Geography (*i.e.* distance) and differences in the availability of capital, knowledge (*e.g.* Japan, South Korea and Taiwan) and labor (China) also have been major drivers of the bilateral trade. It has been observed by many researchers that Latin America aggressively opened up to world trade and investment in the late 1980s and its mixed results have emerged over two decades in expansion, diversification and upgrading its exports. The Asia-Pacific countries have shown extraordinary success in diversifying their exports and in raising their stakes in the world economy, while at the same time their domestic market is largely protected against import competition. Such trade policies of this region have also alarmed the concerns for global partnering and business expansions. Instruments such as tariff, non-tariff barriers, trade related investment measures (TRIMS) and barriers to domestic distribution still play an import role in these countries, although there are important cross-country differences in their timing, scope and importance. Table 2.3 exhibits the tariff dispersion structure among the Mercosur countries.

The last several years have witnessed deep changes in trade policy in the Latin American region; this process has generally been accompanied by other far-reaching macroeconomic reforms. The overhaul of the tariff structure included the reduction of the average rate as well as the reduction in its dispersion. Though the gains along this dimension are not very notable throughout the nineties, there is a significant reduction relative to the levels observed during the second half of the eighties. Relative to Chile's structure –which is almost flat– there is still some room to reduce tariff dispersion by the Mercosur member countries.

It may be observed from the results exhibited in the above Table that tariff structure had high variations in all the countries under study except Chile during 1985 while in the post reforms period such variation in the tariff structure in Latin American countries was reduced. The dramatic change may be experienced when the deviation in the tariff was found to be 7.8 in 1999 as against 36.7 during 1985. It may be seen from the Table that Chile has been the pioneer of trade liberalization since the mid 1980s as it has liberated the tariff regime to lead globalization. Venezuela, and to a lesser extent, Brazil, made considerable progress in trade reform in the late 1980s; all of the remaining countries conducted major trade reforms in the early 1990s. Whereas Brazil and Venezuela liberalized their tariff regime over a few years, Argentina, Colombia, and Peru conducted faster trade liberalizations. It may be stated that the higher the average level and dispersion of tariffs and para-tariffs such as duties and customs fees, the more distorted the trade development. In the specific case of agriculture, although the coverage of non-tariff barriers did fall considerably, in some countries it nevertheless remained for a time more significant than in other sectors. This can be attributed in part due to the desire of governments to protect their farm sectors from world price fluctuations and to counteract export subsidies.

A research study examines the link between tariff changes and manufacturing employment differing across firms with various productivity and leverage characteristics over the period 1988-94 in reference to Canadian trade and economy. The results suggest that the effect of domestic tariff reductions on employment was typically small, but that losses were significantly larger for less productive firms. For instance, firms with average productivity in 1988 responded to domestic tariff changes by cutting employment by 11.3 percent over the period 1988-94, while lower-productivity firms typically shed 20.8 percent of their workforce over the same period. The results also indicates that firms with unhealthy balance sheets— those with relatively too much equity or too much leverage— downsized more in the face of declining domestic tariffs, suggesting that financial constraints became more binding when tariff cuts were implemented and suggest that firms with high productivity and better financial health were better positioned to face the challenge of trade[26]. Another study reveals that positive correlation between real investment rates and real income levels across countries is driven largely by differences in the price of investment relative to output. The high relative price of investment in poor countries is due to the low price of consumption goods in those countries. Investment prices are no higher in poor countries. Thus, the low real investment rates in poor countries are not driven by high tax or tariff rates on investment[27]. Hence, the optimal tariff problem arises under a revenue constraint. It has been analytically presented in a research study that revenue-constrained optimal tariff structure is characterized by the following two rules— the optimal tariff rate is lower for the import good that is a closer substitute for the export good, and the stronger the cross-substitutability between imports, the closer the optimal tariff is to uniformity[28].

Trade, Tariff and Inflation

It has been observed in general that tariffs tend to be inflationary and free trade is deflationary. However, many arguments express that protectionism has generally created inflation in developing economies, though the experience of the developed countries including the United States of America was totally different on this aspect. Tariffs in most of

[26] LaRochelle-Côté, Sébastien (2007), Tariff reduction and employment in Canadian manufacturing, *Canadian Journal of Economics*, 40 (3), 843-860.
[27] Hsieh Chang-Tai and Klenow Peter J (2007), Relative Prices and Relative Prosperity, *The American Economic Review*, 97 (3), 562-585.
[28] Hatta T and Ogawa Y (2007), Optimal Tariffs under a Revenue Constraint, *Review of International Economics*, 15 (3), 560-573.

the developed countries were never associated with rising prices, and trade liberalization with declining prices[29]. High tariffs were always followed by sharp drops in the cost of living. Despite the greater complexities associated with open economy macroeconomics, the policy conclusions for a closed economy remain remarkably unaffected. While Keynesians and heterodox economists believe that government should actively intervene, conservatives remain skeptical about the desirability of such interventions[30]. A study conducted in reference to growth in trade and its impact on inflation in Africa, reveals interesting results stating that inflation drags down growth over the longer term while in the short run, growth above its trend requires accelerating inflation. Thus, in order to pull the economic growth substantially above the low trend, inflation needs to be abandoned. However, this would be counterproductive over the longer term, once the negative relationship between inflation and growth manifests itself[31]. Another argument emphasizes that globalization, taking the form of a higher import component of consumption and a larger export component of GDP, is the cause of the apparent breakdown in the relationship between excess demand and inflation. However, increasing openness of the economy may be one of the significant strategies that developing nations could use to re-establish the relationship between inflation and capacity utilization in all sectors of the economy[32]. On the contrary a long standing proposition states that trade openness is associated with declining prices which makes the protectionism inflationary. The dependency of the central bank is associated with average inflation and the negative relation between trade openness and inflation, is likely to be lower in the countries having independent central banks[33].

It is well established that inflation, for example, is costly and that its elimination is beneficial for the long-run growth. The same is true of structural reforms. Multiple exchange rates, multiple interest rates, protection of domestic products with licenses, quotas, tariffs in the excess of what would have been necessary for infant industries, and a welter of regulations and bureaucratic obstacles to normal business in general have detrimental effects on economic growth. Mainstream economic theory suggests that economic welfare would be maximized when distortions are minimized. Accordingly, a removal of distortions of both macroeconomic and microeconomic nature would have beneficial effects on economic activity and the rate of growth[34]. The growth and development may result in being slower in a country or region in a normal process than with a stirred process of reforms. After years of poor economic management, many Latin American and Caribbean countries are experiencing a process of structural reforms that places them on a path to a superior economic performance[35]. Two basic principles identify this process of economic reforms: fiscal and monetary discipline, and reliance on market forces to determine the allocation and distribution of resources. Some researchers find positive advancements in developing countries in order to improve economic development and analyze the main factors of

[29] Batra, Ravi (2001), Are Tariffs Inflatory, *Review of International Economics*, 9 (3), 373-382.

[30] Stiglitz, Joseph E.; Ocampo, José Antonio; Spiegel, Shari; French-Davis, Ricardo and Nayyar, Deepak (2006), *Open Economy Complications*, Stability with Growth, Oxford Scholarship Online Monographs, 87-105.

[31] Hodge, D (2006), Inflation and Growth in South Africa, *Cambridge Journal of Economics*, 30 (2), 163-180.

[32] Dexter, Albert S; Levi, Maurice D and Nault, Barrie R (2005), International Trade and the Connection between Excess Demand and Inflation, *Review of International Economics*, 13 (4), 699-708.

[33] Romer D (1993), Openness and Inflation: Theory and Evidence, *Quarterly Journal of Economics*, 108, 869-903.

[34] Igor Paunovic: *Growth and Reforms in Latin America and the Caribbean in the 1990s*, United Nations Economic Commission for Latin America and the Caribbean (ECLAC), Working Paper, Economic Division, May, 2000.

[35] Easterly William and Sergio Rebelo (1993): Fiscal Policy and Economic Growth-An Emperical Investigation, *Journal of Monetary Economics*, 32 (3), 417-458.

production that should be improved in order to get a higher degree of development taking into account the results of econometrics models of demand and supply[36].

The social perspectives of economic growth have also been discussed in some studies. A study discussed the importance of education on a sustained economic development strategy, taking into account inter-sector relations and the influence of education in the growth of production per head using three cross-country models[37]. The study recommends the need for evolving new international policies for improving the educative level of the population in less developed countries. Some researchers specializing in economic growth have analyzed the export-led growth in many countries and insist upon the importance of openness to increase real gross domestic product. In this context, one of the studies discusses the important role of human capital, manufacturing and imports to increase real income per inhabitant and non-agrarian employment[38]. The study argues that beyond increasing the degree of openness in order to increase foreign demand, it is also necessary to relate foreign trade with the supply side considering the general positive effects of imports on the domestic growth of industry, building and services. It has been observed that there exists a significant positive impact of political globalization, whereas economic and social globalization does not generate favorable influences when development level and regional differences are operated as controls. Globalization is largely identified by increased global flows and exchanges contributing rather than hampering progress in human welfare[39].

MICROECONOMIC ENVIRONMENT

An environment surrounding a specific product or market concerning the competition rather than a country's overall economic environment refers to the microeconomic environment. A careful analysis of a microenvironment indicates whether a company can successfully enter a specific market. It may be hypothesized that rising prosperity of a nation depends on the productivity with which it uses its human, capital and natural resources. This is manifested in the way in which a nation's firms compete. Productivity, in turn, is a function of the interplay of three factors: the Political, Legal and Macroeconomic Context; the Quality of the Microeconomic Business Environment; and the Sophistication of Company Operations and Strategy. Together they determine the capacity of a nation to produce internationally competitive firms and support rising prosperity. A context that creates pressure for firms continuously to upgrade the source and sophistication of their advantage and at the same time supports the upgrading process is a favorable microeconomic context. Pressure for upgrading is supplied by *demand conditions* featuring sophisticated and demanding customers, whose demands spur the local firms to innovate in order to upgrade their product/service offerings.

[36] Guisan Maria Carmen and Aguayo Eva (2005), Industry and Economic Development in Latin America 1980-2002, *Applied Econometrics and International Development*, 5 (3), 133-142.

[37] Guisan M.C., Aguayo E. and Exposito, P. (2001): Economic Growth and Cycles: Cross-Country Models of Education, Industry and Fertility and International Comparisons, *Applied Econometrics and International Development*, 1 (1), pp 1-18.

[38] Guisan M.C., Malacon C. and Exposito P. (2003): *Effects of Integration of Mexico into NAFTA on Trade Industry, Employment and Economic Growth*, University of Santiago de Compostela, Economic Development Series, Working Paper No. 68, pp 1-24.

[39] Tsai, Ming-Chang (2007), Does globalization affects human well-being? *Social Indicators Research*, 81(1), 103-126.

Particularly valuable is pressure from local customers that anticipate the nature of demand elsewhere in the world. Different competitors, however, might aim to satisfy different types of demand: existing, latent, or incipient. *Existing demand* refers to a product bought to satisfy a recognized need. *Latent demand* applies in a situation where a particular need has been recognized, but no products have been offered. *Incipient demand* describes a projected need that will emerge when customers become aware of it sometime in the future.

Competition may be analyzed in reference to the characteristics of products as breakthrough, competitive, and improved. A *breakthrough product* is a unique innovation that is mainly technical in nature, such as the digital watch, VCR, and personal computer. A *competitive product* is one of many brands currently available in the market and has no special advantage over the competing products. An *improved product* is not unique but is generally superior to many existing brands. For example, let us assume Aubrey Organics is interested in manufacturing shampoo for tender hair in Turkey and seeks entry into the emerging market in the middle-eastern countries. The company finds that in addition to a number of local brands, Johnson & Johnson's baby shampoo and Helene Curtis Industries' Suave Shampoo are the competitive products in the market. Proctor and Gamble has recently entered the market with its Pantene Pro-V brand, which is considered as an improved product. Most of the competition appears to be addressing the existing demand. However, no attempts have been made to satisfy latent demand or incipient demand. After reviewing various considerations, Aubrey Organics may decide to fulfill latent demand with an improved offering through its Camomile Luxurious brand. Based on market information, the company reasons that a hair problem most consumers face in that part of the world is dandruff. No brand has addressed itself to that problem. Even Proctor & Gamble's new entry mainly emphasizes health of hair. Thus, analysis of the competition with reference to product offerings and demand enables Aubrey Organics to determine its entry point into the market of middle-eastern countries. The companies need to analyze some important issues as below while examining the micro-economic environment:

- Who is the competition now, and who will it be in the future?
- What are the key competitors' strategies, objectives and goals?
- How important is a specific market to the competitors, and are they enough to continue to invest?
- What unique strengths do the competitors have?
- Do they have any weaknesses that make them vulnerable?
- What changes are likely in the competitors' future strategies?
- What are the implications of competitors' strategies on the market, the inc. and one's own company?

One of the appropriate ways to examine the competition is to draw up a demographic profile of the industry. Markets dominated by small, single-industry businesses or small regional competitors differ significantly from those dominated by national or multi-industry companies. The competitor strengths may be measured by analyzing various functional indicators in marketing as described below:

- Market share
- Differential advantages

- Cost advantages
- Reputation
- Distribution capabilities
- Core competencies
- Perceptions of target buyers
- Competitors' financial strength, which determines their ability to spend money on advertising and promotions, among other things
- Competitor's ability and speed of innovation for new products and services

It is necessary to list the strengths and weaknesses of the competitors from the customer's viewpoint and analyze how a company can capitalize on their weaknesses and meet the challenges represented by their strengths. The information on the competitor information might be easily obtained by getting a copy of their annual report. It might take analysis of many information sources to understand competitors' strategies and objectives. In an international market, the business takes place in a highly competitive, volatile environment, so it is important to understand the competition. Some questions as illustrated below can help the marketer to map the micro-economic variables in reference to a competitor:

- Who are your five nearest direct competitors?
- Who are your indirect competitors?
- Is their business growing, steady, or declining?
- What can you learn from their operations or from their advertising?
- What are their strengths and weaknesses?
- How does their product or service differ from yours?

The competition in photo film products has been increasing with competitive price and promotion strategies among the major international brands like Kodak and Fuji. The consumers have found a bona fide competitor to Kodak in the name of Fujifilm. Clearly, Fujifilm has emerged from a minor player in the early 1980's in the American market to take a solid number two position within the US market and has caught the attention, as well as the fury, of Kodak. The success of low priced super stores such as Wal-Mart has taught retailers that diversification, scrambled marketing and "one-stop" shopping are important to consumers. As consolidation in the retail industry sweeps in mass marketing, food and drug accounts, retailers realize they must maintain their competitive advantage or close shop. To survive, they are squeezing manufacturers for quality products at competitive prices to capture profit margins for expansion within the industry. This environment has provided an opportunity for Fujifilm to prosper in an otherwise stable and mature photographic industry. Though Kodak and Fuji fight for market share, the real winner and benefactor is the consumer, both the companies officially deny that they are engaging in a price war, but for each move Fuji makes, Kodak counters with a strategic move. Kodak and Fuji traditionally enjoyed healthy margins and treated the market as a mutually profitable duopoly[40]. Then in the spring of 1996, Fuji cut prices on film by 10 to 15 percent after Costco Wholesalers decided to go exclusively with Kodak. Fuji had excess inventory of 2.5 millions rolls of film.

---

[40] Finnerty C Thomas: Kodak vs. Fuji: The Battle for Global Market Share, Institute of Global Business Strategy, Lubin School of Business, Pace University, 2000, pp 4-23.

They distributed the heavily discounted film to other retailers to avoid "expiring" film and thus began a correlation between price cutting and market share. Once consumers tried Fuji, they found they liked the product as long as it was priced lower than Kodak. By 1998 the severe pace of competition between Kodak and Fuji seemed to slow down, with the exception of value packs. However, still the companies are on neck-to-neck competition in the market, though other brands like *Agfa, Konica* have made a dent in the global retailing including American markets.

Competitor analysis is an ongoing process that allows the new entrants to identify their respective strengths and weaknesses. Analyzing the movements of competitors, a firm may develop better understanding of what products or services to be offered in the segmented market; how to market them effectively; and positioning them appropriately in the given market. One way to gauge the strength of a given competitor in your market is to measure its online presence. How often does the competitor's brand appear in all forms on the Internet? In particular, how often does it appear in reference to your market, relative to yours and other companies? There are other, almost limitless, ways to learn about competitors. Competitive intelligence involves legal methods of data collection and analysis, from scouring securities filings and news reports to database research to schmoozing with representatives of rival companies at trade shows.

The soundness of the economy of a country largely governs the consumer confidence, which further determines the buying plans of the consumers. A favorable economic environment helps consumers to optimize their buying decisions and augment propensity to spend money. The reverse occurs when economic conditions are unfavorable. The economic environment in Brazil was not encouraging for the various segments of consumers during the period 1998-1999, though the inflation was under control. The credit restrictions have had a negative impact on consumption during the above referred period. However, after the country exercised appropriate economic measures to stabilize the economy of the country in the recent past, it has been observed that foreign business corporations consider Brazil to be Latin America's most attractive investment target. International marketers should examine the extent to which their business is vulnerable to economic conditions. For example, in a booming economy, consumers tend to buy durable goods, on the contrary in recession they would avoid spending money. The prevailing economic environment is just an indicator to review the business fit in the given region or country. Even if the short-run economic environment is not conducive to profits, a company may decide to enter an overseas market in anticipation of favorable long-term economic prospects in the country such as growing political stability, declining inflation or the low wage rates. However, the long-run perspective is the most critical decision factor, which provides the firm sufficient resources to endure waiting for the future favorable environment. The market attractiveness of Brazil may be described from this point of view.

The microeconomic environment of a product or market also plays a significant role in its market performance in an overseas market. A very successful Asian electronics company, for many years a leader in the electronic home appliances market, launched a cheaper version of its traditional product almost simultaneously in south-east Asia and in Europe. The marketing approach comprising product design, pricing, and advertising was quite similar in both areas. However, the product has been very successful in the home market, but in Europe sales fell far below expectations. The product in the home market was successful as the company's product strategy was in the mature phase of its life cycle, while in Europe it was at its beginning. The brand had stronger penetration in the home market than in the European market that led to the weak consumer perception on the innovativeness of the product in Europe. Besides, the low price without explaining the product concept in the south-east Asian countries market was sensible but this strategy had a negative impact on the European consumers. It may be observed from the above example that the Asian company got into problems in Europe because it could not be competitive in Europe and had a low market share. Besides, the product was new to the European market and at the beginning of the product life cycle it presented an unfamiliar concept to the market. In other words, the Asian company did not orient its marketing program with the product/market environment existing in Europe.

SCREENING THE MICROECONOMIC ENVIRONMENT

In a given perspectives of microeconomic environment, a foreign firm intending to operate marketing activities in the host country may perform an opportunity analysis to determine the suitability to seek entry into a foreign country's market in terms of economic cost-benefit ratio. A conceptual scheme for analyzing economic environment may be drafted and implemented by the firm in order to evaluate existing and potential marketing opportunities in the host country. The conceptual scheme requires consideration of some of the following variables:

Financial Variables
- Capital acquisition
- Interest rates for commercial borrowings
- Payback tenure
- Cash inflow by period
- Cash outflow by period
- Returns on capital employed
- Exchange rate fluctuations
- Repatriation of funds status
- Projected investments linked to productivity
- Functional cost indicators in the business

Marketing Variables
- Market size and potential
- Distribution and logistics
- Competition mapping
- Promotional costs
- Socio-cultural and community factors

Product-market Engineering Variables
- Availability of raw material for building infrastructure
- Raw material for manufacturing
- Physical and environmental factors
- Accessibility factors

- Availability of labor (skilled/unskilled)
- Local management factors
- Regional economic infrastructure
- Quality control and standardization
- Services management indicators

Economic and Political Variables

- Foreign investment policy of the host government
- Capital flow controls
- Inflation status
- Tax regulations
- Internal political stability
- International relations of host country
- Political ideology
- Civil/labor unrest in the host country

Social and Legal Variables

- Demography and household status
- Education, religion and social behavior of the people
- Community and culture
- Ownership restrictions
- Import/export regulations
- Acquisition of immobile assets

There are many other microeconomic variables that may be selected for industry or market analysis in the host country depending upon the specific requirement of the firm. The microeconomic foundations of productivity rest on two interrelated areas, the sophistication with which companies compete, and the quality of the microeconomic business environment. The analysis of the above listed variables would help in determining the scarcity dimensions of the product or services in the selected market in the host country, production possibilities, and opportunity cost that may favor the firm's decision towards entry into the host country market. The careful examination of these variables would also help the firm to know the supply and demand situation, free markets, the price system, and government policy. Microeconomic analysis of business decisions in competitive and noncompetitive markets, labor markets, capital and natural resource markets, and externalities can also be determined by the international firms through the analysis of the spatial and temporal microeconomic variables in the host country. In addition the analysis of the most relevant microeconomic variables may also help in assessing the strategic decision making issues like market breakdown, income redistribution, and role of government, trade and tariff regimes and anticipated gains from international trade over the short and long run. The major microeconomic factors can substantially influence trade forecasts. This can include shortages, strikes, supply problems, defects, capital problems, mergers, consolidations and a wide variety of other factors.

With the use of these variables, analysis of marketing opportunity centers on two sets of criteria: cost/benefit criteria and risk/reward criteria. The cost-benefit criteria should respond to a series of questions towards the efficiencies of markets, competition, and the financial implications of doing business in a foreign country. In view of the microeconomic environment the firm may determine the consumer preferences on products by available segments. More significantly the firm may determine the consumer price sensitivity, propensity of consumption and whether the consumers have enough to pay a price that will yield a profit to the firm. The size of the market may also be known by analyzing the microeconomic variables in the host country. The analysis of these variables would also reveal the kind of competition the firm would face and the possibility of deriving generalizations on the marketing decisions. Such issues of generalization of marketing strategy within a market arise from the modified marketplace competition. Such a situation exists in some countries as they own or subsidize competitors in specific industries like textiles, power generation and petroleum. In such cases, the foreign business usually is at a disadvantage even when it is pitted against an inefficient local business. The analysis of the microeconomic environment would also be helpful to a firm in deciding towards deploying the type of resources in reference to the volume of resources to be mobilized and committed, and at what cost. Such analysis would also reflect upon the expected returns on capital employed and how long it might take to recover the investment. The risk and/or reward criteria emphasize the constantly changing overall mix of situations in the social, political, and economic climates of a host country. In terms of economics, the macroeconomic characteristics of a nation will almost always affect the specific economics of business. The national economic objectives of the country, therefore, also figure in a firm's decision to explore entry there.

The microeconomic environment in reference to territorial infrastructure such as roads, telecommunication and power network contributes significantly to the firm's decision towards entry to any country. The example of the Czech Republic may be described emphasizing the impact of the infrastructural factors of a country on international trading decisions. The Czech Republic ranks rather poorly in international indicators of the administrative requirements to set up a business, and this detracts in particular from the incentives to set up small enterprises. Productivity growth has long since been hampered by a system that allows too many poorly performing firms to continue operating and does not adequately prevent asset stripping. In telecommunications, despite the progress in reform, dominance of previously state-run Cesky Telecom is of a major concern in the country. Prices for some telecommunication services are, on average, high and delay in infrastructure and market development has slowed the spread of high-speed internet. It is intended that this issue, along with others, including the efficiency of the regulator, will be dealt with in a new telecommunications act. Strong market dominance is also an issue in the energy sector. The state-owned gas company was sold entirely to the German company RWE and competition remains weak. In electricity, vertical and horizontal unbundling has to be completed and the incumbent, CEZ, still has significant interests across production, distribution and sales. Across the network industries, unbundling is an important instrument to enhance competition and should be implemented wherever appropriate[41]. Reforms have long-since been planned, and it is welcome that new legislation looks finally set to go ahead. The legislation aims at strengthening the role of creditors, speeding up proceedings and allowing composition to play a bigger role. Likewise, efforts to streamline business registration are welcome and should be implemented as soon as possible. The general business climate is also damaged by issues in

---

[41] OECD: Economic Survey of the Czech Republic-2004, Organization for Economic Cooperation and Development, 2004 www.oecd.org

network-industry competition, as some services, notably internet, are expensive in international comparison. However, growth in the Czech Republic is projected by the OECD to be around 4 percent, marking substantial progress over past performance and reflecting the success of past reforms. Investment and exports are expanding rapidly, taking over from a period of strong increase in domestic consumption. In many areas, good policy has already created healthy conditions for growth. For some years now, inflation has been low and stable and membership of the European Union has prompted further progress in structural reform. The labor market is not performing as well as it should and this is reflected in rising unemployment. The intention to reintroduce legal extensions in wage setting would risk reducing the flexibility of wage determination. Furthermore, the high-tax wedge damps both demand and supply and leads to grey-sector activity. A well-designed competition law, effective law enforcement and competition-based economic reforms promote increased efficiency, economic growth and employment for the benefit of all[42].

EXPANSION OF MICROECONOMIC INSIGHTS

In brief, microeconomics discusses the supply and demand, and the way they interact in various markets. Microeconomic analysis can be carried easily from one topic to another and it holds the core of one of the recognized subfields of economics. Labor economics, for example, is built largely on the analysis of the supply and demand for labor of different types. The field of industrial organization deals with the different mechanisms (monopoly, cartels, and different types of competitive behavior) by which goods and services are sold. International economics discusses the demand and supply of individual traded commodities, as well as of a country's exports and imports taken as a whole, and the consequent demand for and supply of foreign exchange. Agricultural economics deals with the demand and supply of agricultural products, farmland, farm labor, and the other factors of production involved in agriculture. The economics of supply and demand has a sort of moral or normative overtone, at least when it comes to dealing with a wide range of market distortions. In an undistorted market, buyers pay the market price up to the point where they judge further units not to be worth that price, while competitive sellers supply added units as long as they can make money on each increment. At the point where supply just equals demand in an undistorted market, the price measures both the worth of the product to buyers and the worth of the product to sellers. Applied welfare economics is the outgrowth of microeconomics. It deals with the costs and benefits of just about anything—public projects, taxes on commodities, taxes on factors of production (corporation income taxes, payroll taxes), agricultural programs (like price supports and acreage controls), tariffs on imports, foreign exchange controls, different forms of industrial organization (like monopoly and oligopoly), and various aspects of labor market behavior (like minimum wages, the monopoly power of labor unions, and so on). The microeconomic analysis in a host country may also provide an insight about the trade competition in the region in terms of monopoly or oligopoly. Modern monopolies are a bit less transparent, for two reasons. First, even though governments still grant monopolies, they usually grant them to the producers. Second, some monopolies just happen without government creating them, although these are often short-lived.

---

[42] OECD: Background paper, Fifth Global Forum on Competition, February 17-18, 2005, Paris.

In making decision on the international trade firms generally involve in the benefit-cost analysis (BCA), if they feel that the advantages of a particular action are likely to outweigh its drawbacks. In the public arena, formal BCA is a sometimes controversial technique for thoroughly and consistently evaluating the pros and cons associated with prospective policy changes. Specifically, it is an attempt to identify and express in dollar terms all of the effects of proposed government policies or projects. Benefits in a market are measured by the propensity of consumers to pay for the product and services of the firm. The proper calculation of costs is the amount of compensation required to exactly offset negative consequences. Today's dynamic markets and technologies have called into question the sustainability of competitive advantage under pressure to improve productivity, quality, and speed, managers have embraced tools such as TQM, benchmarking, and reengineering. Dramatic operational improvements have resulted, but rarely have these gains translated into sustainable profitability. And gradually, the tools have taken the place of strategy to achieve the competitive advantage by undertaking the careful analysis of the microeconomic environment in the host country. A company's profitability depends in part on the structure of the industry in which it competes. Industry structure resides in five basic forces of competing: the intensity of rivalry among existing competitors; the threat of new entrants; the threat of substitute products or services; the bargaining power of suppliers; and the bargaining power of buyers. Industry structure is relatively stable, but industries are sometimes transformed by changes in buyer needs, regulation, or technology. Companies can shape industry structure rather than passively react to it. Many factors determine the nature of competition, including not only rivals, but also the economics of particular industries, new entrants, the bargaining power of customers and suppliers, and the threat of substitute services or products. A strategic plan of action based on this might include: positioning the company so that its capabilities provide the best defense against the competitive forces; influencing the balance of forces through strategic moves; and anticipating shifts in the factors underlying competitive forces.

It has been observed that the firms are often inclined to identify foreign destinations as a single market, or at least to differentiate very little among individual overseas markets. Another common error is the assumption that product or service concepts suited to a highly developed consumer economy will work as well in any foreign market. This is rarely true. Different markets requires different approaches and under such situations on short listing each country or group of countries to conduct business, the management should formulate a generic marketing strategy with respect to investment, risk, product, and pricing policies—that is, a unified strategic framework applicable to all the countries in each stage of development. This step should lead to a clear understanding of the respective stages of economic development of each country entailed for the marketing strategies of a firm. In developing detailed marketing plans, it is necessary to determine which product lines fit local markets and to allocate resources accordingly. A rough analysis of potential international business, global sales, and profit targets based on the estimates worked out in the first phase will help in assigning product lines. A framework for resource allocation can then be mapped out according to rough comparative figures for investment quotas, management needs, and skilled-labor requirements. This framework should be supplemented by company-specific examples of standard marketing strategies for each group of countries.

MICROECONOMIC ANALYSIS
OF A SUSTAINABLE MARKET STRATEGY

The principal issues towards improvement of microeconomic analysis in host countries may lie in the motivation generated by the inevitable increase in competition. As competition, particularly from Japan, becomes more significant, the recognition of shades of difference and finer distinctions with regard to opportunities becomes more important. It is necessary to build the strategic business mindset to outwit the competitors and gain competitive advantages over the segmented markets. The following factors need to be considered for achieving the strategic business leadership:

- To have a clear sense of desired outcomes before acting. Develop a plan capable of delivering outcomes that will add significant value to a state of affairs.
- Explore possibilities outwards to capture the larger context, to see how the pieces fit together.
- Be adaptive to realities and flexible in choice of tactics. Recognize that once action begins the "game board" is fluid offering both new threats and new opportunities.
- Wherever possible, attempt should be made to achieve multiple objectives through singular actions.
- Plan a couple of steps ahead of competition.
- Anticipate the actions of business rival and strategically rehearse next responses should those contingencies arise.
- To have a core discipline to observe the market moves and rival reactions.
- Capitalize on business crises or behavioural change in the markets in order to turn them to advantage.
- Stay future-focused.
- Plan the business strategy implementation in both sequential and parallel direction to accomplish goals and sustain the impact thereof.
- Develop negotiations with the business intermediaries on win-win platform at an acceptable cost.
- Supplement actions with those of others (allies, partners, joint ventures.)
- Be patient, with a good sense of timing.
- Develop alternate strategies for contingencies
- Use speed and surprise to advantage.
- Form alliances with opponents of his opponents in business.
- Learn the strengths and weaknesses of rivals.
- Be aggressive in pursuing goals, cordon the moves and be ready to take on the next one.
- Assure that everyone in the company knows his role and is equipped with the resources to contribute.
- Monitor activities in the operating environment.
- Use "what if" speculation to stretch thinking in the direction of opportunities and possibilities.

- Study the logic of the opponent's tactics with an eye toward determining what their ultimate end purposes may be.

These are some tested aspects of thinking employed by leaders to gain and hold strategic advantage. They can serve as a checklist for strategic thinking in an organization. Customers want more of everything they value. If they value low cost they want it lower. If they are value convenience they want it easier and faster. If they look for state of the art they want it first and want to push the envelope. If they need expert advice they want more time and dedicated effort and investment. By raising the level of value that customers can expect from everyone, leading companies are driving the market and driving their competitors out of business, or at least into a malaise of mediocrity. The following steps may guide the strategic decision of the company:

- Alter the industry structure to change the basis of competition. Reconfigure the value chain - retailers become wholesalers and suppliers, insurers take over brokerages, banks move into insurance, etc.
- Improve the position of the business within the industry by way of acquisitions and market share. Alter the playing field to achieve an enhanced scale of operations and competitive positioning.
- Innovate and create new opportunities - new products, services, and markets.
- Employ barriers to entry in terms of significant capital investment, proprietary technology, or in the magnitude of resources required to compete effectively.
- Increase the dependence of customers for products and services of the company in terms of the total value for customers or higher costs of switching to alternates.
- Change and enhance supplier relationships to obtain cost and quality improvements, reduced cycle times, and integrated processes.
- Change the basis of competition by creating a service relationship and differentiation. Move away from price to service, software, and customer relationships.
- Centralize into high volume, low cost, automated, 'focused factories', to achieve the lowest cost operations in support of customer value.
- Decentralize into custom, low volume, flexible factories, quick to market, responsive, and customize products to specific customer requirements.

It is necessary to cultivate close and long-term customer relationships and intimate knowledge of customer requirements and create a dependency of customized service and support, and focus on customer retention and satisfaction.

SOME MAJOR CONCLUSIONS ON MICROECONOMIC FACTORS

The economic environment of a foreign country must be explored and analyzed before a firm decides to enter its market. A country facing economic problems may lack stability and become vulnerable to political radicalism while a growing and promising economy usually stimulates business activity and offers new opportunities. The prospects for long-term growth in developing countries have increased relative to the late 1980s, as many countries have become more stable and more open to trade and foreign direct investment, while indicators of health and education have improved. Nevertheless, developing countries face major short-term risks, including the potential for a hard landing of the U.S. economy, further volatility in the oil market, and the continued overhang of non-performing loans in the Asian crisis countries. Many developing countries reduced the level and dispersion of tariffs, dismantled non-tariff trade barriers, and increased reliance on market forces to allocate foreign exchange since 1990. However, weaknesses in trade-related policies continued to impede growth in many of the poorest countries. Appreciated real exchange rates and high real exchange rate volatility have often been associated with a muted export response to trade liberalization; per capita income growth was significantly faster in poor countries with relatively stable real exchange rates. The absence of effective duty exemption/drawback programs, coupled with fiscal reliance on tariffs on intermediate and capital goods, has increased costs for exporters. Finally, weak export infrastructure, inadequate ancillary export services, and high transport costs, often in part the result of policy shortcomings have left many countries at a competitive disadvantage on international markets[43]. Thus, a careful review of economic conditions, both short-and long-term, is a prerequisite for a decision about entering an overseas market. Analysis of microeconomic environment is largely performed with reference to competition. A firm should properly identify different sources of competition and examine its own strengths and weaknesses relative to major competitors. A firm should be able to develop a workable marketing mix in tune to competitive advantage over its rivals. International firms should examine not only the micro- and macroeconomic environment of the host country before preparing to enter its market, but should also take into account the impact of the economic environment of the home country.

BUSINESS OPPORTUNITIES IN DEVELOPING COUNTRIES

In developing countries the business opportunities may be explored for the two prominent reasons. Firstly, a large number of developing countries are pursuing a growth path. South Korea, Taiwan, Singapore, and Hong Kong were first; Brazil and China followed. Most recently, India and Eastern European countries have also opened-up the gates to globalization in consonance with the neo-liberalism concepts. The developing world is beginning to rely on the international market mechanism to attract investment and technology and become industrialized. Such change proneness has given scope to the increasing demand for the technological and environmental products world over. An example of organic products marketing may be appropriately discussed in this context. Most major markets offer good prospects for suppliers of organic products that are not produced domestically, such as coffee, tea, cocoa, spices, tropical fruits and vegetables, and citrus fruits. There are also very good prospects for foods that are produced in the main markets themselves. These opportunities stem from the simple fact that rapidly growing demand in most markets cannot be met by local supply, at least in the short and medium term. Developing countries produce a wide range of organic products and many are exporting them successfully. Secondly, opportunities in developing countries should be even more closely examined than those in advanced countries as the government plays a significant role in business decisions in developing

---

[43] World Bank: Global Economic Prospects and the Developing Countries, World Bank, Washington DC,2001.

countries. This necessitates dealing with the procedural issues therein in foreign investment with considerable sophistication and confidence.

Each year the World Bank Group lends between US$15-20 billion to developing country governments to fund projects for economic development and poverty reduction. This generates around 40,000 contracts ranging in size from a few thousand dollars to multi-million dollar expenditures for the delivery of a vast range of goods and services. Procurement on a World Bank project is the primary way though which companies get involved with the World Bank. The bank lending generates thousands of contracts worth approximately a total of $12 billion annually to firms worldwide. Loans are made to more than eighty governments and government agencies, which are responsible for procurement under World Bank projects. The World Bank develops procurement policy and guidelines (LINK), issues standard bidding documents, supports executing agencies in developing procurement capacity, disseminates information on procurement matters and maintains contacts with industry to ensure that World Bank policies and guidelines reflect current industry standards. The government of the borrowing country is responsible for all procurement steps, including advertising, prequalification evaluation, preparation of bidding documents, evaluation of bids, and contract awards. In its final form, the Country Assistance Strategy (CAS) document outlines the Bank's planned operations in the country lending, analytical work, and technical assistance. Eighty-five countries are covered by the CAS process.

In an effort to create jobs, diversify and grow the economies, many of the countries in the middle-east region have embarked on economic reform and privatization programs to attract foreign direct investment. Algeria, Kuwait and Saudi Arabia are moving toward opening the development of their oil and gas fields to foreign companies and Qatar and the UAE continue to use foreign companies as partners as they expand the development of their oil and gas industries. In the last five years, Egypt, Morocco, Tunisia and the UAE have undertaken one or more new independent power projects. In recent years, most of the countries have implemented new investment laws that allow foreign ownership of domestic enterprises to the full extent. Better laws and stricter enforcement of intellectual property protection in many of the countries have led to increased investment in the pharmaceutical industry in Jordan and in the high tech industries in Israel and the UAE. The Middle East has become an important region for the development of information technology. Several countries, including Egypt, Jordan and Tunisia, are seeking to develop their IT industries. Two countries, Israel and the UAE, have already taken major steps to create vibrant IT sectors. Israel boasts a high-tech sector that is successfully integrated with the global economy. There are more than 200 U.S. high tech companies in Israel today, ranging from the giants, such as Intel and IBM, to "specialty" companies with only a few employees.

An accelerating growth and poverty reduction requires governments to reduce the policy risks, costs, and barriers to competition facing firms of all types, from farmers and micro-entrepreneurs to local manufacturing and multinational companies. A vibrant private sector creates jobs, provides the goods and services needed to improve living standards, and contributes taxes necessary for public investment in health, education, and other services. But too often governments stunt the size of those contributions by creating unjustified risks, costs, and barriers to competition[44]. However, the policy-related risks dominate the concerns of

---

[44] World Bank: World Development Report-2005, News Release 2004/89/S, World Bank, Washington DC.

firms in developing countries. Uncertainty about the content and implementation of government policies is the top-rated concern, with other significant risks including macroeconomic instability, arbitrary regulation, and weak protection of property rights. These risks cloud opportunities and chill incentives to invest productively and create jobs. Nearly 90 percent of firms in Guatemala, and more than 70 percent of firms in Belarus and Zambia, find the interpretation of regulation unpredictable. It has been highlighted in the World Development Report -2005 that more than 80 percent of firms in Bangladesh, and over 70 percent of firms in Ecuador and Moldova, lack confidence in the courts to uphold their property rights. Improving policy predictability alone can increase the likelihood of new investment by more than 30 percent Barriers to competition are also pervasive and dull incentives for firms to innovate and increase their productivity - the key to sustainable growth. High risks and costs restrict competition, while governments also limit competition through policy barriers to market entry and exit. Nearly 90 percent of firms in Poland report strong competitive pressure, more than twice the share of firms in Georgia. Stronger competitive pressure can increase the probability of innovation.

The Tenth Five-Year Plan of Government of India estimates that the Indian economy needs to grow at around 8% per annum over the next decade to create the required 100 million new jobs and reduce the poverty rate to 11%. This would require an increase in agricultural growth from the trend rate of about 3% per annum in the last decade to 4.5% per annum over the next 10 years. Industrial growth would need to increase from 6% per annum in the last decade to 8% per annum in the next decade and services from 7.5% annually in the last decade to 9% per year on an average over the next 10 years[45]. International comparisons indicate that India has intrinsic advantages, such as macroeconomic stability, a large and rapidly growing local market, a large and relatively low-cost labor force, a critical mass of well-educated workers, and abundant raw materials that should allow it to attract and sustain higher levels of private investment, both domestic and foreign. A key challenge for India is to streamline business entry and operation procedures, so as to reduce delays and opportunities for rent seeking.

Promotional efforts to attract foreign direct investment (FDI) have become the focal point of competition among developed and developing countries. This competition is maintained even when countries are pursuing economic integration at another level. And it often extends to the sub-national level, with different regional authorities pursuing their own strategies and assembling their own basket of incentives to attract new investments. While some see countries lowering standards to attract FDI in a "race to the bottom," others praise FDI for raising standards and welfare in recipient countries. Several trends are reinforcing traditional impulses for foreign direct investment, such as access to natural resources, markets, and low-cost labor. Some countries rely on targeted financial incentives, such as tax concessions, cash grants and specific subsidies. Others have chosen a broader approach that focuses on improving their domestic infrastructure and local skills base to meet the demands and expectations of foreign investors. However, many countries have entered into international governing arrangements to increase their attractiveness as investment locations. Although promoting and arranging such investments are complicated, an effective regulatory environment and strong policy framework can make such investments successful.

---

[45] Carter Michael F: Improving the Investment Climate: Challenges for India, Country Director, The World Bank Group, New Delhi, October 19, 2004 (Address delivered in the OECD Investment Conference)

The impact of trade liberalization towards removal of production subsidies and elimination of consumption distortions in world sugar markets using a partial-equilibrium international sugar model calibrated on 2002 market data has reflected on the current trade policies in developing countries. The removal of trade distortions alone induces a 27% price increase while the removal of all trade and production distortions induces a 48% increase in 2011/2012 relative to the baseline. Aggregate trade expands moderately, but location of production and trade patterns change substantially. Protectionist Organization for Economic Co-operation and Development (OECD) countries (the EU, Japan, the US) experience an import expansion or export reduction and a significant contraction of production in unfettered markets. Competitive producers in both OECD countries (Australia) and non-OECD countries (Brazil, Cuba), and even some protected producers (Indonesia, Turkey), expand production when all distortions are removed. Consumption distortions have marginal impacts on world markets and the location of production[46].

The World Trade Organization (WTO) has come-up with the rules of trade between nations. In the area of work on trade and investment, it specially focuses on conducting analytical work on the relationships between trade and investment. There are three main areas of work in the WTO on trade and investment:

- A Working Group established in 1996 conducts analytical work on the relationship between trade and investment.
- The Agreement on Trade-Related Investment Measures ("TRIMs Agreement"), one of the Multilateral Agreements on Trade in Goods, prohibits trade-related investment measures, such as local content requirements, that are inconsistent with basic provisions of GATT 1994.
- The General Agreement on Trade in Services addresses foreign investment in services as one of four modes of supply of services.

This agreement was negotiated during the Uruguay Round, which applies only to measures that affect trade in goods. Recognizing that certain investment measures can have trade-restrictive and distorting effects, it states that no member country of the WTO shall apply a measure that is prohibited. The list of TRIMs includes measures which require particular levels of local procurement by an enterprise (local content requirements) or which restrict the volume or value of imports that an enterprise can purchase or use to an amount related to the level of products it exports (trade balancing requirements). The agreement requires mandatory notification of all non-conforming TRIMs and their elimination within two years for developed countries, within five years for developing countries and within seven years for least-developed countries

The corporate governance is also one of the measures in the microeconomic environment of the country that affect the foreign investor and an overseas firm seeking to enter a developing country. The OECD Principles have become the most widely accepted corporate governance benchmark and have influenced the drafting of other codes issued by international organizations, countries, companies and stock exchanges. Codes of best practice are important tools in corporate governance reform that raise awareness and help build consensus

---

[46] Elobeid A and Beghin J (2006), Multilateral Trade and Agricultural Policy Reforms in Sugar Markets, *Journal of Agricultural Economics*, 57 (1), 23-48.

and ownership of reform processes and outcomes[47]. These codes are non-binding rules that go beyond the law, take specific country conditions into account and often exceed the standards set by international guidelines like the OECD Principles. While adherence to such codes and standards is voluntary, compliance by specific companies sends a signal to investors to help them identify candidates that match their criteria for investment. One of the central Asian republics Uzbekistan is a small country grappling with a legacy of state ownership of enterprises that has contributed to conflicts between government and market-based business objectives, as well as an unclear division of responsibility for corporate governance[48]. The significance of the corporate governance hence may be reviewed as one of the major parameters in evaluating the business opportunities in the developing countries.

REFERENCES

Bharucha N and Kent C: Inflation Targeting in a Small Open Economy, *Research Discussion Paper 9807,* Reserve Bank of Australia, 1998.

Margaret Levi: The Economic Turn in Comparative Politics, *Comparative Political Studies,* Volume 33, August, 2000, pp 822-844.

Michael E. Porter: Location, Competition, and Economic Development: Local Clusters in a Global Economy, *Economic Development Quarterly,* Volume 14, February 2000, pp 15-34.

Jan Svejnar: Microeconomic Issues in the Transition to a Market Economy, *Journal of Economic Perspectives,* Vol. 5, 1991.

Jeffrey M. Perloff: *Microeconomics,* Addison-Wesley, 2004.

Jenkinson Tim: *Readings in Microeconomics,* 2nd Edition, Oxford University Press, 2000.

Luís Moura Ramos and Rita Martins: Privatization in Portugal: Employee Owners or Just Happy Employees? *Economic and Industrial Democracy,* Volume 24, 2004, pp 581-605.

Robert E. Kuenne: *Microeconomic Theory of the Market Mechanism: A General Equilibrium Approach,* Macmillan, New York, 1968.

Ricardo J. Caballero, Eduardo M. R. A. Engel, John Haltiwancer: Aggregate Employment Dynamics-Building from Microeconomic Evidence, *American Economic Review,* Vol. 87, 1997.

Ronald Coase, Dale R. Deboer: The Business-Plan Approach to Introductory Microeconomics, *Journal of Economic Education,* Vol. 29, 1998.

Solomon I Cohen: *Microeconomic Policy,* Routledge, London, 2000.

Walter Nicholson: *Intermediate Microeconomics and its Application,* Thomson Learning, 2004.

William Lazonick: The Theory of the Market Economy and the Social Foundations of Innovative Enterprise, *Economic and Industrial Democracy,* Volume 24, February, 2003 pp 9- 4.

---

[47] OECD: Code of Best Practices, Paris, 1999.
[48] Broadman Harry G: Competition, Corporate Governance and Regulation in Central Asia: Uzbekistan's Structural Reform Challenges, Working Paper 2331. World Bank, Washington, D.C., May 2000.

Justin Tan: The Growth of Entrepreneurial Firms in a Transition Economy-The Case of a
    Chinese Entrepreneur, *Journal of Management Inquiry*, Volume 8, March 1999, pp 83 –
    89.

Chapter 3

POLITICAL RENAISSANCE AND GLOBALIZATION

It is important to understand that the global political environment has a greater role to play in all business and economic matters today, however, it remains in a constant flux. The political system of a country is shaped after passing through major processes of growth, decay, breakdown and a ceaseless ferment of adaptation and adjustment. The magnitude and variety of the changes that occurred in the world's political systems between the 20's and 80's of the 20th century describe the complex dimensions of the problem. It may be observed that during the last century, great empires disintegrated; nation-states emerged, flourished briefly, and then vanished. The two consecutive world wars transformed the international system and seeded new ideologies that swept the world and shook established groups from power-grid nations. However, many developing countries experienced civil and political revolutions during the post-world-ward period in order to determine the most effective governing system and domestic politics in every system was contorted by social strife and economic crisis. In the middle of the 20th century, the nature of political life was changed everywhere by novel forms of political activity as the new means of mass communication, increase of popular participation in politics and the rise of new political issues offered better understanding towards international politics and popular governance in reference to global integration. Besides, the extension of the scope of governmental activity and other innumerable social, economic, and technical developments in the developing countries urged for stability in the government for effective implementation of the international development programs and the trade policies have been one among the international priorities.

There are many factors that influence the ideological transition, development and change in the world's political systems. In the recent past, industrialization, population growth, the "revolution of rising expectations" in the less developed countries, and international tensions have affected the political thinking to a large extent. However, the political instability generally occurs when the distribution of wealth fails to correspond with the distribution of political power. This situation may be described in reference to the classical school of political thought as the political stability in a country is largely based on a large middle class in a country. On the contrary the Marxist theories of economic determinism view all political changes as the result of changes in the mode of production. However, the neo-classical political thinkers discuss that the prime cause of revolutions and other forms of violent political changes are due to power polarization and alienation with the capitalistic economic countries. The majority of the world's political systems have experienced one form or another of internal warfare leading to violent collapse of the governments in power and certain crisis situations seem to increase the likelihood of breakdown in the governing politics of a region or a country. In the politico-economic scenario the economic crisis is another common stimulus to the political setbacks as may be witnessed in the recent Argentinean crisis. The Brazilian economy was also at the cliff in the late 90's due to internal economic instability.

The political situation of a country may be explained in terms of economic growth as reflected in gross domestic product and also towards the social scarcity. However the political environment of a country also contributes in building the social position of individuals. The recent Turkish experience clearly illustrates how markets and politics can interact in producing significant economic transformation. Focus on the new phase of neo-liberal restructuring in Turkey in the post-crisis era, highlights the importance of the European Union (EU) and International Monetary Fund (IMF) as anchors in driving diplomatic moves and the specific domestic and external linkages through which these double external anchors have operated. These anchors played significant and complementary roles in the recent transformation process in Turkey[1]. There have been many shifts in political movements that emerged over the past as a result of the globalization process across countries in the world. It has been observed that the inclination of global politics has shifted from Europe to the Asia-Pacific in recent years with the rise of China and India, gradual assertion by Japan of its military profile, and a significant shift in the US global force posture in favor of Asia-Pacific. The debate now is whether Asia-Pacific will witness rising tensions and conflicts in the coming years with various powers jockeying for influence in the region or whether the forces of economic globalization and multilateralism will lead to peace and stability. Some have asked the question more directly: Will Asia's future resemble Europe's past? It is, of course, difficult to answer this question as of now when major powers in Asia-Pacific such as China, India and Japan are still rising and grappling with a plethora of issues that confront any rising power in the international system[2].

A sense of insecurity and uncertainty for the future, and an aggravation of the relationships among social classes also results in the politico-economic conflicts in a country. A severe national economic crisis develops distrust in the political system of the country and triggers outbreak of revolutions in the political systems. The political unrest in a country triggers the test conditions for the stability of political systems in extremely revealing ways, which often demand either the change in the political leadership or the structure and process of governance in the system. Since the quality of the political leadership is often decisive, those systems that provide methods of selecting able leaders and replacing them possess important advantages towards internal and global political concerns. Unstable political systems are those that prove vulnerable to crisis pressures and that break down into various forms of internal warfare. The fundamental causes of such failures appear to be the lack of a widespread sense of the legitimacy of state authority and the absence of some general agreement on appropriate forms of political action.

The political sovereignty may be referred to as a country's desire to assert its authority over foreign business through various sanctions. Political sovereignty is the assertion of self, determination of its citizens, and the manifestation of their freedom. It is in and through the determination of its sovereignty that the order of the nation is constituted and maintained.

---

[1] Önis, Ziya and Bakır Caner (2007), Turkey's Political Economy in the Age of Financial Globalization: The Significance of the EU Anchor, *South European Society & Politics*, 12 (2), 147-164.

[2] Pant HV (2007), India in the Asia-Pacific: Rising Ambitions with an Eye on China, *Asia-Pacific Review*, 14 (1), 54-71.

Such sanctions are regular and evolutionary, and therefore predictable. An example is an increase in taxes over foreign operations. Many of the developing countries impose restrictions on foreign business to protect their independence. These countries are jealous of their political freedom and want to protect it at all costs, even if it means a slow economic pace without the help of MNCs. Thus, the political sovereignty problem exists mainly in developing countries.

DETERMINING POLITICAL ENVIRONMENT

The political philosophy and the legal environment of a nation largely influence the practice of international marketing. Political globalization is one dimension of a multidimensional process that is beyond economic issues, historical, and transformative in changing institutional structures for a healthier global business. Conceiving the political globalization in evolutionary terms as one centered on innovative sequences of search-and-selection, may make it possible to construct a schedule for global politics, and to derive from it an agenda of priority global problems including global business[3]. The political environment of a country comprises the international environment, host-country environment and the home-country environment. Many studies have shown that dealing with problems in the political arena is the principal challenge facing international managers in developing pro political strategies to run the business successfully in the host country. It is observed that each country has its own set of national goals; most countries also share many common objectives.

Nationalism and patriotism refer to citizens' feelings about their country and its interests. Such feelings exist in every country and the multinational firms, individually or collectively, may be perceived as a threat to that sovereignty. The foreign firms perceive greater threats if they are larger in size and more in number in a country. At the time of any political turmoil, the foreign firms may be targets for attack. Many countries seek "national solutions" to help troubled companies to retain what are perceived to be national champions. International firms need to be sensitive to these issues and to be careful not to be too "foreign." This includes advertising and branding policies as well as ownership and staffing. Establishing local R&D would be perceived favorably in this context. Multinational companies operating in the middle class customer segment in China are learning valuable lessons they need to compete worldwide: multinationals are discovering how to focus products downscale to break out of the premium tier, and domestic firms are building scale and marketing expertise to move up. Both are positioning themselves to export their China offerings to other large emerging markets such as India and Brazil—and, after that, to the developed markets. Multinationals can attack domestic players from above, Chinese firms operating in the low end can burrow up from below, and both can acquire their way into it. The experiences of such players as Colgate-Palmolive, GM, GE, Huawei Technologies, Haier, and Ningbo Bird show how challenging it is to gain a foothold in the middle market but also how much potential there is to use it as a springboard for global expansion[4].

---

[3] Modelski, George and Devezas, Tessaleno (2007), Political Globalization is Global Political Evolution, *World Futures: The Journal of General Evolution*, 63 (5-6), 308-323.
[4] Orit Gadiesh, Philip Leung and Till Vestring (2007), The Battle for China's Good-Enough Market, *Harvard Business Review*, 85 (9), 81-89

The international political environment involves political relations among the countries of common ideologies. The foreign firms need to make all adjustments with the host country's international relations, no matter how non-aligned it may try to be. Such strategic adjustments in tune to the international environment of the host country are required as its operations are frequently related also to the neighboring countries, either on the supply or demand side or both. Another critical factor affecting the political environment is the diplomatic relations of the host countries with others in the region or beyond. If a country is a member of a regional group, such as the EU, NAFTA, ASEAN, its political identity influences the firm's operational and expansion opportunities. If a nation has particular friends or enemies among other nations, the firm must modify its international logistics to comply with how that market is supplied and to whom it can sell. For example, the United States limits trade with various countries, and Arabian countries do not entertain any business activities with Israel. The participation of the host country in the regional trade agreements or with the international trade organizations may affect patents, communication, transportation, and other items of interest to the international marketer. As a rule, the more international organizations a country belongs to, the more regulations it accepts, and the more dependable is its economic, political and legal environment. Globalization has attempted to bridge the cross border political and economic barriers and refocusing the economic activity over the political ideologies. Major factors affecting this politico-economic transformation include people, capital, and information which can be moved across borders quickly. In this process consumers can see how other people live, develop socially, and pressure their governments to give them access to the best and cheapest products. Finally, as governments defer to special interests and try to provide constituents with a civil minimum of services, they invest inefficiently and as a result destroy wealth[5].

> The federal government of Brazil has been more intent on returning its budget to fiscal health than on funding new projects and the result has been decades of underinvestment. From electric power to transportation to housing, the needs are huge. To avoid power shortages such as those that struck in 2001, and to support growth in demand, generating capacity must rise by more than 40 percent during the next ten years. Heartening legislation governing public-private partnerships has underpinned recent successful road projects and should offer favorable conditions for private investment in other projects as well. Yet investors should have a clear perspective on the evolution of the targeted segment's regulatory environment. Before they commit themselves to important capital projects, they should also build strong regulatory-management skills, since tariff review processes continue to be crucial for performance. However, reduction in the country's current-account deficit was achieved on the back of one of the strongest bull markets in commodities. Its collapse could lead to a reversal of the current account and consequently of the momentum toward an investment-grade rating. A weakening commitment to prudent fiscal policy could lead to even greater government participation in the capital markets, essentially crowding out private borrowers[6].

The political environment in the home-country is also an important indicator for a firm to decide its entry into the host country. However, an adverse environment therein may constrain its international operations as well as its domestic operations. The best-known

---

[5] Kenichi Ohmae (1995), Putting global logic first, *Harvard Business Review*, 73 (1), 119-125.
[6] Eduardo Andrade, Roberto Fantoni and William B Jones (2007): What is ahead of business in Brazil, Mckinsey Quarterly, April www.mckinseyquarterly.com

example of the home-country political environment affecting international operations used to be South Africa. Home-country political pressures induced more than 200 American firms to leave that country altogether. In the private sector, the bottom line is shareholder value. In government, the objectives can be harder to pinpoint due to being clouded by political agendas, turf battles, special interests and economics. Some of the key issues in reference to measuring the performance of the government in the given political environment of the home country may be considered by the firm as described below:

- *Measuring performance:* Governments need to continue to focus on gauging performance by what is achieved. Leaders should strive to understand the real results that are being delivered, and how much real progress is being made.
- *Improving through competition:* Government's position is often perceived in a fix by the social pressures. The issues of trade protection, allowing foreign companies to participate in the host country, repatriation of profits and other economic issues are subject to the prevailing political ideology in the host country.
- *Streamlining operations:* It is necessary for a foreign firm to examine the conduct of government activities in the home country. Many government operations can be performed by third parties often at lower cost and with equal or higher quality.
- *Promoting efficiency:* Most government employees are smart, industrious people. But like any workforce, their behavior is largely driven by the organization's rewards and incentives.

Many multinational companies face uncertainty in political environment due to instability of political leadership, coalitions and external pressures. Even if the home country and the host country give them no problems, they can face threats in the neighboring markets. Firms that do not have problems with their home government or the host government may be bothered or boycotted in neighboring countries. Escalation of political conflict in many developing countries and their impact on economic development has been a topical issue in recent development literature. The overwhelming emphasis on 'ethnic conflicts' in this literature has, however, precluded looking at political conflict in the wider context of the development process, going beyond the ethnic dimension. In particular, because of the preoccupation with the ethnic roots as the prime source of these conflicts, reverse causation running from economic policy to political conflict has been virtually ignored in the debate[7]. The effectiveness of the political systems in a country may be analyzed by the foreign firms in reference to the following indicators:

- Democratic effectiveness: capable of deepening democracy and democratic citizenship;
- Policy effectiveness: capable of tackling fundamental developmental problems of poverty and social equality
- Conflict-management effectiveness: capable of channeling conflicts and rendering them less destructive.

---

[7] Sirimal Abeyratne: Economic Roots of Political Conflicts- A Case of Sri Lanka, Australian National University, Australia South Asia Research Centre, Working Paper #03, 2002.

Political conflict in general could be defined as dynamic and manifest conflict processes consisting of certain phases. In this case the term conflict is used in a more specific meaning: a political process (dynamic situation) in which engaged political parties have incompatible attitudes and behaviors. Internal as well as international conflicts have three interrelated components:

- Conflict situation, manifested in expressing various political aims or conflict of interest that cannot be simultaneously achieved and for that reason can be qualified as mutually exclusive;
- Conflict behavior (in the first place aimed at achieving the aforementioned political aims); and
- Conflicting attitudes and perceptions having an emotional dimension (feeling of anger, mistrust, fear, scorn, hatred, etc.) as well as a cognitive dimension.

Many countries in different parts of the world undergo political conflict of various natures like turmoil, internal war, and conspiracy that can be irregular, revolutionary, and/or sporadic. Turmoil refers to instant upheaval on a massive scale against an established political regime. The internal unrest in a country refers to large-scale, organized violence against a government, such as guerrilla warfare. The example may be cited of Vietnam's actions in Cambodia and internal violence by the self proclaimed people's groups like in north-eastern states in India.

Political change in a country sometimes leads to a more favorable economic and business climate. For example, Sukarno's departure from the Indonesian scene improved the business climate there. The political ideology in India after the governance of Late Rajiv Gandhi, the Indian Prime Minister in 1991, became highly favorable for international business as the policy of globalization was adopted and U.S. multinationals found India an attractive place to do business. The political conflict in a country may lead to unstable conditions, but those conditions may or may not affect business. Therefore, political risk may or may not result from political unrest. The international businesses houses must analyze chronologically the occurrence of political conflicts and assess the likelihood of its impact on the business environment.

South Korean agriculture is highly inefficient, and rice farmers feel particularly vulnerable as quotas on imports are gradually lifted. In early 2004 the national assembly approved the trade agreement with Chile after months of delays as thousands of farmers battled riot police outside. The South Korean government signed the free trade agreement with Chile a year ago. The deal was finally ratified in February 2004 after months of bitter argument and a series of violent clashes with farmers. Under the agreement, Chile will lift tariffs on South Korean cars, mobile phones, and electronic goods. In return, South Korea will open its markets to Chilean copper and agricultural goods, including wheat, wool, tomatoes and fish. The farmers have been offered a generous package of subsidies and debt relief, but they say it won't be enough[8].

Many times the political unrest is temporarily focused on the international policies of the government. There have been anti-globalization protests in many countries during the

---

[8] Charles Scanlon: South Korea Shrug's off Farmers Trade Protest, BBC News, February 16, 2004
     http://news.bbc.co.uk/go/pr/fr/-/1/hi/business/3492809.stm

international political movements on pursuing the developing countries to join the World Trade Organization. It is important to understand the nature of political conflict in foreign countries and the motivation behind government actions. If a change in government policy is only symbolic without any indications of the change in implementation process, it represents less risk to foreign firms.

POLITICAL INTERVENTIONS

Political intervention may be described as a decision taken on the part of the government of the host country intended to force a change in the operations, policies, and strategies of a foreign firm in the interest of the country. Such interventions may range from enforcing control to complete takeover, or annexation of the foreign enterprise. The magnitude of intervention would vary according to the company's business existing in the host country and the nature of political decisions taken thereof. In countries where foreign investment plays a significant role in the economy, the possibilities of political interference in the operations of foreign firms would be higher and stringent. The possible political interventions in globalization of trade process have been indicated in Figure 3.1. Besides, the political system of a country like democracy, communism or mixed economies, also indicates the nature of intervention. If a foreign company is prominent in the economy in developing countries such as Zambia, Guinea, Iran, and Tanzania, the possibilities of government intervention are relatively greater in reference to the public policies of the country. The political intervention may affect the marketing-mix functions of a firm in the host country in several ways. The intervention may be observed in a host country to the extent of local content law, technology content, restrictions on the sale of some products, products' functional range, design of products, useful life, and adaptability to local conditions, patent life, local manufacturing and assembling leading to product strategies of a foreign firm. The political directions may also govern the functions related to transfer pricing, price ceiling and price floor, price contracts, price paid for local raw materials and price paid for imported raw materials to be used in production in the host country. Besides the activities of distribution and product retailing may also be subject to political interventions in many developing countries. Advertising and communication is another important area for a foreign firm that is affected by political interference in a country. Of these, local production of commercials, local artists, type of message, type of copy, availability of media and time restrictions on the use of certain media are significant political interventions faced by a foreign firm.

Expropriation, Domestication and Nationalization

The developing countries generally intervene directly in the operations of foreign firms engaged in business in order to pursue their own special interests of their country. Of many different forms of political intervention expropriation, domestication, exchange control, import restrictions, market control, tax control, price control, and labor restrictions are the common ones. *Expropriation* is one of the most stringent and pervasive political interventions that a foreign firm may face in a host country. It may be described as official seizure of foreign property by a host country whose intention is to use the seized property in the public interest. Such intervention is recognized by international law as the right of sovereign states,

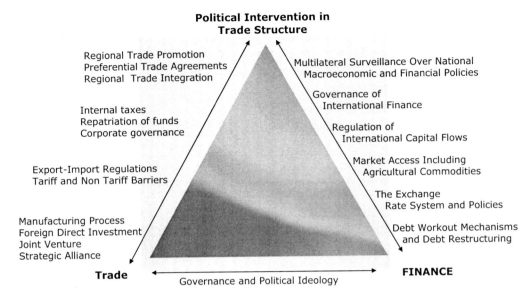

Figure 3.1. Mapping Political Moves towards Global Trade.

provided the expropriated firms are given prompt compensation, at fair market value, in convertible currencies[9]. The act of expropriation without offering any compensation to the foreign or local firms may be described as *confiscation*. In legal terms it may be explained that expropriation occurs when a government takes over property for a purpose deemed to bein the public interest, even though the owner of the property may not be willing to sell it. Any interest in land, plant and machinery and/or value additions thereof, such as permanent constructions, may be expropriated. The business capital may also be subject to expropriation in many countries. However, technology can serve as the defense against expropriation, if the technology of the enterprise cannot be transferred to or duplicated by the host country or despite transfer of technology it cannot be made operational by the expropriators. Further, if a firm is not holding an independent status in the host country and is vertically integrated with the parent firm wherein the supplies for production or the market for the product is controlled by the parent firm located elsewhere, such firms are unlikely to be targeted for expropriation.

Historically, expropriation of private property has been emerged as an example of stringent political intervention. The establishment of the People's Republic marked a sharp change in China's political elite and mode of governance. The degree of central control was much greater than under the Ch'ing dynasty or the KMT. It has reached to the lowest levels of government, to the workplace, to farms and to households. The party was highly disciplined and maintained detailed oversight of the regular bureaucratic apparatus. The military were tightly integrated into the system. Propaganda for government policy and ideology was diffused through mass movements under party control. Landlords, national and foreign capitalist interests were eliminated by expropriation of private property. China became a

---

[9] Eiteman, David K and Stonehill, Arthur I: Multinational Business Finance, Addison-Wesley, Reading MA, 1979, pp 184-188.

command economy on the Soviet pattern. After a century of surrender or submission to foreign incursions and aggression, the new regime was a ferocious and successful defender of China's national integrity, willing to operate with minimal links to the world economy[10].

Recent research has argued that political and regulatory environments have a significant impact on corporate governance systems. In particular, countries with poor investor protection laws and weak law enforcement have low levels of corporate governance that manifests itself in substandard financial performance, management entrenchment, and the expropriation of minority shareholders[11]. Expropriations of foreign direct investment in developing countries are typically blamed on political and economic crises in those countries. A better explanation of expropriation would be opportunistic behavior by host governments when profits of investments are high[12].

Domestication is another form of expropriation, which may be also be conceived as creeping expropriation. In this process of political intervention the controls and restrictions placed by the host country authorities on the foreign firm, gradually reduce the control of owners. The domestication is a slow process of expropriation and a foreign firm may lose its control in all financial, operational and management areas over a period of time. Domestication involves several measures, including gradual transfer of ownership to nationals, promotion of a large number of nationals to higher levels of management, greater decision-making powers accorded to nationals, more products produced locally rather than imported for assembly and specific export regulations designed to dictate participation in world markets.

Traditionally expropriation (in the foreign investment sense) referred to the seizure of property by the host government *e.g.* forced *nationalization* of assets. In recent years, more expansive definitions of expropriation have appeared, such as "creeping expropriation", "regulatory taking over" and "measures tantamount to expropriation", which can sometimes be used as strategy against government measures that might simply dent a foreign investor's profitability. The clause on "measures tantamount to expropriation" has been particularly controversial in the investment related details of NAFTA. The clause argues that expropriation may not necessarily be a taking over of the companies in public interest as it may be unreasonable and do not justify the political interference. However, the regional trade agreements place stress on the investor rights to protect the undue losses to the investing companies in the host country. The governments of countries (Canada, USA and Mexico) under NAFTA are required to compensate the investor for the full market value of the property.

On the contrary, *nationalization* may be described as taking over of assets into state ownership. The process of nationalization refers to a transfer of entire industry within the country from private to public ownership with no discrimination to the foreign or local ownership of firms. This may be explained as policy of bringing a country's essential services and industries under public ownership. It was pursued, for example, by the Labour party ruled

---

[10] OECD Development Centre (2007), Dynamics of Development in the New China, *OECD General Economics & Future Studies*, Volume 2007, Number 5, October, 74-112.

[11] Firth M, Fung Peter M and Rui O M (2006), Firm Performance, Governance Structure, and Top Management Turnover in a Transitional Economy, *Journal of Management Studies*, 43 (6), 1289-1330.

[12] Duncan, Roderick (2006), Price or politics? An investigation of the causes of expropriation, *The Australian Journal of Agricultural and Resource Economics*, 50 (1), 85-101.

government in United Kingdom during 1945–51. Assets in the hands of foreign governments or companies may also be nationalized; for example, Iran's oil industry and US-owned fruit plantations in Guatemala, during the 1950s. The Communist states of Eastern Europe nationalized all industry and agriculture in the period following World War II. Under the Labour government of the period 1945 to 1951, Great Britain nationalized a number of important industries, including coal, steel, and transportation. In non-Communist countries it has been common practice to compensate the owners of nationalized properties, at least in part; however, in the Communist countries, where private ownership is opposed in principle, there usually has not been such compensation. Nationalization of foreign properties has occurred, especially in underdeveloped nations, where there is resentment of foreign control of major industries. Instances include Mexico's seizure of oil properties owned by U.S. corporations (1938), Iran's nationalization of the Anglo-Iranian Oil Company (1951), the nationalization of the Suez Canal Company (1956) by Egypt, and Chile's nationalization of its foreign-owned copper-mining industry (1971). The government of India nationalized fourteen major private commercial banks in 1969 and six more in 1980. Nationalization forced commercial banks increasingly to meet the credit requirements of the weaker sections of the nation and to eliminate monopolization by vested interests of large industry, trade, and agriculture. However, a key issue in nationalization is whether the private owner is properly compensated for the value of the institution.

Exchange Control

In addition to expropriation and domestication, there are various other means of government intervention in foreign enterprise, usually in the form of legislative action or a decree enacted in the best national interest. It has been observed that many countries exercise restrictions on foreign exchange in order to discourage the free and flexible operations of foreign firms. Such strategy may be describes as a government policy designed to restrict the outflow of domestic currency and prevent a worsened balance of payments position by controlling the amount of foreign exchange that can be obtained or held by domestic citizens. Often results from overvalued exchange rates. The process of exchange control emerges as a system of controlling inflows and outflows of foreign exchange, devices include licensing multiple currencies, quotas, auctions, limits, levies and surcharges. Many countries face serious deficits in their balance of payments and are short of foreign exchange. Hence they restrict the use of foreign convertible currency according to their priorities. Foreign firms may be low on that priority list and have difficulty getting foreign exchange for needed imports or profit repatriation. The exchange control regulations are generally introduced by the monetary authorities of governments to control the flow of money. The restriction on the free use of foreign exchange is generally imposed by the countries having imbalances in the import – export ratio leading to problems in the balance of trade. Such countries may enforce restrictions on the remittances from the country involving international convertible currency like US Dollars, Euros and Pounds. This type of exchange control may also be an effort to encourage domestic industry. The exchange-control measures have two major consequences on the foreign business in terms of repatriation of profits and capital to the parent company at will and free imports of raw materials, machinery, spare parts, and the like from other destinations for operating purposes. The foreign exchange restrictions are also imposed by some countries for the off-shore investment by firms of home countries. The State Administration of Foreign Exchange (SAFE) of China has implemented the ceiling on foreign exchange administration in pilot cities to examine foreign exchange sources. It has been found that upon imposing such restrictions in foreign exchange transactions the domestic investment[13] is increased from US$1 million to US$3 million in 2003.

Import Restrictions

Import restriction, is the type of political intervention that primarily intends to support the native industries. Consider a foreign apparel manufacturing company traditionally importing certain synthetic yarn and dyes from the parent company. If the host country places restrictions on imports, the company may be forced to depend on local sources of supply for these new materials. The import restrictions would help the country to encourage domestic industry as a matter of industrial policy; however, such measures tend to jeopardize the functions of foreign business. The globalization and emergence of new international trade order with the emergence of World Trade Organization has reduced the occurrence of import restrictions in many countries. The Chinese government had authorized only a limited number of companies to act as agents for restricted import and export of steel, natural rubber, wool, acrylic fibers and plywood till 2004. After joining WTO in 2001, the Chinese government is gradually relaxing the import restrictions and the above products have been opened for the free trade as an obligation to the WTO agreements. Import restrictions in a country are also subject to the cultural and religious requirements. In Kuwait alcoholic beverages, pork and bacon products, and pigskin are banned for imports on cultural and religious grounds. The general agreements on WTO have emphasized elimination of the import restrictions on all competitive goods and services. Accordingly, in the member countries of WTO, the tariffs on all agricultural products are now bound. Almost all import restrictions that did not take the form of tariffs, such as quotas, have been converted to tariffs, a process known as *"tariffication"*. This has made markets substantially more predictable for agriculture. Previously more than 30% of agricultural produce had faced quotas or import restrictions[14]. However, intervention of WTO in pursuing the member countries towards eliminating the import restrictions had mixed impact in the trade environment of Romania. The development of textile and clothing exports has benefited from link-ups between Romanian production units and companies in France, Germany and Italy. The external environment also became more favorable due to the elimination of long-standing import restrictions by the European Union and Norway; Canada and the United States are two potentially large markets, but they still restrict imports from Romania[15]. The non-tariff barriers imposed by a country also discourages the firms to import the goods. The country's quotas and tariffs limit the firm's ability to import equipment, components, and products, forcing a higher level of local procurement than it may require.

---

[13] Official website of Government of China, SAFE www.chinaonline.com/minitry_profiles
[14] World Trade Organization: Tariffs- More Binding and Closer to Zero, WTO, Geneva, 2004.
[15] World Trade Organization: Trade Policy Review- Romania, WTO, Geneva, 1999, Press Release, PRESS/ TPRB/115

Market Control

The government of a country sometimes imposes market control to prevent foreign companies from competing in certain markets. The market control may be imposed by a country at various phases of the business operations of a foreign form. If allowed to enter the country, the firm may be restricted to the types of industries it may enter. It may be prohibited from acquiring a national firm. It may not be allowed to have total ownership but may be required to enter a joint venture with a national firm. The firm may also be restricted by the government to choose its areas of operation and sell its products. It has been observed that the Japanese government indirectly discourages the foreign firms conducting their business in the country. Until the fall of the 20th century, Japan prohibited foreign companies from selling sophisticated communications equipment to the Japanese government. Thus, AT&T, GTE-Sylvania, and ITT could perform in a limited way in Japan. Besides the operational controls in the market, one of the most common controls that the foreign firms may face is price controls, which limits the profitability of foreign firms in inflationary situations in the host country. Gerber left Venezuela because a decade of price controls prevented a profitable operation. Other regulations may affect advertising or other marketing practices of the firm.

The Export and Import Controls Bureau (EPD) is responsible for administering the *Export and Import Permits Act* (EIPA) which was first enacted in 1947. The EIPA delegates to the Minister of Foreign Affairs (referred to as "the Minister") wide discretionary powers to control the flow of goods contained in specified lists provided for under the Act. Under authority of the *Department of Foreign Affairs and International Trade Act*, the Minister for International Trade provides policy direction in most areas involving market access and trade policy. The Bureau regulates trade in military and strategic dual-use goods, prevents the proliferation of weapons of mass destruction, as we are obliged to do under multilateral agreement, and protect vulnerable Canadian industries such as clothing manufacturing and fulfils other international obligations. The control goods for imports in Canada are textile and clothing, agricultural products, steel products and defense goods while the export restrictions are imposed on agricultural products, textiles, forest timber and wood products, miscellaneous goods including goods of U.S.-origin, items with medical value and all goods destined for countries on the area control list of Angola and Myanmar. Most controlled goods require an Individual Permit for import or export, although some goods may enjoy facilitated treatment under a General Permit. General Permits are not specific to an individual importer or exporter in the manner of Individual Permits. General Permits allow for the pre-authorized export or import of certain eligible goods to/from certain eligible countries, by a simplified process. For instance, the import or exports of household goods are treated in this manner[16].

Sometimes the conflicting political ideologies also let the countries exercise the market controls without strong economic arguments. One of the examples, to be cited in this context may be of the Arabian countries which boycott companies doing business with Israel. The Arab states had not accepted Israel's right to exist and hoped that the boycott eventually would bring about its collapse, which does not seem to be realistic. In April 1998 China ordered all direct-sales operations to cease immediately. The ban, instituted last April,

---

[16] Government of Canada: Export and Import Controls, Export and Import Controls Bureau, Official Web Site, http://www.dfait-maeci.gc.ca/eicb/eicbintro-en.asp

outlawed the direct-sales operations of companies including Avon, Amway, Mary Kay Cosmetics, and Sara Lee. However, China announced provisional plans to phase out ban on direct selling imposed during 1998 by the year 2003. The elimination of such ban on direct sales is contingent upon the development of direct-selling regulations. The consideration of Chinese government on lifting the ban on direct selling has been thought of after the U.S. support in World Trade Organization negotiations[17].

Tax and Human Resources Controls

The governments of some countries may also impose tax control by means of excessive and non-traditional taxes on foreign firms. For example, a new form of tax imposed on a foreign firm towards excessive levy on volume of production, for which no precedent may be placed. Imposing such taxes on the foreign business houses may hold reasons like an out-of-the-way monetary burden on foreign companies, to explore additional sources of revenue to meet the fiscal deficit of the country without putting pressure on the citizens of the country and to construct a tax barrier as a retaliatory measure to voice against the international policies or general dissatisfaction in diplomatic relations with other countries. In many countries like China, labor unions play significant role in political decisions and have great political clout. In such countries labor restrictions are an effective form of government intervention. Traditionally, labor unions in America have been able to prevent layoffs, plant shutdowns, and the like, even when business could not afford to meet their demands.

POLITICAL SYSTEMS

There are three major ideologies that are embedded in the political systems in the world – democracy, communism and capitalism. All political systems are oriented towards the power of ruling with the conventional and modern philosophies in reference to their respective schools of thought. *Democracy* is a political system composed of people, institutions and their relations in regard to the governance of a state under which the power of ruling lies with the people of the country. Under such a system, executive and legislative decisions are made by the people's representatives who act through the consent of the people, as enforced by elections and the rule of law. The direct democracy may be described as any form of government based on a theory of civics in which all citizens can directly participate in the decision-making process. Some adherents want both legislative and executive powers to be handled by the people, but most existing systems only allow legislative decisions. The modern direct democracy comprises of three main constituents- initiative, referendum and recall. The initiative provides a means by which an appeal signed by a certain minimum number of registered voters can force a public vote on a proposed statute, constitutional amendment, charter amendment, or an ordinance. The political system of Switzerland may be described as the strongest example of a modern direct democracy, as it exhibits the first two pillars at both the local and federal levels. In the past 120 years more than 240 initiatives have been put to referendum. The populace has been conservative, granting about 10% of the

---

[17] Institute of Global Ethics: http://www.globalethics.org

initiatives put; in addition, they have often opted for a version of the initiative rewritten by the government. The democratic political system is largely based on the philosophy that describes a governance *of the people, by the people and for the people.*

The *open-closed characteristic* is used broadly to distinguish political systems, as between liberal democracies or polyarchies on the one hand, and dictatorships, autocracies, or totalitarian systems on the other. But this is a characteristic and not a dichotomy. The right of involvement of the people in changing the system is a spectrum. For some states this right may involve full representation through the power to initiate or directly approve laws, as in Switzerland. However, in the United States, the mass may have the power to control the class through the right to elect or reject their incumbency and by opposition to elite-policies, as through interest groups. In some states, such as Spain, people can only produce change or opposition through communal groups like the church, which are participants in the political system. Another type of political system is *authoritarian*. It is closed, with authoritative political positions open to only a few by virtue of birth or other ascribed status, and based on customary law. Groups are autonomous so long as they do not try to alter the traditional status quo, and the elite's goals are concerned with conserving traditions.

As a social system, *communism* would be a type of egalitarian society with no state, no private property and no social classes. In communism, all property is owned by the community as a whole, and all people enjoy equal social and economic status. Perhaps the best known principle of a communist society is *from each according to his ability, to each according to his need.* As an ideology, the word communism is a synonym for Marxism and its various derivatives. In terms of ideology and politics, communism is a sub-category of socialism. Communist ideology is a specific branch of socialist ideology and the communist movement is a specific branch of the larger socialist movement. A person who calls himself or herself a "communist" is a certain kind of socialist; in other words, all communists are socialists but not all socialists are communists. In terms of socio-economic systems, communism and socialism are two different things.

After World War II, a centrally planned socialist system was transplanted to Poland from the Soviet Union without any consideration for the differences in the level of development of the country, its size, resource endowment, or cultural, social, and political traditions. In 1947 Poland became a Communist People's Republic and the elections were denounced by the US as undemocratic. The county went through internal unrest, economic disorders and political problems with its communist ideologies. In 1989 the round-table talks between Solidarity, the Communists and the church took place that allowed having the partially free elections that could achieve widespread success for solidarity, which helped form a coalition government. In the same year Poland became the first of the eastern European countries to overthrow Communist rule. In the following year market reforms, including large-scale privatization were implemented in the country as the new political policies. The Soviet troops made a gradual move to leave Poland and the reformed communists started entering the coalition government. They pledged to continue market reforms and implementation of institutional reforms towards achieving the new goals of the country. Poland ultimately joined NATO in 1999 and the European Union in May 2004[18]. The inception of the democratic transformation in Poland in 1989 evoked high hopes concerning the future of the Polish society. Majority of Poles seemed to expect that incoming changes will consist in expansion of personal freedom and realization of civil rights, introduction of the rules of law

---

[18] The Economist: Country Profile – Poland, The Economist, 19th October 2004.

and social justice, empowerment of ordinary people, attaining national sovereignty, economic progress and significant increase in standards of life. In the post-communist political system people of Poland fostered a development of entrepreneurial spirit and economic (market) rationality that resulted in increase in productivity, decrease in the rate of employment, and dramatic increase in economic polarization. They led to establishment of the strong interdependency between the world of politics and the world of business. As a result, they have faced a fast growth of so called political capitalism[19].

The Islamic revolution in Iran provides a classic case of how the distance between government and people can lead to the total disruption of a country. It is sometimes difficult to ascertain whether the people and the government of a country are in accord. However, media, religious leaders, and internal intelligence of a country can provide some insights into the feelings of the citizens. On the basis of the factors discussed in the pre-text there are many political slants in the political systems of a country. Of these, state-centric international politics, pluralistic national politics, bureaucratic organizational politics, or transnational politics are important. The *state-centric political model* of international politics assumes that national governments seek power and status in relation to one another, that they do so in the context of a competitive, decentralized international political system, and that they utilize whatever international political resources are available in pursuit of their international objectives. The *pluralistic model of national politics* assumes that national governments are responsive to the diverse and conflicting interests and pressures of multiple interest groups within a political system. The assumptions of the *bureaucratic organizational political behavior* hold the notion that the actions of the national government are the result of organizational processes within the bureaucratic setup of the government while the transnational *politics model* emphasizes the increasingly important role played in the world politics by organizations other than those of national governments.

POLITICAL AND RESIDUAL RISKS IN INTERNATIONAL BUSINESS

Political, economic, religious and other tensions can shift at a moment's notice and disrupt business operations for exporters, traders, investors, banks and other organizations involved in international commerce. Companies can be subject to the discriminatory actions—or inaction—of foreign governments and third parties, potentially leading to forced shutdowns, relocations and other unexpected expenses. The political risks in international business are developed with illegitimate use of political power. The way political power is exercised determines government action and the degree of risk that threatens a firm's value. For example, a dramatic political event may pose little risk to a multinational enterprise, while subtle policy changes can greatly impact a firm's performance. Firm-specific political risks are the risks directed at a particular company in reference to its country of origin, nature of activities in the host country, social and economic goals etc. and such risks are by nature discriminatory. The risks specific to the firms may be concerned with the governmental

---

[19] Janusz Reykowski: Unexpected Traps of the Democratic Transformation, Conference on Social Change in Poland, University of Michigan, Ann Arbor, 24-26 September 2003, USA.

policies as well as due to the instability in the political system governing the country. The following risks may emerge from such situations:

Government policy based risk

- Discriminatory regulations
- "Creeping" expropriation
- Breach of contract
- National security
- Structural adjustment
- Internal economic policies

Risk of shooting due to political instability

- Sabotage
- Civil unrest
- Anti-globalization movements
- International relations of the host country
- Firm-specific boycotts

On the contrary, the country-specific political risks are not directed at a firm, but are countrywide, and may affect firm's performance. An example in this context may be given as the decision of the government to forbid currency transfers or the outbreak of a civil war within the host country. The political risks also include government risks and stability risks. The government risks are those that arise from the policies of a governing authority, in reference to the use of authority. A legitimately enacted tax hike or an extortion ring that is allowed to operate and is led by a local police chief may both be considered as government risks. Indeed, many government risks, particularly those that are firm-specific, contain an ambiguous mixture of legal and illegal elements. Instability risks, on the other hand, arise from political power struggles. These conflicts could be between members of a government fighting over succession, or mass riots in response to deteriorating social conditions. The country level risk in reference to the government policies and political instability may vary in its intensity. However, following factors may affect the risks due to government policies and political instability in a country:

Government policy based risk

- Mass nationalizations
- Regulatory changes
- Currency inconvertibility

Risk of shooting due to political instability

- Labor unrest
- Urban rioting
- Protest on international relations
- People's movement on diplomatic moves
- Civil wars

Besides the apparent political risk, a foreign firm may also get exposed to a bundle of different risks. Many of these risks are not unique to the asset owned by a firm but reflect broader possibilities, such as that the stock market average will rise or fall, that interest rates will be cut or increased, or that the growth rate will change in an entire economy or industry.

Residual risk, also known as alpha, is what is left after the firm takes out all the other shared risk exposures. An exposure to such risk can be reduced by the firm through strategic

Table 3.1. Political Risk Platforms in a Country

Area	Risk Factors
Demography	Size and occupational distribution, Economic growth and per capita income, Population growth and control, Income distribution.
Human Resources	Size and composition, Sectoral and geographic distribution, Productivity, Migration and urban unemployment.
Politico-economic	Natural resources, Economic diversification, Topography and infrastructure, Sources and structure of government revenues, Size and growth of the budget deficit, Social expenditure, Price indices, Wage rates, Interest rates, money supply, etc.
International economics and Trade Related Risk	Current account balance and composition, income and price elasticity of exports and imports, Price stability of major imports and exports, Terms of trade, Geographic composition of trade, Outstanding foreign debt, absolute and relative levels, Terms and maturity profile, Debt servicing to income and exports, Size and relative importance, Capital account, Reserve position, Exchange rates (official and unofficial).
Culture and Religion Based Risk	Underlying cultural values and beliefs, Religious and moral values, Sense of alienation with foreign or modem influences, Constitutional principles and conflicts, Resilience of national institutions.
Leadership, International alignment and diplomatic relations	Key leaders' background and attitudes, Main beneficiaries of the status quo, Role and power of the internal security apparatus, Strength, sources of support, effectiveness of opposition political parties, Level and frequency of internal disturbances, Riots and terrorist acts, Bureaucracy and extent of official corruption, International treaties and alignments, Position on international issues, Preferential economic and trade linkages, Border disputes, Diplomatic or commercial conflict with home country.

diversification decisions. The comprehensive political risks in a country may have many dimensions as exhibited in Table 3.1.

Hence, political risk assessment (PRA) is necessary for the foreign firms in order to identify countries that may turn out to be unsafe tomorrow and to identify the actual situation in the countries avoiding any biasness. For example, doing business in Vietnam and Haiti now may not be that unsafe as was felt earlier. Assessing the political risk of a country may also provide a framework to identify the degree of political risk in the selected countries for firm's entry. The political risk may be assessed through some effective methods. In one of the PRA methods, an executive or a team of executives is advised to visit the country in which investment is being considered. A preliminary market research is done to support the visit of the executives in the country. Upon arrival, there are usually meetings with government officials and local businesspersons. This approach is known as *grand tour*. The results emerging out of this approach may be very shallow, representing only selected pieces of information and therefore possibly camouflaging undesirable aspects of the market. The other method relies on the advice of an outside consultant or a person deemed to be an expert. Usually such persons are seasoned educators, diplomats, local politicians, or businesspersons. The capability and experience of the advisor is the factor determining the quality of this report. This approach of political risk assessment, by its very nature is termed as *the old hand*. In another similar approach known as the *Delphi technique*, a few selected experts are asked to share their opinions independently on a given problem, in a form that can be scored in order to produce a statistical distribution of opinion. The experts are shown the resulting distribution and given the chance to alter their original views. In the process of the study the experts are given the task of rating different political factors such as the stability of government, internal and external security issues of the country, and the existing political conflicts. The process is repeated several times and then the results are synthesized. Based on the final expert opinion, the firm takes an entry decision. In addition to the above discussed methods many firms conducts the inquiry into the risk factors in a country using *quantitative methods*. In such studies the statistical analysis is done on the basis of the time series data collected on identified variables. The multivariate analysis, correlations and trend analysis are conducted to measure the magnitude and direction of political risk in a country. The foreign firms decide on the basis of the trend of political risk in a country and its magnitude, which emerges out of the quantitative studies. However, while assessing political stability, the focus should be on the legitimacy of state authority, the ability of that authority to impose and enforce decrees, the level of corruption that spread through the system of authority and the degree of political fractionalization that is present. Where economic policy is concerned, the focus would be more along the lines of the degree of government participation in an economy, the government's external debt burden, and the degree to which interest groups can successfully obstruct the decision-making process.

LEGAL OUTLOOK ON INTERNATIONAL BUSINESS

In addition to the political environment in a country, the legal environment comprising local laws, civil and criminal laws and trade regulations also influences the operations of a foreign firm. It is important for a foreign firm to know the regulatory provisions in each market as such legal environment constitutes the "rules of the game." At the same time, the firm must know the political environment because it determines how the laws are enforced and indicates the direction of new legislation. Thus the legal environment of international marketing has dyadic relationship with political and regulatory systems in a country. Accordingly, for an international firm it is necessary to acquaint itself with host country laws, international law, and domestic laws in each of the firm's foreign markets. Multinational enterprise in its global exercise must cope with widely differing laws. The legal barriers in most of the countries include antidumping laws, tariff structures, horizontal price fixing among competitors, and market division by agreement among competitors, and price discrimination. Hence, the international firms should also understand the arbitration procedures as an alternative to legal recourse. Traditionally, two types of legal systems may be distinguished as common law and code law. *Common law* is based on precedents and practices established in the past and interpreted over time. Common law was first developed in England, and most of the commonwealth countries follow this system. *Code law* is based on detailed rules for all eventualities. Code law was developed by the Roman empires and is popularly practiced by a number of free world countries. The code law is practiced in Italy, France, Germany, Mexico and Switzerland. The distinction between the common law and code law may be described with an example in context to the right to proprietary issues such as trademarks in a country exercising the common-law would largely depend on the chronological use of the property. Under the common law the judicial decision would be favoring the party actually using the trademark on its package and in its advertising campaign, despite not being formally registered the trademark. On the contrary, according to code law, the right of property would rest with party which has actually registered the trademark.

Major problems may face the business firms when a country respects more than one legal system and generates conflicting values. If a business contract contains a clause specifying the jurisdiction, stipulating which country's legal system should be used to settle disputes, the matter can be settled accordingly. However, in absence of any such a provision the disputes can not be settled choosing a legal system or a country in particular. An example may be cited of an accidental leak of poisonous gas that occurred in the chemical plant at Bhopal (India) of Union Carbide, a company of United States of America, causing over 2000 casualties in 1984. In this situation, the Indian government would have preferred to settle the issue of compensation to the survivors in the US court of law than in Indian courts as the decision in India courts may consume time and on the other hand the American judiciary is considered to be liberal in awarding such strictures on humanitarian grounds. Simultaneously the Union Carbide management might have preferred to get the issue settled in the Indian courts in its own economic interest. However, it took over a decade to settle the compensation issues to the survivors of the Bhopal tragedy between the Government of India and the company, and it has been settled as an out-of-court compromise.

TARIFF BARRIERS

The host country laws affect the business operations of a foreign firm. Such regulations may adversely affect the entry of a firm into the host country and may appear in many forms, including tariff, antidumping laws, export/import licensing, investment regulations, legal incentives and restrictive trading laws. A tariff may be defined as the government levies on exports and imports. The tax on export may be determined as export duty while the tax on imports is termed as import duty or customs duty. The objective of imposing an export duty for a country is to discourage selling overseas to maintain adequate supply at home. The heavy import duty is levied in order to protect home industry from penetration by cheap imports, to gain a source of revenue for the government, and to prevent the dilution of foreign exchange balances. A country may decide to impose the tariff barriers for various reasons as mentioned below:

- Control the outflow of national money
- Protect home market products and services
- Equalization of cost of production

- Discourage low cost imports that affect the market stability and quality of goods and services in the home market
- Ensure better home products and services with available technology and manpower
- Wage and employment protection
- Implementing the anti-dumping measures
- Bargaining and retaliation on tariff
- Protecting the infant industry and national security in the home country
- Seeking adjustments in terms of trade and fiscal deficits through optimal tax levies

A country may have a single tariff system for all goods from all sources, which may be termed as *unilinear* or *single column tariff*. Another category of tariff may be described as *general-conventional tariff*, which applies to all the countries in general except the nations that have signed special tax treaties with a particular country or a group of countries. A tariff that is determined on the basis of a tax permit may be classified as *special duty* and a fixed percentage of the value of may be levied as *ad valorem duty*. It may sometimes happen that both special and *ad valorem* duties are levied in a country as a combined duty. The ways to control the penetration of foreign goods and services in the home country without imposing the financial compensation or taxes may be categorized as non-tariff barriers. Such non-tariff barriers include quotas, import equalization taxes, road taxes, laws giving preferential treatment to domestic suppliers, administration of antidumping measures, exchange controls, and a variety of *invisible* tariffs that impede trade. These measures are comprehensively discussed as under:

- Specific limitations on trade comprising quotas, licensing, proportion restrictions of foreign goods to domestic goods, minimum price limitations on import goods and embargos that restrict the import of specific products from restricted countries.
- Customs and entry procedures include valuation of imports, anti-dumping practices, tariff classifications of imported goods, imposing complex and lengthy documentation procedure involving bureaucratic requirements, comprehensive service by service fee structure.
- Standards include undue discrimination towards health, sanitation, hygiene, safety, and imposing higher standards on imported goods than on domestic products. Also applying packaging, labeling, and marketing standards of the country to imported goods in an excessively stringent and discriminatory way.

Besides the above *non-tariff barriers*, a country may directly participate in the trade activities with an objective to discourage imports as well as participation of foreign firms in the home country in any manner[20]. Under such measures, the government gets involved in the trade activities though procurement policies favoring the products of home country over the products of other countries. The government may also impose export subsidies in terms of tax incentives to the domestic firms and implementing the *countervailing duties* that may be described as taxes levied to protect domestic products from the imported products that had been given export subsidy by the exporting country's government. A country may also

---

[20] Cao A D: non-tariff Barriers to US Manufactured Exports, Columbia Journal of World Business, Summer, 1980, pp 93-102.

proceed to various types of other charges levied on imports to make them less competitive against the domestic goods. Such non-tariff measures include prior import deposit requirement, administrative fee, supplementary duties and other variable levies.

ANTI-DUMPING LAWS

The act of exporting a product by an international firm at a price lower than the price it normally charges on its own home market is defined as "dumping" the product. Dumping is a type of pricing strategy for selling products in foreign markets below cost, or below the price charged to domestic customers. Such strategy is adapted to capture a foreign market and to damage rival foreign national enterprises. The legal definitions are more precise, but broadly the WTO agreement allows governments to act against dumping where there is genuine ("material") injury to the competing domestic industry. In order to do that the affected country's government shows that dumping is taking place, calculates the extent of dumping as how much lower the export price is compared to the exporter's home market price, and shows that the dumping is causing injury or threatening to do so. The subsidies that require recipients to meet certain export targets, or to use domestic goods instead of imported goods are prohibited under the WTO agreement because they are specifically designed to distort international trade, and are therefore likely to hurt other countries' trade[21]. The agreement further specifies to the member countries that the countervailing duty, which is parallel to anti-dumping duty, can only be charged after the importing country has conducted a detailed investigation similar to that required for anti-dumping action. The argument against dumping is largely on the price differentials that are intended strictly to weaken competition and over the long run uproot the native products from the market. Hence, all countries pass antidumping laws to secure their home markets from any undue foray by foreign firms.

Though dumping is commonly not regarded as a healthy business strategy for the foreign forms, there are sometimes good management reasons for doing that. A typical case describing the positive side of this strategy may be to survive in a large competitive market by selling at very low prices, another case is when a company has overproduced and wants to sell the product in a market where it has no brand franchise to protect. However, if the firms have implemented the dumping, they can well reverse it. The "reverse dumping" refers to the less-common practice of selling products at home at prices below cost. This would be done in extreme cases where the share at home needs to be protected while monopolistic market positions abroad can be used to generate surplus funds. Regardless, dumping is considered to be illegal since it is destructive of trade, and competitors can take an offender to court to settle a dumping case. The usual penalty for manufacturers whose products are found to violate the antidumping laws is a countervailing duty, an assessment levied on the foreign producer that brings the prices back up over production costs and also imposes a fine.

There was a growing uproar in 2001 among the business communities in construction sector in America about the foreign firms riding over the steel prices. This steel trade war was all about how Europeans and Asians are "dumping" on America. In literal sense dumping is the export of goods at prices below their cost of production, but it is meant to evoke the

---

[21] The World Trade Organization: Understanding WTO – The Agreements, WTO Headquarter, Geneva, 2004
www.wto.org

dishonest foreign firms building their strategy to maneuver to undersell honest locals or even drive them out of business. However, one of the arguments in defense of dumping which was put forth by the foreign companies dealing steel in America emphasized that prices always cover costs and are the same everywhere for all customers. Although, this logic did not stand strong as generally no customer expects the same price for a car, insurance, apples or a hamburger from any two dealers. In response to complaints from U.S. steelmakers, the U.S. International Trade Commission recommended a hike in tariff for steel up to 40 percent. The situation turned serious with major steel manufacturing countries world over to find alternatives to sell the 250 million tonnes of overproduced steel at lower prices, as it may lead to bankrupting manufacturers all over the world. Negotiators from Europe and Asia warned that the American tariff threats could provoke retaliation, even a "trade war." However, the business analysts at various forums felt that this may not be a right moment for a trade fight over anything as the WTO discussions in Doha, Qatar, has brought hopes to develop a new agenda for global trade. The threat of US in decreasing the price of steel however has been criticized as unethical over the Doha round of discussions of WTO[22].

By the end of 2000, there were 450 antidumping cases involving tens of billions of U.S. dollars against Chinese producers, and the number was expected to increase with China's entry to WTO. One problem has been that without a true market economy, the cost basis for determining potential dumping practices does not exist. Foreign governments have used third country prices to arrive at a proper cost figure. The argument is that in China, where state-owned exporters receive subsidies and bank loans they never have to repay, under a system that is largely secret, there is no basis to assess costs. Most countries and regional groupings have established their own particular version of antidumping regulations. Under the trade laws coordinated by WTO, the antidumping rules that are to apply to all members are more liberal than usual, making penalties more difficult to assign. The new rules, developed with the intent to support emerging countries' exports, feature stricter definitions of injury, higher minimum dumping levels needed to trigger imposition of duties, more rigorous petition requirements, and dumping duty exemptions for new shippers.

IMPORT LICENSING

Many countries have laws on the books that require exporters and importers to obtain licenses before getting into the international deals. Import licensing is imposed by the nations to control the unnecessary purchase of goods from other countries. Such restrictions would help the government to save foreign exchange balances for other important purposes like the import of pharmaceuticals, chemicals, and machinery. India, for example, has strict licensing requirements against the import of cars and other luxury goods. A member country of WTO may restrict imports of a product temporarily (take "safeguard" actions) if its domestic industry is injured or threatened with injury caused by a surge in imports. Here, the injury has to be serious. Safeguard measures were always available under GATT (Article 19). However, they were infrequently used, some governments preferring to protect their domestic industries through "grey area" measures using bilateral negotiations outside the aegis of GATT; they

---

[22] For details see Tony Emerson, Paul Mooney, Lee B. J. and Rich Thomas: Dumping in America, The Newsweek International, December 24, 2001

persuaded exporting countries to restrain exports "voluntarily" or to agree to other means of sharing markets. Agreements of this kind were reached for a wide range of products, for example automobiles, steel, and semiconductors[23]. It has been envisaged in the new directives of the agreement that member countries must not seek, take or maintain any voluntary export restraints, orderly marketing arrangements or any other similar measures on the export or the import side. The bilateral measures that were not modified to conform to the agreement were phased out at the end of 1998. Countries were allowed to keep one of these measures an extra year (until the end of 1999), but only the European Union for restrictions on imports of cars from Japan made use of this provision. This agreement is called as *safeguards.*

The agreement sets out the criteria for assessing whether "serious injury" is being caused or threatened, and the factors which must be considered in determining the impact of imports on the domestic industry. When imposed, a safeguard measure should be applied only to the extent necessary to prevent or remedy serious injury and to help the industry concerned to adjust. Where quantitative restrictions (quotas) are imposed, they normally should not reduce the quantities of imports below the annual average for the last three representative years for which statistics are available, unless clear justification is given that a different level is necessary to prevent or remedy serious injury. The import licensing systems are subject to disciplines in the WTO. The Agreement on Import Licensing Procedures says import licensing should be simple, transparent and predictable. For example, the agreement requires governments to publish sufficient information for traders to know how and why the licenses are granted.

REFERENCES

Amsden A H: The *Rise of "The Rest": Challenges to the West from Late Industrializing Economies*, Oxford University Press, Oxford & New York, 2001.

Bairoch P: *Economics and World History: Myths and Paradoxes*, University of Chicago Press, 1993, pp 184.

Chang H J: State, Institutions and Structural Change, *Structural Change and Economic Dynamics*, 5 (2), December, 1994, pp 293-313.

Collier P and Hoeffler A: On the Incidence of Civil War in Africa, *Journal of Conflict Resolution*, 46 (1), 2001, pp 13-28.

Finger J M and Schuler P: *Implementation of Uruguay Round Commitments: The Development Challenge*, World Bank Staff Working Paper # 2215, Washington DC, World Bank, October 1999, pp 1-53.

Huber, Walt. *California State and Local Government in Crisis,* Fourth Edition, Covina, CA: Educational Textbook Co., 2000.

Lall S and Lastch W: Import Liberalization and Industrial Performance: The Conceptual Underpinning, *Development and Change*, 29 (3), July, pp 473-465.

Light, Paul: *A Delicate Balance: An Introduction to American Government,* Second Edition, New York, NY: Saint Martin's Press, 1999.

Peter Kobrak: Political Environment of Public Management, Longman, 2002.

---

[23] World Trade Organization: Understanding the WTO, 3rd Edition, Information and Media Relations Division, WTO headquarters, Geneva, 2003, pp 48-49.

Rimmerman, Craig A. *The New Citizenship: Unconventional Politics, Activism, and Service,* Second Edition, Boulder, CO: Westview Press, 2001.

Robert A. Gorman: *Biographical Dictionary of Marxism,* Westport, CT: Greenwood Press, 1986.

Wayne Ellwood and Andy Crump: *The A to Z of World Development,* Oxford, England: New Internationalist, 1998.

Welton, David A., and John T. Mallan: *Children and Their World: Strategies for Teaching Social Studies,* Seventh Edition, Boston, MA: Houghton Mifflin, 2001.

World Trade Organization: *Understanding WTO, Information and Media Relations Division,* WTO Headquarters, Geneva, 2003.

Chapter 4

TRADE COMPETITIVENESS
IN DEVELOPING COUNTRIES

Regional trade has emerged as an important move of globalization which has been induced collectively with shared norms and political leadership in respective regions. Informality has appeared to be a representative common norm which played a catalytic role in first nurturing communication for a regional cooperation framework to enhance the international trade opportunities with emerging countries as business partners. The political leadership shown by China and Japan has played a vital role in promoting the regional integration initiatives. There has been a rapid proliferation of bilateral free trade agreement (FTA) in East Asia and the Asia-Pacific regions since the 1990s and this trend has further intensified enhancing the scope of advanced regional co-operation and integration. However, after experiencing the regional financial crisis of 1997–98 many Asian economies underscored the need of expanding their trade and economy consciously and aggressively moved towards exploring alternative liberalization paths. At this juncture the new regionalism or new regional trade agreements became relevant[1]. Since the late 1980s, Mexican firms have faced a variety of environmental changes including the privatization of state-owned firms, opening of markets to foreign trade and investment, increased domestic and foreign competition, political change, and economic crises. Mexican firms have increasingly undertaken new strategies and have expanded into foreign markets while others have "restructured" their portfolios of diversified subsidiaries[2].

India has emerged today as the largest producer of milk in the world crossing 80 million tonnes. This has been achieved largely through a smallholder economy in which "Operation Flood", one of the world's largest dairy development programs, played an important role. All this happened largely under autarkic framework and regulated public policy dictated by import-substitution strategy. Until 1991, the Indian dairy industry was highly regulated and protected through quantitative restrictions (QRs) and stringent licensing provisions. Since early 1990s, India embarked upon liberal policy framework, which got reinforced with the signing of Uruguay Round Agreement on Agriculture (URAA) in 1994. This opening-up

---

[1] Rajan Ramkishen S (2005), Trade Liberalization and the new Regionalism in the Asia-Pacific: Taking Stock of Recent Events, *International Relations of the Asia-Pacific*, 5(2), 217-233.
[2] Wood T and Caldas M P (2007), *Brazilian Firms and the Challenge of Competitiveness*, Can Latin American Firms Compete? Oxford Scholarship Online Monographs October, 232-250.

increasingly exposed the Indian dairy sector to the global markets, which in-turn is distorted by export subsidies, domestic support and prohibitive tariffs in developed countries[3].

The development of international trade in the eastern and central Europe has been found to be slow due to transition in the regional economy and political situations. Major crises observed in Central and Eastern European countries (Czech Republic, Hungary, and Slovak Republic) and two CIS countries (Russia and Ukraine) can be explained by inconsistencies in the domestic policy mix and by the deterioration of macroeconomic fundamentals. The transitional economies in eastern and central Europe are emerging with a new agenda for inter-regional trade development promoting a liberal internationalist agenda[4]. The paper reviews the approach to trade policy in early development research and evolution of thoughts integrating the economic and structural reforms in Latin America and analyzes economic integration between two economies—one central, with a large local market, and the other peripheral, with a small local market. With the recent enlargement of the European Union (EU), ten new member states have entered the borderless Single European Market (SEM) and adopted common EU policies in trade with third countries. This policy change causes trade creation effects within the borderless SEM and trade diversion effects in trade with third countries. Slovenia is a typical example of trade creation effects within the enlarged EU-25 and trade diversion effects particularly with traditional former Yugoslav markets. However, it has been observed that the trade creation effects are found to be much more significant in Slovenian imports than exports, indicating lack of Slovenian export competitiveness[5]. As the global economy has become increasingly open to 'free' trade, European industry and international firms across the developed world have found threat of growing competition from low cost, emerging market countries. Media headlines suggest that effort has been focused on raising trade barriers to keep competition at bay. However, such actions are a thin veneer over the very real, structural changes that are rapidly taking place[6].

The economic reforms thus will not have a constant speed and will often be subject to modifications in the policies that bring changes in the performance and structure of economic activities. The economic reforms can be assessed by examining their corresponding policy measures and implications. However, entire economic progress may not be interpreted as an outcome of the reforms. The growth and development may result in being slower in a country or region in a normal process than stirred process of reforms. After years of poor economic management, many Latin American and Caribbean countries are experiencing a process of structural reforms that places them on a path to a superior economic performance[7]. Two basic principles identify this process of economic reforms—fiscal and monetary discipline, and reliance on market forces to determine the allocation and distribution of resources. Traditional economic theory and business practice have tended to pose a contradiction or trade-off

[3] Sharma VP and Gulati A (2003), *Trade liberalization, market reforms and competitiveness in Indian dairy sector*, MTID Discussion Paper #61, International Food Policy Research Institute.
[4] Söderbaum, Fredrik, StÅlgren, Patrik and Van Langenhove, Luk (2005), The EU as a Global Actor and the Dynamics of Inter-regionalism: a Comparative Analysis, *Journal of European Integration*, 27 (3), 365-380.
[5] Majkovic D, Bojnec, S and Turk J (2007), Development of New Members' EU Trade: Evidence from the Slovenian Agri-Food Sector, *Post-Communist Economies*, 19 (2), 209-223.
[6] Economic Outlook (2006), European industry: the emerging market competitiveness challenge, *Economic Outlook*, 30 (3), 11-17.
[7] Easterly William and Sergio Rebelo (1993), Fiscal Policy and Economic Growth-An Empirical Investigation, *Journal of Monetary Economics*, 32 (3), 417-458.

between efficiency and equity: what is good for one may be bad for another. Yet recent years have seen the emergence of a group of business and other actors, particularly at the regional scale, that have begun to highlight the important of paying attention to fairness, inclusion, and sustainability in their economic strategies and planning[8]. The rapid liberalization of the world's trading system has obliged all firms (micro, small, medium and large) to participate in the international trading system. The competitiveness of these enterprises is very important if developing economies are to secure their economic survival in this era of rapid market liberalization and erosion of trade preferences[9].

MACROECONOMIC FACTORS

The structural reforms have been initiated in the macro areas including economic activity, international trade, financial markets, generation and use of public resources, governance, and labor markets. It has been observed in the previous studies that the economies that have advocated for open international trade have gained higher rates of growth influenced by the higher rate of investment and factor productivity[10]. The tariff and quantitative restrictions often impede the process of trade liberalization. The higher the average level of dispersion of tariffs and para-tariffs in terms of custom duties and taxes, the greater is the distortion of international trade. The measure applied to evaluate the level of tariffs and para-tariffs is the weighted average rate of tariff and para-tariff charges that is used to weigh their respective shares in regional or global imports[11].

The current developments in competitiveness of Russia towards global merchandise export markets are a critical factor to determine its trade specialization and comparative advantage in a global context. It is observed that government efforts to stimulate export growth in sectors needs more vigorous push in Russia's trade profile and assesses prospects for improvement in the balance of Russia's export profile[12]. Upon analyzing Russia's economy and its oil and gas-producing sectors it may be stated that the country's Revealed Comparative Advantage, Revealed Comparative Disadvantage, and Trade Specialization Index, which is compiled by Russia's Federal Customs Service, the focus is changing in comparative advantage of Russia's major export and import commodities over the 1994-2005 period. The results of the analyses make it possible to test the assertion that the increasing competitiveness of oil and gas exports and secondarily those of armaments, selected base metals, round wood, and fertilizers, must compensate for declining competitiveness in meat, plastics, and automobile production and stagnation in the machinery sectors and increasing imports thereof[13]. Russia has shown an impressive increase in labor productivity has been achieved

---

[8] Organization for Economic Co-operation and Development (2007), Cohesion and Competitiveness: Business Leadership for Regional Growth and Social Equity, *OECD Governance*, 18, 788-830.

[9] Williams D A (2007), Competitiveness of small enterprises: Insights from a developing economy, *The Round Table*, 96 (3), 347-363.

[10] Harrison A (1996), Openness and Growth – A Time-series, Cross-country Analysis for Developing Countries, *Journal of Development Economics*, 48 (2), 419-447.

[11] Pritchett L and Sethi G (1994), Tariff Rates, Tariff Revenue and Tariff Reforms- Some New Facts, *World Bank Economic Review*, 8 (1), 1-16.

[12] Cooper, Julian (2006), Can Russia Compete in the Global Economy? *Eurasian Geography and Economics*, 47 (4), 407-425.

[13] Tabata, Shinichiro (2006), Observations on Changes in Russia's Comparative Advantage, 1994-2005, *Eurasian Geography and Economics*, 47 (6), 747-759.

since 1997, especially during the post-crisis period. This has been true for all major sectors, with the exception of those which are still predominantly state-controlled or which suffer from strong state interference and there have been significant relative adjustments within the industrial sector, as labor productivity increased more in less productive sectors. Since the crisis, relative unit labor costs have also adjusted considerably, as less competitive sectors experienced larger labor force reductions. However, international trade competitiveness as measured by revealed comparative advantage remains limited to a small number of sectors that mainly produce primary commodities (particularly hydrocarbons) and energy-intensive basic goods. Also, there has been a tendency for further specialization in resource-based exports in recent years[14].

The most common pattern of economic reforms in Latin America has been, first, radical liberalization, and second, implementation of prudential norms that moderated the initial liberalization. The policy changes related to the financial system (namely, the removal of interest-rate controls, elimination of mandated credit to "priority" sectors, privatization of state banks, liberalization of the foreign investment regime, and more recently, improvements in the regulatory framework) have improved both the banking system and the stock market. The traditional view about fiscal and monetary policies in developing countries (and particularly in LAC) is that they are pro-cyclical, contributing to deepen business cycles[15]. Trade policy reform in LAC in the 1990s has been both widespread and extensive, and the region now shows a fairly open trade regime. Such a sharp policy reversal clearly had an impact on trade flows, and those effectively underwent significant changes in the past decade[16]. The Latin American countries with higher GDP, faster growth, more cropland and a longer period of time since reform had more empathy to support free trade[17]. In looking at the effects of the economic crisis of the 90's on the larger countries of Latin America, Brazil appears as the most vulnerable economy. It has been observed that move towards liberalization stimulated privatization in Latin American countries. However, most cases of privatization failure can be linked to poor contract design, opaque processes with heavy state involvement, lack of re-regulation and a poor corporate governance framework[18].

FREE TRADE AGREEMENTS

There have been varying arguments on the impact of trade agreements on the economy and welfare measures. It has been concluded in one of the studies that the preferential trade agreements are mostly welfare reducing since the partner countries might end up with severe

---

[14] Ahrend, Rudiger (2006), Russian Industrial Restructuring: Trends in Productivity, Competitiveness and Comparative Advantage, *Post-Communist Economies*, 18 (3), 277-295.

[15] Talvi Ernesto and Végh Carlos (2000), *Tax Base Variability and Procyclical Fiscal Policy*, NBER Working Paper, No. 7499, January.

[16] Loser Claudio M and Guerguil Martin (1999), Trade and Trade Reform in Latin America and the Caribbean in the 1990's, *Journal of Applied Economics*, 2 (1), 61-96.

[17] Beaulieu, Eugene, Yatawara, Ravindra and Wang, Wei Guo (2005), Who Supports Free Trade in Latin America?, *The World Economy*, 28 (7), 941-958.

[18] Lopez de Silanes, Florencio and Chong, Alberto (2003): *The Truth about Privatization in Latin America*, Yale ICF Working Study No. 03-29, October.

welfare losses due to substantial amount of trade diversion[19]. Since 2001, the American administration has pursued a trade policy known as Competitive Liberalization. This policy envisages a series of mutually-reinforcing and sequential steps to open markets abroad to US companies, to strengthen market-oriented laws and regulations overseas, and to place the United States at the centre of the world trading system. Among other administrative considerations, foreign and security policy considerations have influenced US trade policy making, perhaps more so than in the 1990s. Till recently, the principal outcome of this policy has been the negotiation by the United States of numerous free trade agreements, mainly with developing countries, individually or in sub-regional groupings[20].

Free Trade Areas constitute a potential threat to the world trading system because these types of agreements are; in general, trade diverting and they lead to formation of new interest groups who oppose the multilateral tariff reductions[21]. Regionalism in Asia, particularly in the form of free-trade areas, is a recent trend that is becoming increasingly important. This has been disturbing to many, given the significance of trade and investment in Asian economic growth and development and the region's key role in global commerce. However, more advanced regional accords generally receive high grades, with the notable exception of rules of origin, which tend to be even more problematic in the context of accords in which a member country of OECD is a party[22]. The examination of the compatibility of exchange rate systems across trading partners is also very revealing. Part of the success of NAFTA since the late 1990s and the "impasse" of Mercosur during 1999-2001 had to do with the choices of exchange rate regimes. In both trade areas the share of trade among the partners is very high, and in NAFTA, this includes significant financial transactions[23] while another study draws attention on the historical context of economic institutions in the region, and on how these institutions have influenced competition policy enforcement[24].

New estimates of export and import equations are studied using a broader set of variables than previous studies and distinguishing trade between the member countries of Mercosur and trade with non-Mersocur member countries[25]. It has been observed that Latin American countries are moving in sensible directions by emphasizing well-publicized actions against price fixers, by undertaking competition advocacy programs, and by targeting public sector restraints on competition[26]. Mercosur is not likely to develop supranational governance institutions present in the European Union, as policy elites in Mercosur member states desire to maintain a great deal of domestic policy autonomy. However, Latin American countries

---

[19] Bhagwati, J. and A. Panagariya (1996), Preferential trading areas and multilateralism: strangers, friends or foes?, in J. Bhagwati and A. Panagariya (eds.), *Free Trade Areas or Free Trade? The Economics of Preferential Trading Agreements* AEI Press.

[20] Evenett S J and Meier M (2008), An Interim Assessment of the US Trade Policy of `Competitive Liberalization', *The World Economy*, 31 (1), 31-66.

[21] Krueger, A O (1995), Free Trade Agreements versus Customs Unions, NBER WP#5084.

[22] Plummer M G (2007), 'Best Practices' in Regional Trading Agreements: An Application to Asia, *The World Economy*, 30 (12), 1771-1796.

[23] Rojas-Suarez, Liliana (2002), Toward a Sustainable FTAA: Does Latin America Meet the Necessary Financial Preconditions? Institute for International Economics Working Study No. 02-4.

[24] Leon Igancio de (2001), *A Market Process Analysis of Competition Policy in Latin America*, Catholic University of Adres Bellow (UCAB), Venezuela, Working Paper.

[25] Catao Luis and Falcetti Elisabetta (2002), Determinants of Argentina's External Trade, *Journal of Applied Economics*, 5 (1), 19-57.

[26] Owen, Bruce M (2003), *Competition Policy in Latin America*, Stanford Institute for Economic Policy Research (SIEPR) Stanford Law and Economics Olin Working Study No. 268, October.

have recently made impressive progress in trade reforms; there has been limited use of competition policies[27] (Rajapatirana, 1994).

TRADE AND MONETARY REFORMS

Besides World Trade Organization and various economic unions of common interest nations, International Monetary Fund (IMF) has been supporting international monetary cooperation among the member countries for expansion and balanced growth of international trade, exchange rate stability, elimination of restrictions on the international flow of capital, and the orderly adjustment of balance of payment (BOP) imbalances. At the Bretton Woods conference, the IMF was embedded with the task of coordinating the system of fixed exchange rates to help the international economy recover from two world wars and the instability in the interwar period caused by competitive devaluations and protectionist trade policies. IMF has steadily incorporated microeconomic factors such as institutional and structural reforms into its activities and designed strategies to provide short-term balance of payments (BOP) lending and monitoring member countries macroeconomic policies[28]. The exchange rate regulations positively correlate with the amount of overall structural reforms of the developing nations and of trade liberalization in particular.

Recent international experience has shown that excessively complex administrative procedures required to establish and operate a business discourage inflows of foreign direct investment. The cost of administrative procedures varies significantly across countries. The most important barriers appear to be the delays associated with securing land access and obtaining building permits, which in several countries take more than two years. Countries that impose excessive administrative costs on entry tend to be equally intrusive in firm operations, thereby weakening the argument that barriers to entry are a substitute for the unwillingness government of the or inability to regulate enterprise operations[29]. Upon analyzing the policies of the industrialized countries, the economic crises in emerging markets appears to be in the areas including the macroeconomic policies of the country which determine the global financial environment and efforts to reform the international financial architecture, with the aim of lessening the frequency and severity of future crises[30].

The analysis of the distributional impact of policy reforms on the well-being or welfare of different stakeholder groups, particularly on the vulnerable sectors, has an important role in the elaboration and implementation of economic growth strategies in developing countries. In recent years this type of work has been labeled as Poverty and Social Impact Analysis (PSIA) and is increasingly implemented to promote evidence-based policy choices and foster debate on policy reform options[31]. Over the 1990s macroeconomic policies improved in most developing countries, but the growth dividend from this improvement fell short of

[27] Kaltenthaler Karl and Mora Frank O (2002), Explaining Latin American Economic Integration – The Case of MERCOSUR, *Review of International Political Economy*, 9 (1), 72-97.

[28] Sanford, Jonathan E. and Weiss, Martin A (2004), International Monetary Fund: Organization, Functions, and Role in the International Economy, Working Paper, U.S. Congressional Research Service, April, 1-24.

[29] Morisset, J P and Lumenga-Neso O (2002), Administrative Barriers to Foreign Investment in Developing Countries, World Bank Policy Research Working Paper No. 2848, May, 1-21.

[30] Frankel, J A and Roubini N (2001), The Role of Industrial Country Policies in Emerging Market Crises, Harvard University, KSG Working Paper No. RWP02-002, November.

[31] World Bank (2005), *Analyzing the Distributional Impact of Reforms*, June, 1-295.

expectations, and a policy agenda focused on stability turned out to be associated with a multiplicity of financial crises. The main lesson learnt by these countries reveal that more often, slow growth and frequent crises resulted as the major concern in the agenda of economic reforms in 1990s in the developing nations. These issues posed limitations in the depth and scope of the reform agenda, its lack of attention to macroeconomic vulnerabilities, and its inadequate attention to complementary reforms outside the macroeconomic sphere[32].

REGIONAL TRADE AND ECONOMY OF EEC

In the beginning of the transition process it was presumed that the newly liberalized economies in Central and Eastern Europe would experience high rates of sustained economic growth, with rapid convergence towards trade and economy of the major industrialized economies in the West. However, Hungary, Poland, Lithuania and Latvia have experienced transition recessions and have grown at a relatively slower rate. There has been considerable heterogeneity in outcomes, with some transition economies recovering rapidly so that by the end of the 1990s their level of output was at or above pre-transition levels. A key factor of the transition process is the structural change consisting in the reallocation of resources on the basis of market incentives. Product variety is therefore a potentially useful concept in analyzing the structural changes that have actually occurred in Eastern European transition economies. Using contemporary econometric methods and data which provide a new dimension for testing the implications of alternative growth models, an empirical study reveals that there exists a strong evidence of export fostering in economic growth of the East European transition economies. The results show that export in capital-intensive industries and investment are spearheading the growth process in an export-led growth model[33].

It may be observed from Table 4.1 that the transitional economies of Central and Eastern Europe suffered severe transitional recessions with negative growth of GDP. Among the Central and Eastern European countries the Polish transition can be viewed as the most successful one in terms of growth levels. It was the first of the transition economies to record positive levels of growth following the recession, growing by 2.7 percent in 1992. Slovenia entered its recovery a year later, but Hungary and the Czech Republic did not show positive growth until 1994, and Estonia until 1995. Russia recorded weak positive growth for the first time in 1997, but the financial crisis of 1998 pushed it back into recession. The growth of aggregate GDP in Eastern Europe was lower (3.0 per cent) than in the CIS but was basically unchanged from the previous year. The flexibility of domestic demand induced future prospects of these economies on the part of both consumers and investors. This also reflects the considerable progress that some of these countries have made in their market reforms, as evidenced by the invitation to eight east European countries to join the European Union in 2004.

---

[32] Montiel P and Serven L (2006), Macroeconomic Stability in Developing Countries: How Much Is Enough? *The World Bank Research Observer*, 21 (2), 151-178
[33] Ventura J (1997), Growth and interdependence, *Quarterly Journal of Economics*, 112, 57–84.

Table 4.1. Growth of GDP in Eastern European Countries
(in percent)

Country	1990	1995	1999	2002
Czech Republic	-1.2	6.0	-0.2	2.5
Estonia	-8.1	4.2	-1.4	5.7
Hungary	-3.5	1.4	4.4	3.2
Poland	-11.6	7.1	4.0	1.3
Russia	-3.0	-4.1	3.2	4.3
Slovenia	-8.1	4.2	4.9	3.2

Source: UNEEC (2003) and IMF (2000).

The recent reduction of tariffs in Eastern Europe is consistent with welfare-maximizing trade policy in response to the substantial changes in the market structure of these countries[34]. It has been observed by the European Bank for Reconstruction and Development that impact of disintegration on trade among the former constituent republics of three demised federations in central and Eastern Europe, the Soviet Union, Yugoslavia, and Czechoslovakia has been followed by a sharp fall in trade intensity, although the legacy of a common past remains strong. However, the process of integration into the world economy has not been uniform across transition countries. Integration has been rapid and deep in the countries of Central Europe and Baltic states. The countries of South-eastern Europe and Commonwealth of Independent States (CIS) are far less integrated into the world's product and capital markets for different reasons. CIS trade is limited by obstructive domestic and regional policies and distance from other markets. Restrictions to market access remain significant in several sectors compared with those faced by many other countries. Moreover, with the completion of accession, remaining EU trade barriers against the accession countries will be lowered. As a result, trade with the non-accession countries may be reduced unless their market access is improved[35].

The Central –European Free Trade Agreement (CEFTA) has been instrumental for sub-regional trade alliance and cooperation, however, the constraints to both further internal and external development of CEFTA are such that it is unlikely to move to a redefined role in the future[36]. After long inward-looking trade policies and import-substituting industrialization, several Latin American countries undertook comprehensive trade liberalization and macroeconomic adjustment in the 1980s and the experience of these countries has been relevant for the economies in Eastern Europe and the former Soviet Union in transition from socialism to market economies. The inward-looking trade policies have been the principal attribute of Latin American economy, which has gradually transformed towards trade openness. Similar situation prevailed in the countries Eastern Europe and the former Soviet Union as they belonged to the Council for Mutual Economic Assistance (CEMA), a regional

---

[34] Egli Dominik and Westermann Frank (2004), Optimal Tariffs and Subsidies and Changes in Market Structure, *Review of Development Economics*, 8 (3), 406-412.

[35] EBRD (2003): *Trade and Integration in Transition Countries*, Transition Report, European Bank for Reconstruction and Development, 73-88.

[36] Dangerfield, Martin (2001), Sub-regional Cooperation in Central and Eastern Europe: Support or Substitute for the 'Return to Europe'?, *Perspectives on European Politics and Society*, 2 (1), 55-77.

trading arrangement with many limitations on outward movements[37]. Russia did trade significantly, but largely with other members of the CMEA. Such trade rarely reflected underlying comparative advantages and soon disappeared once the transition process began[38].

CEMA was officially dissolved in early 1991 and future trade among the former CEMA countries has taken place on a radically different basis, and the region will be in search of new partners. The reorientation of Central European trade is likely to be gradual rather than dramatic, as trade negotiation in the western countries may not be easy. It has been observed that the trade reforms policies in former CEMA countries would be able to drive changes in production as these countries begin to produce according to their comparative advantage alike countries in Latin America. In addition, the traditional state trading structures are being dismantled, with individual enterprises increasingly able to search out their own foreign partners. Since the start of economic transformation more than a decade ago, a number of east European economies have had massive inflows of FDI, a significant part of which have been undertaken by large, export-oriented multinational companies. These new and expanding capacities exploit the comparative advantages of these economies in low-cost labor (particularly, low-cost skilled labor) as well as their proximity to the major markets of Western Europe. This fundamental competitive edge appears to have been one of the factors that allowed east European exporters to continue to gain export market share in some particular products despite the weakness of western demand.

Trade and Economic Growth in Latin American Countries

In the 1990s macroeconomic policies improved in a majority of developing countries, but the growth dividend from such improvement fell short of expectations, and a policy agenda focused on stability turned out to be associated with a multiplicity of financial crises[39]. The economic advancement of a country may be reviewed in reference to its fiscal, monetary, and exchange rate policies over time, and the effectiveness of the changing policy framework in promoting stability and growth. There are large differences in gross domestic products by sectors among Latin American countries, and the majority of these differences are due to the value of industrial and service sectors. Although the economic activities in different development sectors have been increased, in per capita terms this value decreased due to the demographic growth that Latin American countries (mainly Mexico and Brazil) had experienced during the last decades. In terms of external trade, it has been found that the outward orientation as the ratio between total exports and gross domestic product (GDP) increased from 16.1% in 1990 to 32.7% in 2000. Panama had the highest level in this area (66.5%). Modest growth returned to Latin America and the Caribbean in 2003 and regional GDP advanced by an average 1.3 percent, after a contraction of 0.6 percent in 2002. Argentina continued recovering rapidly after its acute crisis. Brazil and Uruguay shared in the broadening of economic recovery during the year while Chile, Colombia and Peru recorded

---

[37] De Melo Jaime and Dhar Sumana (1992), *Lessons of Trade Liberalization in Latin America for Economies in Transition*, Policy Research Working Paper Series #1040, World Bank, November.

[38] Michalopoulos C(1999), *The integration of the transition economies into the world trading system*, World Bank Policy Research Working Paper # 2182, World Bank.

[39] Luis Servén, and Peter J. Montiel (2004), *Macroeconomic Stability in Developing Countries: How Much Is Enough?* Working Study # 3456, World Bank, November.

growth above 3 percent. However, ongoing political uncertainties caused Venezuela's economy to deteriorate further during the first half of the year. Central America grew by an average 3.1 percent and looks set to sustain growth, thanks to the recently signed Central America Free Trade Agreement (CAFTA). The rate of change in the merchandize export in the Latin American countries during 2002 shows that most of the countries in the region except Costa Rica and Peru, have shown a downward trend[40]. The Latin American and Caribbean countries that have shown low growth in exports have suffered from macroeconomic imbalance and in some cases a virtual economic chaos in the pre-reform period. In many countries inflation rates evolved into hyperinflations during the 1980s, while fiscal deficits continued to burst[41].

The Central American Free Trade Agreement (CAFTA) negotiated between the U.S. and Central America offers opportunities and challenges for the five countries including El Salvador, Guatemala, Honduras, and Nicaragua that joined in 2003 and Costa Rica that was included in January 2004. Mexico, Nicaragua, Jamaica and Honduras always were over the mean. During the years 1990, 1995 and 2000, Mexico, Cuba, Panama, Argentina, Brazil, Chile and Uruguay reached incomes above 2000 dollars per capita in the service sector[42]. On the other hand, there are some countries like Haiti, Honduras, Nicaragua and Bolivia with incomes below 500 dollars per capita. Latin America's merchandise exports increased slightly as the decline in intra-regional trade was balanced by increased shipments to other regions. The recovery of commodity prices in the course of the year and the upturn in the US economy contributed to this rise. While most Latin American countries saw a reduction or stagnation in their imports, those of Costa Rica increased by 9 per cent. Mexico benefited from the recovery of the US market while for Costa Rica; the recovery in semi-conductor shipments boosted both imports and exports. Despite the continuation of low prices for a number of primary commodities, exports of many Central American and Caribbean countries recovered strongly. Economic activity in Western Europe remained subdued as Germany, the largest economy, experienced declining domestic demand. Domestic demand growth remained positive in the rest of the region, but was sluggish in several other countries. In the euro zone, public consumption was the most dynamic expenditure category while private consumption slowed down and fixed investment in the enterprise sector fell nearly 3 per cent. In the midst of this poor economic situation, further progress was made in the process of European integration[43].

Starting in the mid-sixties of the 20th century, the European example inspired a number of trade-oriented integration arrangements in the Latin American region such as the Latin American Free Trade Association, which later became the Latin American Integration Association (ALADI), the Central American Common Market (MCCA), the Caribbean Community and Common Market (CARICOM), the Andean Group, later the Andean Community; and more recently, the Southern Common Market (Mercosur), the Group of Three (G3) and the Association of Caribbean States (ACS). The main objective of Mercosur is to improve the efficiency of the four member economies through the process of opening

---

[40] World Bank: Report on Latin America and Caribbean, Regional Overview, 2003.

[41] Rajagopal (2007), Dynamics of Growth in Foreign Trade in Transitional Economies: Analysis of European, Latin American and Asian Countries, *Journal of East-West Business*, 13 (4), 37-64.

[42] Guisan, M C and Aguayo (2000), Education, Industary, Trade and Development of American Companies in 1980-99, *Applied Econometrics and International Development*. Vol. 2(1), 83-106.

[43] World Trade Organization: World Trade Report 2003, pp 30-42.

markets and accelerating economic development. The common history shared by the member countries facilitates the integration process and the group is recognized as the third largest regional trading bloc in the world.

There are many bilateral alliances as well. Latin American countries have been living a renaissance since the 80's. Most economies are stabilized, living standards are higher, direct foreign investment has surged, democracy has been institutionalized and most countries have demonstrated a desire to integrate themselves into the new global economy by opening their economies to international trade and investment. In the 90's the Latin American countries have liberalized their economies, which has been followed by a significant increase in their imports. This improvement was due primarily to three factors including lower inflation, less government intervention, and fewer trade barriers[44].

International trade has been the key indicator of the overall economic growth of Latin American countries. Several regional free trade agreements signed over the past decade—such as Mercosur, the Central American Common Market, the Andean Community, and the Caribbean Common Market-demonstrate the region's understanding of the benefits of free trade. Countries like Chile have gone even further in their trade liberalization efforts, signing bilateral agreements with Mexico and Canada after being unable to sign an agreement with the entire NAFTA bloc. In terms of scope, sectors of interest and coverage, there are three levels of sub-regional arrangements: (i) customs unions currently being finalized, e.g., the Andean Community, Mercosur, MCCA and CARICOM, (ii) first-generation free trade accords with a commercial emphasis, and (iii) new-generation free trade pacts encompassing such sectors as services, investment, intellectual ownership, and state acquisitions. Chile successfully engaged in negotiations for broader scope aimed at furthering their association with Mercosur, establishing free trade areas and bringing other sectors and issues into the accords.

With investor confidence returning in Latin America and domestic conditions improving, gross private financial inflows in 2003 increased by 40 percent over 2002. Moreover, interest rate spreads on sovereign bonds over US treasuries reached record lows. Net foreign direct investment (FDI), however, continued its decline from a peak of $88 billion in 1999 to an estimated $36 billion in 2003. This is partly explained by the end of the privatization boom and the profit crisis in Brazil and Argentina. Export growth outpaced import growth for most countries in 2003, leading to surplus positions on trade and a big improvement in the region's current account deficit, down to 0.5 percent of GDP (compared to 4.5 percent in 1998). Tourism revenues and workers' remittances also improved, and commodity prices were generally strong. Consequent upon falling trade and investment barriers and high growth prospects, the countries of Latin America represent attractive alliance prospects for an increasing number of global firms. The typical objective for these strategic alliances is a basic trade-off wherein local firms seek access to technology and capabilities that are critical for their survival in an environment of increased competition and in return, they offer prospective multinational partners access to a large and growing market.

The macroeconomic policy refers to the top-down strategy developed and implemented in a country by the government and central banks, usually intended to maximize growth while keeping down inflation and unemployment. The growth factors determining the incentives

---

[44] Rajagopal (2007), Dynamics of International Trade and Economy: An Inquiry into Emerging Markets, Nova Science Publishers, Happague, NY.

towards investing in human capital for developing new products include government policies. Countries with broadly free-market policies, in particular free trade and the maintenance of secure property rights typically have higher growth rates. By 1990, most developed countries reckoned to have long-term trend growth rates of 2-2.5% a year. Elsewhere, among Latin American countries, the reforms did bring lasting benefits. In Chile, an early reformer, fast growth saw poverty halved, to 23%, between 1987 and 1996.

A positive trend in the behavior of trade flows has been observed during the reforms period, resulting from the increased openness of these economies to international markets. There is a striking difference between the behavior of export and import volumes around the devaluation episodes. Exports tend, on average, to increase in the year of the devaluation and the following two years. Only in Argentina, Peru and Venezuela do we observe negative export growth in the second year after the devaluation, and this probably has more to do with the circumstances in world markets at that time, especially in the United States. In all other cases, exports continue to increase. Import volume, in contrast, behaves quite differently. In most of the devaluation episodes, import volume contracted, e.g. devaluation of currency in Brazil in the mid 1990s has driven substantial growth in imports. In all other cases, the import contraction was short-lived. Exports increase faster than average to countries in the region, and especially towards countries that are partners in regional trading agreements. Brazil and Argentina increased their trading flows with each other significantly, and also with other countries in the region such as Chile and Paraguay.

INTERNATIONAL TRADE AMONG LATIN AMERICAN AND ASIAN COUNTRIES

It may be stated that the higher the average level and dispersion of tariffs and para-tariffs such as duties and customs fees, the more distorted the trade development. In the specific case of agriculture, although the coverage of non-tariff barriers did fall considerably, in some countries it nevertheless remained for a time more significant than in other sectors. This can be attributed in part due to the desire of governments to protect their farm sectors from world price fluctuations and to counteract export subsidies. Expansion of international trade from Latin American countries to Asia-Pacific countries is exhibited in Table 4.2.

Latin America's total exports grew by an annual average 8.9 percent between 1990 and 2003 raising its share of world exports from 3 to 5.4 percent as exhibited in Table 4.2. It may be observed from the data that Chile has the largest share of its exports (29.5 percent) to the Asia- Pacific countries in terms of percent share to the world exports followed by Peru (17.3 percent) during 2003. Mexico has been the indisputable driver of Latin America's export growth, with its share of the regional total rising from a fifth in the early 1980s to 45 percent in 2003. It may be observed from the exhibited data that four big countries which include Brazil, Argentina, and Venezuela-today generate more than three-fourths of Latin America's exports. Even with Latin America struggling with anemic economic growth, the region's imports rose by more than exports (an annual average of 10.1 percent in 1990-2003), perhaps reflecting the region's rather aggressive opening and episodes of exchange rate appreciation.

Table 4.2. Exports from Latin American Countries to Asia-Pacific (1990-2003)
(US $ millions)

Trade Bloc	Country	Japan	Korea Republic	China	Hong Kong	Taiwan	Singapore	ASEAN	Asia-Pacific (A)	World (B)	Percent Share (A/B)
Mercosur	Argentina	344 (395)	434 (51)	2478 (241)	98 (60)	126 (48)	10 (409	1098 (329)	4588 (1164)	29566 (12352)	15.5 (9.4)
	Brazil	2311 (2349)	1223 (543)	4533 (382)	694 (271)	689 (432)	338 (250)	1113 (790)	10900 (5016)	73084 (31412)	14.9 (16.0)
	Paraguay	5 (21)	0 (6)	17 (67)	9 (17)	12 (3)	1 (5)	9 (5)	53 (123)	1242 (1708)	4.3 (7.2)
	Uruguay	12 (21)	6 (6)	95 (67)	14 (17)	5 (3)	2 (5)	63 (5)	197 (123)	2198 (1708)	9.0 (7.2)
Prospecting for Mercosur	Chile	2243 (1384)	1006 (258)	1817 (34)	0 (41)	583 (279)	39 (33)	254 (132)	5922 (2162)	20077 (8522)	29.5 (25.4)
	Colombia	202 (259)	76 (13)	82 (2)	16 (16)	52 (1)	11 (3)	18 (9)	456 (303)	13092 (6765)	3.5 (4.5)
	Peru	390 (420)	176 (65)	675 (55)	30 (19)	147 (50)	16 (0)	76 (18)	1511 (628)	8749 (3313)	17.3 (19.0)
	Venezuela	135 (505)	15 (6)	165 (6)	11 (34)	37 (57)	201 (125)	9 (44)	571 (777)	24974 (18044)	2.3 (4.3)
Overall	LAC	6473 (6958)	3367 (1091)	10470 (866)	1278 (507)	1786 (967)	832 (495)	3029 (1376)	27234 (12261)	363707 (120916)	7.5 (10.1)

Figures in parentheses indicate values for 1990.

Source: IDB-INT calculations based on UN/COMTRADE data published in the official document AB-2370, March 21, 2005: "Asia and Latin America and the Caribbean: Economic Links, Cooperation and Development Strategies".

   The dynamism of trade notwithstanding, the volume of Latin American exports to Asia-Pacific starts from a relatively low base and is well below the region's exports to North America, the European Union, and intra-regional commerce. In fact, while increasing substantially up to 1991, the importance of Asia-Pacific as a market for Latin America has declined over the past decade. Latin American exports to Asia-Pacific stood at $24 billion in 2003, with the Asia-Pacific accounting for 6.6 percent of Latin America's total exports to the world—a marked drop from Asia-Pacific's share of 9 percent in 1990. Central America did, however, experience slight growth in the share of the Asia-Pacific in total exports in 1990-2003. Of the individual countries, Argentina, Chile, Colombia, Paraguay, Peru, Uruguay, and Venezuela have experienced a rise in the share of Asia-Pacific in their exports between 1990 and 2003.

   The importance of the Asia-Pacific is most marked for Chile, which exported 29 percent of its exports to Asia-Pacific, as well as for the Mercosur countries, which sent 15 percent of their exports to the Asia-Pacific basin in 2003. Arguably, the most vulnerable region right now is Latin America, where most countries are trying to cope with an environment of high economic fragility, partly resulting from the current global slowdown but also reflecting internal political trouble and policy mismanagement. The region's problems are of a more long-term nature than merely cyclical and therefore need to be tackled accordingly, taking into account country-specific circumstances. Latin America's large distance from world markets, the region's complicated topography, and the tropical climate pose particularly important challenges. On the macroeconomic front, the fiscal policy stance has deteriorated significantly in several countries, sending them into a dangerous spiral of increasing debts and deficits despite important efforts to generate primary surpluses in the public budget. However, that encouraging reforms have been implemented in some areas, notably regarding foreign trade and financial liberalization. As a result, exports have deepened and become more diversified, which bodes well when the external environment becomes more favorable again.

Architecture of Business Partnering among Asian-LA Countries

The Latin American and Caribbean countries have a long history of bilateral and sub-regional preferential agreements on trade and economic integration. Dating from the 1960s and early 1970s, the Latin American Free Trade Area (LAFTA), the Andean Community (AC), the Caribbean Common Market (Caricom) and the Central American Common Market (CACM) rarely met their goals, because of the inherent clash between integration and import substitution industrialization. However, a new wave of preferential agreements rocked the region in the 1990s, now linked to a re-hauling of trade and development strategies. Traditional arrangements, such as the Latin American Integration Association (LAIA) — LAFTA's successor — and the AC, gained strength and Mercosur broke off as an important sub-regional initiative in South America. Various bilateral agreements (many of them under the Montevideo Treaty that created LAIA in 1981) were struck, generally with the goal of establishing free trade areas.

In the process of bi-regional business negotiations among the Latin American and Asian countries, the Free Trade Agreements (FTAs) were up until recently and signed mainly in reference to the geographically proximate countries. In 2003, Chile and South Korea signed the first comprehensive FTA between an Asian and Latin American country; the agreement went into effect in April 2004. Latin American and East Asian partners have launched negotiations for three further bi-regional FTAs, including Chile-Singapore-New Zealand. Chile and Japan have formed a joint study group to explore the feasibility of launching formal FTA negotiations. Latin America-Asia trans-continentalism has spanned the Asia Pacific basin, with Brazil and India negotiating an FTA. Moreover, plans have been expressed for Chile-Japan, Mexico-New Zealand, Mercosur-India, Mercosur-China, and Chile-China FTAs.

These agreements often managed to form sub-regional free trade areas; many even explicitly seek to become common markets. For example, Mercosur was created with the intention of gradually evolving towards a common market and the AC has reaffirmed its goal of forming a common market in 2005. Neither has the Caricom abandoned its strategic goal of building a common market, evidenced by member statements in the Protocol of Guatemala in 1993. With ambitious integration goals and modest results, taken together the initiatives present similar trends and prospects, most remain in a free trade, a stage incapable of turning into full-fledged customs unions. Divergent foreign policies, domestic political and economic restraints, and border conflicts plague nearly all. Conflicts flare up from disparities in size, economic structure and patterns of trade, in addition to often contradictory cost-benefit evaluations of undertaking a common external tariff.

Prospects in Foreign Trade

After many years of effort, a global preferential trade agreement was negotiated in the form of the Global System of Trade Preferences (GSTP), which entered into force in 1989. The Preamble of the GSTP Agreement embodies the belief that the system is a major instrument of south-south cooperation, for the promotion of collective self-reliance as well as for the strengthening of world trade as a whole. Participation in the GSTP is limited to members of the Group of 77 and only those developing countries that have exchanged concessions are eligible for its benefits. Developing countries, as members of the Group of 77, can become parties to the Agreement individually or as a sub-regional, regional or interregional grouping. The Agreement envisages arrangements relating to tariffs; para-tariffs; non-tariff measures; direct trade measures, including medium and long-term contracts, and sectoral agreements. The negotiations can be conducted in accordance with one or any combination of the following modalities:

- Product-by-product negotiations;
- Across-the-board tariff reductions;
- Sectoral negotiations; and
- Direct trade measures.

The GSTP Agreement also contains special benefits for the least developed countries by granting exclusive preferential concessions and by stipulating that they must not be required to make concessions on a reciprocal basis. Concessions have been exchanged among 45 developing countries in the first round of GSTP negotiations, which concluded on 30 April 1988 and involved important trading nations from all regions. Among the countries were Argentina, Brazil, Chile, Colombia, and Peru from Latin America, and India, Indonesia, Malaysia, Pakistan, Philippines, Republic of Korea, Singapore and Thailand from the Asian and Pacific region. Some main features of the concessions granted in the first round of GSTP negotiations were:

- Concessions were confined to tariffs
- Use of product-by-product negotiations as the modality
- Limited coverage of concessions for most participants. For example, Argentina had five tariff lines at the 10-digit level; Chile had 10 tariff lines at the eight object level; Indonesia had one tariff line at the seven-digit level; Malaysia had one tariff line at the seven digit level; Philippines had three tariff lines at the seven-digit level and Thailand had 11 tariff lines at the six-digit level. Somewhat more extensive but still quite modest concessions were given by Brazil, 93 tariff lines at the eight-digit level; and India gave 32 tariff lines at the six-digit level.
- Concessions were generally in terms of a margin of preference over a range of 10 to 50 per cent.

The first and by far the most significant is Mercosur, with Argentina, Brazil, Paraguay and Uruguay as members. Mercosur introduced a common external tariff (CET) in 1995, to be phased over a six-year period. The aim is to eventually create a common market with free movement of goods, labor, services and capital. A feature of the Mercosur policy is that it has either formed a free trade area with other countries (such as Chile) or is actively negotiating such an accord (such as with the EU). Colombia and Venezuela formed another free-trade area, known as the Group of Three in 1994, to be phased over a 10-year period.

In Asia, the most significant arrangement is among the countries of South-East Asia. ASEAN was formed in 1967 to promote economic, social and cultural cooperation among Indonesia, Malaysia, Philippines, Singapore and Thailand. In 1978, ASEAN put into force a preferential trading arrangement granting a margin of preference to members of 10 to 15 per cent on selected products. In the early 1990s, the arrangement was upgraded into the ASEAN. Free Trade Area (AFTA) and in 1994 it was decided to fully implement the arrangement in 2003. ASEAN membership has also expanded to include Brunei Darussalam, Viet Nam, Lao People's Democratic Republic, Myanmar and Cambodia. Another integration arrangement among the developing countries of the region that is potentially significant is the South Asian Association for Regional Cooperation (SAARC), whose membership includes Bangladesh, Bhutan, India, Maldives, Nepal, Pakistan and Sri Lanka. A decision was taken in 1992 to form the SAARC Preferential Trading Arrangement (SAPTA) and in 1995, the group agreed to move towards a free trade area. However, political differences between India and Pakistan have impeded the effectiveness of the arrangement. In the meantime, India and Sri Lanka have moved separately to form a free trade area.

The economic integration arrangements in the Latin American and Asian regions have been established mainly at the sub-regional level. There are initiatives in the Latin American region to link together some of the Sub-regional arrangements. This leads to the question of what are the possibilities for economic integration arrangements linking the two regions. In the Asian and Latin American regions, some cross-regional free trade areas are almost at the point of being established. Preferential arrangements have also been envisaged between Taiwan Province of China and some countries in Central America. Besides the countries of Asia, membership in APEC includes Peru and Chile. However, their membership has so far been only a consultation forum and not an integration arrangement.

The best opportunity for countries of Asia and Latin America may be to intensify their commercial exchanges by continuing to rely on non-discriminatory trade relations. To expand interregional trade, the countries of the two regions should look at barriers to trade for products of interest to them from countries of the other region and negotiate for reduction or elimination on the basis of most favored nations (MFN) at a future round of multilateral trade negotiations. Apart from this, other cooperative action could be taken to overcome impediments due to such factors as distance, lack of traditional trade relations and even linguistic differences that have inhibited interregional trade exchanges. Consultative forums among governments and among businesses should be set up where they do not exist. Such forums have to be strengthened where they already exist. Periodic consultations have to be coordinated with full use of the internet to disseminate information about production capabilities and the supply needs in the two regions.

Expansion of Latin America-Asia Trade Links

The trade performance of Asian and Pacific countries had been outstanding up to 1997. In 1980, the region exported less than US$ 280 billion, by 1990 that total had increased to almost US$ 700 billion and in 1995 more than US$ 1,230 billion. Results on the export side were matched by an exceptional performance on the import side. Total imports jumped from US$ 292 billion in 1980 to more than US$ 700 billion 10 years later and over US$ 1,300 billion in 1995. These values indicate an average annual growth rate between 1990 and 1995 of about 12 per cent for exports and over 13 per cent for imports. However, the Asian crisis had a negative effect on the region's trade performance. Between 1996 and 1998, the average annual growth of total exports was -0.2 per cent, while on the import side the decrease was more pronounced, at -4.2 per cent. The result for the period 1990-1998 shows that annual growth for exports reached only 7.5 per cent as compared to 11.5 per cent for the period of 1980-1990. Growth of Asian and Pacific exports to the countries belonging to Latin American Integration Association (LAIA) increased 19 per cent a year between 1990 and 1995, growth that was even more pronounced than intra-Asian trade. This was a clear indication that trade liberalization in Latin America offered a special opportunity for Asian and Pacific countries to increase their share in this expanding market.

Inter-regional cooperation has intensified on the trans-Pacific agenda in recent years. Latin America and Asia-Pacific have created various business platforms to deal with bilateral economic and political issues. The most comprehensive in terms of bi-regional membership is the Forum for East Asia-Latin America Cooperation (FEALAC) launched at a Ministerial Meeting in March 2001 in Santiago, Chile. Comprising of 17 Latin American and 15 Asia-Pacific economics, FEALAC is an informal mechanism for dialogue and cooperation among the countries of the two regions to meet political, cultural, social, economic and international issues of common concern. Two further major venues of trans-Pacific cooperation are the Pacific Basin Economic Council (PBEC) and the Pacific Economic Cooperation Conference (PECC). The Latin American partners in each are Colombia, Chile, Ecuador, Mexico and Peru. PBEC is an association of senior business leaders from more than 1,100 major corporations in 20 economies around the Pacific Basin Region aimed at expanding trade and investment flows through open markets. In its next International General Meeting (IGM) in June 2005 in Hong Kong, PECC will focus on the Pacific Basin's role in the next stages of globalization, such as the Doha Development Round. Meanwhile, the 25-member PECC promotes trade, investment, financial stability, and development around the Pacific Rim. It comprises senior representatives from business, government, and the academia. PECC has recently focused on the proliferation of regional integration agreements as a potential way for achieving the Bogor Convention Goals of APEC[45].

Japan and Latin America have deep-seated cooperation. Japan has alone, contributed to Latin America's development through economic and technical cooperation aimed particularly at economic reform, poverty reduction, and environmental protection. It is one of Latin America's main sources of Official Development Assistance (ODA). Japan was one of the key actors in helping Latin America debt crisis of the early- 1980s, and also involved in the Central American peace processes. More recently, Japan has supported the electoral processes in Latin America, including joining the dispatch of election observers from the Organization of American States (OAS). Japan has also pursued active cooperation with the Caribbean through the Japan-CARICOM Consultation, which centers on fostering bilateral relations,

---

[45] Inter-American Development Bank (2005), IDB Official document # AB-2370, March 21, 2005: "Asia and Latin America and the Caribbean: Economic Links, Cooperation and Development Strategies".

and economic cooperation, cultural exchanges, and collaboration in international business associations.

It is interesting to note that this was the highest rate of growth compared to other regions. On the other hand, Asian and Pacific imports from LAIA were the most affected among the regions. Even before the Asian crisis, Latin America was a minor partner in Asia's export and import flows. In 1998, only 2.2 per cent of total Asian and Pacific exports went to Latin America, and only 1.8 per cent of their imports originated in LAIA countries. It is even more significant that 18 years earlier, the share of LAIA countries in total Asian and Pacific exports and imports was higher. During the first five years of the 1990s, growth of exports from Asia and the Pacific to LAIA was high. Eight countries had annual average growth rates over 20 per cent during this period. Three countries that included China, Indonesia and Thailand had increases of over 40 per cent in their exports to the region.

The average annual growth rate for imports to East Asian countries from LAIA countries actually increased slightly over the rate for 1990-1995. However, New Zealand's imports from the world which had increased on average by 8 per cent between 1990 and 1995 decreased almost 6 per cent between 1996 and 1998. Before the crisis, the most dynamic Asian market for Latin American products was Malaysia, followed closely by Indonesia. The import demand of these two countries declined drastically after the crisis. During this period, Latin America represented more than 2 per cent of total imports for only five Asian and Pacific countries, Latin America absorbed more than 2 per cent of total exports for only three countries. Latin America had the highest average market share of total exports for Japan, while the region's imports were more relevant for the Republic of Korea. South Korea maintains important institutional ties with the countries of Latin America and the Caribbean. It was one of the first Asian countries to join the OAS as a permanent observer, and has made efforts to contribute to Latin America's economic and social development through ODA and technical cooperation. South Korea has recently sought to deepen its economic ties with Latin America. Besides the FTA with Chile, in 2003 South Korea staged with various Latin American countries the South Korea-Latin America and Caribbean Business Forum, which drew a host of government officials and analysts. South Korea and Mexico are joined by the 21st Century Commission, a private-level consultation forum created to explore possibilities for longer-term bilateral collaboration.

China and Latin America have strengthened cooperation ties markedly over the past decade. The Rio Group and China launched political dialogue in 1990, and in 1994 China became the first foreign country to be admitted as an observer to the Latin American Integration Agreement (LAIA or ALADI). In 1997, China was admitted to the Caribbean Development Bank. China has also held official talks with Mercosur following the establishment of a bilateral dialogue mechanism. Furthermore, much like Japan and South Korea, China collaborates with various Latin American countries in APEC and FEALAC. It also has expressed interest in a non-borrower membership in the Inter-American Development Bank.

India and Chile have signed a Preferential Trade Agreement (PTA) in early 2006 as part of initiatives to increase trade and investment between the two countries. The PTA strategically positions Chile to access and to capitalize on the Indian market and its technological assets. The agreement provides tariff preferences ranging from 10 to 50 per cent on 178 products to Chile and a similar range of preferences on 296 items to India. It would benefit 98 per cent of items being exported by Chile to India and 91 per cent of the goods being exported by India to Chile. The Indian products, which would benefit include textiles, chemicals, pharmaceuticals, engineering and agricultural machinery while Chilean products include copper, newsprint, iodine, fish meal and salmon. Both countries have also discussed the draft reports of the Joint Study Group and agreed to submit their findings to consider further action on a Free Trade Agreement.

TRADE POLICY IMPLICATIONS

The business partnership strategies should be developed keeping in view the heterogeneity in economic development, culture and institutional modalities that exist in both regions, while seeking globally balanced relations. The relationship should be based on fundamental shared principles and values, which in turn can be translated into clear political messages and a general sustained process of dialogue and cooperation. Relationships can be deepened at the bi-regional, regional or bilateral levels, taking advantage of the special circumstances of country groupings. Building relationships should proceed at different levels and speeds among the countries of the region. Considering the multiplicity of forums it is necessary to focus the trade partnering negotiations at bilateral and multilateral levels and avoid overlap between distinct dialogues and similar initiatives taken at other forums.

Bilateral negotiations should be strategically pursued in removing/ reducing the non-tariff and investment barriers. The trade related negotiations among the Latin America-East Asian countries should also focus on the technical norms and standards; rules of origin, anti-dumping, subsidies, countervailing measures; other liberalization and deregulation measures (privatization); sub-regional, regional and hemispheric integration processes; and convergence and divergence between regional integration and multilateral trade regimes. The negotiations should also be dealt on simplifying the customs rules and procedures, including non-transparent and inefficient infrastructures; differing customs; improper application of rules of origin, customs valuation, pre-shipment inspection and import licensing. Customs problems can be especially difficult for small and medium enterprises that have less experience and fewer resources for handling these problems.

The trade integration between most of the largest Central and Eastern European countries and the euro area is already relatively advanced, while the Baltic countries as well as the South Eastern European countries still have significant scope for integration. The necessity of foreign investments in the transition countries is the result of industrial restructuring in post-socialist Eastern Europe and the Baltic countries. New markets, lower production costs and higher profit rates have been the main motivators in investing to the transition countries. Bi-regional multilateral trade needs to be encouraged among the Latin America and East Asian countries which would enable them to promote liberalization which is conducive to increasing the traditional trade flows among the participating countries. The bi-regional diplomatic negotiations should be evolved towards developing an action plan aiming at reducing non-tariff barriers and transaction costs, as well as promoting trade and investment opportunities between the two regions. Such a plan could provide concrete goals to be achieved in identified priority areas such as customs procedures, standards, testing, certification and accreditation, public procurement, intellectual property rights and mobility of business people.

GLOBAL BUSINESS PARTNERING

Triad Market

The new global marketplace accelerates competition, thereby reducing the lead time for companies with new products, services or technologies to reach and service their target market. To survive and grow in this type of economic environment, a business will need strategic markets where it can expand its sales and be competitive. Businesses, both large and small, are turning to niche markets where competition is reduced. Economic globalization is a new worldwide economic order, in which a majority of nations prescribe to the free enterprise system. The triad market refers to the United States and Canada, Japan and Western European countries. This group of countries accounts for approximately 14 percent of the global population and represent about 70 percent of world gross product and absorb the major proportion of capital and consumer products. There are about 92 percent of world computers used by the triad countries. Since 1980 three major international trading areas emerged in the world economy in the form of triad that aims at developing uniformity in the markets and currency parity differences across the countries.. One of the appealing characteristics of the triad market is the globalization of needs. There are similarities in the demand and lifestyle patterns of triad consumers. The purchasing power of triad residents is more than 10 times higher than the buyers of the developing countries. The technology infrastructure of this group of countries is advanced as over 70 percent of the households possess modern telecommunication tools and services. The level of buyers in the triad countries is higher as compared to other regions in the world and the social infrastructure like roads, electricity and communication, health and sanitation, housing and transport services are highly advanced. All these factors stimulate the triad to be powerful in doing business among its affiliates and global marketplace.

Global business leaders are largely emerging with the convergent and divergent technologies and marketing strategies. A convergent technology strategy is defined as the development and synergistic integration of all technologies necessary to achieve worldwide leadership for a new product. A typical example is the first laptop computer by Toshiba. A divergent technological strategy is defined as the development of alternative technologies, related or unrelated, that will assure leadership in a given market. A typical example is General Electric Medical Systems. A convergent market strategy is defined as the utilization of all marketing efforts to gain worldwide leadership in a specific market segment, as for example General Electric Medical Systems. Finally, a divergent market strategy is defined as targeting a broad spectrum of customers across many industries, with a great variety of diverse applications. A typical example is the Toray Company of Japan which has achieved worldwide leadership in the application of carbon fibers[46]. However, significant differences are known to exist among organizations operating in different countries due to different national and organizational cultures, strategic orientations, and management styles. Though it is less clear whether there are significant patterns of differences in how marketing-related factors drive performance in the most successful firms regardless of country. Successful firms appear to transcend differences in national culture and develop a common pattern of drivers of

---

[46] Abetti PA (2003),Convergent and divergent technological and market strategies for global leadership, *International Journal of Technology Management*, 14 (6-7), 635-657.

success which include primary focus on organizational innovativeness, a participative work climate, and an externally oriented organizational culture[47].

The triad power may be described as the group of countries performing business operations on a predetermined framework. A Japanese triad power is operative in the United States of America, European community and the Southeast Asia with Japan as a foul point of business operations. Likewise the American triad power consists of the NAFTA countries (United States, Canada and Mexico), European community and Japan. The triad powers essentially function in the countries of their spatial spread and the other regions become less important for survival and are considered as marginal or less opportunistic. In the triad market time and distance play a major role in helping the executives to make quick and appropriate strategic decisions. This factor of time and distance may be termed as an *anchorage* perspective in international marketing[48]. However this base pattern may not be uniform for all the companies of the triad region and there may be some exceptions. For many European companies like Volkswagen, Latin America may be a more attractive market than Africa and for a British Chocolate company like Cadbury's; India, Australia, Africa and part of Canada may be a more attractive market than others. Some American companies heavily depend on the Middle-East markets. The relative strengths of Triad partner countries also reflect on their resource allocation and corporate spending on the research and development and strategic alliances in terms of capital tie-ups, joint ventures and technical tie-ups with the multinational companies of the partnering countries. Although foreign multinational firms from the Triad regions increasingly use mainland China as both a sourcing and a marketing location, no study has directly examined the sourcing strategy–performance linkage. Using resource complementarity and resource dependence theory, we extend the sourcing literature and apply these perspectives to an important transitional economy of China. These two theoretical perspectives suggest that product and uncertainty factors moderate the relationship between strategic alliance-based sourcing of major components and market performance[49].

Asia- Caribbean- Pacific Rim Countries

The countries of Pacific Rim are emerging in the 21st century as the new international business power over the developing countries. The Pacific Rim composed of South Korea, Singapore, Taiwan, Hong Kong, Malaysia, Thailand, Indonesia and the Philippines is growing as an economic powerhouse by improving the regional trade treaties and exports to European and North American countries. These countries have created a strong manufacturing potential in electronics and natural resources. The consumption of construction materials like steel is higher in the region than in the United States and also the demand for semiconductors are increasing over the European Union. The Committee on Trade and Investment (CTI) of Asia Pacific Economic Cooperation (APEC) organization works to reduce impediments to business activity in 15 key areas outlined in the Osaka action agenda -

---

[47] Deshpande R, Farley J U and Webster F E (2001), Triad lessons: Generalizing results on high performance firms in five business-to-business markets, *International Journal of Research in Marketing*, 17 (4), 353-362.
[48] Ohmae Kenichi: Triad Power-The coming shape of global competition, Free Press, New York,1985, 35-54.
[49] Murray J Y, Kotabe M and Zhou J N (2005), Strategic alliance-based sourcing and market performance: evidence from foreign firms operating in China, *Journal of International Business Studies*, 36 (2), 187-208.

tariffs and non-tariff measures, services, standards and conformance, customs procedures, intellectual property rights, competition policy, government procurement, deregulation, rules of origin, dispute mediation, mobility of business people and implementation of World Trade Organization (WTO) obligations. The committee[50] is focusing on the following priority areas during 2004:

- Trade and investment facilitation (including IPR).
- Implementation of the APEC Transparency Standards.
- Implementation of Pathfinder Initiatives
- Contribution to the APEC Structural Reform Action Plan, and
- Support for World Trade Organization

Promoting Trade and Investment Liberalization in Asia Pacific rim countries: Major Proposals

To advance the Doha Development Agenda (DDA) and the Bogor (Indonesia) Goals of free and open trade and investment, as well as their supporting conditions, we agreed to:

- Press for an ambitious and balanced outcome to the DDA, reiterating that the development dimension is at its core.
- Re-energize the negotiation process, building on flexibility and political will are urgently needed to move the negotiations toward a successful conclusion.
- Work towards the abolition of all forms of agricultural export subsidies, unjustifiable export prohibitions and restrictions, and commit ourselves to work in the negotiating group on rules in accordance with the Doha mandate.
- Advance free trade in a coordinated manner among multilateral, regional and bilateral frameworks so that they are complementary and mutually reinforcing.
- Extend our continued support for the early accession of the Russian Federation and Viet Nam to the WTO.
- Continue APEC's work on WTO capacity and confidence building in areas where APEC can best add value, while reviewing past performance to improve its effectiveness.
- Instruct Ministers to take concrete steps to make APEC's trade agenda more supportive of the work of the WTO and report on their progress in 2004.
- Work with the APEC Business Advisory Council (ABAC) and the business community to continue to implement the Shanghai Accord and Los Cabos directives to facilitate business activity in the APEC region, including the reduction of transaction costs 5% by the year 2006.
- Advance all pathfinder initiatives, including the APEC Sectoral Food MRA and Digital Economy Statement to, e.g., stop optical disk piracy and allow technology choice for business.
- Fight corruption, and develop specific domestic actions to combat it. Promote transparency by implementing our general and area-specific transparency standards through our Transparency by 2005 Strategy.

Source: Bangkok Declaration on Partnership for the Future, Bangkok, Thailand (21 October 2003), APEC online document, http://www.apecsec.org.sg/apec/leaders__declarations/2003.html

---

[50] Asia Pacific Economic Cooperation: APEC Secretariat www.apecsec.org.sg

APEC Member Economies are working to eliminate tariff and non-tariff barriers to trade. Elimination of these barriers will help Asia-Pacific countries to achieve the common goals resolved in various ministerial meetings of the APEC member countries, encourage greater and freer trade and investment flows and create new business opportunities and jobs in the Asia-Pacific region. It has been further resolved by the APEC nations that sustainable economic development requires empowering people and strengthening societies for globalization. This process requires more effective, better focusing and strengthening global economic and technical cooperation. Also it has been envisaged that increasing the interaction of Asia-Pacific rim countries with international financial institutions, the private sector, and other outside organizations would pay long-run gains of globalization.

The Pacific Rim offers a variety of opportunities for American and European companies for the products and services that range from telecommunication instruments to the aircraft seats and banking services and a host of other products. Although it is a competitive market, the region is growing economically cohesive that attracts production sharing possibilities with the industrial countries. The Asian producers outside Japan have gained more than one fourth of the global market share for personal computers. Japan and the Pacific emerging triad comprising Singapore, Taiwan and South Korea provide most of the capital and expertise for the rest of the countries of the region that have enormous labor and natural resources. Hong Kong also contributes significantly for the development of international trade in the Pacific region. Japan is Canada's second largest national trading partner (after the United States), taking 2.1 percent of total exports, and is the fifth largest source of foreign direct investment (FDI) in Canada. Canada is a leading supplier to Japan of a number of products of key export interest, such as lumber, pulp and paper, coal, meat, fish, oilseeds and prefabricated housing. While resource-based exports continue to represent much of our trading relationship, Canada is an increasingly important source of sophisticated, value-added, technology-driven products and services imported by Japan. In 2003, Canada's total merchandise trade with Japan was $22 billion. Canadian exports to Japan have declined steadily since the mid 1990s, Canadian exports to Japan declined again to $8.1 billion in 2003 from $8.4 billion in 2002 while imports were decreased by 10 percent in 2003 to $14 billion. In 2003, Canada exported $1.4 billion in services and imported $1.9 billion[51]. The long-term trend in Japan is toward a growing demand for cost-competitive and innovative imports, which represents a significant market opportunity for Canadian exporters. The Asia Pacific region has been the fastest growing trade block over past three decades though it had experience downturn in 1998 and extended after shocks. East Asia is the principal export market for American goods. The transpacific trade has grown over 50 percent of its transatlantic trade by the end of 20th century.

A recent research investigation reveals that the growing economic and political interaction between two important Pacific Rim players-Chile and New Zealand is very much in discussion among international community. There are many issues emerging out this prospecting relationship between these countries which need to be analyzed in reference to the rationale for the closer economic partnership in the Pacific region. It is observed that the trade between the countries may turn as a mix of strategic, symbolic geopolitical and geo-economic drivers towards driving the agreement to increase bilateral commodity exchange.

---

[51] Government of Canada: Report on Canada's International Market Access Priorities- 2004, Department of Foreign Affairs and International Trade, Opening doors to the world, Chapter 6, 2004.

As it is presently constructed, the agreement is likely to bestow disproportionate benefits on specific corporate actors in certain sectors[52]. However, findings of a survey on non-tariff trade barriers (NTBs) indicate that firms in the Pacific Rim region frequently encounter. NTBs are categorized into restrictions on market access, restrictions on personnel movement and transparency of regulatory information. Such barriers seem to be particularly prominent in the region, given the diverse character of the economies there. Many NTBs are implicit in the sense that they restrict trade by cumbersome administrative procedures and by various problems arising from interpreting or implementing government regulations. The non tariff barriers have a significant impact on firms' production costs, revenue and expansion plans of international trade in the countries of Pacific Rim[53].

Post-Communist Countries

The dynamics of the political transformations have always swept eastern Europe and the former Soviet Union. By the change of government systems in the countries of these regions the trade patterns are affected and reshaped over the preventive trade protocols. These frayed and ungrouped countries are moving towards the western economic orbits of North American and west European countries to rebuild their trade and economy. The largest economies like Czech Republic, Hungary and Poland are making headway. On the contrary Yugoslavia is concentrating on controlling the ethnic conflicts as the top priority over the trade matters and the less developed Romania and Bulgaria have been finding a better administration for moving ahead with their economic development agenda. In the wake of the Soviet bloc's collapse, various post-Communist countries rushed to gain greater access to foreign markets. Many of them have made substantial progress in liberalizing commerce, but the movement toward free trade has been by no means universal. One prominent view is that the establishment of democratic institutions has stimulated economic reform in the post-Communist countries[54]. The post-Communist transition was associated with specific phenomena including political liberalization and economic reforms which were initiated simultaneously. During the economic transition process instead of a short J-shaped adjustment, most transition countries experienced deep and protracted recessions. Some analysts suggest that the early introduction of democracy was in fact harmful for economic growth. Similarly, proponents of reemerging authoritarian regimes claim that a strong hand is needed to restore order and reinvigorate the economy[55].

The economies of the post-Communist countries are in "transition" and are leading to reform and liberalize their trade programs to allow freer trading among countries. After the fall of Communism in 1989, foreign investors diverted their investments to eastern European countries which is still continuing. Once the changeover of the market economy is complete the countries that have emerged in the post–Communist era may offer attractive trade terms.

---

[52] Murray W and Challies E (2004), New Zealand and Chile: partnership for the Pacific century? *Australian Journal of International Affairs*, 58 (1), 89-103.

[53] Ching S, Wong CY P and Zhang A (2004), Non-tariff barriers to trade in the pacific rim, *Pacific Economic Review*, 9 (1), 65-73.

[54] Fray T and Mansfield E D: Timing is everything: Elections and trade liberalization in the Post-communist world, *Comparative Political Studies*, May 2004, 37 (4), 371-398.

[55] Fidrmuc J (2003), Economic reform, democracy and growth during post-communist transition, *European Journal of Political Economy*, 19 (3), 583-604.

Import liberalization forms are part and parcel of trade reforms in transition economies. There are, however, significant differences among post-Communist countries in the degree of import liberalization. In the last decade, free trade affected the post-communist countries and predominantly among them those which had a maturated level of stability, economic development and their geopolitical situation was favored[56]. Russia is taking strong steps to liberalize its economy as fast as it can in order to achieve quicker stability of its collapsed economy. It has adopted high risk averse and austerity based programs to support its international trade policies. It has been viewed by western economies as a challenge and opportunity both to extend their trade operations.

Eastern Europe is a perceived grouping of countries on the European continent. Their populations do not see themselves as Eastern Europeans, and many consider it a pejorative term. Most countries prefer to include themselves in other groups, associating themselves with Germany in Central Europe, with Scandinavia in Northern Europe or with Italy and Greece in Southern Europe. For many years Europe was divided on a North South axis. With the southern Mediterranean states having much in common, and the northern Atlantic Ocean and Baltic Sea bordering states also having much in common. The term *Baltic* first arose in the 18th and 19th century and to describe an area that was falling behind the rest of Europe economically. Much of Eastern Europe has ties with both the east and west. While all of the countries were heavily influenced by Roman Catholic or Protestant Christianity and have very close historical and cultural ties to Germany, Italy, France or Scandinavia (e.g. the Hanseatic league in the Baltics), many countries also had relations with the East. The concept of Eastern Europe was greatly strengthened by the domination of the region by the Soviet Union after the Second World War and the takeover of the nations of the region by Communist governments. The idea of an "Iron Curtain" separating Eastern and Western Europe was an extremely common view throughout the Cold War.

Since Estonia, Latvia and Lithuania have been liberated in 1991, these countries struggled to transform into market-oriented economies. During a decade, the Baltic countries have accomplished an impressive reorientation of foreign trade, and today the European Union represents the most important trading partner of the Baltic countries. However, foreign trade is still far from fully developed, which leaves opportunities for new international players to participate in trade activities to augment the volumes of business operations of the Baltic countries[57]. Since 1989 the largest islands in the Baltic Sea have formed a common interest group- "The Islands of the Baltic Sea", also called Baltic Sea Seven Islands, or just B7. The member islands are Bornholm (Denmark), Gotland (Sweden), Hiiumaa (Estonia), Saaremaa (Estonia), Åland (Åland/Finland), Öland (Sweden) and Rügen (Germany). The Baltic countries have enough opportunities to get into the European trade arena and also take advantage of the emerging Russian market. Five of the former Soviet republic countries namely Azerbaijan, Uzbekistan, Turkmenistan, Kyrgyzstan and Tajikistan have joined Iran, Turkey and Pakistan to become a part of an Islamic market[58]. Simultaneously in the most advanced post-Communist countries of Europe, including Poland, the dynamic growth of the small business sector has been the principal factor driving economic growth since 1992, and

[56] Rédei Mary: Regional specialization in a transition country-Hungary, European Regional Science Association, *ERSA conference paper*, August 2001.
[57] Larson, Karin and Wikström, Jenny.: *The Development of Foreign Trade in The Baltic Countries*, Graduate Business School, Göteborg, 2002.
[58] Jain Subhash: *International Marketing*, South Western, Ohio, USA, 2001, 55-63.

has been accompanied by a number of public programs supporting Small and Medium-sized Enterprise (SME) development. Most former Soviet republics have fallen into an economic and political under-reform trap. An intrusive state imposes high tax rates and drives entrepreneurs into the unofficial economy, which further aggravates the pressure on official businessmen. Tax revenues and public goods dwindle, further reducing incentives to register business activity[59].

African Marketplace

Various initiatives have been undertaken to strengthen Africa's production and trade capacity including mechanisms such as debt cancellation, improved regional cooperation, the Cotonou Agreement and various trade preference schemes. A recent example is the African Growth and Opportunity Act (AGOA) of the United States, which improves the access of African products to US markets. Although the largest part of US imports from Africa is accounted for by fuels, there are some indications that a number of non-oil exporting countries have experienced markedly higher shipments to the United States in 2002. While overall imports of the United States from Africa decreased by 20 per cent, imports from non-oil exporting countries which are full beneficiaries of AGOA preferences rose by 6 per cent. The strongest increases in shipments to the United States were reported by Kenya, Swaziland and Lesotho[60]. However, the available studies suggest that they have not yet succeeded in bringing about sustained growth in trade to the beneficiary countries. This reflects in part the reality that various supply-side constraints are also key to Africa's growth and trade performance. The US-African trade is being nurtured under AGOA and the primary U.S. cross-border service exports to Africa included tourism, business services, education, and freight transport. U.S. service imports from Africa were mainly travel and tourism, passenger transport, business services, and freight transport. The largest share of U.S. imports under AGOA came from Nigeria (60.2 percent), followed by South Africa (14.9 percent) and Gabon (12.7 percent). Other major suppliers included Lesotho, Kenya, Cameroon, Mauritius, and the Republic of the Congo during 2001-03.

Africa's trade growth lagged behind global trade expansion. In 2002, Africa's merchandise and commercial services trade lagged behind the global trade expansion. Merchandise exports and imports recorded only marginal gains. Financial development policies in emerging market economies have been shaped by a fundamental shift toward market-based financial systems and the lessons learnt from financial crises, in the recent decades. However, there is a growing consensus today that financial development depends on financial stability and convergence toward international standards. These issues are being further debated in reference to policy thinking which are evidenced by recent experiences. South Africa is one of the largest countries as well as the largest economy on the African continent. The country's history, including its economic and social development, is exceptional in many respects. Since the watershed of 1994, marked by the end of apartheid and the beginning of democratization, South Africa has undergone fundamental changes in

---

[59] Andres Aslund, Peter Bonne and Simon Johnson: Escaping the under-reform trap, IMF Staff Papers, Vol.48, Special Issue, 2001, 88-108.
[60] World Trade Organization: World Trade Report 2003, pp 36-42.

political, economic and social terms.[61]. Regional trade arrangements (RTAs) in Africa have been ineffective in promoting trade and foreign direct investment. Relatively high external trade barriers and low resource complementarity between member countries limit both intra- and extra-regional trade. Small market size, poor transport facilities and high trading costs make it difficult for African countries to reap the potential benefits of RTAs[62].

South African exports and imports recovered by 2 per cent to 3 per cent from the preceding year's decline. Exports of the other non-oil exporting African countries were much stronger and expanded by about 6 per cent. A strong rebound in exports in 2002 from the preceding years' decline in a number of countries (including Morocco, Egypt, Côte d'Ivoire and Ghana) accounted for most of this strength in the export growth of non-oil exporters in Africa. It has been observed that increase in the prices of cocoa and gold helped export recovery in Côte d'Ivoire and Ghana. However, it is estimated that only six out of 53 African countries comprising Equatorial Guinea, Lesotho, Mozambique, Seychelles, Sierra Leone and Tanzania achieved a sustained expansion of their exports over the 1999-2002 period. Europe is South Africa's biggest source of investment, accounting for almost half of South Africa's total foreign trade. The recently concluded trade agreement between the EU and South Africa removes 90 percent of all trade barriers over the next decade, 95 percent of SA goods (including agricultural products), and 86 percent of EU imports. Africa's overall merchandise import growth was held back by import contraction in Nigeria and Egypt, the third and second largest merchandise importers in Africa in 2001. The European Union is currently negotiating Economic Partnership Agreements (EPAs) with six African, Caribbean and Pacific country groupings, aiming at establishing mutual free trade. In this international trade negotiation process moderate trade effects can be expected, relatively large budget effects are likely to occur in a number of these countries, exposing them to considerable structural and financial adjustment requirements. In addition, EPAs would strengthen the need to consolidate overlapping intra-regional integration schemes[63]. However, African countries need to undertake more broad-based liberalization and streamline existing RTAs to increase regional trade and investment supported by improvements in infrastructure and trade facilitation. Early action to strengthen the domestic revenue base would help address concerns over revenue losses from trade liberalization.

GROUPING OF COUNTRIES

The countries of the world can be grouped using similar criteria to that of domestic markets. A multinational company may group the countries on the basis of a single variable like per capita GNP or geographic factors. Similarly the other variables like political system, religion and culture may also be considered as the criterion for grouping the countries. The choice of an appropriate grouping technique will depend on the nature of products and

[61] Organization for Economic Co-operation and Development (2008), Economic Performance and Structural Adjustment, *OECD Science & Information Technology*, 14, February, 118-170.

[62] Yang, Y and Gupta S (2007), Regional Trade Arrangements in Africa: Past Performance and the Way Forward, *African Development Review*, 19 (3), 399-431.

[63] Borrmann A, Busse M and De La Rocha M (2007), Consequences of Economic Partnership Agreements between East and Southern African Countries and the EU for Inter- and Intra-regional Integration, *International Economic Journal*, 21 (2), 233-253.

services of the company. The following methods are commonly used by the multinational companies in grouping the countries for developing appropriate business strategies:

- Economic status grouping
- Geographic grouping
- Political grouping
- Grouping by religion
- Cultural classification
- Multiple variable grouping
- Inter-market segmentation
- Portfolio approach

The grouping of the countries by *economic status* is a simple approach based on the GNP per capita ranks. Accordingly the countries may be grouped into three categories of low income, middle income and high income classifications. The fast-growing countries are defined as those that have an annual average growth rate above the median and the slow-growing countries grow less than the median. The grouping of countries with this criterion assumes that market behavior is directly related to income. In the case of discrepancies of GNP per capita among the countries or a tie between two or more countries, the parameter of purchasing power might be considered by the multinational companies in forming the groups of the countries. In these clusters each activity benefits from access to inputs produced by others located in the same area and to a pool of skills, infrastructure and business services. A sufficiently large market allows for extensive specialization while each company is still able to exploit economies of scale. Furthermore, when manufacturers have access to a broad variety of specialized inputs their productivity improves, their costs are reduced and they can expand sales. As the market expands, room for more specialized producers is created with a further lowering of costs. The countries that form the consortium on the basis of the economic factors may further lead to various business advantages through economic diplomacy. Another common method that is followed by the multinational companies in grouping the countries is their geographic position and possible networking. Many international companies organize worldwide operations on the basis of *geographically* determined regions like, South-east Asian, Far-East; eastern, central and western European countries, Pacific and Caribbean countries and the like. The proximity of the countries in such regions help in establishing functional trade blocs and the activities can be monitored and controlled by the predetermined locations. All the countries in the Latin American region may be well managed by having the business headquarters at Brazil as its proximity to other countries allows the company to establish better transport and communication networking. The regional trade agreements are also made largely on the basis of the geographic locations of the countries like APEC, ASEAN, NAFTA, CAFTA, MERCOSUR. These organizations possess regional economic characteristics and lead to the common business arrangements.

Another way of grouping the countries may be in reference to the commonality in the *political systems* and diplomatic relations. Such a consortium may refer to the countries of a democratic republic, Communist and post-Communist governing systems and monarchy. The international trading system has been shaped by a blend of Social, Legal, Economic, Political and Technological (SLEPT) factors and pragmatic thinking for mutual benefit. Trade relations cannot be determined solely on the basis of simple grouping techniques consisting of economic, geographic proximity, political and technological convergence that are defined and agreed upon in a general sense. Practical considerations, politics and particular expressions of the national interest inevitably intervene to determine positions taken by governments. Some commentators reflect this reality when they refer to a government measure or policy approach as "bad economics but good politics". The existing literature on international relations and the theory of politics would offer many rich hypotheses and explanations as to why governments might favor international co-operation. The reasons for such engagements include reciprocity in trade liberalization negotiations, co-operation involving participation, expansion of trade and profit and entering into the stronger international relations for protecting the economic interests of the country and the region against all odds. Grouping the countries by *religion* constitutes an important factor of the society in most of the dominating cultures across the countries. The religion influences the lifestyles and also impedes the liberal decision making as it influences and determines the societal values to a large extent. As the effect of religion on lifestyle is a relevant criterion for grouping the countries, the Islamic countries exhibit common consumer preference for better trade alliances. The religious conglomeration of countries thus provides a better scope for international relations.

The *cultural* grouping also makes sense since culture plays a significant role in developing lifestyle. Some societies are associated with the power distance attributes that refers to the degree of acceptable inequality. In societies where a few people make decisions that are followed by a large number of people, this may be termed as high-power distance groups and in the societies where the decisions are made in a decentralized way, this may be referred to as cultures of low power distance. Some countries would like to play safe and avoid any risks. Countries dominated by such cultural behavior may be grouped or otherwise the societies that possess a high risk-high benefits culture may be constituted as a group. However, there are also cultures that exhibit individualism and function in isolation. Alternatively, the *multiple variable approach* of grouping the countries attempts to combine countries with similar socio-economic and political perspectives into segments. However, it assumes that countries are indivisible and are heterogeneous.

The recent segmentation approach followed by the multinational companies is that the consumers who are alike in different countries form homogeneous segments. Such segments are called *inter-market* segments. This segmentation approach may be explained in reference to the pharmaceutical industry that caters to the common needs of the consumers of different countries for its innovative drug formula. Similarly, Mercedes-Benz has a worldwide market niche among the customers of the same class. Besides, there are some common characteristics of buyers across the countries that include deal makers, price seekers, loyalists, the luxury oriented and experimentalists. The deal makers are value oriented, price seekers exist mainly in competitive and developed markets, the brand loyalists are widespread and the consumers with luxurious values and innovators generally refer to the developed countries. The *portfolio approach* of country grouping may be explained through a three-dimensional matrix comprising the factors of country potential, competitive strength and risk. The country potential approach refers to the market potential for the product or services of the company in a given country based on all economic factors. The internal and external factors determine the competitive strength of the market. In a given country the internal factors constitute the market share of company, resources and facilities while the external factors include industry attractiveness and competition. The risk factor has a broad range of factors that include principally, financial, political and business risk in a given country.

REFERENCES

Derek S Pugh and Allan R Plath: *International Business and Management*, Internationalization and International Strategy (Vol.1), Sage, London, 2003.

Geert Hofstede: *Cultural Consequences-International Differences in Work Related Values*, Sage, London, 1980.

Henbig P and Day K: Outgrowth of ASEAN- A common market for Pacific, *European Business Review*, 93 (2), 1995, pp 12-23.

Jeannet J P and Hennessey H: *International Marketing Management*, Houghton Mifflin, 1992.

Kenichi Ohmae: *Triad Power*, The Free Press, New York, 1985.

Krugman Paul R: *Geography and Trade,* MIT Press, Cambridge, MA, 1988.

Porter Michael E: *The Competitive Advantage of Nations*, Macmillan, 1990.

Lane Kelley and Reginald Worthley: The Role of Culture in Comparative Management: A Cross Culture Perspective, *Academy of Management Journal*, Vol.1, 1981, pp 164-173.

Lawrence John D: *Can We Compete in the Global Marketplace*, Iowa State University, Department of Economics, Staff General Research Papers, June 2003.

Louis Kraar: The Rising Power of the Pacific, *Fortune*, Pacific Rim Issue, 1990, pp 80-84.

McCallum John: National Boarder Matters: Canada-US Regional Trade Patterns, American Economic Review, 85 (3), 1995, pp 615-623.

Vandermevwe S: Strategies for a Pan European Market, *European Journal of Management*, 7 (2), 1989.

Yip George: *Total Global Strategy*, Prentice Hall, Englewood Cliffs, New Jersey, 1992.

Chapter 5

INTERNATIONAL TRADE IN EMERGING MARKETS

Emerging economies are characterized by an increasing market orientation and an expanding economic foundation, and entrepreneurship plays a key role in this economic development. The success of many of these economies is such that they are rapidly becoming major economic forces in the world. In the regime of global competition, several shocks have recently hit the emerging economies of developing countries towards financial turmoil, cooling housing markets, and higher prices of energy and other commodities. Fortunately, they have occurred at a time when growth was being supported by high employment that boosts income and consumption; by high profits and strong balance sheets that underpin investment and resilience in the face of financial losses and tighter credit; and by still buoyant world trade driven by robust growth in emerging economies[1]. Developing countries are the fastest-growing market in the world for most products and services. However, many multinationals have fears about tapping the potential of these markets. The multinational companies are concerned about lack of market institutions including consumer-data experts, logistics providers which are required to do business in the developing countries. To mitigate the risks of investing in developing countries, it is necessary to assess potential target countries' market institutions. Consider whether changing the business model can help you work around gaps. Dell Computer, for instance, decided to sell its products in China through local distributors and systems integrators after discovering that Chinese consumers do not buy over the Internet. Also, the global players need to learn how emerging contenders cope with weak market institutions at home and gain traction on the global stage[2].

Since the 1990's there has been a sea change in trade and related policies in emerging markets. This results from autonomous reforms undertaken in conjunction with macro-economic stabilization programs. Many non-tariff measures have been eliminated and tariffs, now the principal trade instrument, have been rationalized and reduced[3]. The real dynamism in trade is observed in the global trade pattern of developing counties where Brazil, China, India, Malaysia, Mexico and Thailand all posted double-digit growth in exports. These emerging markets have not only expanded their global market place, Africa too has staked its

---

[1] Organization for Economic Co-operation and Development (2008), Editorial, *OECD Economic Outlook-2007 Number 2*, January, 10-18.
[2] Khanna T, Palepu K G, Sinha J, Zeng M, Williamson P J (2006), Winning in the World's Emerging Markets (HBR Article Collection), Harvard Business School Press, Boston, MA.
[3] Zdenek Drabek and Sam Laird (1997), *The New Liberalism: Trade Policy Developments in Emerging Markets*, World Trade Organization, Working Paper, ERAD-97-007.

claim to a bigger share of the global trade by posting export growth in excess of 25 percent since 2005. However, businesses entering early into new Eastern European markets are believed to attain crucial competitive advantages over later entrants. However, this contention receives only mixed support in the empirical literature, in part because performance is measured in different ways. It has been found that market share is strongly related to order of entry, but we did not find a positive relationship between order of entry and perceived performance. We found general support for early mover advantages in Hungary and Poland but a strongly negative relationship for Lithuania, suggesting that early entry is a trade off between risk and return[4].

There are large differences in gross domestic products by sectors among Latin American countries, and the majority of these differences are due to the value of industrial and service sectors. Although the sectoral economic activity has been increased, in per capita terms this value decreased due to the demographic growth that Latin American countries (mainly Mexico and Brazil) had experienced during the last decades. Argentina continued recovering rapidly after its acute crisis. Brazil, Mexico and Uruguay shared in the broadening of economic recovery during the year. The rate of change in the merchandize export in the Latin American countries during 2002 shows that most of the countries in the region except Costa Rica, Ecuador, Peru and St. Kit Islands the have shown a downward trend. There are many countries apart from Latin America and Caribbean region categorized as emerging markets. Among various countries competitive in the global race of trade and economic development, Brazil, India, Russia and China are prominent in the category of emerging markets. It has been observed that value of exports and imports are growing as exhibited in Table 5.1.

The 1997 Asian financial crisis principally affected Thailand, Indonesia, Malaysia, and Korea, as well as other East Asian countries heavily dependent on intra-regional trade. Banks and other financial institutions quickly became insolvent, and heavily indebted industrial firms went bankrupt. Many of these firms were affiliated with the business groups of this region, yet most groups did not immediately collapse, indeed they proved remarkably robust, some surviving and even prospering. The Asian Crisis affected the inter-relationships among the socio-cultural environment, the state, and the market of each country quite differently and had distinct effects on the operations of these countries' business groups. This slow yet divergent pattern of development counters globalization theorists' arguments about rapid global convergence. Yet East Asian business groups face an uncertain future. The influence of foreign investors has increased substantially since the crisis. Governments supervise banks more closely and have loosened restrictions on mergers and hostile takeovers, further strengthening the discipline of the market. Various entry barriers that had inhibited foreign multinationals from competing in national markets were lifted. Under these new conditions, business groups in East Asia should reconfigure their business structures and adjust their corporate governance systems to regain momentum for further growth[5].

---

[4] Jakobsen, Kristian (2007), First Mover Advantages in Central and Eastern Europe: A Comparative Analysis of Performance Measures, *Journal of East-West Business*, 13 (1), 35-61.

[5] Chang Sea-Jin (2006), Emerging Market Countries (Part II), *Business Groups in East Asia*, Oxford Scholarship Online Monographs, March, 117-119.

Table 5.1. Merchandise Trade in Emerging Markets (2000-2006)
(Billion dollars and Percentage)

Countries	Value	Exports				Value	Imports			
		Annual Percentage change					Annual Percentage change			
	2006	2000-06	2004	2005	2006	2006	2000-06	2004	2005	2006
Mexico	250	7	14	13	17	268	7	16	13	15
Brazil	137	16	32	23	16	88	7	31	17	14
South Africa	58	12	27	12	13	77	17	35	17	24
China	969	25	35	28	27	792	23	36	18	20
Japan	647	5	20	5	9	578	7	19	13	12
India	120	19	30	30	21	174	23	37	41	25
World	11762	11	22	14	15	12080	11	22	13	14

Source: World Trade Report, 2007.

Trade globalization always makes crashes less likely, financial globalization may make them more likely, especially when trade costs are high. Such a crash comes with a current account reversal and drops in income and investment. Lower-income countries are more prone to such demand-based financial crises[6]. The major attributes of the emerging markets may be understood as below:

- Political Stability in the development process (Diplomatic relations, domestic policies, growth related development)
- Industrial reforms including infrastructure, free trade, licensing and patenting policies, trade related intellectual property (TRIPs) and trade related investment measure (TRIMs)
- Economic and legal reforms (FDI, Foreign exchange regulation, tariff, transfer and repatriation of funds
- Planning and entrepreneurship
- Factors of production
- Outward orientation (Export promotion)
- Economic incentives on investment
- Privatization
- Regional trade agreements (RTAs)
- Technology development – diffusion and adaptation
- Infrastructure

CHINA AN EMERGING MARKET

China has emerged as a key player in the determination of global macroeconomic balances and as a major point of reference in the production strategies of the world's major transnational corporations. At present, 400 of the Fortune 500 companies have set up

---

[6] Martin P and Rey H (2006), Globalization and Emerging Markets: With or Without Crash? *The American Economic Review*, 96 (5), 1631-1651.

operations in China. This is not only because of China's attractive market of 1.3 billion consumers. China has ambitious medium- and long-term goals designed to transform it into an industrial power by 2010 and a technological power by 2015. A particularly noteworthy aspect of Chinese trade development is that, between 1990 and 2004, high-technology exports grew faster than those of other sectors in the economy, while commodity exports fell steeply. China's emergence is having differential effects on Asia's advanced and developing countries and the region's advanced countries are benefiting from the existence of a large and rapidly growing Chinese market for their capital goods, components and technology, whereas its developing countries compete head to head with China in third markets. These attributes create additional challenges for late-industrializing Asian countries seeking to catch up with the region's industrial leaders. Asian regionalism will be open in order to prevent a rise to expensive trade diversion. An early move toward a common exchange rate regime with the associated common monetary stance will be problematic. And, in the absence of these common policies, pressure for the development of powerful regional institutions to formulate the common monetary stance will be at best modest[7]. Political and pro-globalization ideologies of China are intending to help provide global public goods, particularly the strengthening of the multilateral free-trade system, and the protection of the global environmental commons. Specifically, China should work actively for the success of the Doha Round and for an international research consortium to develop clean coal technology[8]. Traditionally, foreign multinationals have dominated the premium market segment of China, while many domestic companies have served the low end market of the country for low profits. However, as middle-class buying power is apparently growing and the tolerance for high markups have increased among customers; the middle market segment is growing rapidly. The competition in this particular arena has more far-reaching implications, and companies that flourish in China's middle market today are learning valuable lessons they need to compete worldwide. Multinationals are discovering how to focus products downscale to break out of the premium tier, and domestic firms are building scale and marketing expertise to move up and both types of firms are positioning themselves to export their China offerings to other large emerging markets such as India, Russia and Brazil[9].

The principal trading partners of China are its neighbors in Asia and the Pacific, especially Japan and the nations belonging to the Association of Southeast Asian Nations (ASEAN). These countries supply 56 percent of China's imports and buy 45 percent of its total exports. Manufactures represent an extremely high percentage to the extent of 95 percent of these trade flows. The composition of China's trade with other developing countries, primarily of Latin America, Africa and the Middle East, complements these flows, as it is concentrated in commodities and natural resource based manufacturers. These developing nations are thus its main suppliers of copper, iron ore, Soya, petroleum, fishmeal, sugar and a range of other products. China's trade deficit with Latin America alone jumped from US$ 6.37 billion to US$ 10.969 billion between 2003 and 2004. China has emerged as the largest investors among Asian countries. Chinese firms are investing via mergers and acquisitions in

[7] Eichengreen B (2006), China, Asia, and the World Economy: The Implications of an Emerging Asian Core and Periphery, *China & World Economy*, 14 (3), 1-18.
[8] Woo W T (2007), The Challenges of Governance Structure, Trade Disputes and Natural Environment to China's Growth, *Comparative Economic Studies*, 49 (4), 572-602.
[9] Gadiesh Orit, Leung Philip, Vestring Till (2007), The Battle for China's Good-Enough Market, *Harvard Business Review*, 85 (9), 80-89.

well-positioned technology intensive enterprises that possess the necessary know-how and have good reputations backed up by established brand names. They are also making green field investments in strategically located research and development centers. This strategy has permitted some firms to enhance their credibility and penetrate more deeply into new markets[10].

The growing expansion of trade of China has been associated with its deepening but contrasting trade relations with its two groups of key trading partners. China's trade surpluses with the USA and the EU have risen rapidly, reaching US$144 Billion and US$91 Billion in 2006, respectively one hand and China is importing heavily from its Asian neighbors, on the other. This diverging pattern of trade relations between China and its main trading partners reflects the continuous expansion and intensification of a complex cross-border production network in Asia, particularly for consumer electronics. In the process of deepening manufacturing sharing, China serves as an essential export platform for firms headquartered in the more advanced economies[11].China has been increasing its share in Latin American trade during the course of this decade, and by 2003 it accounted for almost 3 percent of the total exports of the region and percent of its total imports, thus becoming largest Asian trading partner of the Latin American and Caribbean region. After a period of flat growth that lasted until 1999, Chinese imports from Latin America and the Caribbean began to soar, jumping to almost US$ 5.4 billion in 2000 and to US$ 21.668 billion in 2004. This represented an annual growth rate of 42 percent between 2000 and 2004, which far outstripped the growth rates of China's imports of about 26 percent from the world as a whole. China is an extremely important trading partner for many of the countries in the region today. China absorbs just over 10 percent of exports of Chile compared with less than 1 percent a decade ago. Other countries, including Argentina, Brazil and Peru, are also similarly placed. China is now the third-largest trading partner of Brazil, after the United States and Argentina, and competes with Japan for second place. China's trade with Mexico, the Bolivarian Republic of Venezuela and Costa Rica, though still quite limited, has also increased significantly in recent years[12].

As the international trade is being liberalized in many developing countries, China is a competitive threat to Latin America in trade in manufactured goods. The direct threat to exports to third country markets appears small: Latin America and the Caribbean's (LAC's) trade structure is largely complementary to that of China. In bilateral trade, several LAC countries are increasing primary and resource-based exports to China. However, the pattern of trade, with LAC specializing increasingly in resource-based products and China in manufactured goods, seems worrying. Given cumulative capability building, China's success in increasingly technology-based products with strong learning externalities can place it on a higher growth path than specialization in "simpler" goods, as in LAC. China may thus affect LAC's technological upgrading in exports and industrial production. The issue is not so much current competition as the "spaces" open for LAC in the emerging technology-based world[13].

---

[10] Economic Commission for Latin America and Caribbean (2004): Latin America and Caribbean in the World Economy, ECLAC Publication, 145-180.

[11] Tong S Y and Zheng Y (2008), China's Trade Acceleration and the Deepening of an East Asian Regional Production Network, *China & World Economy*, 16 (1), 66-81.

[12] *Ibid.*

[13] Lall, S, Weiss J and Oikawa H (2005), China's Competitive Threat to Latin America: An Analysis for 1990-2002, *Oxford Development Studies*, 33 (2), 163-194.

Comparative indicators reveal that four key issues affect the trade and economy of LAC countries which include the impact of fiscal performance on democratic legitimacy, relevance of pension fund reform and governance for national saving and capital markets deepening, the role market-seeking investments by the private sector can have at improving access to telecommunication services, and growing trade with China and India as an incentive to boost the competitiveness of Latin American countries[14].

Economic growth of China since the mid 80's has generated ripple effects in the world economy. Its search for natural resources to satisfy the demands of industrialization has pushed China to move into Sub-Saharan African trade negotiations. Trade between China and Africa accounted for more than $50 billion during 2006 in reference to Chinese companies importing oil from Angola and Sudan, timber from Central Africa, and copper from Zambia. Demand from China has contributed to an upward swing in prices, particularly for oil and metals from Africa, and has given a boost to real GDP in Sub-Saharan Africa. Chinese aid and investment in infrastructure are bringing desperately needed capital to the continent. At the same time, however, strong Chinese demand for oil is contributing to an increase in the import bill for many oil-importing Sub- Saharan African countries, and its exports of low-cost textiles, while benefiting African consumers, is threatening to displace local production. China poses a challenge to good governance and macroeconomic management in Africa and presents both an opportunity for Africa to reduce its marginalization from the global economy and a challenge for it to effectively harness the influx of resources to promote poverty-reducing economic development at home[15].

INDIA IN GLOBAL TRADE COMPETITION

In Asia, the most significant arrangement is among the countries of South-East Asia. ASEAN was formed in 1967 to promote economic, social and cultural cooperation among Indonesia, Malaysia, Philippines, Singapore and Thailand. In 1978, ASEAN put into force a preferential trading arrangement granting a margin of preference to members of 10 to 15 per cent on selected products. In the early 1990s, the arrangement was upgraded into the ASEAN. Free Trade Area (AFTA) and in 1994 it was decided to fully implement the arrangement in 2003. ASEAN membership has also expanded to include Brunei Darussalam, Viet Nam, Lao People's Democratic Republic, Myanmar and Cambodia. Another integration arrangement among the developing countries of the region that is potentially significant is the South Asian Association for Regional Cooperation (SAARC), whose membership includes Bangladesh, Bhutan, India, Maldives, Nepal, Pakistan and Sri Lanka. A decision was taken in 1992 to form the SAARC Preferential Trading Arrangement (SAPTA) and in 1995, the group agreed to move towards a free trade area. However, political differences between India and Pakistan have impeded the effectiveness of the arrangement. In the meantime, India and Sri Lanka have moved separately to form a free trade area.

---

[14] Organization for Economic Co-operation and Development (2008), Latin American Economic Outlook, *OECD Emerging Economies*, Number 18, November 2007, pp. 1192.

[15] Zwane, Alix Peterson *et al* (2007), The Growing Relationship Between China and Sub-Saharan Africa: Macroeconomic, Trade, Investment, and Aid Links, *World Bank Research Observer*, 22 (1), pp. 103-130.

As restrictions on trade and competition have been reduced, constraints associated with infrastructure and regulatory bottlenecks have become increasingly evident and need to be addressed urgently both through regulatory reform and through increased investment. Despite further liberalization of the FDI regime, India's record in attracting investment remains disappointing, with FDI accounting for some 1 percent of GDP. The government has also taken various steps to improve enforcement of intellectual property rights which should help to attract FDI. Tariff and tax reform are also crucial to address the problem of high fiscal deficits, which have continued to grow despite efforts to reduce public spending. Moreover, with the customs tariff accounting for some 30 percent of net government tax revenue, further reform of the tariff may depend on major tax reform. It has been observed that the customs tariff has become the main form of border protection. There have been significant recent efforts to rationalize the tariff, but, with numerous exemptions based on end-use, it remains complex and applied tariffs, which averaged some 32 percent in 2001/02, remains relatively high. As a result of additional bindings taken by India in the WTO, the share of tariff has increased since the previous review, from 67 percent to 72 percent. The average (final) bound rate is 50.6 percent, higher than the applied Most Favored Nations (MFN) rate; this gap provided ample scope for applied rates to be raised recently on a few agricultural products.

Major structural adjustments in the trade and economy appeared in the country towards removal of all import restrictions maintained for balance-of-payments reasons. As a result, the customs tariff has become the main form of border protection. There have been significant recent efforts to rationalize the tariff, but with numerous exemptions based on end-use, it remains complex. Tariffs are relatively high, but the average applied MFN rate fell from 35.3 percent to 32.3 percent between 1997-98 and 2001-02 and is expected to fall further, to 29 percent in 2002-03, as the "peak" rate of tariff is reduced from 35 percent to 30 percent. The tariff shows substantial escalation in some sectors, especially for paper and printing, textiles and clothing, and food, beverages and tobacco. The Government announced recently that it intends to simplify and lower the tariff to two tiers by 2004-05; 10 percent for raw materials, intermediates and components, and 20 percent for final products. In addition to the tariff, importers must pay additional and special duties on a number of products[16]. In the context of the Association of Southeast Asian Nations (ASEAN) market the evaluation of competition between India and China has been undertaken with special reference to the prior implementation of the ASEAN-China Free Trade Area relative to the ASEAN-India Free Trade Area. The results suggest that threat perceptions at the product level might currently prevail for both economies from each other across all sectors in both markets even though the intensity of the competitive threat varies across products. However, long-term trend analysis shows that the patterns of comparative advantage of India and China are evolving along divergent paths and, therefore, competition between the two economies might not be a major issue[17].

India plays key role in regional trade and cooperation among the South-east Asian countries. The ASEAN-India Comprehensive Economic Cooperation covers the issues of strengthening and enhancing economic, trade and investment co-operation. The trade

---

[16] World Trade Organization: Trade Policy Review of India- June 2002, WTO Headquarters, Geneva, Press release # Press/TPRB/195.

[17] Batra A (2007), Structure of Comparative Advantage of China and India: Global and Regional Dynamics, *China & World Economy*, 15 (6), 69-86.

agreement also envisages the cooperation towards the progressive liberalization and promotion of trade in goods and services as well as the creation of a transparent, liberal and facilitative investment environment. Under the agreement it has been emphasized to explore new areas and develop appropriate measures for closer economic co-operation in the region. The role may also be viewed towards facilitating the more effective economic integration of the new ASEAN Member States and bridging the development gap among ASEAN member countries and India. Under the Framework Agreement, ASEAN and India committed to progressively reduce and eliminate tariffs on a reciprocal basis. During January 2006 to December 2011 Brunei, Indonesia, Malaysia, Singapore, Thailand and India would honor the agreement of progressive reduction of the tariffs on reciprocal basis while Cambodia, Lao PDR, Myanmar, Vietnam, Philippines and India would engage in the process of tariff elimination during January 2006-December 2016. A total of 177 manufactured goods from Malaysia are eligible for the preferential tariff treatment under the EHP. The main EHP products exported by Malaysia to India include cocoa butter, cocoa powder, cyclic hydrocarbons, chemical products and preparations, tin and fiber board of wood. Such free trade agreement enables ASEAN and India to share the huge resources available through joint collaboration to promote the further growth of both the manufacturing and services industries[18].

There appears to have been an increase in other border measures such as anti-dumping with some 250 cases initiated since 1995, though import licensing and tariff restrictions are generally declining. Internal reforms have concentrated on improving efficiency and competition in the economy. Thus, while industrial policy remains important, its scope seems to have been reduced significantly. In addition, since the previous review, there has been a reduction in the number of activities reserved for the public sector and for the small scale industry. The need for increased competition is being addressed by gradually reducing the degree of direct government involvement in economic activities, including through a program to restructure and privatize state-owned companies. The privatization program has experienced limited success and must also be stepped up to address the fiscal deficit. In addition, price controls, currently maintained on several products including fertilizers, petroleum products and in agriculture, add to the fiscal burden of subsidies (implicit and explicit subsidies were estimated at some 14.5 percent of GDP in the mid-1990s).

During the last 10 years there has been a significant shift in the composition of the export basket. The share of manufactured goods in total export of India has increased from 76 percent in 1991-92 to 83 percent in 2000-2001. Chemicals & related products, Engineering goods, Electronic goods, Gems & Jewellery, Marine products and Textiles have witnessed steady export growth, barring some inter year variations, during the period. The growth rates of Agricultural & allied products and Leather & manufactures have lagged behind during the last 10 years. The export growth rates of items within the manufactured goods groups have shown an increasing trend throughout the decade and include items like Gems & Jewellery, Manufactures of Metals, Pharmaceuticals & Chemicals and Textiles. Another important sector is that of Petroleum products export in which the share has risen from a level of 2.58 percent to 4.10 percent.

India's exports during February, 2005, grew 8 percent over the same period last year but the trade deficit widened during the first 11 months of this fiscal year to about $23.83 billion. Exports during the month stood at $6.7 billion compared to $6.2 billion in the same month last year,

---

[18] Directorate of ASEAN Economic Cooperation, Malaysia.

according to the latest data released by the government. The trade deficit for April-February, 2004-05, grew 73 percent to $23.83 billion as against $13.72 billion in the corresponding period in 2003-04. Exports during April-February this fiscal grew 27.03 percent to $69.7 billion compared to $54.94 billion in the same period in the previous fiscal. This has raised hopes of achieving the export target of $75 billion this fiscal year[19]. The average annual growth of exports during the five-year period 1999-2004 has been 14.68 percent. Out of India's total merchandise exports during the previous financial year 2003-04, textiles accounted for 18.86 percent; followed by gems & jewellery with 16.56 percent and engineering goods with 16.41 percent share. The other key contributors were chemicals & related products (15.43 percent share in total exports); agricultural products (8.39 percent); petroleum products (5.5 percent); ores & minerals (3.69 percent); leather & manufactures (2.74 percent); and marine products (2.08 percent). The significant increase in exports during the current financial year has been on account of the growing competitiveness of the Indian manufacturing sector[20].

Destination-wise, the share of India's exports to Asia & Oceania region has improved significantly over the decade from 30 percent in 1990-91 to 37.48 percent in 2000-01. Similarly, North America's share has increased substantially from 16 percent to 24.73 percent and Africa's share has more than doubled from 2.61 percent to 5.3 percent. However, the West European region has slipped from its top position as India's main export destination to the second position with its share falling from 33.64 percent in 1990-91 to 27.7 percent in 2000-01. Another important trading partner of India whose share has fallen substantially is that of East European region. India's exports to this region have declined from a level of 17.87 percent in 1990-91 to 2.95 percent at the end of the decade. In terms of growth performance, high growth rates have been recorded in the case of Asia & Oceania, Africa, America and Latin American Countries (LAC). Low growth rates have been seen in Indian exports to West Europe and East Europe. Country-wise, share of Hong Kong in India's total exports has shown an increase from 3.29 percent to 5.94 percent in the decade. The share of India's exports to China to the total has also increased from 0.10 percent to 1.87 percent. Other countries to which India's exports during the last decade have increased are Bangladesh, Sri Lanka, Indonesia and Malaysia. The growth of foreign trade of India is exhibited in Table 5.2.

There are some key strategic policies and issues which will impact India's ability to effectively adopt the product market strategies in the new world trade order. Fifteen such main policies have been examined for the merchandise sector. To achieve overall export competitiveness, the broad economic and trade related issues include tariff issues affecting Indian exports price competitiveness, macro economic issues such as FDI and exchange rate mechanism, procedural issues such as export related tax rebates, transaction costs and also infrastructure issues such as export infrastructure, marketing support etc. All these play their part in affecting the overall competitiveness of India's exports in the international arena. A strategic tariff policy for each industry is required, which focuses on maintaining the real effective exchange rate of the rupee at a level appropriate for ensuring price competitiveness of exports. The economic growth in various sectors in India during the post-independence period is exhibited in Table 5.3.

---

[19] The Economic Times: April –Feb Trade Deficit, 14th March 2005.
[20] The Economic Times: Export Cross $70 Billion Mark, 12th March, 2005.

Table 5.2. India's Foreign Trade (In US $ Million)

Year	Exports	Growth Rate	Imports	Growth rate	Trade deficit
1991-92	17865	-1.5	19411	-19.4	-1546
1992-93	18537	3.8	21882	12.7	-3345
1993-94	22237	20.0	23306	6.5	-1069
1994-95	26330	18.4	28654	22.9	-2324
1995-96	31797	20.8	36678	28.0	-4881
1996-97	33470	5.3	39132	6.7	-5662
1997-98	35006	4.6	41484	6.0	-6478
1998-99	33219	-5.1	42389	2.2	-9170
1999-2000	36822	10.8	49671	17.2	-12849
2000-2001	44560	21.0	50537	1.7	-5976
2001-02(P) (Apr-Nov.)	28851	0.5	34724	1.19	(-) 5873

Source: Computed based on the DGCI&S data. P denotes provisional.

Table 5.3. Sectoral Growth Rates in India (Average Growth in Percent Per Annum)

Sector	Period		
	1951-1980	1981-1990	1991-2000
Agriculture	2.1	4.4	3.1
Industry	5.3	6.8	5.8
Services	4.5	6.6	7.5
GDP	3.5	5.8	5.8

Source: Computed on the data provided by Central Statistical Organization (CSO) Data for respective periods.

Various business surveys show capacity utilization at record levels, while monthly data show both the import and domestic production of capital goods sustaining double digit annual growth rates for over one year. FDI flows have also perked up, rising by over 70 percent in the first quarter of 2003 after years of lackluster performance. Growth in Indian merchandise exports has exceeded 20 percent per annum in three of the last four years. Software service exports have expanded by almost 30 percent per annum over the past two years. Comparing India's growing integration with that of China, Japan, the new industrial economies (NIE) and the ASEAN-4, when their output and growth first started exhibiting sustained growth highlights a number of similarities as well as challenges. India's growth rate is just below that experienced by other Asian economies in the initial phases of take-off. However, India's share of world trade, at 0.8 percent, is still well below that of the other Asian economies at corresponding phases of their integration process when their share of world trade ranged from 1 percent (China) to about 2 percent[21] (Japan, NIEs, ASEAN-4). India, for some time now the focal point of the global trend toward strategic off-shoring, has simultaneously become appealing as a market in its own right. With GDP growth more than double that of the United States and the United Kingdom during the past decade, and with forecast continued real

---

[21] International Monetary Fund: World Economic Outlook, 2004, IMF.

annual growth of almost 7 percent, India is one of the world's most promising and fastest-growing economies, and multinational companies are eagerly investing there. In another estimate *The Economist Intelligence Unit* forecasts 6.9 percent real GDP growth for India from 2003 to 2008. However, India's per capita income is half of China's and one-fourth of Brazil's, and as much as 80 percent of Indian demand for any industry's products will be in the middle or lower segments. In Indian business, it looks like the more successful companies have invested time and resources to understand local consumers and business conditions: tailoring product offers to the entire market, from the high-end to the middle and lower-end segments; reengineering supply chains; and even skipping the joint-venture route[22].

There are signs of a recovery in domestic and external investment in India, and exports of goods and services are growing rapidly as it becomes more integrated into the global economy. India is also set to benefit from a rapid expansion in its labor force. The challenge ahead will be to capitalize on these promising beginnings by accelerating the structural reform process. The literature shows that as an economy matures, its sectoral growth pattern typically evolves in two stages. In the first stage, both industry and services grow faster than agriculture, and consequently the share of industry and services in output increases. In the second stage, services grow faster than the rest of the economy, and its share in GDP continues to increase, accompanied by a stagnant or declining share of the industrial sector. Though the Indian experience fits in this pattern well, the sectoral transformation in the last decade was more rapid, and occurred at a lower level of income, than in other countries. Consequently, India's services share of GDP is now higher than the average for other low-income countries.

LATIN AMERICAN AND CARIBBEAN COUNTRIES AS EMERGING MARKETS

The principal trading partners of China are its neighbors in Asia and the Pacific, especially Japan and the nations belonging to the Association of Southeast Asian Nations (ASEAN). These countries supply 56% of China's imports and buy 45% of its total exports. Manufactures represent an extremely high percentage (95%) of these trade flows. The composition of China's trade with other developing countries, primarily of Latin America, Africa and the Middle East, complements these flows, as it is concentrated in commodities and natural resource based manufacturers. These developing nations are thus its main suppliers of copper, iron ore, Soya, petroleum, fishmeal, sugar and a range of other products. China's trade deficit with Latin America alone jumped from US$ 6.37 billion to US$ 10.969 billion between 2003 and 2004. China has emerged as largest investors among Asian countries. Chinese firms are investing via mergers and acquisitions in well-positioned technology intensive enterprises that possess the necessary know-how and have good reputations backed up by established brand names. They are also making green field investments in strategically located research and development centers. This strategy has

---

[22] Jain Kuldeep P, Nigel A. S. Manson, and Sankhe Shirish: The Right Passage to India, The McKinsey Quarterly, February 2005.

permitted some firms to enhance their credibility and penetrate more deeply into new markets[23].

China has been increasing its share in Latin American trade during the course of this decade, and by 2003 it accounted for almost 3% of the total exports of the region and 5% of its total imports, thus becoming the largest Asian trading partner of the Latin American and Caribbean region. After a period of flat growth that lasted until 1999, Chinese imports from Latin America and the Caribbean began to soar, jumping to almost US$ 5.4 billion in 2000 and to US$ 21.668 billion in 2004. This represented an annual growth rate of 42% between 2000 and 2004, which far outstripped the growth rates of China's imports from the world as a whole (26%). China is an extremely important trading partner for many of the countries in the region today. China absorbs just over 10 percent of exports of Chile compared with less than 1 percent of decade ago. Other countries, including Argentina, Brazil and Peru, are also similarly placed. China is now the third-largest trading partner of Brazil, after the United States and Argentina, and competes with Japan for second place. China's trade with Mexico, the Bolivarian Republic of Venezuela and Costa Rica, though still quite limited, has also increased significantly in recent years[24].

The Central American Free Trade Agreement (CAFTA) negotiated between the U.S. and Central America offers opportunities and challenges for the five countries including El Salvador, Guatemala, Honduras, and Nicaragua that joined in 2003 and Costa Rica that was included in January 2004. Mexico, Nicaragua, Jamaica and Honduras always were over the mean. During the years 1990, 1995 and 2000, Mexico, Cuba, Panama, Argentina, Brazil, Chile and Uruguay reached incomes above 2000 dollars per capita in the service sector[25]. On the other hand, there are some countries like Haiti, Honduras, Nicaragua and Bolivia with incomes below 500 dollars per capita. Latin America's merchandise exports increased slightly as the decline in intra-regional trade was balanced by increased shipments to other regions. The recovery of commodity prices in the course of the year and the upturn in the US economy contributed to this rise. While most Latin American countries saw a reduction or stagnation in their imports, those of Costa Rica increased by 9 percent. Mexico benefited from the recovery of the US market while for Costa Rica, the recovery in semi-conductor shipments boosted both imports and exports. Despite the continuation of low prices for a number of primary commodities, exports of many Central American and Caribbean countries recovered strongly. Economic activity in Western Europe remained subdued as Germany, the largest economy, experienced declining domestic demand. Domestic demand growth remained positive in the rest of the region, but was sluggish in several other countries. In the euro zone, public consumption was the most dynamic expenditure category while private consumption slowed down and fixed investment in the enterprise sector fell nearly 3 percent. In the midst of this poor economic situation, further progress was made in the process of European integration[26].

Starting in the mid-sixties of the 20th century, the European example inspired a number of trade-oriented integration arrangements in the Latin American region such as the Latin American Free Trade Association, which later became the Latin American Integration

---

[23] Economic Commission for Latin America and Caribbean (2004): Latin America and Caribbean in the World Economy, ECLAC Publication, 145-180.
[24] Ibid.
[25] Guisan, M.C. and Aguayo (2000): Education, Industry, Trade and Development of American Companies in 1980-99, Applied Econometrics and International Development. Vol. 2-1, pp. 83-106.
[26] World Trade Organization: World Trade Report 2003, pp 30-42.

Association (ALADI), the Central American Common Market (MCCA), the Caribbean Community and Common Market (CARICOM), the Andean Group, later the Andean Community; and more recently, the Southern Common Market (Mercosur), the Group of Three (G3) and the Association of Caribbean States (ACS). There are many bilateral alliances as well. Latin American countries have been living a renaissance since the 80's. Most economies are stabilized, living standards are higher, direct foreign investment has surged, democracy has been institutionalized and most countries have demonstrated a desire to integrate themselves into the new global economy by opening their economies to international trade and investment. In the 90's the Latin American countries have liberalized their economies, which has been followed by a significant increase in their imports. This improvement was due primarily to three factors: lower inflation, less government intervention, and fewer trade barriers. International trade has been the key indicator of the overall economic growth of Latin American countries. Several regional free trade agreements signed over the past decade— such as Mercosur, the Central American Common Market, the Andean Community, and the Caribbean Common Market—demonstrate the region's understanding of the benefits of free trade. Countries like Chile have gone even further in their trade liberalization efforts, signing bilateral agreements with Mexico and Canada after being unable to sign an agreement with the entire NAFTA bloc. In terms of scope, sectors of interest and coverage, there are three levels of sub-regional arrangements: (i) customs unions currently being finalized, e.g., the Andean Community, Mercosur, MCCA and CARICOM, (ii) first-generation free trade accords with a commercial emphasis, and (iii) new-generation free trade pacts encompassing such sectors as services, investment, intellectual ownership, and state acquisitions. Chile and Bolivia are successfully engaged in negotiations for broader scope aimed at furthering their association with Mercosur, establishing free trade areas and bringing other sectors and issues into the accords.

With investor confidence returning in Latin America and domestic conditions improving, gross private financial inflows in 2003 increased by 40 percent over 2002. Moreover, interest rate spreads on sovereign bonds over US treasuries reached record lows. Net foreign direct investment (FDI), however, continued its decline from a peak of $88 billion in 1999 to an estimated $36 billion in 2003. This is partly explained by the end of the privatization boom and the profit crisis in Brazil and Argentina. Export growth outpaced import growth for most countries in 2003, leading to surplus positions on trade and a big improvement in the region's current account deficit, down to 0.5 percent of GDP (compared to 4.5 percent in 1998). Tourism revenues and workers' remittances also improved, and commodity prices were generally strong. Consequent upon falling trade and investment barriers and high growth prospects, the countries of Latin America represent attractive alliance prospects for an increasing number of global firms. The typical objective for these strategic alliances is a basic trade-off wherein local firms seek access to technology and capabilities that are critical for their survival in an environment of increased competition and in return, they offer prospective multinational partners access to a large and growing market.

The region is becoming more attractive to multinationals, as product patent protection is implemented and, more importantly, enforced, in Latin American countries. Mexico, in particular, as a member of NAFTA, is attracting substantial inward investment. This is likely to grow even more rapidly in the future, given the recent signing of a trade deal with the European Union. The recent recovery of oil prices has shown a positive sign of growth for a number of countries in the region, particularly Venezuela, Mexico and Colombia.

ECONOMIC ENVIRONMENT

In the 1990s macroeconomic policies improved in a majority of developing countries, but the growth dividend from such improvement fell short of expectations, and a policy agenda focused on stability turned out to be associated with a multiplicity of financial crises[27]. The economic advancement of a country may be reviewed in reference to its fiscal, monetary, and exchange rate policies over time, and the effectiveness of the changing policy framework in promoting stability and growth. The contemporary concepts of economic advancement for developed countries include entire range of governmental functions, including sectoral policy reform, economic integration, privatization, public sector enhancement, labor market competitiveness, investment climate enhancement, e-government, soft infrastructures for developing a knowledge economy, macroeconomic management and effective long-range planning. The weight of the public sector constitutes a serious impediment to more rapid growth for many countries. Importantly the large expenditure burden it requires does not always translate into an efficient and equitable distribution of services. Such performance is reflected by the public sector efficiency and governance in promoting the economic advancement of a country. The challenges of employment generation, economic growth and societal advancement in changing demographic contexts can only be addressed through productive investment and value building. The climate for investment is therefore critical for the countries which need a strategic direction and an economic concentration on value building rather than value trading, which leads towards the higher degree of economic advancement in a country.

Economic advancement is directly proportional to the educational and training facilities available in the country. Human resources are not only producers of goods and services, which also play a multifold role in economic development. Economic advancement is characterized by the following factors:

- Allocation of labor force to agriculture
- Energy available in large amounts at low cost per unit
- High level of GDP and income
- High levels of per capita consumption
- Relatively low rates of population growth
- Complex modern facilities for transportation, communication, and exchange
- Substantial amount of capital for investment
- Urbanization based on production as well as exchange
- Diversified manufacturing that accounts for an important share of the labor force; and technology that includes ample media and methods for experiment.

These factors may be utilized to examine economic standing of the host country and analysis of a large variety of information on these variables may help to categorize the countries on an economic development scale. Besides, there are many historical, geographic, political, and cultural factors intimately related to the economic well-being of a nation.

---

[27] Luis Servén, and Peter J. Montiel (2004): *Macroeconomic Stability in Developing Countries: How Much Is Enough?* Working Paper # 3456, World Bank, November.

Large nominal exchange rate changes affect the behavior of trade flows through their impact on the relative prices of tradable goods in the economy. A change in the nominal exchange rate affects the prices of export and import goods relative to domestically produced goods, which implies changes in the real exchange rate. There is a striking difference, as regards the behavior of the real exchange rate, between the two sets of countries indicated above. In Brazil, Peru, and Argentina home currency goods became more expensive during this episode, due to an even higher domestic inflation rate. For the remaining countries large nominal exchange rate devaluations were transmitted into real exchange rate devaluations. With the notable exception of Brazil and Argentina, all countries had experienced a relative convergence to their initial long-term real exchange rates, with rates of real depreciation much lower than those experienced only two years after the devaluation. In Brazil the five-year period ended just after the large real depreciation resulting from the collapse of the Real Plan in February of 1999 and some of this depreciation was corrected shortly after that. The adjustment of trade flows to their new equilibrium level does not happen immediately. Exporters and importers need to identify new markets for their products, establish relationships, and develop sales and distribution networks that allow them to find substitutes for their current international partners

The macroeconomic policy refers to the top-down strategy developed and implemented in a country by the government and central banks, usually intended to maximize growth while keeping down inflation and unemployment. The growth factors determining the incentives towards investing in human capital for developing new products include government policies. Countries with broadly free-market policies, in particular free trade and the maintenance of secure property rights typically have higher growth rates. By 1990, most developed countries reckoned to have long-term trend growth rates of 2-2.5% a year. However, during the 1990s, growth rates started to rise, especially in the United States. Some economists said it was the result of the birth of a new economy based on a revolution in productivity, largely because of rapid technological innovation but also (perhaps directly stemming from the spread of new technology) due to increases in the value of human capital. In the end of the 20th century, it has been argued that developments in information technology and globalization leading towards free trade through the regional trade agreements, has given birth to a new economy initiated in United States. These developments have shown a higher rate of productivity and growth than the previous economy it replaced. Open economies have grown much faster on average than closed economies.

The main instruments of macroeconomic policy are deviations in the interest rates and money supply, taxation and public spending, known as fiscal policy. It has been observed that with the rise of the rate of unemployment and inflation, the growth rate of the economy declines and the GDP of the country falls[28]. This may be an evidence of poorly planned macroeconomic policy and implementation thereof. Higher public spending relative to GDP is generally associated with slower growth. The rise in the rate of inflation is contributed by the high social expenditure and political instability in a country. However, business cycles may simply be an unavoidable fact of economic life that macroeconomic policy, however well conducted, can never be sure of conquering. The long run pattern of growth and recession in the business that may be explained as boom and bust of the economy of a country or a region may be described as business cycle. There are two main versions of the new

---

[28] The Economist: Insecurities, November 11, 2004.

paradigm that have attracted followers in America lately over the reactions of the previous business cycles[29]. Of these, one version states that the country's long-term growth rate has shifted upwards while the other reveals that the old pattern of boom and bust has disappeared in the light of the free trade and globalization movement by 2000.

Elsewhere, the reforms did bring lasting benefits. In Chile, an early reformer, fast growth saw poverty halved, to 23%, between 1987 and 1996. Overall, macroeconomic management in the region improved dramatically compared with, say, the 1970s. Partly because governments pulled back from running steelworks and factories, they spent more on education and health. In some countries, such as Brazil and Mexico, new, targeted, anti-poverty programs were introduced. Where income inequality worsened, it was mainly because of recession, not reform. Privatization was not the blanket failure painted by the critics. There is little argument over the sale of state industries. Public utilities are more controversial. In some countries, their sale was badly handled: either tainted by corruption, or by private monopolies, or because regulation has been poor. But private provision of telephones, electricity and water has vastly increased their coverage and quality. However, that has generally come at a price: as subsidies were withdrawn, tariffs often rose, before later starting to fall[30].

A positive trend in the behavior of trade flows has been observed during the reforms period, resulting from the increased openness of these economies to international markets. There is a striking difference between the behavior of export and import volumes around the devaluation episodes. Exports tend, on average, to increase in the year of the devaluation and the following two years. Only in Argentina, Peru and Venezuela do we observe negative export growth in the second year after the devaluation, and this probably has more to do with the circumstances in world markets at that time, especially in the United States. In all other cases, exports continue to increase. Import volume, in contrast, behaves quite differently. In most of the devaluation episodes import volume contracted; only in the two devaluations by large countries in the mid 1990s (Mexico and Brazil) was there substantial positive import growth. In all other cases, the import contraction was short-lived. Exports increase faster than average to countries in the region, and especially to countries that are partners in regional trading agreements. Brazil and Argentina increased their trading flows with each other significantly, and also with other countries in the region such as Chile and Paraguay. There was also a significant increase in regional trade among Central American countries: Honduras, El Salvador and Guatemala, despite suffering an exchange rate crisis, increased their bilateral trade with one another at a rate significantly above the average of their overall trade growth.

INTERNATIONAL COMPETITION

Competition may be analyzed in reference to the characteristics of products as breakthrough, competitive, and improved. A *breakthrough product* is a unique innovation that is mainly technical in nature, such as the digital watch, VCR, and personal computer. A *competitive product* is one of many brands currently available in the market and has no

---

[29] The Economist: Beyond the business Cycles, October 21, 1999.
[30] The Economist: Wanted: A new regional agenda for economic growth, April 24, 2003.

special advantage over the competing products. An *improved product* is not unique but is generally superior to many existing brands. For example, let us assume Aubrey Organics is interested in manufacturing shampoo for tender hair in Turkey and seeks entry into the emerging market in the middle-eastern countries. The company finds that in addition to a number of local brands, Johnson & Johnson's baby shampoo and Helene Curtis Industries' Suave Shampoo are the competitive products in the market. Proctor and Gamble has recently entered the market with its Pantene Pro-V brand, which is considered as an improved product. Most of the competition appears to be addressing the existing demand. However, no attempts have been made to satisfy latent demand or incipient demand. After reviewing various considerations, Aubrey Organics may decide to fulfill latent demand with an improved offering through its Camomile Luxurious brand. Based on market information, the company reasons that a hair problem most consumers face in that part of the world is dandruff. No brand has addressed itself to that problem. Even Proctor & Gamble's new entry mainly emphasizes health of hair. Thus, analysis of the competition with reference to product offerings and demand enables Aubrey Organics to determine its entry point into the market of middle-eastern countries. The companies need to analyze some important issues as below while examining the micro-economic environment:

- Who is the competition now, and who will it be in the future?
- What are the key competitors' strategies, objectives and goals?
- How important is a specific market to the competitors, and are they enough to continue to invest?
- What unique strengths do the competitors have?
- Do they have any weaknesses that make them vulnerable?
- What changes are likely in the competitors' future strategies?
- What are the implications of competitors' strategies on the market, the inc. and one's own company?

One of the appropriate ways to examine the competition is to draw up a demographic profile of the industry. Markets dominated by small, single-industry businesses or small regional competitors differ significantly from those dominated by national or multi-industry companies. The competitor strengths may be measured by analyzing various functional indicators in marketing as described below:

- Market share
- Differential advantages
- Cost advantages
- Reputation
- Distribution capabilities
- Core competencies
- Perceptions of target buyers
- Competitors' financial strength, which determines their ability to spend money on advertising and promotions, among other things
- Competitor's ability and speed of innovation for new products and services

It is necessary to list the strengths and weaknesses of the competitors from the customer's viewpoint and analyze how a company can capitalize on their weaknesses and meet the challenges represented by their strengths. The information on the competitor information might be easily obtained by getting a copy of their annual report. It might take analysis of many information sources to understand competitors' strategies and objectives. In an international market, the business takes place in a highly competitive, volatile environment, so it is important to understand the competition. Some questions as illustrated below can help the marketer to map the micro-economic variables in reference to a competitor:

- Who are your five nearest direct competitors?
- Who are your indirect competitors?
- Is their business growing, steady, or declining?
- What can you learn from their operations or from their advertising?
- What are their strengths and weaknesses?
- How does their product or service differ from yours?

The competition in the photo film products has been increasing with competitive price and promotion strategies among the major international brands like Kodak and Fuji. The consumers have found a bona fide competitor to Kodak in the name of Fuji film. Clearly, Fuji film has emerged from a minor player in the early 1980's in American market to take a solid number two position within the US market and has caught the attention, as well as the fury, of Kodak. The success of low priced super stores such as Wal-Mart has taught retailers that diversification, scrambled marketing and "one-stop" shopping are important to consumers. As consolidation in retail industry sweeps in mass marketing, food and drug accounts, retailers realize they must maintain their competitive advantage or close shop. To survive, they are squeezing manufacturers for quality products at competitive prices to capture profit margins for expansion within the industry. This environment has provided an opportunity for Fuji film to prosper in an otherwise stable and mature photographic industry. Though Kodak and Fuji fight for market share, the real winner and benefactor is the consumer, both the companies officially deny that they are engaging in a price war, but for each move Fuji makes, Kodak counters with a strategic move. Kodak and Fuji traditionally enjoyed healthy margins and treated the market as a mutually profitable duopoly[31]. Then in the spring of 1996, Fuji cut prices on film by 10 to 15 percent after Costco Wholesalers decided to go exclusively with Kodak. Fuji had excess inventory of 2.5 millions rolls of film. They distributed the heavily discounted film to other retailers to avoid "expiring" film and thus began a correlation between price cutting and market share. Once consumers tried Fuji, they found they liked the product as long as it was priced lower than Kodak. By 1998 the severe pace of competition between Kodak and Fuji seemed to slow down, with the exception of value packs. However, still the companies are in neck-to-neck competition in the market, though other brands like *Agfa, Konica* have made a dent in the global retailing including American markets.

The soundness of the economy of a country largely governs the consumer confidence, which further determines the buying plans of the consumers. A favorable economic environment helps consumers to optimize their buying decisions and augment propensity to

---

[31] Finnerty C Thomas: Kodak vs. Fuji: *The Battle for Global Market Share, Institute of Global Business Strategy*, Lubin School of Business, Pace University, 2000, pp 4-23.

spend money. The reverse occurs when economic conditions are unfavorable. The economic environment in Brazil was not encouraging for the various segments of consumers during period 1998-1999 though the inflation was under control. The credit restrictions have had a negative impact on consumption during the above referred period. However, after the country exercised appropriate economic measures to stabilize the economy of the country in the recent past, it has been observed that foreign business corporations consider Brazil to be Latin America's most attractive investment target. International marketers should examine the extent to which their business is vulnerable to economic conditions. For example, in a booming economy, consumers tend to buy durable goods, on the contrary in recession they would avoid spending money. There are many areas in emerging markets as listed below which attract business partnering opportunities with developed countries.

- Turnkey projects
- Process consultancy
- Consortium production and marketing
- Cooperative ventures
- Strategic alliances
- Buyback agreements
- Corporate chains-Technology, retail, consultancy
- Custom hiring- production, branding
- Technology diffusion- creating demand
- Green marketing

The prevailing economic environment is just an indicator to review the business fit in the given region or country. Even if the short-run economic environment is not conducive to profits, a company may decide to enter an overseas market in anticipation of favorable long-term economic prospects in country such as growing political stability, declining inflation or the low wage rates. However, the long-run perspective is the most critical decision factor, which provides the firm sufficient resources to endure waiting for the future favorable environment. The market attractiveness of Brazil may be described from this point of view. The big emerging markets like Brazil, China, Russia and India have enhanced economic and political attributes as discussed below:

- Physically large markets
- Growing population
- Representing wide range of products
- Strong growth rate
- High participation in economic reforms
- Regional/global political importance
- Regional development drivers
- Lead managers in neighborhood and regional trade
- Contemporary infrastructure
- Liberal policies

An accelerating growth and poverty reduction requires governments to reduce the policy risks, costs, and barriers to competition facing firms of all types, from farmers and micro-entrepreneurs to local manufacturing and multinational companies. A vibrant private sector creates jobs, provides the goods and services needed to improve living standards, and contributes taxes necessary for public investment in health, education, and other services. But too often governments stunt the size of those contributions by creating unjustified risks, costs, and barriers to competition[32]. However, the policy-related risks dominate the concerns of firms in developing countries. Uncertainty about the content and implementation of government policies is the top-rated concern, with other significant risks including macroeconomic instability, arbitrary regulation, and weak protection of property rights. These risks cloud opportunities and chill incentives to invest productively and create jobs.

POLITICAL FACTORS IN INTERNATIONAL TRADE ALLIANCES

An accelerating growth and poverty reduction requires governments to reduce the policy risks, costs, and barriers to competition facing firms of all types, from farmers and micro-entrepreneurs to local manufacturing and multinational companies. A vibrant private sector creates jobs, provides the goods and services needed to improve living standards, and contributes taxes necessary for public investment in health, education, and other services. But too often governments stunt the size of those contributions by creating unjustified risks, costs, and barriers to competition[33]. However, the policy-related risks dominate the concerns of firms in developing countries. Uncertainty about the content and implementation of government policies is the top-rated concern, with other significant risks including macroeconomic instability, arbitrary regulation, and weak protection of property rights. These risks cloud opportunities and chill incentives to invest productively and create jobs. Nearly 90 percent of firms in Guatemala, and more than 70 percent of firms in Belarus and Zambia, find the interpretation of regulation unpredictable. It has been highlighted in the World Development Report -2005 that more than 80 percent of firms in Bangladesh, and over 70 percent of firms in Ecuador and Moldova, lack confidence in the courts to uphold their property rights. Improving policy predictability alone can increase the likelihood of new investment by more than 30 percent Barriers to competition are also pervasive and dull incentives for firms to innovate and increase their productivity - the key to sustainable growth. High risks and costs restrict competition, while governments also limit competition through policy barriers to market entry and exit. Nearly 90 percent of firms in Poland report strong competitive pressure, more than twice the share of firms in Georgia. Stronger competitive pressure can increase the probability of innovation

The reforms were implemented in a relatively unfavorable external environment. The effect of implementing the reforms during 1991–95, instead of in the previous five-year period, was to associate them with an international context that by itself reduced the average growth rates of the reforming countries by about 1 percent. Latin America has not yet reached the levels of performance achieved in faster-growing regions. The results of the study highlights that only about half of the annual growth gap of about 7 percent between Latin

---

[32] World Bank: World Development Report-2005, News Release 2004/89/S, World Bank, Washington DC.
[33] World Bank: World Development Report-2005, News Release 2004/89/S, World Bank, Washington DC.

America and East Asia during the reform period can be closed by doing more of the same that is, intensifying the reform effort along the lines already undertaken. This remaining gap suggests that the scope of reform in Latin America will need to be broadened. Improvements in macroeconomic management are simply not sufficient for Latin America to achieve long-run growth rates comparable to those achieved in East Asia. Such results have also been evidenced by other research studies[34].

TRADE AND TARIFF STRUCTURES

The trade among the Latin American and East Asian countries certainly exhibit enormous potential and apart from the trading of physical goods the services trade in terms of consultancy, transfer of technology and managerial training may also be explored bi-regionally. However, there exist differences among both the regions in factor endowment between the generally natural-resource-abundant Latin America and the natural resource-scarce Asia-Pacific Geography (*i.e.* distance) and differences in the availability of capital, knowledge (*e.g.* Japan, South Korea and Taiwan) and labor (China) also have been major drivers of the bilateral trade. It has been observed by many researchers that Latin America is aggressively opened up to world trade and investment in the late 1980s and its mixed results have emerged over two decades in expansion, diversification and upgrading its exports. The Asia-Pacific countries have shown extraordinary success in diversifying their exports and in raising their stakes in the world economy, while at the same time their domestic market is largely protected against import competition. Such trade policies of this region have also alarmed the concerns for global partnering and business expansions. Instruments such as tariff, non-tariff barriers, trade related investment measures (TRIMS) and barriers to domestic distribution still play an import role in these countries, although there are important cross-country differences in their timing, scope and importance. China has clearly the more protected market, despite the progress made since the WTO accession in 2001, whereas in the other countries protection is particularly high for agriculture. There still exist wide differences in dynamism between these economies. Latin America has yet to resume the high growth rates of the 1950s-60s, whereas most of the Asian Pacific countries, particularly China, have been growing at a breakneck speed, led by exports.

The involvement of Central America's major trading partner, the USA in a trade agreement benefiting neighboring Mexico could have been a source of disruption in the direction and pattern of trade flows in the region. Despite the implementation of NAFTA in 1994, a number of Central American countries (Costa Rica, Guatemala, Honduras, Nicaragua and the Dominican Republic) witnessed throughout the decade an unprecedented increase in trade, both in import and export trade, with the USA[35]. This implies that NAFTA preferential treatment, with its potential trade diversion effect, was to some extent effectively counter balanced. It is notable that only Costa Rica experienced a decline in its market share, but this was probably due to export growth in other sectors of the economy of Costa Rica.

---

[34] Fernandez-Arias Eduardo and Montiel Peter (2001): Reforms and Growth in Latin America: All Pains, No Gains? *IMF Staff Working Paper*, 48 (4), pp 1-25.

[35] Leaderman Daniel, Perry Guillermo and Suescun Rodrigo (2002): *Trade Structure, Trade Policy and Economic Policy Options in Central America*, The World Bank, Office of the Latin American and Caribbean Region, Working Paper, November.

Latin America's total exports grew by an annual average 8.9 percent between 1990 and 2003 raising its share of world exports from 3 to 5.4 percent as exhibited in Table 5.4. Mexico has been the indisputable driver of Latin America's export growth, with its share of the regional total rising from a fifth in the early 1980s to 45 percent in 2003. It may be observed from the exhibited data that four big countries— which include Mexico, Brazil, Argentina, and Venezuela— today generate more than three-fourths of Latin America's exports. Imports mirror the export patterns. Even with Latin America struggling with anemic economic growth, the region's imports rose more than exports (an annual average of 10.1 percent in 1990-2003), perhaps reflecting the region's rather aggressive opening and episodes of exchange rate appreciation.

The dynamism of trade notwithstanding, the volume of Latin American exports to Asia-Pacific starts from a relatively low base and is well below the region's exports to North America, the European Union, and intra-regional commerce. In fact, while increasing substantially up to 1991, the importance of Asia-Pacific as a market for Latin America has declined over the past decade. Latin American exports to Asia-Pacific stood at $24 billion in 2003, with the Asia-Pacific accounting for 6.6 percent of Latin America's total exports to the world— a marked drop from Asia-Pacific's share of 9 percent in 1990. Central America did, however, experience slight growth in the share of the Asia-Pacific in total exports in 1990-2003. Of the individual countries, Argentina, Chile, Colombia, Costa Rica, El Salvador, Guatemala, Jamaica, Paraguay, Peru, Uruguay, and Venezuela did experience a rise in the share of Asia-Pacific in their exports between 1990 and 2003.

Table 5.4. Exports from Latin American Countries to Asia-Pacific (1990-2003)
(US $ millions)

Country	Japan	Korea Republic	China	Hong Kong	Taiwan	Singapore	ASEAN[a]	Asia-Pacific (A)	World (B)	Percent Share (A/B)
Argentina	344 (395)	434 (51)	2478 (241)	98 (60)	126 (48)	10 (409	1098 (329)	4588 (1164)	29566 (12352)	15.5 (9.4)
Brazil	2311 (2349)	1223 (543)	4533 (382)	694 (271)	689 (432)	338 (250)	1113 (790)	10900 (5016)	73084 (31412)	14.9 (16.0)
Chile	2243 (1384)	1006 (258)	1817 (34)	0 (41)	583 (279)	39 (33)	254 (132)	5922 (2162)	20077 (8522)	29.5 (25.4)
Colombia	202 (259)	76 (13)	82 (2)	16 (16)	52 (1)	11 (3)	18 (9)	456 (303)	13092 (6765)	3.5 (4.5)
Costa Rica	58 (15)	11 (5)	89 (0)	132 (2)	39 (6)	24 (1)	244 (5)	596 (34)	5800 (1456)	10.3 (2.4)
Ecuador	86 (51)	242 (23)	14 (0)	3 (0)	4 (65)	1 (0)	3 (2)	353 (142)	6038 (2714)	5.8 (5.2)
Mexico	607 (1442)	95 (102)	463 (65)	258 (42)	106 (0)	183 (33)	91 (26)	1803 (1711)	165395 (26345)	1.1 (6.5)
Paraguay	5 (21)	0 (6)	17 (67)	9 (17)	12 (3)	1 (5)	9 (5)	53 (123)	1242 (1708)	4.3 (7.2)
Peru	390 (420)	176 (65)	675 (55)	30 (19)	147 (50)	16 (0)	76 (18)	1511 (628)	8749 (3313)	17.3 (19.0)
Uruguay	12 (21)	6 (6)	95 (67)	14 (17)	5 (3)	2 (5)	63 (5)	197 (123)	2198 (1708)	9.0 (7.2)

Venezuela	135 (505)	15 (6)	165 (6)	11 (34)	37 (57)	201 (125)	9 (44)	571 (777)	24974 (18044)	2.3 (4.3)
LAC	6473 (6958)	3367 (1091)	10470 (866)	1278 (507)	1786 (967)	832 (495)	3029 (1376)	27234 (12261)	363707 (120916)	7.5 (10.1)

Figures in parentheses indicate values for 1990.
Source: IDB-INT calculations based on UN/COMTRADE data published in the official document AB-2370, March 21, 2005: "Asia and Latin America and the Caribbean: Economic Links, Cooperation and Development Strategies".

The importance of the Asia-Pacific is most marked for Chile, which exported 29 percent of its exports to Asia-Pacific, as well as for the Mercosur countries, which sent 15 percent of their exports to the Asia-Pacific basin in 2003. Arguably, the most vulnerable region right now is Latin America, where most countries are trying to cope with an environment of high economic fragility, partly resulting from the current global slowdown but also reflecting internal political trouble and policy mismanagement. The region's problems are of a more long-term nature than merely cyclical and therefore need to be tackled accordingly, taking into account country-specific circumstances. Latin America's large distance from world markets, the region's complicated topography, and the tropical climate pose particularly important challenges. On the macroeconomic front, the fiscal policy stance has deteriorated significantly in several countries, sending them into a dangerous spiral of increasing debts and deficits despite important efforts to generate primary surpluses in the public budget. However, that encouraging reforms have been implemented in some areas, notably regarding foreign trade and financial liberalization. As a result, exports have deepened and become more diversified, which bodes well when the external environment becomes more favorable again.

ARCHITECTURE OF BUSINESS PARTNERING AMONG ASIAN-LATIN AMERICAN COUNTRIES

The Latin American and Caribbean countries have a long history of bilateral and sub-regional preferential agreements on trade and economic integration. Dating from the 1960s and early 1970s, the Latin American Free Trade Area (LAFTA), the Andean Community (AC), the Caribbean Common Market (Caricom) and the Central American Common Market (CACM) rarely met their goals, because of the inherent clash between integration and import substitution industrialization. However, a new wave of preferential agreements rocked the region in the 1990s, now linked to a re-hauling of trade and development strategies. Traditional arrangements, such as the Latin American Integration Association (LAIA) — LAFTA's successor — and the AC, gained strength and Mercosur broke off as an important sub-regional initiative in South America. Various bilateral agreements (many of them under the Montevideo Treaty that created LAIA in 1981) were struck, generally with the goal of establishing free trade areas. Moreover, Mexico negotiated NAFTA with the US and Canada during the 1990s.

India and Chile have signed a Preferential Trade Agreement (PTA) in early 2006 as part of initiatives to increase trade and investment between the two countries. Chile is a major

Latin American country with a GDP of 76.3 billion dollars and a trade of 53.2 billion dollar during 2004. India-Chile trade during 2004-05 stood at 447 million dollars. The PTA strategically positions Chile to access and to capitalize on the Indian market and its technological assets. This marks business ties between the two countries as it will impart a new dimension to trade relations in times to come. The PTA also provides tariff preferences ranging from 10 to 50 per cent on 178 products to Chile and a similar range of preferences on 296 items to India. It would benefit 98 per cent of items being exported by Chile to India and 91 percent of the goods being exported by India to Chile. The Framework Agreement also provided for a Joint Study Group to identify the potential for cooperation in trade in goods and services, investments and other areas. The Indian products, which would benefit include textiles, chemicals, pharmaceuticals, engineering and agricultural machinery while Chilean products include copper, newsprint, iodine, fish meal and salmon[36].

In the process of bi-regional business negotiations among the Latin American and Asian countries, the Free Trade Agreements (FTAs) were up until recently signed mainly in reference to the geographically proximate countries. Today, however, FTAs are becoming trans-continental. Reflecting this trend are, for example, the US-Australia, US-Singapore, and Mexico-Israel FTAs, as well as the EU's FTAs with Chile, Mexico, and South Africa. Also Latin America and Asia have established trans-continental FTAs. In 2003, Chile and South Korea signed the first comprehensive FTA between an Asian and Latin American country; the agreement went into effect in April 2004. Japan and Mexico have also recently concluded FTA talks. Latin American and East Asian partners have launched negotiations for three further bi-regional FTAs, including Chile-Singapore-New Zealand, Mexico-South Korea, and Mexico- Singapore FTAs. Chile and Japan have formed a joint study group to explore the feasibility of launching formal FTA negotiations. Latin America-Asia trans-continentalism has spanned the Asia Pacific basin, with Brazil and India negotiating an FTA. Moreover, plans have been expressed for Chile-Japan, Mexico-New Zealand, Mercosur-India, Mercosur-China, and Chile-China FTAs. The Table 5.5 exhibits the successful trade and economic negotiations since 1980 among the Latin American and Asian countries.

These agreements often managed to form sub-regional free trade areas; many even explicitly seek to become common markets. For example, Mercosur was created with the intention of gradually evolving towards a common market and the AC has reaffirmed its goal of forming a common market in 2005. Neither has the Caricom abandoned its strategic goal of building a common market, evidenced by member statements in the Protocol of Guatemala in 1993. With ambitious integration goals and modest results, taken together the initiatives present similar trends and prospects, most remain in a free trade, a stage incapable of turning into full-fledged customs unions. Divergent foreign policies, domestic political and economic restraints, and border conflicts plague nearly all. Conflicts flare up from disparities in size, economic structure and patterns of trade, in addition to often contradictory cost-benefit evaluations of undertaking a common external tariff. Moreover, regional agreements risk being drowned out by the deepening of unilateral preferential trade schemes in the US and the EU that benefit the small economies of Central America and the Caribbean.

---

[36] Times of India, Wednesday, March 08, 2006.

Table 5.5. Concluded Trade and Economic Partnership among the Latin American and Asian Countries (1980-2004)

Trade and Economic Agreements	Year of Entry
Asia-Pacific Economic Cooperation (APEC)	1989
South Korea-Chile	2003
Taiwan-Panama	2004
Japan –Mexico	2004

Prospects

After many years of effort, a global preferential trade agreement was negotiated in the form of the Global System of Trade Preferences (GSTP), which entered into force in 1989. The Preamble of the GSTP Agreement embodies the belief that the system is a major instrument of south-south cooperation, for the promotion of collective self-reliance as well as for the strengthening of world trade as a whole. Participation in the GSTP is limited to members of the Group of 77 and only those developing countries that have exchanged concessions are eligible for its benefits. Developing countries, as members of the Group of 77, can become parties to the Agreement individually or as a sub-regional, regional or interregional grouping. The Agreement envisages arrangements relating to tariffs; para-tariffs; non-tariff measures, direct trade measures, including medium and long-term contracts, and sectoral agreements. The negotiations can be conducted in accordance with one or any combination of the following modalities:

- Product-by-product negotiations;
- Across-the-board tariff reductions;
- Sectoral negotiations; and
- Direct trade measures.

The GSTP Agreement also contains special benefits for the least developed countries by granting exclusive preferential concessions and by stipulating that they must not be required to make concessions on a reciprocal basis. Concessions have been exchanged among 45 developing countries in the first round of GSTP negotiations, which concluded on 30 April 1988 and involved important trading nations from all regions. Among the countries were Argentina, Brazil, Chile, Colombia, Mexico and Peru from Latin America, and India, Indonesia, Malaysia, Pakistan, Philippines, Republic of Korea, Singapore and Thailand from the Asian and Pacific region. Some main features of the concessions granted in the first round of GSTP negotiations were:

- Concessions were confined to tariffs;
- Use of product-by-product negotiations as the modality;
- Limited coverage of concessions for most participants. For example, Argentina had five tariff lines at the 10-digit level; Chile had 10 tariff lines at the eight object level; Indonesia had one tariff line at the seven-digit level; Malaysia had one tariff line at

the seven digit level; Philippines had three tariff lines at the seven-digit level and Thailand had 11 tariff lines at the six-digit level. Somewhat more extensive but still quite modest concessions were given by Brazil, 93 tariff lines at the eight-digit level; India gave 32 tariff lines at the six-digit level and Mexico gave 26 tariff lines at seven-digit level. Only the concession granted by Yugoslavia was quite extensive; and

- Concessions were generally in terms of a margin of preference over a range of 10 to 50 percent.

The first and by far the most significant is Mercosur, with Argentina, Brazil, Paraguay and Uruguay as members. Mercosur introduced a common external tariff (CET) in 1995, to be phased in over a six-year period. The aim is to eventually create a common market with free movement of goods, labor, services and capital. A feature of the Mercosur policy is that it has either formed a free trade area with other countries (such as Chile) or is actively negotiating such an accord (such as with the EU). Colombia, Mexico and Venezuela formed another free-trade area, known as the Group of Three in 1994, to be phased in over a 10-year period.

Table 5.6. Trade and Economic Negotiations among the Latin American and Asian Countries: In Process and Newly Proposed

Latin American Country	Asian Countries	
	Negotiations in Process	Newly Planned Proposals
Chile	Singapore-New Zealand	Japan
	China	-
Guatemala	Taiwan	-
Panama	Singapore	-
Peru	Singapore	-
	Thailand	
Mexico	Singapore	New Zealand
	-	South Korea
Mercosur	-	China
	-	India

Source: IDB, Integration and Regional Programs Department.

Argentina, Brazil and Chile (ABC) have succeeded in the post-reforms period attracting substantial amounts of foreign direct investment, though these countries have mainly targeted the investment in the primary sectors where competitive advantages already exist. The foreign investments are also promoted by the ABC group of countries to specific segments of the non-tradable sector consisting of mainly infrastructure and banking. Agricultural and food products are the largest contributor to exports in the ABC group of countries and continue to have a strong potential for expansion. First of all, in Argentina and Brazil there is still a large amount of permanent pasture that can be converted into arable cropland. ABC also has room to increase labor and land productivity, and exports of processed food products. In this regard, Chile has succeeded somewhat in developing differentiated products out of primary clusters, the wine industry being a notable, but not unique, example. Competition policy in ABC has evolved from the enforcement of competition on the basis of private claims, to competition advocacy and its contribution to the design of regulatory reforms. However, ABC group of countries still need to strengthen their competition policies and regulatory frameworks, particularly in infrastructure[37].

The economic integration arrangements in the Latin American and Asian regions have been established mainly at the sub-regional level. There are initiatives in the Latin American region to link together some of the Sub-regional arrangements. This leads to the question of what are the possibilities for economic integration arrangements linking the two regions. In the Asian and Latin American regions, some cross-regional free trade areas are almost at the point of being established. The one between Chile and the Republic of Korea is more advanced, but other bilateral initiatives are under way between Japan and Chile, Colombia and Mexico. Preferential arrangements have also been envisaged between Taiwan Province of China and some countries in Central America. Besides the countries of Asia, membership in APEC includes Mexico, Peru and Chile. However, their membership has so far been only a consultation forum and not an integration arrangement. The trade and economic negotiations which are lying under process and newly planned have been exhibited in Table 5.6.

The best opportunity for countries of Asia and Latin America may be to intensify their commercial exchanges by continuing to rely on non-discriminatory trade relations. To expand interregional trade, the countries of the two regions should look at barriers to trade for products of interest to them from countries of the other region and negotiate for reduction or elimination on the basis of MFN at a future round of multilateral trade negotiations. Apart from this, other cooperative action could be taken to overcome impediments due to such factors as distance, lack of traditional trade relations and even linguistic differences that have inhibited interregional trade exchanges. Consultative forums among governments and among businesses should be set up where they do not exist. Such forums have to be strengthened where they already exist. Periodic consultations have to be coordinated with full use of the internet to disseminate information about production capabilities and the supply needs in the two regions.

Expansion of Latin America-Asia Trade Links

The trade performance of Asian and Pacific countries had been outstanding up to 1997. In 1980, the region exported less than US$ 280 billion, by 1990 that total had increased to almost US$ 700 billion and in 1995 more than US$ 1,230 billion. Results on the export side were matched by an exceptional performance on the import side. Total imports jumped from US$ 292 billion in 1980 to more than US$ 700 billion 10 years later and over US$ 1,300 billion in 1995. These values indicate an average annual growth rate between 1990 and 1995 of about 12 percent for exports and over 13 percent for imports. However, the Asian crisis had a negative effect on the region's trade performance. Between 1996 and 1998, the average annual growth of total exports was -0.2 percent, while on the import side the decrease was more pronounced, at -4.2 percent. The result for the period 1990-1998 shows that annual

---

[37] OECD (2004): *Trade and Competitiveness in Argentina, Brazil and Chile*, Agriculture and Food, Organization for Economic Co-operation and Development, Vol. 2004, No. 9, 1-233.

growth for exports reached only 7.5 percent as compared to 11.5 per cent for the period of 1980-1990. Growth of Asian and Pacific exports to the countries belonging to Latin American Integration Association (LAIA) increased 19 percent a year between 1990 and 1995, growth that was even more pronounced than intra-Asian trade. This was a clear indication that trade liberalization in Latin America offered a special opportunity for Asian and Pacific countries to increase their share in this expanding market. In the following three years, Asian and Pacific exports to Latin America increased over 7 percent per year[38].

Inter-regional cooperation has intensified on the trans-Pacific agenda in recent years. Latin America and Asia-Pacific have created various fora to deal with bilateral economic and political issues. The most comprehensive in terms of bi-regional membership is the Forum for East Asia-Latin America Cooperation (FEALAC) launched at a Ministerial Meeting in March 2001 in Santiago, Chile. Comprising 17 Latin American and 15 Asia-Pacific economies, FEALAC is an informal mechanism for dialogue and cooperation among the countries of the two regions to meet political, cultural, social, economic and international issues of common concern. Two further major venues of trans-Pacific cooperation are the Pacific Basin Economic Council (PBEC) and the Pacific Economic Cooperation Conference (PECC). The Latin American partners in each are Colombia, Chile, Ecuador, Mexico and Peru. PBEC is an association of senior business leaders from more than 1,100 major corporations in 20 economics around the Pacific Basin Region aimed at expanding trade and investment flows through open markets. In its next International General Meeting (IGM) in June 2005 in Hong Kong, PECC will focus on the Pacific Basin's role in the next stages of globalization, such as the Doha Development Round. Meanwhile, the 25-member PECC promotes trade, investment, financial stability, and development around the Pacific Rim. It comprises senior representatives from business, government, and the academia. PECC has recently focused on the proliferation of regional integration agreements as a potential way for achieving the Bogor Convention Goals of APEC[39].

Japan and Latin America have deep-seated cooperation. Japan has alone, contributed to Latin America's development through economic and technical cooperation aimed particularly at economic reform, poverty reduction, and environmental protection. It is one of Latin America's main sources of Official Development Assistance (ODA). Japan was one of the key actors in helping Latin America debt crisis of the early- 1980s, and also involved in the Central American peace processes. More recently, Japan has supported the electoral processes in Latin America, including joining the dispatch of election observers from the Organization of American States (OAS). Japan has also pursued active cooperation with the Caribbean through the Japan-CARICOM Consultation, which centers on fostering bilateral relations, and economic cooperation, cultural exchanges, and collaboration in international fora.

It is interesting to note that this was the highest rate of growth compared to other regions. On the other hand, Asian and Pacific imports from LAIA were the most affected among the regions. Even before the Asian crisis, Latin America was a minor partner in Asia's export and import flows. In 1998, only 2.2 percent of total Asian and Pacific exports went to Latin America, and only 1.8 percent of their imports originated in LAIA countries. It is even more significant that 18 years earlier, the share of LAIA countries in total Asian and Pacific exports

---

[38] World Trade Reports, 1999, 2001, 2003 and 2004, World Trade Organization.
[39] Official document Inter-American Development Bank (IDB) # AB-2370, March 21, 2005: "Asia and Latin America and the Caribbean: Economic Links, Cooperation and Development Strategies".

and imports was higher. During the first five years of the 1990s, growth of exports from Asia and the Pacific to LAIA was high. Eight countries had annual average growth rates over 20 percent during this period. Three countries that included China, Indonesia and Thailand had increases of over 40 percent in their exports to the region.

The average annual growth rate for imports to East Asian countries from LAIA countries actually increased slightly over the rate for 1990-1995. However, New Zealand's imports from the world which had increased on average by 8 percent between 1990 and 1995 decreased almost 6 percent between 1996 and 1998. Before the crisis, the most dynamic Asian market for Latin American products was Malaysia, followed closely by Indonesia. The import demand of these two countries declined drastically after the crisis. During this period, Latin America represented more than 2 percent of total imports for only five Asian and Pacific countries, Latin America absorbed more than 2 percent of total exports for only three countries. Latin America had the highest average market share of total exports for Japan, while the region's imports were more relevant for the Republic of Korea. South Korea maintains important institutional ties with the countries of Latin America and the Caribbean. It was one of the first Asian countries to join the OAS as a permanent observer, and has made efforts to contribute to Latin America's economic and social development through ODA and technical cooperation. South Korea has recently sought to deepen its economic ties with Latin America. Besides the FTA with Chile, in 2003 South Korea staged with various Latin American countries the South Korea-Latin America and Caribbean Business Forum, which drew a host of government officials and analysts. South Korea and Mexico are joined by the 21st Century Commission, a private-level consultation forum created to explore possibilities for longer-term bilateral collaboration.

China and Latin America have strengthened cooperation ties markedly over the past decade. The Rio Group and China launched political dialogue in 1990, and in 1994 China became the first foreign country to be admitted as an observer to the Latin American Integration Agreement (LAIA or ALADI). In 1997, China was admitted to the Caribbean Development Bank. China has also held official talks with Mercosur following the establishment of a bilateral dialogue mechanism. Furthermore, much like Japan and South Korea, China collaborates with various Latin American countries in APEC and FEALAC. It also has expressed interest in a non-borrower membership in the Inter-American Development Bank. Business between East Asia and Latin America is small. East Asia is largely represented by the countries Brunei, Cambodia, Indonesia, Laos, Malaysia, Myanmar, the Philippines, Singapore, Thailand and Vietnam, along with Australia, China, Japan, South Korea and New Zealand. Latin-American countries export only $23 billion worth of products to East Asia from total annual exports of $350 billion with an even smaller amount of Asian exports going the other way. Total trade, on the other hand, between the Philippines and Latin America was around $800 million in 2002. Trade between the Philippines and Mexico paced these economic ties. Our other major export markets are Panama, Brazil, Chile and Costa Rica. The relations between the Philippines and Mexico started with the Galleon Trade. Through the centuries, bilateral trade ties have developed between Manila and Latin-American capitals. There was a time when the Philippines was considered part of the Hispanic community. The potential for bigger trade and investments is great. Latin America with 500 million consumers is a major market for Philippine goods and services. Manila promises to be a big investment partner and regional headquarters for Latin America in Asia. Philippine visibility is strong in most of Latin America, although there is a need to establish full-fledged embassies in many countries to speed up economic and cultural ties. Figure 5.1 exhibits the possible trade agreements among the Latin America and Southeast Asian countries.

In fact, Latin America was the only region that presented positive growth rates for exports from Asia and the Pacific. The solid nature of Latin American import demand has at its roots the process of deep transformation in the region. The depth in the recent crisis in Latin America has not entirely stopped this process. However, Latin American exports to Asia and the Pacific were the most strongly affected by the crisis. This creates a challenge for countries of both regions to find ways to establish solid trade and economic relation that are less vulnerable to fluctuations in the international economic environment. During the 1990s, Latin America improved its trade ties with most regions of the world. From 1990 to 1998, total exports increased from US$ 113 billion to US$ 248 billion. Total imports, which stood at US$ 83 billion in 1990, reached US$ 282 billion in 1998. These values indicate an average annual increase of almost 17 percent for imports and 11 percent for exports. These statistics represent a drastic change from the 1980s when the debt crisis caused a slowdown for Latin America's external trade, particularly in imports. As shown in the tables, LAIA imports stagnated in the period 1980-1990, growing at an average of 4 percent annually. In the same period, the yearly average increase of world exports was 6 percent.

DEVELOPMENT OF TRADE RELATIONSHIPS AMONG ASIAN-LAC COUNTRIES

The trade partnering between Latin America and Asia is yet to be explored while trade between the European Union and Latin America is growing in importance, currently amounting to $100 billion a year. However, there are potential problems for European businesses seeking to move into this market. The North American Free Trade Agreement linking Canada and the USA with Mexico has had a serious impact on European trade with Mexico and the Free Trade Area of the Americas, which aims to further the economic integration of the western hemisphere, and an increasing tendency towards dollar orientation in Latin America will pose additional challenges to European trade and investment in the region. The historical perspective of the trade agreements in the global market place is exhibited in Table 5.7.

The countries of the Pacific Rim are emerging in the 21st century as the new international business power over the developing countries. The Pacific Rim comprising South Korea, Singapore, Taiwan, Hong Kong, Malaysia, Thailand, Indonesia and Philippines is growing as an economic powerhouse by improving the regional trade treaties and exports to European and North American countries. These countries have created a strong manufacturing potential in electronics and natural resources. The consumption of construction materials like steel is in electronics and natural resources. The consumption of construction materials like steel is higher in the region than in the United States and also the demand for semiconductors are increasing over the European Union. The Committee on Trade and Investment (CTI) of Asia Pacific Economic Cooperation (APEC) organization works to reduce impediments to business activity in 15 key areas outlined in the Osaka action agenda - tariffs and non-tariff measures, services, standards and conformance, customs procedures, intellectual property rights

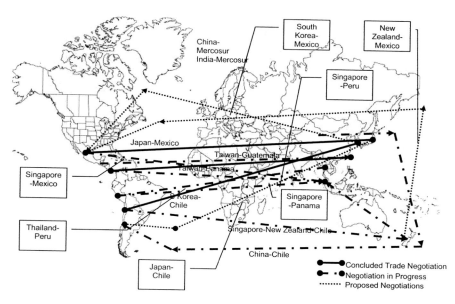

Figure 5.1. Bi-regional Trade and Economic Partnership Between Latin American Countries and Asia.

Table 5.7. Regional Trade Agreements in Global Market Place
(as of January 2003)

Period	Developed-Developed	Developed-Developing	Developed-Transition	Developing-Developing	Developing-Transition	Transition Transition	Total
1958-1964	2	0	0	1	0	0	3
1965-1969	0	0	0	0	1	0	1
1970-1974	5	3	0	2	0	0	10
1975-1979	0	5	0	1	0	0	6
1980-1984	2	1	0	1	0	0	4
1985-1989	1	1	0	2	0	0	4
1990-1994	3	3	12	5	0	6	29
1995-1999	3	7	10	4	12	28	64
2000-2002	0	11	4	5	4	6	30
Total	16	31	26	21	17	40	151

In this table, developed countries include Canada, USA, EU, EFTA, Japan, Australia, and New Zealand; transition countries include the former Soviet Union, Eastern and Central Europe, the Baltic States and the Balkans; the remaining countries are classified as Developing.

Source: World Trade Report-2003, WTO, P 47.

competition policy, government procurement, deregulation, rules of origin, dispute mediation, mobility of business people and implementation of World Trade Organization (WTO) obligations. The committee[40] is focusing on the following priority areas during 2004:

- Trade and investment facilitation (including IPR).
- Implementation of the APEC Transparency Standards.
- Implementation of Pathfinder Initiatives
- Contribution to the APEC Structural Reform Action Plan, and
- Support for World Trade Organization

APEC Member Economies are working to eliminate tariff and non-tariff barriers to trade. Elimination of these barriers will help Asia-Pacific countries to achieve the common goals resolved in various ministerial meetings of the APEC member countries, encourage greater and freer trade and investment flows and create new business opportunities and jobs in the Asia-Pacific region. It has been further resolved by the APEC nations that sustainable economic development requires empowering people and strengthening societies for globalization. This process requires more effective, better focusing and strengthening global economic and technical cooperation. Also it has been envisaged that increasing the interaction of Asia-Pacific rim countries with international financial institutions, the private sector, and other outside organizations would pay long-run gains of globalization.

The United Nations Economic Council for Latin America and Caribbean (ECLAC) observed that Latin America and the Caribbean accumulated a surplus in goods and services of about $25.5 billion, and a current account surplus of about $2.8 billion during 2003 as exports from the countries of this region grew by 8.3 percent in the same reference period due to better prices and higher-volume sales for basic goods such as copper, oil, coffee, cotton, wool and sugar. Chile secured a "major advance" with its recently implemented free-trade agreement with the United States. El Salvador, Honduras, Guatemala and Nicaragua successfully concluded negotiations in 2003 for a free-trade pact with the United States, joined by Costa Rica and the Dominican Republic in 2004[41]. Productive activities in Caribbean community and common market (CARICOM) also reflect the changing mode of doing business in a globalization environment with Trinidad and Tobago, Jamaica, Bahamas and Barbados being ranked at 1, 11, 23 and 24 respectively with regard to the "transnationality index" of developing economy host territories for the year 1996. The transnationality index is based on the average of the share of FDI inflows as a percentage of gross fixed capital formation for the last three years; FDI inward stock as a percentage of GDP; value added of foreign affiliates as a percentage of GDP; and employment of foreign affiliates as a percentage of total employment and the rankings of the above mentioned four countries in 1997 were 1, 15, 20 and 24, respectively[42].

The performance of merchandize trade in Latin America during the past five decades has been exhibited in Table 5.8 The data reveals that Mexico is the largest exporting countries among the other LAC countries. The recovery in the region's merchandise trade was held

---

[40] Asia Pacific Economic Cooperation: APEC Secretariat www.apecsec.org.sg
[41] UN Economic Commission on Latin America and Caribbean (ECLAC): Caribbean Trade and Investment Report, 2000.
[42] World Investment Report, 2000, p 25.

back by the sluggish growth of shipments to North America, its principal market, and the failure of some countries in the region to grasp the opportunities provided by the rise in global demand for primary commodities, in particular fuels. The recovery in intra-regional trade, by 9 percent in 2003, did not fully offset its contraction in 2002. The share of intra-regional trade in exports stayed at 15.6 percent in 2003 or more than five percentage points below the 1977 peak level of 21 percent. Merchandise shipments to Western Europe and Asia advanced by 17 percent and 20 percent, to new record levels. Exports to China, the region's largest market in Asia, surged to $9.2 billion, only slightly less than the region's shipments to Africa and the Middle East combined. Exports to the transition economies and Africa rose by more than one third, but even combined account for less than 3 percent of the region's merchandise exports.

Table 5.8 Merchandize Trade in Latin America (1963-2003)
(Share in Percentage)

Country/ Region	1963		1973		1983		1993		2003	
	E	I	E	I	E	I	E	I	E	I
Mexico	0.6	0.8	0.4	0.6	1.4	0.7	1.4	1.8	2.3	2.4
Brazil	0.9	0.9	1.1	1.2	1.2	0.9	1.1	0.7	1.0	0.7
Argentina	0.9	0.6	0.6	0.4	0.4	0.2	0.4	0.4	0.4	0.2
Latin America & Caribbean	7.0	6.8	4.7	5.1	5.8	4.5	4.4	5.1	5.2	4.8
North America	19.3	15.5	16.9	16.7	15.4	17.8	16.6	19.7	13.7	20.5
World	100	100	100	100	100	100	100	100	100	100

E=Exports, I=Imports.
Source: World Trade Statistics 2004, WTO.

Canadian companies have been able to expand their sales in the US thanks to innovative design and high quality products. Exports of men's and boy's tailored clothing have been particularly successful abroad, accounting for 32.5% of total foreign shipments. Besides these products, Canada is also renowned for its outerwear, furs, leather goods and children's wear. With NAFTA, the apparel industry has become very trade-oriented: exports represented over 41.0% of total shipments in 2000 compared to 17.4% in 1994 and only 5.0% in 1989. Exports of Canadian apparel have risen over 180% since the inception of the North American Free Trade Agreement (NAFTA), mostly as a result of increasing shipments south of the border. In 2000, Canadian shipments made up 1.9% of the US import market (up from 1.2% in 1994). Exports to the European Union, Canada's second market, have increased more moderately (17.1%) in the past five years and have actually declined since 1998, as a combination of trade barriers, strong local industry, and a relative depreciation of the Euro (especially in the past two years) have dampened the competitiveness of Canadian firms. Since NAFTA, American companies have been restructuring their operations by shifting a growing part of their productive capacity to Mexico and the Caribbean (there is a bilateral trade agreement with the region), decreasing their dependence on supplies from Asia. As a result, imports from Mexico to the US have grown strongly since 1994, causing their share of the American import market to rise from 5.7% to 15.8% in 2000. By the same token, US-bound shipments from Asia made up 19.4% of that market in 2003, down from 34.0% in 1994. Unlike their American and European counterparts, Canadian apparel companies have not resorted extensively to offshore production[43].

In the framework of the external co-operation and development policies of European Union, the European Investment Bank (EIB) operates in 77 African, Caribbean and Pacific (ACP) countries. The ACP countries, with a population of some 600 million, have established a special relationship with the European Union through successive Conventions; the latest is the 2000 Cotonou Agreement signed in June 2000. The EIB has been the developing partner of most of the ACP countries over 25 years and as many as 40 countries of the region. Under parallel provisions EIB also supports investments in 20 overseas countries and territories mainly in the Caribbean and Pacific which have constitutional links with certain European community countries. The Pacific Rim offers a variety of opportunities for American and European companies for the products and services that range from telecommunication instruments to aircraft seats and banking services and a host of other products. Although it is a competitive market, the region is growing economically cohesive and that attracts production sharing possibilities with the industrial countries. The Asian producers outside Japan have gained more than one fourth of the global market share for personal computers. Japan and the Pacific emerging triad comprising Singapore, Taiwan and South Korea provide most of the capital and expertise for the rest of the countries of the region that have enormous labor and natural resources.

Hong Kong also contributes significantly to the development of international trade in the Pacific region. Japan is Canada's second largest national trading partner (after the United States), taking 2.1% of total exports, and is the fifth largest source of foreign direct investment (FDI) in Canada. Canada is a leading supplier to Japan of a number of products of key export interest, such as lumber, pulp and paper, coal, meat, fish, oilseeds and prefabricated housing. While resource-based exports continue to represent much of our trading relationship, Canada is an increasingly important source of sophisticated, value-added, technology-driven products and services imported by Japan. In 2003, Canada's total merchandise trade with Japan was $22 billion. Canadian exports to Japan have declined steadily since the mid 1990s, Canadian exports to Japan declined again to $8.1 billion in 2003 from $8.4 billion in 2002. In 2003, Canada exported $1.4 billion in services and imported $1.9 billion[44]. The long-term trend in Japan is toward a growing demand for cost-competitive and innovative imports, which represents a significant market opportunity for Canadian exporters. The Asia Pacific region has been the fastest growing trade block over the past three decades though it had experienced a downturn in 1998 and extended after shocks. East Asia is

---

[43] Export Development Council: The Canadian Apparel Industry, EDC, 2000 (http://www.edc.ca).

[44] Government of Canada: Report on Canada's International Market Access Priorities- 2004, Department of Foreign Affairs and International Trade, Opening doors to the world, Chapter 6, 2004.

the principal export market for American goods. The transpacific trade has grown over 50 percent of its transatlantic trade by the end of the 20th century.

REFERENCES

Barro Robert J (1991), Economic Growth in a Cross Section of Countries, *Quarterly Journal of Economics*, 106, pp 407-443.

Beaulieu, Eugene, Yatawara, Ravindra and Wang, Wei Guo: Who Supports Free Trade in Latin America?, *The World Economy*, Vol. 28, No. 7, 2005, 941-958.

Bruce Owen M (2003): *Competition Policy in Latin America, Institute of Economic Policy Research*, Stanford University, Working Paper # 268.

Collie David and Hviid Morten(1993), Export Subsidies as Signals of Competitiveness, *Scandinavian Journal of Economics*, Vol.95, No.3, pp 327-339.

Edwards S (1992), Trade orientation, Distortions and Growth in Developing Countries, *Journal of Development Economics*, 39, pp 31-57.

Frankel Jaffery A and Romer David (1999): Does Trade Cause Growth? *American Economic Review*, Vol. 89, No. 3, pp 379-399.

Haar Jerry and Buonafina Moria Ortiz (2002), Entrepreneurial Exporters: The Canadian Experience, *The International Trade Journal*, Vol. 16, No.1. pp 31-71.

Kamin Steven B(1998), *A Multi Country Comparison of the Linkages between Inflation and Exchange Rate Competitiveness*, Federal Reserve bank of US, International Finance Discussion Paper No. 603.

Omen C (1999): *Policy Competition and Foreign Direct Investment*, OECD Development Centre, OECD, Paris.

Perroni Carlo and Whalley John (1996), How Severe is the Global Retaliation Risk under Increasing Regionalism, *American Economic Review*, Vol. 86, No. 2, pp 57-61.

Rajagopal (2005), Institutional Reforms and Trade Competitiveness in Latin America, *Applied Econometrics and International Development*, Vol. 5, No.1 pp 45-64.

Sanchez Blanca R and Clavo Marta Bengoa (2003): Foreign Direct Investment, Economic Freedom and Growth, *European Journal of Political Economy*, Vol. 19, No. 3, September, pp. 529-545.

Tussie, Diana (1987): *The Less Developed Countries and the World Trading System: A Challenge to the GATT*. New York: St. Martin's Press.

Vogel David (1997): Trading Up and Governing Across – Transnational Governance and Environment Protection, *Journal of European Public Policy*, Vol.4, No.4, pp 556-571.

Zheng Ping, Siler Pamela and Giorgioni G (2004): FDI and the Export Performance of Chinese Indigenous Firms: A Regonal Approach, *Journal of Chinese Economic and Business Studies*, Vol. 2, No.1, pp 55-71.

Chapter 6

MODES OF ENTRY IN A GLOBAL MARKETPLACE

A firm, which would like to involve itself in international business, may look for its entry into international marketing in many possible ways including exporting, licensing, franchising, or as a production firm with multi-national plant locations. However, at any level of market entry the managerial trade-off lies between extent of risk and operational control. The low intensity modes of entry minimize risk, *e.g.* contracting with a local distributor requires no investment in the destination country market as the local distributors may own offices, distribution facilities, sales personnel, or marketing campaigns. Under the normal arrangement, whereby the distributor takes title to the goods or purchases them as they leave the production facility of the international company, there is not even a credit risk, assuming that the distributor has offered a letter of credit from his bank. At the same time such arrangement to enter a destination country may minimize control along with the risk factor. In many cases, low-intensity modes of market participation cut off the international firm with information network while operational controls can only be obtained through higher-intensity modes of market participation, involving investments in local executives, distribution, and marketing programs.

Breakfast cereal, a relatively new introduction to the Bulgarian market, is the fastest growing sector in the Bulgarian bakery products market. According to a research study[1], ready-to-eat breakfast cereals grew by 90 percent in value terms during 2000-2005 and the market grew by approximately 14 percent just in 2005. Despite this impressive growth, cereal consumption in Bulgaria is low compared to other countries, which illustrates the immaturity of the market and its potential for the future. Besides the "novelty" of breakfast cereals, a key reason for the success of breakfast cereals in Bulgaria is their healthy image, which manufacturers have carefully created by illustrating that their products are part of a balanced diet. Although the concept of health and wellness is growing in popularity in Bulgaria, consumers still need additional education on the subject. The foreign cereal manufacturing companies like Nestle, Kraft, Kellogg and General Mills etc. have therefore invested heavily in radio and television advertising to promote a healthy image for their products and attract health conscious consumers. These companies have also set up demonstrations in supermarkets that are designed to educate consumers on the health benefits of breakfast cereals. By using samples and other promotional materials, manufacturers have tried to inspire trials and eventually repeat purchases of their products. These campaigns mainly

---

[1] Euromonitor (2006): Breakfast Cereals Boom in Bulgaria, January.

targeted the bigger cities, where consumers are generally more willing to try new products. The entry of foreign brands in the breakfast cereals in Bulgaria is further moved ahead by the fast expansion of supermarkets and the development of this distribution channel over the next several years will play a crucial role in making breakfast cereals more widely available[2].

Many companies begin their internationalization opportunistically through a variety of arrangements that may be described as "piggybacking," because they all involve taking advantage of a channel to an international market rather than selecting the country-market in a more conventional manner. Piggybacking is an interesting development. The method means that organizations with little exporting skill may use the services of one that has. Another form is the consolidation of orders by a number of companies in order to take advantage of bulk buying. Normally these would be geographically adjacent or able to be served, say, on an air route. The fertilizer manufacturers of Zimbabwe, for example, could piggyback with the South Africans who both import potassium from outside their respective countries. Such practices may be noticed as American breakfast cereal products like Post from the owners of the leading US brand, which entered the Mexican market via their subsidiary Kraft rather than directly from USA, thus leading to the rather bizarre situation of packs of breakfast cereals with English language packaging covered with stickers in Spanish. The most common form of piggybacking is to internationalize by serving a customer who is more international than the vendor firm. Thus, a customer requests an order, delivery, or service in more than one country, and the supplier starts selling internationally in order to retain the customer and increases its penetration of the account. This is particularly common in the case of business-to-business companies and technology-oriented start-ups[3]. The innovative concept of market entry strategy is based on moving with *consumer space* which indicates that foreign firms enter the destination market by developing adequate consumer awareness on the products and services prior to launch. This strategy is followed largely by the fast moving consumer goods manufacturing companies and such practice is termed as go-to-market strategy. Go-to-market planning enables the firm to achieve higher margins, accelerated revenue growth and increased customer satisfaction through existing sales channels. An effective go-to-market strategy aligns products & services, processes, and partners with customers and markets to deliver brand promise, the desired customer experience, and tangible value. Go-to-market strategy services help technology suppliers overcome market challenges.

Anti-ageing products are driving growth in Hong Kong's skin care market, on the back of increasing consumer interest in premium products and the development of consumer-focused cosmetics retailing. Consumer interest in premium products has been spurred, in part, by recent media reports on the safety of chemicals present in some skin care products. Catching on to this consumer trend, manufacturers have been introducing more premium anti-ageing products containing rare ingredients, and products benefiting from more advanced technology, to the market. This has generated greater consumer interest in premium quality products and has provided a further boost to the market. Guerlain, for example, is expected to launch a new skin care cream in 2006, which is based on a rare orchid extract and is expected to retail for more than US$350. Further, a recent entrant to Hong Kong's skin care market, Sulwhasoo which is a premium herbal based brand from Amore Pacific of Korea that draws on Oriental medicine by using a unique compound of five herbs to deliver a range of products targeted at

---

[2] *Ibid.*
[3] David Arnold (2003): *The Mirage of Global Marketing: How Globalizing Companies can Succeed as Markets Localize*, Financial Times Prentice Hall, Upper Saddle River, NJ, 24-65.

women over 35. The value driver of growth in the anti-ageing products market in Hong Kong is the trend towards concept stores and beauty boutiques, which are retail outlets designed to emphasize the experiential aspects of premium cosmetic products. Developed to attract new customers and gain their loyalty in Hong Kong's increasingly competitive market, these brand-specific beauty salons and spas, not only engage in a highly personalized product sales process, but also provide make-up and skin care services. Since 2004, major players, such as Kose, L'Oréal, H2O and cult brand Aesop, have set up concept stores around the city, in the hopes of developing a loyal customer base[4]. Such retail strategy where concept of the product is delivered with practical experience on it establishes the go-to-market strategy on consumer space.

Some firms who are aggressive have clearly defined plans and strategy, including product, price, promotion, and distribution and research elements. Passiveness versus aggressiveness depends on the motivation to export. In countries like Tanzania and Zambia, which have embarked on structural adjustment programs, organizations are being encouraged to export, motivated by foreign exchange earnings potential, saturated domestic markets, growth and expansion objectives, and the need to repay debts incurred by the borrowings to finance the programs. The type of export response is dependent on how the pressures are perceived by the decision maker. The degree of involvement in foreign operations depends on "endogenous versus exogenous" motivating factors, that is, whether the motivations were a result of active or aggressive behavior based on the firm's internal situation (endogenous) or a result of reactive environmental changes (exogenous)[5]. There is certainly no single strategy that fits all firms, products and markets. The competitive strategy for an established firm to start a new venture and launch a new product must be shaped by the characteristics of the firm, the market, and other environmental factors. Market entry through expansion of the company draws many challenges to firms considering new business options. Capitalizing on overseas markets often opens doors to new levels of top and bottom line growth. Moreover, introducing a new product or service into a new market is an even bigger strategic challenge. A Successful Entry strategy may conceptualize and implement well structured entry processes to drive future growth, explore diversified stream of revenues and augment profit margins. It also addresses new competitors, customers, partners, suppliers and other market dynamics. However, there are five major modes which a foreign firm may apply to enter in the international markets. These modes of entry include exporting, contractual agreement, joint venture, strategic alliance and wholly owned subsidiaries.

EXPORTING

A firm may organize indirect export through the intermediaries or export agents of the parent country. On the contrary, in direct exporting foreign markets are reached by exporters through agents located outside their parent markets. Exporting is a low risk-low investment strategy wherein a company may minimize the risk of dealing internationally by exporting domestically manufactured products either by minimal response to inquiries or by systematic

---

[4] Olivier Hofmann (2006), Anti-ageing Skin Cream Booms in Hong Kong, Euromonitor, May (online edition).
[5] Piercy, N (1982), Company Internationalization: Active and Reactive Exporting". *European Journal of Marketing*, 15 (3), 26-40.

development of demand in foreign markets. Exporting activity requires small capital for quick start. Exporting is also a good way to gain international experience. A major part of the overseas involvement of large firms is through export trade managed by the various channels involved in the process. The channels involved in direct and indirect exporting are listed in Table 15.1.

Some companies, which occasionally carry out export activities typically, use the services of the broker. Brokers are the middlemen who bring buyers and sellers in contact for a negotiated commission or brokerage. They are just the trade facilitators and do not take the ownership of the product. These brokers operate in international markets independently and do not belong to any firm. The manufacturer's export agent (MEA) may be an exclusive agent engaged by the firm to offer services as desired by the firm. The MEA's are vested with the right to take marketing decisions on behalf of the firm, arrange negotiations and trade agreements and the delivery of the consignment to the buyer.

Table 15.1. Export Channels

Indirect Exporting	Direct Exporting
Broker	Representative
Manufacturer's Export Agent	Merchant Middlemen
Combination Export Manager	Company Sales Manager
Group Export Forum	Own Distribution Network
Domestic Middlemen	
Company Based Managers	

The Combination Export Manager (CEM) provides services over and above the broker and the MEA by way of taking over the entire export operations of a firm on a commission basis. The export operations involve a variety of activities like identifying the country, markets, analyzing consumer behavior, product designing, technological improvements, competitive pricing, distribution, promotion, negotiations with the governments of countries, public relations and collecting marketing information. The group export forums are associations of exporters who collectively manage to export activities. These forums are recognized by the government of the parent country and provide admissible concessions on export activities like licensing, taxes and duties infrastructure, etc. Middlemen who have a base in the parent country of the exporting firm also function as one of the channels for indirect exports. The company-based managers are the salaried personnel of the exporting firm and possess the responsibility of total export management. In direct exporting activities, the firm appoints its own export representatives for conducting the export operations in the respective markets or countries. The Merchant Middlemen are a type of intermediary based in foreign markets that buy products on their own and resell these to the identified countries functioning with substantial operational managers. They may also take up export activities without involving any indirect channel. Such offices may also be networked as an effective distribution channel for a region in order to cater to identify countries thereof.

Li & Fung, Hong Kong's largest export trading company, has been an innovator in supply-chain management. It performs the higher-value-added tasks such as design and quality control in Hong Kong, and outsources the lower-value-added tasks to the best possible locations around the world. To produce a garment, for example, the company might purchase yarn from Korea that will be woven and dyed in Taiwan, then shipped to Thailand for final assembly, where it will be matched with zippers from a Japanese company. The corporate philosophy of Li & Fung envisages that for every order, the goal is to customize the value chain to meet the customer's specific needs. The organizational approaches that keep the company towards growth in profits and size largely set around small customer-focused units, competitive incentives and compensation structure and it's leaning towards venture capital strategy as a vehicle for business development[6]. The company operates in partnership with customers to cater to their needs of competitive pricing, quality, on-time delivery, as well as ethical sourcing. The company manages the logistics of producing and exporting private label consumer goods across many producers and countries[7].

The firms choosing to enter the international markets through exporting activities may choose to engage the goods listed under open general license which does not involve heavy documentation process. However the goods that are not controlled, regulated or prohibited by other government departments need to be reported to customs prior to export by means of export declaration. On the contrary regardless of their value, export of all goods that are controlled, regulated, or prohibited need to be supported by valid permits, licenses, or certificates required by the government departments or agencies that regulate the export of these goods. A firm also opts for direct exporting as a platform to enter into the destination country. This approach is the most ambitious and difficult as the exporting firm handles every aspect of the exporting process independently from market research and planning to foreign distribution and collections. Consequently, a significant commitment of management time and attention is required to achieve good results. However, this approach may lead to maximum profits, higher control and long-term growth.

CONTRACTUAL AGREEMENT

There are several types of contractual agreements including patent licensing agreement, turnkey operation, co-production agreement, management contract, and licensing. The patent licensing agreement is based on either a fixed fee or a royalty-based agreement and delivering managerial training on manufacturing and quality control process. The plant construction, personnel training, and initial production runs on a fixed-fee or cost-plus arrangement and are be covered under a turn-key operation agreement. The co-production agreement was one of the popular practices among the Soviet-bloc countries, where plants were built and then paid for with part of the output. In the Middle East, the management contract requires that an MNC provide key personnel to operate the foreign enterprise for a fee until local people acquire the ability to manage the business independently.

---

[6] Fung Victor and Magretta Victor (1998), Fast Global and Entrepreneurial: Supply Chain Management- Hong Kong Style, Harvard Business Review, September.
[7] Corporate website, Li & Fung http://www.lifung.com

LICENSING

This is one of the common tools of franchising a firm to set quality and operational control standards. In the past, multinational companies used licensing for many reasons. One of the major reasons may be towards the use of a trademark of the company. Licensing may be understood as one of the varieties of contractual agreements whereby a multinational firm makes available intangible assets such as patents, trade secrets, know-how, trademarks, and company name to foreign companies in return for royalties or other forms of payment. Transfer of these assets is usually accompanied by technical services to ensure their proper use. It also helps in regulating the import and export operations of firms in such countries or regions where trade restrictions prohibit the movement of products. Some of the advantages of licensing are as follows:

- Licensing is a quick and easy entry tool with little capital investment in the foreign markets
- Some countries offer licensing as the only means of tapping the market.
- Licensing is also considered to be an effective tool for life extension of products during their stage of maturity in order of their life cycle.
- Licensing is a good alternative to start foreign production and marketing activity in a destination country which has economic inflation, shortages of skilled-labor, increasing domestic and foreign governmental regulation and restriction, and severe international competition.
- In the licensing arrangement periodic royalties are guaranteed, whereas shared income from investment fluctuates and stays risky.
- The company which has a strong domestic base can benefit through licensing arrangement in developing customized products without expensive research.
- Licensing provides an alternative when exports are no longer profitable because of intense competition.
- Licensing can reduce transportation costs and help promoting exports in non-competitive markets.
- One of the major advantages of licensing is the immunity over stringent political intervention as expropriation.

On the contrary, the economic liberalization policy envisages the de-licensing of goods and services (notified) for mutual business growth. Under contract manufacturing, a firm gets its products manufactured by an independent local firm as per the agreement. Such export mechanism is chosen by the firms typically where the marketing potential seems to be low with tariff walls that are too high. Assembling involves the import of raw material and mechanical parts for manufacturing any product. Such an operation is usually labor intensive, despite high capital investment in business. This mode of entry into international marketing would be advantageous in countries which do not impose heavy import duties and which encourage free exports. Assembling firms take the benefit of low wage rates by shifting labor intensive operations to the foreign market that results in a lower final price of the product. Largely, local laws of a country play a big role in the decision-making for setting up an assembling unit in foreign country.

Procter & Gamble offered most of its exceptional growth through continuous innovation and building global research facilities. The company lagged behind in achieving its growth objectives by spending greater and greater amounts on research and development for smaller and smaller payoffs during 2000. This situation revolutionized the strategic management process of the company to dispense with the company's age-old *invent it ourselves* approach and reorient to innovation following *connect and develop* model. Now, the company collaborates with suppliers, competitors, scientists, entrepreneurs, and others, systematically scouring the world for proven technologies, packages, and products that P&G can improve, scale up, and market, either on its own or in partnership with other companies. The *connect and develop* approach, brought P&G an increase of about 60 percent productivity through research and development. In the past two years, P&G launched many new products for which some aspect of development came from outside the company[8]. Among most successful connect-and-develop products of the company include Oil of Olay, Tide, Crest dental products and Mr. Clean Magic Eraser. The success of this strategy further revealed in launching a unique portfolio in the US Market. The company that revolutionized the laundry industry with the launch of Tide(R) in 1946 has begun offering an on-premise laundry (OPL) and daily cleaners program to hotels in select markets across the United States. Marketed under the P&G Pro Line(TM) brand name, the Lodging Program aims to leverage reputation of the company as a leader in home and commercial cleaning products to help hotel housekeeping staffs discover how the company's top-performing brands maximize productivity and increase guest satisfaction. The program is built around popular household-name laundry brands including Tide, Downy(R), and Clorox(R) Bleach, as well as daily cleaners including Spic and Span(R) 3-in-1 Disinfecting All-Purpose Spray and Glass Cleaner and Comet(R) Disinfecting Bathroom Cleaner. The Lodging Program presents an alternative to the housekeeping departments of lodging establishments[9].

Technology licensing is a contractual arrangement in which the licensor's patents, trademarks, service marks, copyrights, trade secrets, or other intellectual property may be sold or made available to a licensee for compensation that is negotiated in advance between the parties. A technology licensing agreement usually enables a firm to enter a foreign market quickly, and poses fewer financial and legal risks than owning and operating a foreign manufacturing facility or participating in an overseas joint venture. In considering the licensing of technology, it is important to remember that foreign licensees may attempt to use the licensed technology to manufacture products in direct competition with the licensor or its other licensees.

FRANCHISING

The practice of franchising is widely experienced by multinational retail food chains particularly in the fast food sector. Franchising is emerging as a highly effective strategy for business growth, local employment, and regional economic development. However, the quest for global markets through franchising has traditionally relied on employing just three generic

---

[8] Also see Hustom Larry and Sakkab Nabil (2006), Connect and Develop: Inside Proctor and Gamble's New Model for Innovation, Harvard Business Review, May.

[9] Proctor and Gamble Corporate web site: P & G Launches Loading Program in Selected US Markets, News November 14, 2005 http://www.pg.com

franchising options including direct franchising, master franchising and area development[10]. Significantly large percent of retail sales pass through chains that engage in franchising as many industries are being transformed as chains replace the mom-and-pop proprietors that used to sit on every street corner. Franchising strategy as a tool for managing restaurants in North America was initiated in the 1930s and in the mid-1940s Dairy Queen was set-up followed by McDonald's, Pizza Hut and Kentucky Fried Chicken in the 1950s and 1960s. These firms observed quick expansion of their business through franchising operations[11]. Franchising is primarily seen as a foreign concept in emerging markets which attracts both positive and negative attention. Franchisees evaluate such business negotiation in reference to the well-being of small businesses, socio-economic, socio-cultural well-being, and employment opportunity as major decision factors. Some of these factors were associated with patronage behavior and the associated residual feeling[12].

Traditional franchise research suggests that there is a dichotomy in the sources of power available to franchisors, that is, coercive or non-coercive sources of power. Hence, franchise partner selection, the franchise relationship and the use of master/area franchising emerge from the qualitative findings as further control mechanisms available to international retail franchisors. In selection of franchisees, overseas firms face many cultural problems which require firms to acquire significant knowledge on the social and cultural diversities to choose a retailer. The greater the cultural distance, the more challenges the firm has to face in terms of upgrading and adapting its prior knowledge to local needs[13]. As international retailers continue to employ franchising as a major method of market entry, management and control of these international retail franchise networks becomes of significant importance to measure their business performance[14]. In franchisee stores, customer satisfaction is a key to brand growth, while the positive effect of customer satisfaction on brand revenue performance is moderated by the extent of franchising within each brand. However, despite business convenience for the overseas firms and economic importance of franchising to the region, not enough contributions were made to evaluate the factors influencing franchisee value, generating store attractiveness, customer satisfaction and services quality through empirical investigation[15].

Franchise Administration

Multinational retail chains have successfully adopted franchising as an expansion tool in overseas markets after examining its advantages. The advantages of franchising include allowing the firm to overcome resource constraints of limited capital and thin the ranks of

---

[10] Preble, J F and Hoffman, R C (2006), Strategies for business format franchisors to expand into global markets, *Journal of Marketing Channels*, 13 (3), 29-50.

[11] Bradach J L (1998), *Franchise organizations*, Harvard Business School Press, Boston, MA.

[12] Paswan A K and Kantamneni P S (2004), Public opinion and franchising in an emerging market, *Asia Pacific Journal of Marketing and Logistics*, 16 (2), 46-61.

[13] Altinay, L and Wang, C L (2007), The role of prior knowledge in international franchise partner recruitment, *International Journal of Service Industry Management*, 17 (5), 430-443.

[14] Doherty, A M and Alexander, N (2006), Power and control in international retail franchising, *European Journal of Marketing*, 40 (11-12), 1292-1316.

[15] Rajagopal (2007), Optimizing Franchisee Sales and Business Performance, *Journal of Retail and Leisure Property*, 6 (4), 341-360.

experienced managers. Franchising also provides a means of trading off complex transfer functions, and franchisees are more efficient in performing functions whose average cost curve turns up relatively quickly. It obviates the need for monitoring and its attendant costs because franchisees have invested their own capital and are motivated to work hard for profitability[16]. The franchise contract, support mechanisms, franchise partner selection, the franchise relationship and the use of master/area franchising were found to be the major methods by which international retail franchisors exert control over their franchise networks. While coercive and non-coercive sources of power were identified in the form of the franchise contract and support mechanisms, the paper also identifies sources of relationship power and organizational power[17].

Although franchisors value the benefits of the mix of ownership types and do maintain that mix over time, there is some evidence of a greater tendency to permanently convert existing franchised outlets to company-owned outlets as fast food systems mature and gain greater access to resources. Franchising offers substantial efficiencies in promotion and advertising by leveraging the value of a trademark and brand image. Moreover, it helps in managing one's risks, because franchisors can eventually convert profitable franchise locations into company-owned operations though this strategy raises certain ethical concerns. Globalization has moved the multi-brand concepts and co-branding in franchising as a strategy to stimulate and rejuvenate growth in a mature retail food franchising sector. Development trends such as multiple unit franchising, mobile franchising and co-branding, occur because of the sector's need to find new means of expansion beyond the standard model of franchising[18].

Franchising and Customer Value

It has been observed that franchisees often do not recognize that what influences customer satisfaction is not the same as what engenders store loyalty, and consequently do not allocate scarce resources systematically among tactics influencing one or the other. Unless they are vigilant to changing consumer behavior patterns, they will not be able to isolate in their strategy the elements of the retail mix that could insulate their loyal customers from responding to competitors' special offers[19]. The growth of franchising is regarded as having significant implications for development of retailing. Shopping behavior at franchisee outlets prompts sequential relationship among tourists leading to shopping satisfaction through the perceived values on recreational attractions and store loyalty. Thus, managers may think of significant franchisee expansion on demographic and territorial basis for enhancing the loyalty in shopping behavior. Franchising in sub-urban marketplace is a relatively recent phenomenon which demands new retail infrastructures and recreational facilities to attract leisure shopping. The customer satisfaction has become one of the

---

[16] Tikoo S (1996), Assessing the franchise option, *Business Horizon*, 39 (3), 78-82.
[17] Doherty, A M and Alexander, N (2006), Power and control in international retail franchising, *European Journal of Marketing*, 40 (11-12), 1292-1316.
[18] Wright O; Frazer L and Merrilees, B (2007), McCafe: The McDonald's co-branding experience, *The Journal of Brand Management*, 14 (6), 442-457.
[19] Miranda M, Konya L and Havira I (2005), Shopper's satisfaction levels are not only the key to store loyalty, *Marketing Intelligence and Planning*, 23 (2), 220-232.

measures of retailing performance. Leisure eating behavior in restaurants and buying souvenirs, fashion products and high value products indicates that the retailing strategy is becoming more customer-centric at franchisee outlets[20].

The customer value concept is utilized to assess product performance and to determine the competitive structure of the new products. The analytical approach to the franchisee-based retailing structure based on customer value may be fitted well within the microeconomic framework. The measure of customer value as the product efficiency may be viewed from the customer's perspective towards a ratio of outputs (e.g., perceived use value, resale value, reliability, safety, comfort) that customers obtain from a product relative to inputs (price, running costs) that customers have to deliver in exchange. The efficiency value derived can be understood as the return on the franchisees investment. Franchisee stores offering a maximum customer value relative to all other alternatives in the market are characterized as efficient. Different efficient products may create value in different ways using different strategies (output-input combinations). Each efficient product can be viewed as a benchmark for a distinct sub-market. Jointly, these products form the efficient frontier, which serves as a reference function for the inefficient products[21].

In the most optimistic settings, such value measures are observed to be generated by franchisor firms for new franchisees in view of augmenting the business-to-business relationship and market expansion strategies of the firm. The fast moving food sector has a quick shelf turnover at relatively low cost and quick buying decisions of consumers. The rate of change within this market sector continues apace, particularly in the areas of innovation and value addition to the customers. A firm may combine innovation and technologies in the franchising strategy to create business value and competitive gains. New and modern franchisees have moved rapidly into the growing fast moving consumer goods retail market. The fast food retailing sector is largely attracted by the innovations in product attributes and packaging besides the price sensitivity. It has been observed that the effects of the franchising decisions of foreign firms are systematically moderated by elements of the marketing strategy associated with the innovative retailing and customer relationship competencies of franchisee firms[22].

Performance Measures in Franchising

The success of franchising also depends on the compensation arrangements followed in the franchise relationship. Consistent with predictions suggested by agency theory, the compensation arrangements studied appear to function as substitutes. It has been observed that the value of the services provided by franchisors to franchisees strongly affects the compensation arrangements studied, so a capital goal of these arrangements is to recover the costs of the services offered by franchisors[23]. In addition, two dimensions of transactional

[20] Rajagopal (2006[b]), Leisure shopping behavior and recreational retailing: a symbiotic analysis of marketplace strategy and consumer response, *Journal of Hospitality and Leisure Marketing*, 15 (2), 5-31.
[21] Bauer H H, Hammerschmidt M and Staat M (2004), A*nalyzing product efficiency: A customer oriented approach*, University of Mannheim, February.
[22] Steenkamp Jan-Benedict E M and Gielens K (2003), Consumers and market drivers of trial probability of new consumer packaged goods, *Journal of Consumer Research*, 30 (3), December, 368-384.
[23] Vázquez, L (2005), Up-front franchise fees and ongoing variable payments as substitutes: an agency perspective, *Review of Industrial Organization*, 26 (4), 445-460.

quality are identified from the franchisee perspective that includes contents and assistance. On the other hand, these dimensions of transactional quality from the franchisor's point of view refer to formality and identify business opportunities while the relationship quality identifies variables such as trust between cooperation partners, mutual commitment, and relational sensitivity. The franchise system has assumed great importance as a pattern for the expansion of services and, just like any other organization, needs to preserve the quality of the business concept to achieve overall success[24].

The success of franchise systems is usually explained by referring to franchisees' incentives, that is, residual claims to profit and empowerment through delegation. Of many human factors, psychological and social dimensions of franchisees' incentives, employed managers' self-efficacy, system commitment, and system conformity performance plays distinct roles in driving the franchisee outlets successful and sustain competitive pressures. Franchising has met or exceeded the growth expectations, generating very high annual sales in the developing countries. However, considerable regional differences in franchising activities do exist. The business sectors experiencing the most franchising growth are retail and restaurants. Franchising firms tend to export their business formats to neighboring countries or to countries with similar cultural characteristics[25]. As franchisees are perceived to be independent and self-employed entrepreneurs, their ongoing development is frequently overlooked or poorly managed; particularly compared with the development opportunities for corporate staff in their support offices. However, the concern is that franchisees do not prioritize their own professional development due to their inability to diagnose and source appropriate training, their focus on immediate operational needs and a lack of free time to undergo development activities. As primary income generators of franchise businesses organizational effectiveness and growth of the entire organization rests on the abilities of the franchisees[26].

Franchising is not a business itself, but a way of doing business. It is essentially a marketing concept introducing an innovative method of manufacturing and distributing goods and services. Franchising is a business relationship in which the franchisor (the owner of the business providing the product or service) assigns to independent entrepreneur (the franchisee) the legal right to manufacture, market and distribute the franchisor's goods or service using the brand name for an agreed period of time. The International Franchise Association defines franchising as a continuing relationship in which the franchisor provides a licensed privilege to do business, plus assistance in organizing training, merchandising and management in return for a consideration from the franchisee. Franchising has become popular because it allows a much greater degree of control over the marketing efforts in the foreign country. In franchising, product lines and customer service are standardized, two important features from a marketing perspective though cultural differences might require adaptation. Franchising can offer people looking at self-employment a greater chance of success than starting their own businesses, but it is a path that many people are not aware is open to them. A franchisor's main ongoing commitment to his franchisees is to provide

[24] Monroy, M F and Alzola, L M (2005), An analysis of quality management in franchise systems, *European Journal of Marketing*, 39 (5-6), 585-605.
[25] Hoffman R C and Preble J F (2004), Global franchising: current status and future challenges, *Journal of Services Marketing*, 18 (2), 101-113.
[26] Paul D (2004), Maximizing productivity and capability: issues of professional development for franchisees, *International Journal of Productivity and Performance Management*, 53 (4), 345-352.

support. A support program should be well defined prior to joining a given franchise group and is likely to cover areas such as staff issues, marketing and system compliance. There are four possible models of franchising as discussed below :

- Manufacturer-Retailer: Where the retailer as franchisee sells the franchisor's product directly to the public. (e.g. Automobile dealerships).
- Manufacturer-Wholesaler: Where the franchisee under license manufactures and distributes the franchisor's product (e.g. Soft drink bottling arrangements).
- Wholesaler-Retailer: Where the retailer as franchisee purchases products for retail sale from a franchisor wholesaler. (e.g. Hardware equipments and automotive product stores)
- Retailer-Retailer: Where the franchisor markets a service, or a product, under a common name and standardized system, through a network of franchisees.

The first two categories cited above are often referred to as product and trade name franchises. These include arrangements in which franchisees are granted the right to distribute a manufacturer's product within a specified territory or at a specific location, generally with the use of the manufacturer's identifying name or trademark, in exchange for fees or royalties. The business format franchise, however, differs from product and trade name franchises through the use of a format, or a comprehensive system for the conduct of the business, including such elements as business planning, management system, location, appearance and image, and quality of goods.

Papa John's has recently expanded its business in Edinburgh and Glasgow (UK). Its new-look stores compete with more established names like Pizza Hut and Domino's Pizza. The competition in the fast food market is fierce and challenging for potential franchisees. Papa John's operates a comprehensive marketing and public relations campaign for all stores. Launch events typically include a 'grand opening' day with entertainment, free pizzas and visits from local dignitaries. It also runs national marketing campaigns and special offers, backed up by a marketing team to help franchisees promote their stores at a local level. Franchisees can expect to pay extra for those services. The prospective franchisees need to undergo a three-stage interview process which includes an initial telephone interview to ascertain suitability and solvency of applicants, an informal meeting and presentation of factual details including an outline of potential working hours and staffing requirements and a more formal gathering to discuss site positioning and to release paperwork, including a legal/franchise agreement and a business plan template to present to the bank. The company has proposed a 5 percent royalty fee on the store's weekly net sales figures, and a 4 percent marketing fee is also charged on its weekly net sales[27].

There are many benefits to becoming a franchisee; the major ones are listed below:

- The franchisor provides detailed consultation and training in operating the business as well as choosing locations for the business

---

[27] For details on the case study please see Case Study:Papa John's, New Business.Com http://www. newbusiness.co.uk/cgi-bin/showArticle.pl?id=3562

- The franchisee benefits from operating under the established brand image and reputation of the franchisor

- The franchisees usually need less capital than they would if they were setting up a business independently because the franchisors, through their pilot operations and buying power, will have eliminated unnecessary expenses.

- The franchisor helps the franchisee obtain occupation rights to the trading location, comply with planning (zoning) laws, prepare plans for layouts, plan ergonomics and refurbishment, and provide general assistance in calculating the correct level and mix of stock for the opening launch of the business.

- The franchisee taps into the bulk purchasing power and negotiating capacity made available by the franchisor by reason of the size of the franchised network.

- The franchisee has access to use of the franchisor's patents, trade marks, copyrights, trade secrets, and any secret processes or formulae.

- The franchisee has the benefit of the franchisor's continuous research and development programs, which are designed to improve the business and keep it up-to-date and competitive.

One of the drawbacks of franchising is the need for careful and continuous quality control. Such close supervision of the various aspects of distant operations requires well-developed global management systems and labor-intensive monitoring. Inevitably, the relationship between the franchisor and franchisee must involve the imposition of controls. These controls will regulate the quality of the service or products to be provided or sold by the franchisee to the consumer. As the effective managerial skills are required, international franchising has become successful largely among those enterprises which have long experience with franchising at home before venturing out in international markets.

JOINT VENTURES

A joint venture involves partnership between two or more business firms interested in pooling their resources and expertise to achieve a common goal. The risks and rewards of the enterprise are also shared. The reasons for forming a joint venture may include business expansion, development of new products or moving into new markets, particularly overseas. The joint venture may offer more resources, increased capacity of production, enhanced technical expertise and established markets and distribution channels. Entry into an international market would be possible either as a wholly owned subsidiary of any firm or as a joint venture. Joint ventures provide the best partner-like manner of obtaining foreign trade income if the firm chooses to begin a business relationship with a firm in the host country. These two partners could agree upon a contract setting out the terms and conditions of how this will work. Alternatively, joint ventures may be set up as a separate joint venture business, possibly a new company. A joint venture company can be a very flexible option wherein partners own substantial resources in the company, and agree on a managing strategy. Firms of any size can use joint ventures to strengthen long-term relationships or to collaborate on short-term projects. A successful joint venture can offer:

- Access to new markets and distribution networks
- Increase in production capacity
- Risk sharing and control process policies among business partners
- Working with specialized staff and technology

However, partnering in business may also be complex. It may consume time and effort to build the right relationship while operational problems may grow with the following ideological and functional discrepancies:

- The objectives of the venture are not clear and communicated among the partnering firms
- There exists an imbalance in levels of expertise, investment or assets set into the venture by the different business partners
- Coordination problems of cross- cultural issues and management styles affecting the functional integration and workplace co-operation
- Lack of sufficient leadership and support in the early stages

Success in a joint venture depends on thorough research and analysis of aims and objectives. This should be followed up with effective communication of the business plan to everyone involved. International joint ventures are used in a wide variety of manufacturing, mining, and service industries and frequently involve technology licensing. The company looking for a joint venture invites foreign firms by issuing by a regional or global invitation to share stock ownership in the new unit. However, the control of the unit will rest with the companies accepting either a minority or a majority position. Largely, multi-national companies prefer wholly owned subsidiaries for effective control. A major potential drawback of joint ventures, especially in countries that limit foreign companies to minority participation, is the loss of effective managerial control. This can result in reduced profits, increased operating costs, inferior product quality, exposure to product liability, and environmental litigation and fines. When firms decide to create a joint venture, the terms and conditions need to set out in a written agreement. This will help prevent any misunderstandings once the joint venture is up and running. A written agreement should cover:

- The structure of the joint venture
- The objectives of the joint venture
- Financial contributions, liabilities, distribution of profit, and other matters related to corporate finance and accounts
- Protocol on transfer assets or employees in or out of the joint venture
- Ownership of intellectual property created by the joint venture
- Management and control of operational issues
- Responsibilities, tasks and processes to be followed in production and operations activities
- Protocol on managing liabilities, sharing of profits and losses
- Policy and process of disputes settlement between the partnering firms in the joint venture, and

- Exit policies to being the joint venture to an end and cause and effect management at post-closure.

Ranbaxy Laboratories Limited (Ranbaxy) has raised its equity stake in Nihon Pharmaceutical Industry Co., Ltd. (NPI), a Joint Venture between Ranbaxy and Nippon Chemiphar Co. Ltd. (NC), from the present 10% to 50%. With this enhancement, NPI will become a 50:50 Joint Venture between Ranbaxy and NC. Ranbaxy and NC have signed the agreement on November 11, 2005. The increasing financial stakes of Ranbaxy in the shareholding of the joint venture reinforces the Company's strong commitment to the Japanese market. Further, the new structure recognizes the equal commitment of both partners and their intent to grow the generics business in Japan, in a collaborative manner. Ranbaxy and NPI have had a successful relationship. This logical move by Ranbaxy to enhance its stake flows from the increased comfort level of both partners and take the business to higher levels of performance. The 50:50 JV exemplifies the synergy and the strengths, which the respective companies bring to the Joint Venture. In Japanese ethical pharmaceutical industry, NC is one of the first companies to recognize the importance of generics and to make the generic business a pillar of the company's business. NC intends to be a leading company in Japan's generics market. Both partners have a complementary role to play. NC provides the regulatory know how and in-depth knowledge of the Japanese market, while Ranbaxy brings to the table, its diversified and rich generics product pipeline along with its astute understanding of the global generics business[28].

Smaller firms often want to access a larger partner's resources such as a strong distribution network, specialist employees, and financial resources. The larger company might benefit from working with a more flexible, innovative partner or simply from access to new products or intellectual property (IP). Joint ventures offer mutual advantages for domestic and foreign firms to operate in a global competitive business environment sharing both capital and risk and by making use of mutual technical potentials. Japanese companies, for example, prefer entering into joint ventures with American firms as such arrangements help them to ensure against possible trade barriers. American firms, on the other hand like to venture with Japanese firms to explore product innovation at low-cost Japanese manufacturing technology, and make pace to enter a wide Asian market. The joint venture in this ways helps both the international firms to utilize established channels and to outperform potentially tough competitors in respective countries. House Foods and Takeda Pharmaceutical have signed a joint venture agreement on their beverage and food businesses. Under the terms of the agreement, the two companies will establish a new company, House Wellness Foods Corporation, with a capital of 100 million yen ($840,000), on April 2006. House Foods will have a 66% stake in the new company while Takeda Pharmaceutical will retain the remaining 34%. After the initial 18-month joint venture period, the new company will become a wholly owned House Foods subsidiary[29]. A joint venture serves as a center of resource appropriation and making a foreign firm's entry into a new terrain easier than other modes. It should not be viewed as a handy vehicle to reap money without effort, interest, or additional resources. In view of the above benefits, the joint ventures stand as a popular mode to seek entry in a foreign country.

---

[28] Ranbaxy Laboratorios Ltd.: Ranbaxy Consolidates Relationship with Japan JV Partner Nippon Chemiphar, Rainbaxy Press Release, November 11, 2005 http://www.ranbaxy.com/newsroom
[29] Aki Tsukioka: Joint venture agreement on food and beverages, Japan Corporate News Network, Feb. 27, 2006.

STRATEGIC ALLIANCE

A strategic alliance for international marketing is developed by pooling resources directly in collaboration. This strategy is more advantageous than joint venture. In this process the business partners bring together the specific skills of production, marketing and control in order to maximize their profit and have a major stake in the international business scenario. Many organizations have come to rely on alliances with key players in the marketplace as strategic ventures for maintaining a competitive advantage. These key relationships can help foster organizational learning, thus giving an edge over the competition. This serves as a primary motivation for alliance formation. A new trend of collaborative strategy in international business has gained popularity based on strategic alliance through which leading firms, particularly in high-tech industries gain mutual benefit. Strategic alliances are partial merger, but have comprehensive impact on the performance of the firm. They involve mutual dependence and shared decision making between two or more separate firms. Strategic alliances differ from joint ventures as they encompass selected activities within time limits. Strategic goals pursued through strategic alliances are product exchange or supply alliances, learning alliances in research and development and market positioning alliances[30]. There are some important types of alliance that can be set-up for optimizing the business. They are:

- Technology based alliances
- Production based alliances
- Distribution based alliances
- Resource based alliances

One way for a firm to enter into a foreign market is to create a strategic alliance. A global strategic alliance is an agreement among two or more independent firms to cooperate for the purpose of achieving common goals such as a competitive advantage or customer value creation. Strategic partnerships may emerge in many forms including research and development consortium, co-production alliance, co-marketing partnerships, cross-licensing and cross-equity arrangements. Such alliances do not result in formation of a separate corporate entity but equity joint ventures form new strategic allies as legal entities to do specified business. The emergence of strategic alliances in Canada and other industrialized countries are related to economies of scale or scope, resource pooling, and risk and cost sharing among alliance partners. They include globalization of the world economy, systemic technological change, and the growing acceptance of the view that competition, by itself, does not necessarily ensure optimum, innovation-led growth. While international alliances provide firms with strategic flexibility, enabling them to respond to changing market conditions, they can also be effective paths for achieving global scale in enterprise operations along with mergers and acquisitions and green field investment. The driving forces behind international strategic alliances include cost economizing in production and research and development, strengthening market presence, and accessing intangible assets[31]. In the recent trends of

---

[30] Schoenmakers, Wilfred and Duysters, Geert (2006), Learning in Strategic Technological Alliances, *Technology Analysis and Strategic Management*, 18 (2), 245-264.
[31] Nam-Hoon Kang and Kentaro Sakai (2005), International Strategic Alliances: Their Role in Industrial Globalisation; OECD, STI Working Paper # 2000/5

globalization, the practice of entering the international market through such alliances seems to be gearing up along with political support from developing countries. However, the companies having a larger share in the international market still reserve the right to entertain or not, any such alliances. Strategic alliances offer many advantages in business, of which some significant ones are as indicated below:

- The organizational efficiency will be improved with the flexibility and informality in strategic alliances
- Alliances developed strategically offer access to new markets and technologies
- The risk and expenses are shared among the allies reducing the impact of risk on the participating members
- The alliance would help the partners build their independent brand and manage retailing of goods and services
- Alliances can take various forms, from simple research and development deals to heavy budget projects.

Strategic alliances are especially useful for seeking entry into emerging markets. Foreign firms in emerging markets seek to optimize the market performance in global economy and strategic alliances appear to be the obvious solution for mutual benefit. Given this pattern of benefit, the strategic alliances of US and European manufacturing firms account for over half of the market entries into Latin America and Asia.

ING is one of the largest financial services companies among the prominent global firms, offering banking, insurance and asset management in over 50 countries. It has spread over its business to 60 million private, corporate and institutional clients in 60 countries with a workforce of over 115,000 people as in 2003. ING was founded in 1991 by a merger between *Nationale-Nederlanden* and *NMB Postbank Group* to become the first *bancassurer* of Netherlands. During the past 15 years ING has become multinational with very diverse international activities. The company holds insurance operations and asset-management activities in the Americas. It is well-established in the United States with retirement services, annuities and life insurances and has leading positions in non-life insurance in Canada and Mexico. Furthermore, the company is active in Chile, Brazil and Peru. The operating profits for the company in Americas have been increasing in €1310 million in 2003 to €1669 in 2004 before tax. In 2004, ING successfully repositioned itself in the wholesale banking market. The insurance business of the company in the Netherlands introduced a far-reaching plan to improve its customer service, with positive results so far. The business lines of the company further sharpened their focus on profitable top line growth, managing costs and risks and showing good bottom-line results. These four pillars are all equally important to generate above-average returns for shareholders. ING has diversified business activities in developing markets which offer a broad range of services in the fields of banking, insurance and asset management and has made its identity obvious in Asia/Pacific, Latin America and Central Europe amidst the competing local and multinational companies. In Latin America, ING is the largest insurer in Mexico and has important businesses in Chile and Brazil[32].

---

[32] Rajagopal (2005), Virtual Sales Offices for Insurance Services in Mexico: A Case of ING Comercial America, Discussion Case, ITESM, Mexico.

The convergence of business practices of the partnering firms often emerges as a major challenge to perform the alliance task as in international business arena partnering firms belong to different socio-cultural environments. Alliance managers must make difficult decisions about when to partner and with whom, as well as how to structure and manage the partnership. Managers who can leverage information and knowledge across each stage of the alliance process will find that a knowledge-based approach is critical to the success of any partnership. In U.S.-Japanese alliances in the past, for example, Japanese companies saw these partnerships as a way to learn from their partner, while their U.S. counterparts used these alliances as a substitute for more competitive skills, ultimately resulting in an erosion of their own internal skills. Therefore, with companies that look on alliances as a way of learning from their partners, practices that enable knowledge sharing, creation, dissemination and internalization become critical[33]. Cisco Systems and Polycom Inc. have a strategic agreement for joint development, licensing, and sales of Internet protocol (IP) telephony solutions. The objective of the alliance is to deliver enhanced IP telephones to enterprise customers; this agreement combines Polycom's leadership in audio conferencing technologies and Cisco's industry-leading expertise in IP networking and IP telephony. Based on this agreement, Polycom and Cisco have brought a Voice over IP (VoIP) conference phone to market that provides customers with industry-leading group conferencing capabilities within the Cisco IP Telephony environment[34].

WHOLLY-OWNED SUBSIDIARIES

The multi-national companies also plan to enter into a new international market establishing themselves in overseas markets by direct investment in a manufacturing or assembly subsidiary company. In view of the frequently changing economic, social and political conditions globally, these wholly-owned subsidiaries are highly risk averse. A wholly owned subsidiary in manufacturing can involve investment in a new manufacturing or assembly plant or the acquisition of an existing plant (such as Coca-Cola Company purchases local bottling plants in developing countries). The presence of actual manufacturing operations helps support marketing activities. As manufacturing is established abroad through direct investment, parts and components are often exported from the home country. Besides manufacturing subsidiaries, establishing a sales subsidiary requires relatively low levels of capital investment which leads to low risk. HP Financial Services has emerged in 2002 as the parent company Hewlett Packard's (HP) new leasing and financial services subsidiary. HP Financial Services (HPFS) is designed to enhance the worldwide sales efforts of the parent company by delivering a broad range of financial services and asset management capabilities that can positively impact the customer and partner relationships and shareowner value of the parent company. The HPFS represents approximately 4 percent of total revenue of the parent company. This new subsidiary brings a centralized business model for the financial services offered to customers as part of a total HP solution[35].

[33] Salvatore Parise and Lisa Sasson (2002), Leveraging Knowledge Management across Strategic Alliances, IBM Institute for Business Value Study, Cambridge, Massachusetts. USA.

[34] Polycom Corporate Website: Information on strategic ally partners, http://www.polycom.com

[35] Hewlett Packard Development Company: HP Financial Services as Wholly Owned Subsidiary, News Release, Corporate Office, Aug 13, 2002 http://www.hp.com/hpinfo/newsroom/press/2002/020813a.html

Cadbury's played an excellent strategic move by acquiring Green & Black's (G&B), organic food products, which has been leading with 90 percent market share in organic chocolates. In the global marketplace for organic products, the organic chocolate market in United Kingdom was worth £24 million in 2004 and growing on an average by a phenomenal 30% each year since 2002. With this acquisition G &B has enabled Cadbury to enter both the organic and premium chocolate markets, which are growing faster than chocolate confectionery overall, with a well-established brand that already enjoys significantly wider distribution than many other organic products. G & B is the fastest growing chocolate confectionery brand in the UK and will also benefit from Cadbury's strong presence in impulse channels such as newsagents, where distribution of their products is still relatively weak. Nonetheless the company's sales have more than quadrupled between 2001 and 2004 thanks to a combination of other factors, including good distribution across various channels from foodservice to supermarkets, the premium image of the brand and the company's fair trade policies[36].

The parent ventures, which are managed by wholly-owned subsidiaries, are more successful than shared management ventures, where both companies-parent and subsidiary-contribute on operational strategies. Problems often arise in shared situations because managers of international ventures have communication problems and different attitudes regarding time, job performance and the desirability of change[37]. Firms become multinational companies by setting up manufacturing or marketing subsidiaries overseas and transferring knowledge, which embodies its advantage, from one country to another. That is, knowledge flows from headquarters to overseas subsidiaries. Venturing is serious business, requiring skill, patience, and entrepreneurial flair. Most new ventures involve entering unfamiliar markets, employing unfamiliar technology, and implementing an unfamiliar organizational structure. An approach of particular promise is the new-style joint venture, in which a small company with vigor, flexibility, and advanced technology joins forces with a large company with capital, marketing strength, and distribution channels[38]. In order to determine the fit between the parent company and its subsidiaries, corporate strategists should evaluate the operational areas which includes the critical success factors of the business, the parenting opportunities in the business, organizational attributes of the parent company, and the financial results[39].

DEVELOPING AN ENTRY PLAN

An international marketing plan is prepared considering various factors that determine marketing functions across various countries. However, the marketing plan primarily needs to be designed considering the principal business components as stated below:

- Commitment on decisions taken by the marketing firm

---

[36] Christiana Benkouider (2005), Going Organic: Cadbury Acquires Green and Black's, *Euro Monitor*, 20 May.
[37] Killing Peter J (1982), How to make a Global Joint Venture Work, Harvard Business Review, May.
[38] Rajagopal (2006), Innovation and Business Growth through Corporate Venturing in Latin America: Analysis of Strategic Fit, *Management Decision*, 44 (5), 703-718.
[39] Andrew Campbell, Michael Goold, Marcus Alexander (1995), Corporate Strategy-The Quest for Parenting Advantage, *Harvard Business Review*, March.

- Selection of country or cluster of countries (trade region)
- Mode of entry in the market
- Appropriate marketing strategy in tune with the marketing environment of the identified country or region.
- Building effective marketing organization

The selection of a country is a critical exercise that involves the examination of all the above variables besides undertaking the demand analysis and financial estimates. The commitment of the firm to its trading decisions in the selected country, cost-benefit ratio study, and market operational methods largely determine the mode of entry of the firm into the international marketing avenue. The marketing strategy needs to be evolved assessing the objectives of the firm in the local markets in order to acquire differential advantage. Once the marketing-mix is critically analyzed, an implementation strategy can be formulated by the marketing firm. However, to ensure effective implementation of marketing policies, the marketing organization needs to be strengthened first. The decentralized organizational structure at regional levels (like Central Asia, South-East Asia, Middle-East, Far-East, etc.) would be appropriate for a marketing firm when planning for international marketing in more than one country. Such an organizational set-up would facilitate monitoring of demand, supply, price trend and political interventions more comprehensively. The centralized set-up would be of greater cost but less effective in exercising the marketing implementation and control measures.

A two stage selection process is required for the firm in identifying the product, market and services for international marketing. In this process, first, potential international markets need to be explored. Secondly, comparison of the domestic market of the firm with those abroad needs to be carried out in order to ensure that marketing at the international level has cooperative advantages over the domestic market[40]. Identifying a marketing region is always better than restricting to an individual country for the purpose of cost effective distribution networking. In addition, the tariff walls at the border countries need to be studied carefully. The firm involved in the international marketing should also make efforts to develop export markets in the initial stage. This would help in product specialization. International business firms have found that exporting is cheaper than manufacturing in overseas markets. There still remain some basic issues to be examined by the firm engaged in international marketing. These are:

- Size and growth
- Marketing potential of a country or region
- Similarities in host countries
- Free trade area, customs, common market
- Economic and political unions
- Appropriate economies of scale in managing business
- Accessibility, infrastructure and its cost
- Possibilities of decentralizing business activities

---

[40] Rajagopal (2004), Conceptual Analysis of Brand Architecture and Relationships within Product Category, *Journal of Brand Management*, 11(3), 233-247.

- Geographical boundaries of the markets
- Long run market segmentation

Exporting firms should understand that the export operations are subordinate to the domestic market policies and that the policy of the business firm to market the surplus home produce in the international market, would largely be determined by the opportunities offered by the host country or regional markets. However, the considerations on —(i) the firm's extent of awareness on varying requirements of consumers (ii) market response to the design and packaging of the product (iii) the impact of the pre-launch promotion among the focus groups and (iv) the size of the market which influences the adaptation process of goods and services at the international markets level.

Roche is a pharmaceutical research, technology and market-driven company, whose unique portfolio of products and services creates superior value for the customers. The products of the company are delivered through its affiliates located all over the world. Affiliates or regional representations are direct links to the customers and local markets of the company. Roche Diagnostics integrates its own know-how with that of selected partners from a wide range of specialized areas. With this objective in mind, Roche Diagnostic's strategic alliances and collaborative partnerships are aimed at combining potential with an innovative and ambitious approach. Best known examples of successful and long lasting partnerships are the global alliances with Hitachi (since 1978) for clinical chemistry and immunoassay systems, with Sysmex (since 1998) for hematology systems and with Stago (since 1973) in selected countries for coagulation systems. Roche Centralized Diagnostics (formerly Roche Laboratory Systems) directs its products and services at private labs, laboratory associations and central hospital laboratories, offering high-performance analysis systems to measure hundreds of different parameters in clinical specimens as well as programs to optimize lab processes, from sample down to result management. In cooperation with its partners Hitachi, Sysmex and Stago, Roche Centralized Diagnostics offers a full line of solutions for laboratories of all workloads. Roche Centralized Diagnostics' ultimate goal is to improve patients' health through the application of modern laboratory diagnostics as an integrated part of health management systems. In another alliance Roche-Syntex Mexico is engaged in selling the diagnostic reagents and equipments to the government and private clinics. The company also provides the diagnostic equipments to these health institutions and hospitals on lease. The business environment of the diagnostic market in Mexico is highly competitive and distributor oriented. The laboratory diagnostics supplier base in Mexico is confined to the selected suppliers dominating 80% of the total market[41].

The firms preparing for international marketing should also keep track of the international subsidies provided to the developing countries. A strong political and economic information system would help the firms in preparing international marketing plans more effectively. The synthesis of these inputs for planning is essential in pursuing global strategies. Thus integration of this information with the border-country profiles is a pre-requisite for sound plans. The selection of a market place at international level is a critical

---

[41] Rajagopal (2003), *Sales Force Re-organization for Maintaining Profitable Growth: A Case of Roche Diagnostics Mexico (A),* Discussion case, ITESM, Mexico City Campus, 1-19.

process and is required to be filtered at many intermediate levels to select the core business country.

CONTROL MANAGEMENT

A control feedback system is one of the core components of international marketing management and it serves to assess performance. Monitoring is one of the tools to measure the degree of the success of international marketing and needs to be incorporated in the plan itself. The marketing plans need to specify the periodicity of the control exercises and its prime objective. The monitoring calendar for international marketing firms may be designed keeping the following checks in mind:

- Budgetary control
- Plan implementation
- Performance of marketing functions (11Ps) which include product, price, place, promotion, packaging, pace, people, performance, psychodynamics, posture and proliferation
- Periodical appraisals of marketing information
- Social, cultural and political changes

The overall objective of these checks and controls is to determine the achievement of targeted results on time. These points need to be administered from the corporate office of the business firm in a centralized manner in order to enable effective planning and execution process. The standardization of marketing-mix is usually centralized to ensure the quality of all the components of the mix across the markets in the operational region. Besides, it is important to provide a common business language across markets which would help in understanding local markets more analytically. The checks need to be exercised at different levels of the marketing plan execution and to build-up a strong communication and information system. A consolidated document of the target group index (TGI) may be an appropriate tool for information processing and analysis. The variables which need to be covered in the TGI include consumer goods, industrial goods, services, spatial and temporal trend of demand and price, distribution patterns, marketing budgets, response to advertising, communication services and the like. International marketing research needs to be conducted on specific issues of interest and inferences may be tagged along with the Monitoring and Evaluation (M&E) process. Nevertheless, M&E should be conducted periodically as a tool of control.

EXIT POLICY

It is essential that the firm entering into the international market needs to analyze the level of profitability, asset-production ratio, production costs, sales projections, and the risk factors in the short and long run. Further, it is very important that the firm should make all possible arrangements for a smooth ejection from the international business in case of an unavoidable loss to property, brand or functional markets. The firm usually faces exit barriers after entry. A firm will be reluctant to commit on non-recoverable investments that have been made, people hired, contracts signed if there is likelihood of a forced exit. Another consideration for the marketer is the potential loss of goodwill accompanying withdrawal from an important and visible market. The French automaker Peugeot probably lost a great deal of brand equity and money in the U.S. market before finally exiting in 1992. The specific exit reasons for international firms to leave the operational stream are listed below:

- Shut down of specific operations
- Labor scarcity and high wage rates
- Market speculation and its impact
- Employees' demand, labor problems and threats
- Changing government regulations
- International trade policies
- Total mismanagement

Hence, exiting strategy should also be carefully designed together with the approaches for entering the international market. Enough capital cushions are to be built or insured against risks in the world markets and against abrupt exits. In the era of global marketing, the company needs sufficient resources and capability to nurture and sustain its products and brands, thus surmounting exit barriers by never having to face them.

MARKET UNCERTAINTIES AND ENTRY DECISIONS

In turbulent markets the competitive strategy provides the conceptual magnitude that integrates various functional activities and marketing programs for sustaining the competitive threats. The effective competitive strategies have a direct bearing on possessing the relative market share and growth of the business organization. The strategies are the directional statements and need to be converted into the step-by-step plan of action for effective plan implementation. The strategic directions have four options that can be expressed by 4As - arena, advantage, access and activities. The arena may be defined as serving the targeted market segment through an appropriate scale of operations and scope of activities to be performed for competitive advantage. The advantages in the process consist of positioning the products theme that differentiates the business from competitors. The access may be referred to the communication and distribution channels used to reach the market in the uncertain business conditions. These activities are interdependent and are affected by the change in any of the factors. The arena of the market largely dictates the customers to be served by the company, the competitors to by-passes and the key success factors to be considered. Each market has a distinctive profile of key success factors developed by the attributes of the market. The recent development of corporate strategies shows that many multi-national companies are considering their choice of the market arena based on the following factors:

- There is an increasing trend of market fragmentation. New segments with specific needs are emerging and are being served by the specialist competitors by offering tailor-made goods and services.

- The traditional market boundaries are disappearing as a consequence of the rush of substitutes emerging due to the technological growth.

- The transformation of existing self-contained regional and national markets into global markets.

In the above discussed situations the challenge for the corporate sector management may be observed as to find the right balance of global reach and standardization of the activities versus the traditional strategies or local adaptation. The companies need to find out the competitive advantages within the chosen arena of business. The core issue associated with the competitive advantage is positioning of the theme that sets a business apart from the rivals in the way that is meaningful to target the customers. It is necessary for the companies to move aggressively against the competitors to retain their market territories and build a strong defense. Thus Kodak asserted itself in the film market against the strategies of Fuji in the American market. The supply gluts also put pressure on advantages. The markets for pharmaceuticals, electronics and automobiles suffer chronic global overcapacity to the extent of 15-40 percent. Such a problem situation demands the companies develop strategies of competitive advantage to hold the key success factors and become the market leader. Such strategies are required as there are too many firms competing and the customers may back integrating their marketing requirement rather than buying them. This situation reduces the volume of market demand relative to supply and the customers may sell their excess capacity on competition with their one-time supplier. The need for the competitively advantageous strategies may further be justified as a large number of firms are increasingly productive in reference to the rapid diffusion of the technologies. The customers' bargaining power also works out to be an instrument to either broaden or narrow the differences between the competitors. The companies that use intermediaries often encounter having to balance the power of distribution and delivery of services. In consumer markets the retail trade is forcing major concessions on the multi-national brands. Such strategies hold the access to the retail network through a long chain of channels. Conventionally the choice of appropriate scale in business and scope thereof were guided by the concepts of *the bigger is better* and *umbrella control of activities*. In the current era of globalization the decentralization of activities and production sharing have become more effective tools in marketing. The profit centre approach (PCA), control circles and total quality management practices has endorsed the success of small integrated units operating in a well defined market. In view of promoting the PCA concepts and maintaining the control circles, the large companies are increasingly creating the autonomous, small and entrepreneurial units to find responsive solutions to the customer problems in the well defined market niches[42]. Corporate structures are changing in order to accommodate the concept of PCA and control circles and are exploring for the long-term advantages by way of heavy investment to develop the core competencies.

---

[42] Frederick E Webster Jr.: It's 1990- Do you know where your marketing is?, Mass Marketing Science Institute, Cambridge 1989.

BMW, Honda, and Toyota, among other companies, begin with a strong brand that imparts sales momentum to each model. Brands that are weak—because their products have acquired a reputation for shoddy workmanship, their designs are not evocative, or their models bear little relationship to one another—cannot pursue this top-down approach. But a company stands a good chance of selling more cars and, step by step, of rehabilitating the brand if managers take pains to match each model to the consumer segments most likely to be interested in it, identify and overcome the obstacles that keep browsers from becoming purchasers, and emphasize both the functional and the process and relationship benefits of the model in question. BMW Direct is an initiative of BMW (GB) to help selected company car fleet buyers streamline their service for employees. BMW Direct is a web based, fully personalized, car configuration and ordering system for the purchase of new BMWs. This highly efficient rules based web application delivers a level of information previously unavailable outside of a showroom. The BMW Direct solution provides users with the ability to view details on all eligible cars online and then go on to configure them against a full menu of accessories. BMW Direct is truly 'CRM' compliant, providing two-way communication via automated alerts and e-mails and incorporating a Contact Centre to ensure immediate access to trained product advisors. Users can track online the status of their individual orders whether by web, phone, fax or email. The call centre functionality includes phone and e-campaign generation, customer enquiry handling and profiling to customised promotions[43]. Post-sales support is delivered using a thin client solution, (using Citrix) to BMWs contact centre in Croydon and order management centre in Bracknell in UK.

The technological changes are the main impetus behind new market opportunities. The extent of such change may be explained from super technologies to the appropriate and intermediate technologies. The strategic choices have wide ranging ripple effects through the organization that determine the key success factors and growth performance. Some companies would be making right strategic choices by improving the implementation process of competitive advantages. These companies are guided by the shared strategic vision and are driven by the responsive attitude towards the market requirements. They emphasize the continuous striving to satisfy the customers. A strategic vision in managing markets may be understood as the guiding theme that explains the nature of business and the future projections thereof. These projections or business intentions depend on the collective analysis of the environment that determines the need for the new developments or diversifications. The vision should be commissioned on a concrete understanding of the business and the ability to foresee the impact of market forces on the growth of business. The vision will motivate the organization for collaborative business planning and implementation. The powerful visions are also the statements of intent that create an obsession with winning throughout the organization[44]. The business strategy broadly incorporates the following dimensions:

- Customer needs
- Consumer segments
- Technology and resources
- Activities in the value added chain

---

[43] Rajagopal (2003), *Building Customer Loyalty Through Relationship Networking: A Case of BMW Mexico, Discussion Case*, ITESM, Mexico City Campus, 1-16.

[44] Day Geogr. S (1990), *Market Driven Strategy: Process for Creating Value*, The Free Press, New Cork, 10-18.

The strategic thrust has a significant magnitude and direction in sailing the business through the turbulent situation. The factors associated with the competitive advantage and business investments uphold the strategic thrust to achieve the business objectives though the positive channel efforts. The competitive advantage may be assessed in reference to the superior customer value and lowest delivered cost. Such combination of the strategies may be termed as competitive superiority that explains cost effective delivery strategy to enhance the customer value. An overall edge is gained by performing most of the activities at a lower cost than competitors. This would enable the company to optimize its cost of delivery of the new products and simultaneously enhance the value of customer value to uphold the strategic thrust of the company.

Canon delivers innovative digital business solutions to ensure that its customers achieve and maintain the information edge. The increasingly competitive global marketplace, and the fact that the organizations must store, process and share immense volumes of information with both speed and accuracy have been the key areas of the company to penetrate in the territorial gateways like Mexico for the Latin American market. The company functions with four key areas in the Mexican market that include marketing, logistics, sales and services operations. The marketing activities of the company consist of planning and budgeting, pricing, forecasting, purchases, marketing research and developing promotional strategies. The company is also engaged in developing attractive media –mix and advertising campaigns and launches the loyalty programs for its major brands. The virtual shopping network is also a major part of the marketing functions performed by the company in the country. The company feels that the loyal, ongoing customers are the backbone of every business and in the prevailing highly competitive environment, these shoppers cannot be ignored or else they may be won over by competitors. The consumers might have bought such products many times in their life or some might have purchased one at least once in their life time. There is no single way to segment a market. The most important factors influencing a consumer's involvement level are their perceived risks. The purchase of any product involves a certain amount of risk, which may include product failure, financial, operational, social, personal and psychological. The repeat customers are more apt to buy a full range of merchandise, not merely items that are under promotional programs. This means that the dealers and retailers of the company can reach profit margin goals. The logistics functions of the company are largely international trade oriented as the Canon Mexico is a part of Canon USA and many products of the company are acquired from its USA counterpart as inbound logistics. The import process has been one of the major activities of the company in Mexico. The logistics of the company further involves the key activities of transport, inventory management and developing appropriate overseas trade and information strategies[45].

There are major types of strategies catalogued and given various names by different authors. Often these strategies and tactics are so bold and innovative that they "change the rules of the game." Leaders are increasingly being advised to seek that objective in planning and executing their strategies. The pace of change today is dizzying with new technological breakthroughs occurring at shorter intervals and global competition putting the heat on. Mergers and acquisitions change the competitive landscape unexpectedly, and strategic alliances develop even among the companies that were, or still are, competitors. The concept of *Hyper-competition* explains the highly aggressive form of competition that characterizes

---

[45] Rajagopal (2003), *Striving with Competition in Global Imaging Market: Canon in Mexican Business Environment*, ITESM, Mexico City Campus, 1-22.

hi-tech industries today. Hyper-competition is said to be increasingly making its way into other industries as well. They speak in terms of surprise, speed and mobility, terms suggestive of the military approach. Not that aggressive action is new in business so much so as the level, intent and severity of business "combat" have changed dramatically. It is necessary to build the strategic business mindset to outwit the competitors and gain competitive advantages over the segmented markets. The following factors need to be considered for achieving the strategic business leadership:

- A clear sense of desired outcomes before acting. Develop a plan capable of delivering outcomes that will add significant value to a state of affairs.
- Explore possibilities outwards to capture the larger context, to see how the pieces fit together.
- Adaptive to realities and flexible in choice of tactics. Recognize that once action begins the "game board" is fluid offering both new threats and new opportunities.
- Wherever possible, attempt to achieve multiple objectives through singular actions.
- Plan a couple of steps ahead of the competition.
- Anticipate the actions of a business rival and strategically rehearse the next responses should those contingencies arise.
- Core discipline to observe the market moves and rival reactions.
- Capitalize on business crises or behavioural change in the markets in order to turn them to advantage.
- Stay future-focused.
- Plan the business strategy implementation in both sequential and parallel direction to accomplish goals and sustain the impact thereof.
- Develop negotiations with the business intermediaries on win-win platform at an acceptable cost.
- Supplement actions with those of others (allies, partners, joint ventures.)
- Be patient, with a good sense of timing.
- Be able to scrap or alter plans when information indicates actions are not attaining their intended results.
- Develop alternate strategies for contingencies
- Use speed and surprise to gain advantage.
- Form alliances with opponents of his opponents in business.
- Learn the strengths and weaknesses of rivals.
- Be aggressive in pursuing goals, cordon the moves and be ready to take on the next one.
- Assure that everyone in the company knows one's role and is equipped with the resources to contribute.
- Monitor activities in the operating environment.
- Use "what if" speculation to stretch thinking in the direction of opportunities and possibilities.
- Study the logic of the opponent's tactics with an eye toward determining what their ultimate end purposes may be.

These are some tested aspects of thinking employed by leaders to gain and hold strategic advantage. They can serve as a checklist when responsibilities include thinking strategically. Customers want more of everything they value. If they value low cost they want it lower. If they value convenience they want it easier and faster. If they look for state of the art they want it first and want to push the envelope. If they need expert advice they want more time and dedicated effort and investment. By raising the level of value that customers can expect from everyone, leading companies are driving the market and driving their competitors out of business, or at least into a malaise of mediocrity. Here are a few options for managerial consideration:

- Alter the industry structure to change the basis of competition. Reconfigure the value chain—retailers become wholesalers and suppliers, insurers take over brokerages, banks move into insurance, etc.
- Improve the position of the business within the industry by way of acquisitions and market share. Alter the playing field to achieve an enhanced scale of operations and competitive positioning.
- Innovate and create new opportunities—new products, services, and markets.
- Employ barriers to entry in terms of significant capital investment, proprietary technology, or in the magnitude of resources required to compete effectively.
- Increase the dependence of customers for products and services in terms of the total value for customers or higher costs of switching to alternates.
- Change and enhance supplier relationships to obtain cost and quality improvements, reduced cycle times, and integrated processes.
- Change the basis of competition by creating a service relationship and differentiation. Move away from price to service, software, and customer relationships.
- Centralize into high volume, low cost, automated, 'focused factories', to achieve the lowest cost operations in support of customer value.
- Decentralize into custom, low volume, flexible factories, quick to market, responsive, and able to customize products to specific customer requirements.

Controls may be considered as checkpoints used to verify performance progress by comparison with some standard in a given competitive environment. Generally the business standards are established by top management in the planning process. The control and analysis process needs to be revised with the growing size of the firm and its business operations. Controls must go along with the expansion process and tight control should ensure consistency in product and marketing performance. Since multinational companies typically have several foreign subsidiaries in different parts of the world, a good control system is important to ensure that these subsidiaries move together toward a common goal, spelled out by the corporate strategic plan to meet any market uncertainties. These issues need to be considered in anticipation by the international firms while deciding the entry strategies in foreign markets.

REFERENCES

Albrinck J, Hornery J, Kletter D and Neilson G (2001), Adventures in Corporate Venturing, *Strategy and Business*, 22, pp 119-129.

Biggadyke R (1979), The Risky Business Diversification, *Harvard Business Review*, 57, pp 103-111.

Frost P J and Egri CP (1990), Influence of Political Action on Innovation: Part I, *Leadership and Organization Development Journal*, 11(1), pp 17-25.

Ghemawat P (1991), *Commitment: The Dynamics of Strategy*, New York, Free Press.

Suarez Feranando F and Lanzolla Gianvito (2005), The Half Truth of First Mover Advantage, *Harvard Business Review*, April, pp 1-8 (Ref R 0504J).

Tushman M and Nadler D (1986), Organizing for Innovation, *California Management Review*, 3(1), pp 73-84.

Zahra S A (1993), Environment, Corporate Entrepreneurship and Financial Performance: A Taxonomic Approach, *Journal of Business Venturing*, 8(4), pp 319-340.

Zahra S A (1996), Governance, Ownership and Corporate Entrepreneurship: The Moderating Impact of Industry's Technological Opportunities, *Academy of Management Journal*, 39(6), pp 1713-1735.

Chapter 7

GLOBAL COMPETITION AND COMPETITORS

Productivity differs across individual, monopolistically competitive firms in each country. Firms face some initial uncertainty concerning their future productivity when making an irreversible investment to enter the domestic market. In addition to the sunken entry cost, firms face both fixed and per-unit export costs. Only a subset of relatively more productive firms export, while the remaining, less productive firms only serve their domestic market. This microeconomic structure endogenously determines the extent of the traded sector and the composition of consumption baskets in both countries. Exogenous shocks to aggregate productivity, sunken entry costs, and trade costs induce firms to enter and exit both their domestic and export markets, thus altering the composition of consumption baskets across countries over time[1]. The microeconomic features have important consequences for macroeconomic variables. Macroeconomic dynamics, in turn, feed back into firm level decisions, further altering the pattern of trade over time. The aggregate picture of world economic growth shows a remarkable diversity in growth performance, both geographically and across time. There exist high growth countries and low growth countries on the panorama of global economy. Some countries have grown rapidly over time while others have experienced growth spurts for a decade or two. What is the role of policy in this diversity? How can policy help transform this picture? However the increasing globalization tries to answer these questions in terms of catalyzing the economic growth and institutional innovations in the developing countries. Analysis of the success story of China, with an astonishing annual growth rate of 8.0 percent since the late 1970s, together with other well-known East Asian experiences that have taken place in countries such as South Korea and Taiwan, provide the basis to build some stylized facts about the take-off and the process of sustaining economic growth. On the other hand, the experience of liberalization, deregulation and privatization in countries such as Mexico, Argentina, Brazil, Colombia, Bolivia, and Peru have offered substantial evidence that allows us to question the standard formulae used to propel and maintain economic growth[2].

---

[1] Fabio Ghironi and Marc Melitz:International Trade and Macroeconomic Dynamics with Heterogeneous Firms, Society for Economic Dynamics, Annual Meeting Papers, 2004.

[2] Pessoa Argentino: Institutional Innovations, Growth Performance and Policy, Conference Paper, European Regional Science Association, 2004.

UNDERSTANDING COMPETITION

Competition may be defined as an object-centered process in business performance. Competition may be semantically described as a combination of two distinct Latin words- *com* (together) and *petere* (to seek). Similarly conflict is derived from *com* (together) and *fligere* (to strike). This distinction between the quest and the blow, to strive or to strike seems precisely the pertinent one for clarity and efficiency in social science[3]. Competition may be characterized as striving together to win the race not to destroy the other competitors from the point of view of the supporters of globalization. The local market competition is targeted towards the customers and the competitors strive to win the customer, temporarily or permanently. However, in business-to-business process, the competition may turn more tactical and strategic in order to outperform the rivals firms. In this way competition can be seen as regulated struggle. There are rules of economic competition and they do not generally include the destruction of competitors. The technology of marketing research is devoted to the difficult tasks of discovering customer needs, and the sub-disciplines of consumer and organizational buying behavior attempt to provide theoretical bases for the results. In this process the emphasis is on determination to win customers where competitors turn tactical towards brand or product positioning.

The emergence of virtual shopping, liberalization of economic policies in the developing countries all over the world competition has become like a traditional derby in which many companies participate for neck-to-neck race. In this business game the rules are subject to change with out notice, the prize money may change in short notice, the route and finish line is also likely to change after the race begins, new entrants may join at any time during the race, the racers may form strong alliances, all creative strategies are allowed in the game and the governmental laws may change without notice and sometimes with retrospective effect. Hence to win the race any company should acquire the strategies of outwitting, outmaneuvering and outperforming the competitors. In this process a company must understand thoroughly all the moves of the rival firms from various sources. The locales of the business rivalry have to be spotted to assess their strengths. An intriguing aspect of the marketplace is that the nature of competition can change over time. A technology, company, or product does not need to remain prey to another forever. Competitive roles can be radically altered with technological advances or with the right marketing decisions. External light meters, used for accurate diaphragm and speed setting on photographic cameras, enjoyed a stable, symbiotic (win–win) relationship with cameras for decades. As camera sales grew, so did light-meter sales. But eventually, technological developments enabled camera companies to incorporate light meters into their own boxes. Soon, the whole light-meter industry became prey to the camera industry. Sales of external light meters diminished while sales of cameras enjoyed a boost, and the relationship passed from win–win to *predator–prey*[4]. Table 1.1 exhibits the competitors' arena, which has to be studied comprehensively, and strategies to be built accordingly.

---

[3] Mack R F: The Components of Social Conflicts, *Social Problems*, 22 (4), 1965, 388-397.
[4] Modis Theodore: Conquering Uncertainty, McGraw-Hill, New York, 1998.

Table 1.1. Possible Locales of Business Rivalry

Business Factors	Customer Locale	Geography	Channels	Institutions and Patrons
– Supply Chain – Promotion – Investment	– Market Place – Segments – Individual	– Spread – Regional	– C&F Agents – Retailers – Wholesalers – Franchisees – Mailers	– Government agencies – Cooperatives

The access to the infrastructure, raw material, the process, supplies and the other vital business factors is the most vulnerable to the competition. The competing firms pay more attention to the sources of factors, quality thereof, cost and management of the factors in order to prove better over each other. Customer, the end user, is the ultimate target of competitor for building aggressive and defensive strategies in business. The competing firms try to attract the customers by various means to polarize business and earn confidence in the marketplace. It is necessary for the successful business companies to look for such a place of business that provides them more location advantage and hold the customers for their goods and services. The business cordoning or securing the trade boundaries is an essential decision to be taken for building competitive strategies to attack rivals across regions. Even a small business company can compete globally with the firms of all sizes through the Internet. The distribution channels, franchisees, carrying and forwarding agents, retailers and mailers with value added services represent an increasingly intense business rivalry or competition in all markets or competitive domains. Many firms like Godrej (Diversified Products), Proctor and Gamble (Consumer Goods), Compaq (Computers) reward their managers handsomely for winning the business battles in their channel wars. In succeeding to the market competition, the institutional and political patronage provides long run support to the companies. Winning in the product, channel and factor marketplace in many instances may not last long in building relationships with the customers. Many business firms have found themselves outmaneuvered in various functional aspects of business by the adept actions of rivals in the institutional arena. An intriguing aspect of the marketplace is that the nature of competition can change over time. A technology, company, or product does not need to remain prey to another forever. Competitive roles can be radically altered with technological advances or with the right marketing decisions. The need of the moment is to apply scientific methods to manage competition. Only then could modern corporations withstand the pressures of intense competition of a dynamic business era. The paper examines issues involved in the scientific approach of managing competition

The struggle between fountain pens and ballpoint pens had a different ending. The substitution of ballpoint pens for fountain pens as writing instruments went through three distinct stages. Before the appearance of ballpoint pens, fountain pen sales grew undisturbed to fill the writing- instrument market. They were following an S-shaped curve when the ballpoint technology appeared in 1951. As ballpoint sales picked up, those of fountain pens declined in the period 1951 to 1973. Fountain pens staged a counterattack by radically dropping prices. But that effort failed. Fountain pens kept losing market share and embarked on an extinction course. By 1973, their average price had dropped to as low as 72 cents, to no avail. Eventually, however, the prices of fountain pens began rising. The fountain pen underwent what Darwin would have described as a character displacement to the luxury niche of the executive pen market. In the early 1970s, the strategy of fountain pens became a retreat into non-competition. By 1988, the price of some fountain pens in the United States had climbed to $400. The Volterra-Lotka model indicates that today the two species no longer interact but each follows a simple S-shaped growth pattern. As a consequence, fountain pens have secured a healthy and profitable market niche. Had they persisted in their competition with ballpoint pens, they would have perished[5].

Many factors determine the nature of competition, including not only rivals, but also the economics of particular industries, new entrants, the bargaining power of customers and suppliers, and the threat of substitute services or products. A strategic plan of action based on this might include positioning the company so that its capabilities provide the best defense against the competitive forces, influencing the balance of forces through strategic moves and anticipating shifts in the factors underlying competitive forces[6]. In outwitting the competitors the companies must detect the changes in the strategy game in reference to the market players' status in gaining more knowledge, networking, entrepreneurship and increasing ambitions. The changes that are taking place in all the arenas as discussed in Table 1.1 have to be considered. The driving forces of competing firms, their organization and micro-economic environment need to be studied carefully by the company planning to overtake competitors in the business. Further in the process of winning the battle of rivals it would be helpful for a company to understand the changing stakes of the competitors and the forces after such developments. A company can outmaneuver the rival by being more skillful in particular tasks and reshaping the stakes in one or more business arenas. Outmaneuvering the rivals is the core of changing the rules of the marketplace. The strategy for outperforming the competitor is largely based on two basic issues- the performance parameters and assessment criteria of the performance. However the critical parameters may include a probe for the following information as *who is*:

- Creating new customer needs that do not exist
- Developing and establishing the new attributes of the product
- Establishing new channels to reach all the existing and potential customers
- Reinventing stakes to make others confined to play catch-up roles
- Creating new capabilities as the source of new products and customer needs
- Creating knowledge base for driving the capabilities for the new goods and services
- Establishing new relationships with the channels, institutions and customers
- Winning or loosing in the business battle
- Establishing new chain of customer delight
- Leading the product
- Dominating the price-value relationship

---

[5] Modis Theodore: A Scientific Approach to Managing Competition, *The Industrial Physicist*, 9 (1), 25-27.
[6] Porter Michael E: How Competitive Forces Shape Strategy? *Harvard Business Review*, March, 1979.

The parameters and assessments of the above actions would help in focusing both the thinking and strategy building process for sailing through the competition successfully. The current and future strategy of competitors must be considered by any company planning to outwit, outmaneuver and outperform them.

THEORETICAL FRAMEWORK OF COMPETITION

The philosophy of the free enterprise system has been laid on the basics of competition. Competition is found in all marketing functions which include the prices at which products are exchanged, the attributes and qualities of products manufactured, the volume of products exchanged, the methods of distribution and promotion. The school of thought, which has constructed the competition related theories, may be categorized in two groups— economic theory and industrial organization perspective. The economists of the former group have discussed many different models of competition. The focus of their work is the model of perfect competition, which is based on the premise that, when a large number of buyers and sellers in the market are dealing in homogeneous products, there is complete freedom to enter or exit the market and everyone has complete and accurate knowledge about everyone else. The latter group from the school of thought on competition in reference to industrial organizations postulates that a firm's position in the marketplace depends critically on the characteristics of the industry environment in which it competes. The industry environment comprises structure, conduct, and performance. Structure refers to the economic and technical perspectives of the industry in the context in which firms compete. It includes concentration in the industry such as the number and size distribution of firms, barriers to entry and product differentiation. The competition theories have further laid emphasis also on the market competition on functional dimensions, which include non-price competitions towards the product differentiation and quality competition. Products are differentiated when the products of different firms are not perfect substitutes and companies may compete by changing the characteristics of the product they sell. Such a strategy may not be necessarily to make a product better than the competitor, but just to differentiate it in order to create an appeal to a different *market niche*.

Niche strategies provide a classic instance of such situations. No market is entirely homogeneous. There are always groups of customers which differ in terms of their needs. The environment thus created may well be fragmented; at the very least it will be structured. There exists the possibility of the occurrence of niches which individual competitors may occupy. Niches are unlikely to be complete, separate and well-defined. There will always be overlap. However if such niches are rather subtly defined they may not always be obvious to all the players. Thus niche players may appear to compete but in practice do not do so or at least not fully. The competitive strategy of product differentiation helps the company in enhancing the product-mix by introducing many varieties, which increase the range of consumer choice. However, it divides up the market, leading to higher prices and costs for the firm. From an economist's point of view this definition of competition most closely resembles the category of monopolistic competition. In this case it is assumed that a large number of buyers and sellers exist, with each seller producing a variety of the essentially differentiated product which characterizes the product group. The distinctive features of each attribute yield the firms to gain small but nevertheless positive monopolistic advantage. This in turn accords the firms in question some of the features of the monopoly described earlier, but at a more modest level. The precise level of monopoly power enjoyed by each of the firms depends crucially upon the number of competing varieties in the market, and the distribution of consumers' preferences.

Since the 1960s, however, sophisticated economic theories of how firms work have been developed. These have examined why firms grow at different rates and tried to model the normal life cycle of a company, from fast-growing start-up to lumbering mature business. The more competition there is, the more likely are firms to be efficient and prices to be low. Economists have identified several different sorts of competition. In perfect competition every firm is competitive and plays in the market as a price taker. Where there is a monopoly, or firms have some market power, the seller has some control over the price, which will probably be higher than in a perfectly competitive market. By how much more will depend on how much market power there is, and on whether the firm(s) with the market power are committed to profit maximization. Firms earn only normal profits, the bare minimum profit necessary to keep them in business. If firms earn more than this (excess profits) other firms will enter the market and drive the price level down until there are only normal profits to be made. The market power may be stated as when one buyer or seller in a market has the ability to exert significant influence over the quantity of goods and services traded or the price at which they are sold. Market power does not exist when there is perfect competition, but it does when there is a monopoly, *monopsony*[7] or oligopoly. The basic attributes of the monopolistic competition include:

- Many buyers and sellers
- Differentiated products
- Sufficient knowledge
- Free entry

Hair dressing industry may be a good example to understand monopolistic competition. There are many hairdressers in the country, and most hairdressing firms are quite small. There is free entry and it is at least possible that people know enough about their hairdressing options so that the "sufficient knowledge" condition is fulfilled. But the products of different hairdressers are not perfect substitutes. At the very least, their services are differentiated by location. A hairdresser in the downtown of Mexico may not be a perfect substitute for a hairdresser in the suburbs, although they may be good substitutes from the point of view of a customer who lives in the suburbs but works in downtown. Hairdressers' services may be differentiated in other ways as well. Their styles may be different; the decor of the salon may be different, and that may make a difference for some customers; and even the quality of the conversation may make a difference. A customer of a hair dressing firm may change hairdressers because an old hairdresser was an outspoken market protectionist.

In the contemporary analysis of competition and related strategies thereof, it is observed that the competitive firms intend to ascertain a continuous organizational learning process with respect to the value creation chain and measure performance of the new products

---

[7] Monopsony may be described as the market dominated by a single buyer unlike the monopoly wherein there exists a single seller.

introduced in the market. In the growing competitive markets the large and reputed firms are developing strategies to move into the provision of innovative combinations of products and services as 'high-value integrated solutions' tailored to each customer's needs than simply 'moving downstream' into services. Such firms are developing innovative combinations of service capabilities such as operations, business consultancy and finance required to provide complete solutions to each customer's needs in order to augment the customer value towards the innovative or new products. It has been argued that the provision of integrated solutions is attracting firms traditionally based in manufacturing and services to occupy a new base in the value stream centered on *systems integration* using internal or external sources of product designing, supply and customer focused promotion[8]. Besides the organizational perspectives of enhancing the customer value, the functional variables like pricing play a significant role in developing the customer perceptions towards the new products.

Most markets exhibit some form of imperfect or monopolistic competition. There are fewer firms than in a perfectly competitive market and each can create barriers to entry to some degree. A firm may own a crucial resource, such as an oil well, power generation, or it may have an exclusive operating license, which restricts other competitors to enter in the business. Operating on economies of scale for a large firm may also have a significant competitive advantage as it may enjoy a large volume of production at lower costs which may further lead to the price leadership with low retail prices. Such strategy would also prevent the potential competitors to enter in the business. An incumbent firm may make it hard for a would-be entrant by incurring huge sunk costs with high budget advertising. In view of such strategy any new entrant may match to compete effectively but may lose the market share if the attempt to compete would fail. The sunk costs are costs that have been incurred and cannot be reversed such as spending on advertising or researching a product idea. They can be a barrier to entry. If potential entrants would have to incur similar costs, which would not be recoverable if the entry failed, they may be scared off. Another radical strategy may be used by the powerful firms to discourage entry by raising exit costs, for example, by making it an industry norm to hire workers on long-term contracts, which would build the escalated cost barriers for rival companies. Thus firms can earn some excess profits without a new entrant being able to compete to bring prices.

For more comprehension on the functional efficiencies of high performing companies see Mankins Michael C and Steele Richmond: Turning great strategies into great performance, *Harvard Business Review*, July 2005

The least competitive market is a monopoly, dominated by a single firm that can earn substantial excess profit by controlling either the amount of output in the market or the price but not both. In this sense it is a price setter. When there are few firms in a market (oligopoly) they have the opportunity to behave as a cartel. A cartel may be described as an agreement among two or more firms in the same industry to co-operate in fixing prices and/or carving up the market and restricting the volume of production they handle. A market dominated by a single firm does not necessarily have monopoly power if it is a contestable market. In such a market, a single firm can dominate only if it produces as efficiently as its competitors and does not earn excess profits. If it becomes inefficient or earns excess profits, another more efficient or less profitable firm will enter the market and dominate it instead.

---

[8] Davies Andrew (2004), Moving Base into High-value Integrated Solutions: A Value Stream Approach, *Industrial and Corporate Change*, 13(5), October, pp 727-756.

Organizational Competencies and Competitive Efficiency of Multinational Companies

The high-performing companies like Barclays, Cisco, Dow Chemical, 3M, and Roche drive to establish some basic rules for setting and delivering strategy which include simple executable strategy, realistic, short-run result oriented and transparency in process of strategy implementation. The above companies work on debating over the assumptions, and do not construct strategic frameworks on forecasts. The high performing companies create cross-functional teams drawn from strategy, marketing, and finance to ensure the assumptions underlying your long-term plans which reflect both the real economics of the company's markets and its actual performance relative to competitors. It has been observed that rigorous analytic framework is used by the high performing companies. Such companies as above ensure that the dialogue between the corporate office and the business units about market trends and assumptions is conducted within a rigorous framework, such as that of *profit pools*. These companies manage the resources deployments early to support the scheduled production and marketing activities. Proper resources management would in turn help the company create more realistic forecasts and more executable plans by discussing up-front the level and timing of critical deployments. The companies like Barclays, Cisco, Dow Chemical, 3M, and Roche clearly identify priorities and prioritize tactics so that employees have a clear sense of where to direct their efforts and continuously monitor performance. Tracking resource deployment, monitoring and evaluating results against plans, using continuous feedback to reset assumptions and reallocate resources have been principal activities performed by the business monitoring centers of these companies. The monitoring and evaluation reports are directly reported to the top management periodically. The Reward is set for the best strategy, product, brand and sales managers who achieve the targets and non-planned market shares in the up-stream markets. These companies also develop execution capabilities and motivational tools for the staff. Following these rules strictly the high performing companies narrow the strategy-to-performance gap and achieve sustainable growth among the competitors.

Source: Euro Monitor Online www.euromonitor.com

An environment surrounding a specific product or market concerning the competition rather than a country's overall economic environment refers to the microeconomic environment. A careful analysis of a microenvironment indicates whether a company can successfully enter a specific market. It may be hypothesized that rising prosperity of a nation depends on the productivity with which it uses its human, capital and natural resources. This is manifested in the way in which a nation's firms compete. Productivity, in turn, is a function of the interplay of many factors including political, legal and macroeconomic context; the quality of the microeconomic business environment; and the sophistication of company operations and strategy. Together they determine the capacity of a nation to produce internationally competitive firms and support rising prosperity. A context that creates pressure for firms continuously to upgrade the source and sophistication of their advantage and at the same time supports the upgrading process is a favorable microeconomic context. Pressure for upgrading is supplied by *demand conditions* featuring sophisticated and demanding customers, whose demands spur the local firms to innovate in order to upgrade their product/service offerings. Particularly valuable is pressure from local customers that anticipate the nature of demand elsewhere in the world. Different competitors, however, might aim to satisfy different types of demand: existing, latent, or incipient. *Existing demand* refers to a product bought to satisfy a recognized need. *Latent demand* applies in a situation where a particular need has been recognized, but no products have been offered. *Incipient demand* describes a projected need that will emerge when customers become aware of it sometime in the future.

Competition may be analyzed in reference to the characteristics of products as breakthrough, competitive, and improved. A *breakthrough product* is a unique innovation that is mainly technical in nature, such as the digital watch, VCR, and personal computer. A *competitive product* is one of many brands currently available in the market and has no special advantage over the competing products. An *improved product* is not unique but is generally superior to many existing brands. For example, let us assume Aubrey Organics is interested in manufacturing shampoo for tender hair in Turkey and seeks entry into the emerging market in the middle-eastern countries. The company finds that in addition to a number of local brands, Johnson & Johnson's baby shampoo and Helene Curtis Industries' Suave Shampoo are the competitive products in the market. Proctor and Gamble has recently entered the market with its Pantene Pro-V brand, which is considered as an improved product. Most of the competition appears to be addressing the existing demand. However, no attempts have been made to satisfy latent demand or incipient demand. After reviewing various considerations, Aubrey Organics may decide to fulfill latent demand with an improved offering through its Camomile Luxurious brand. Based on market information, the company reasons that a hair problem most consumers face in that part of the world is dandruff. No brand has addressed itself to that problem. Even Proctor & Gamble's new entry mainly emphasizes health of hair. Thus, analysis of the competition with reference to product offerings and demand enables Aubrey Organics to determine its entry point into the market of middle-eastern countries.

The contemporary ideology on the competition puts emphasis largely on the competitive environment which contributes to various dimensions of rivalries. It has been observed that the low-end competitor indulging a company in offering much lower prices for a seemingly similar product, has been the common fear of each industry leader managing his business among competitors. The vast majority of such low-end companies falls into one of the four broad categories which include strippers, predators, reformers, or transformers[9]. Each of these is defined by the functionality of product and the convenience of purchase. Strippers, for instance, typically enter a market with a bare-bones offering, reduced in function and usually in convenience. Industry leaders have significant advantages for combating low-end competition, but they often hesitate because they're afraid their actions will adversely affect their current profit margins. The solution then may be to find the response that is most likely to restore market calm in the least disruptive way. An industry leader could choose to ride out the challenge by ignoring, blocking, or acquiring the low-end competitor or it could decide to strengthen its own value proposition by adding new price points, increasing its level of benefits, or dropping its prices. Such tactics can be effective in the short term, but the industry leader also needs to consider strategic retreat, particularly when certain conditions make future low-end challenges inevitable.

---

[9] Potter Don: Confronting Low-end Competition, *Harvard Business Review*, July, 2004.

COMPETITOR ANALYSIS
LEARNING MODEL

- **STAGE 1**

  <u>ASSESSMENT</u> : CURRENT, PREVIOUS, NEED
  FOR KNOWLEDGE BASE
  <u>DECISIONS AND ACTIONS</u>: SITUATION BASED,
  ACTION PLAN, STRENGTH

- **STAGE 2**

  <u>CAPTURING</u> : BUILDING INFORMATION BASE

- **STAGE 3**

  <u>PROCESSING</u> : INFORMATION ANALSYIS AND
  INTERPRETING RESULTS

- **STAGE 4**

  <u>CRAFTING</u> : SHAPING OUTPUT, REVIEWING,
  COMMUNICATING OUTPUT

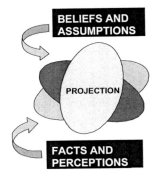

Figure 7.1.

COMPETITOR LEARNING

There are many ways of competitor learning process. Comparative learning occurs when two or more competitors are compared and contrasted. It especially entails analysis of outputs which is necessary frequently to compare and contrast the projections of two or more competitors' future strategies as a means of anticipating which competitors are likely to do what and when. It is also often necessary to compare and contrast how competitors are responding to the focal firm's own initiatives. The process of descriptive learning of competitors involves learning about the individual competitors at the basic level in reference to capturing the processing data and information about the competitor to identify the facts and features. This learning tool supports the inputs to comparative learning. Many of the concepts and analysis tools such as marketplace strategic activity, value chain, assumptions, resources, and competency facilitate comparisons across two or more competitors. The comparative learning process generates insights and inferences that cannot be derived by examining individual competitors in isolation. Learning is a cognitive process as customer decisions make sense of the world around them. They select and array the information, permeate data with meaning, draw inferences from incomplete data and portray the results. Thus, the wide variety of analysis tools and techniques presented throughout the remaining chapters are intended as aids to interpretation. Learning also is a collective process though transforming individual learning into organizational learning is a difficult task. Learning truly occurs when individuals share their knowledge, challenge each other, and reflect on each other's judgments and assessments.

Understanding and analyzing each move of the competitor and using the output to developing counter strategy may be defined as the process of the competitor learning. This integrates the process of knowledge management through four stages as exhibited in Figure 7.1. The company must make assessment of the existing needs, historical perspectives and develop the knowledge bank accordingly to help in decision making and scheduling the actions. The actions need to be taken by the company as required for the situation in view of projecting the facts and beliefs more effectively among the customers. The learning exercises may take place with individuals and groups who are engaged in decision-making. It is necessary to build-up strong, comprehensive and reliable database for capturing the activities of any business rival or competitor. Data is thus the basic input for competitor learning. In the process of capturing the competitor's moves the first task is to determine the data requirement and issue clear instructions to the data base managers (DBM). The DBMs have to first identify the data sources, prepare a checklist of information, collect data and submit it for analysis to the competent department or agency. The information collection is a very vulnerable issue and there may be many companies looking for the similar sets of information. Hence taking the opportunity first is always advantageous in the business. The major task in processing the data is proper interpretation of results. There should be no biases and the results of the analysis should be able to detect some signals. The crafting of the information outputs is one of the important tasks which should give a shape to the output. The outputs are crafted to inform the decision makers and influence decision-making in the interest of the business.

The two core concepts of the competitor learning process are *efficient and effective* learning. The former refers to the learning input-output ratio. The input for the learning process is the competitor data and the output includes the change in knowledge level. The effective competitor learning addresses the output-decision relationship. In the process of competitor learning both efficiency and effectiveness need attention and require data, information and intelligence. Data constitute the basic input in the process of competitor learning. The data about any competitor may be put into three broad categories *viz.* behavioral pattern of the competitor, statements pertaining to the competitor, and organization change. The individual actions of competitors or the patterns displayed thereof are referred as the competitor behavior. The actions may be analyzed in reference to the market place strategy, customer relationship, brand management, sales and promotion of the products and services in the region. The statements of the competitors may be of various types such as the performance data, announcements, annual reports and the like. These constitute formal business communications made in the public periodically. The informal communications on the other hand are largely oral comments delivered by the channels, competitors' personnel and high profile rivals, though these statements are not authentic. However, such informal information may be very useful to build strategies down to reality for outwitting the competitors in the market. The changes in the business strategies, financial status, business credentials and production and sales data represent the data on organizational change. Such information plays a significant role in understanding the latest moves of the competitor in the market and allows the new entrants to build a shield for their business as well as develop strategies to overcome the competitive blockades. It is essential that the data on the competitor's strategies should have the following attributes for efficient and effective analysis:

- Quantification
- Temporal values *i.e.* time series data
- Precision, and
- Description and opinion

Race of Cosmetics Companies in China

The Chinese cosmetics and toiletries industry certainly presents an attractive proposition for any business, valued at US $7.9 billion. It is the world's eighth largest market for the industry and second largest of Asia which has registered 12 percent growth in 2004. Increased disposable income has meant that more consumers can afford higher value products and so, are increasingly buying into the growing 'upper mass' sector or are trading up from mass brands to premium ones. Distribution has been affected by chained retailers, such as Wal-Mart, Carrefour and Hong Kong based Sa Sa, extending their retail networks in China. Skin care is the most valuable cosmetics and toiletries sector in China, accounting for 38 percent of all industry sales during and demonstrating significant potential for further expansion. Key to the growth of skin care was a rise in the up take of anti-ageing or nourishing facial care products, which form part of a the emerging 'upper-mass' segment. Such brands command higher prices as they adopt attributes that were once confined to premium products therefore offering consumers added value above their usual moisture products.

With dynamism and high value, skin care was the sector that presented the maximum opportunity for brands to establish themselves in China. This sector attracts western brands which are keen to make their presence, particularly when local markets are proving to be stagnant. However, cultural differences can often make it harder for them to establish themselves. Chinese skin care draws inspiration from the abundance of herbs and plant life in the country and this is one way in which companies have tried to become closer to understanding the market. Multinationals are quick to establish partnerships with local scientists and doctors so as to increase their understanding of the medicinal properties of skin care in native herbs and plants and their effects on the skin. The improving situation in China has led companies like Procter & Gamble (P&G) and L'Oréal to step up their investment in the market. Procter & Gamble's Olay brand has a strong established presence in China, which is maintained through an extensive product range, affordable pricing and strong national advertising, often endorsed with celebrities. Procter & Gamble launched, Olay brand in China during April 2005 as a test market for their make up brands while Max Factor and Cover Girl also set to fortify their dominant presence in the market by using the channels established on the strength of the Olay brand of P&G. During 2004 L'Oreal made two acquisitions in the Chinese cosmetics and toiletries market, firstly with Mininurse, a well loved domestic skin care brand, and then Yue-Sai. L'Oréal will benefit from the strong and extensive distribution channels these brands hold and is challenging Olay's dominance in the market through development of the *Mininurse* brand image. L'Oréal has already introduced the Garnier Naturals range under the *Mininurse* name, which has proved popular with young and trendy consumers and their market share, particularly in the skin care sector, is building rapidly. Procter & Gamble and L'Oréal's increased presence in China has helped the expansion of the 'upper-mass' segment in skin care too, which creates higher value sales for their products.

Source: Euro-monitor International On line, September 2005.

It is necessary to look into some of the information errors that may occur during the data collection process. The fallacy of misplaced facts is most common among various problems in data collection. The information on the projections of the cash flows, sales and production levels are more vulnerable for the competitors as well as the customers and investors in business. The information error also constitutes the misconstrue pattern or underlying structure in a set of information or data. Such information errors are based on the assumptions drawn by the information collectors and disseminators. However, the exaggerated information provided to the strategy builder or decision-makers is also one of the common information errors that occur often in the process of outwitting the competitor from the market. Evidence for the success of relationship marketing remains contradictory, with practitioners reporting that most relationship marketing efforts fail, and academic researchers suggesting that further exploration of the boundary conditions of relationship marketing are needed. A number of researchers have identified changes in the competitive environment as the basis for the adoption of relationship marketing, although recent research suggests a more complex, contingent view[10].

At the turn of the twentieth century, American and Chinese millers were locked in a fiercely contested battle for control of China's flour market. Imported American flour had dominated Chinese urban markets since the early 1880s, but the founding of a modern native milling industry in 1900 had initiated a commercial war that pitted the great flour corporations of the Pacific Coast against the independent mill owners near Shanghai. Although the anti-American boycott of 1905 had boosted sales for Chinese mills and sparked growth in the native industry, the period between 1905 and 1909 severely tested the ability of the young industry to survive foreign competition. A high silver/gold rate, low transpacific shipping rates, and bumper wheat harvests in the Pacific Northwest lowered the relative cost and enhanced the market appeal of American flour to Chinese brokers. Conversely, severe flooding in China's wheat-producing regions forced curtailment or even cessation of production for some native mills. Facing catastrophic reductions in their wheat supplies and markets saturated with American flour, Chinese millers devised alternative business strategies and implemented collaborative measures to ensure the solvency of their mills. A study[11] examines the details and dynamics of the competition between native and imported flour and highlights the decisive measures Chinese mill owners employed to assure the survivability of the modern milling industry in China. If there were any question or doubt about the Chinese becoming a flour-eating people to a considerable extent, the building of a mill by the Fou Foong Flour Mills Co. at Shanghai would dispel it. It is not in the nature of things for Chinese businessmen to act hastily, so that the erection of this mill may be regarded as an index of the future.

A common mistake many firms make is to start by collecting information without thinking how the information will be used such junk data has no value and it will be just shelved. The information needs to be comprehensive and adequate to help analysis of the strategic or tactical decisions on the role of competitors and vita indicators. If a firm is planning a new product, information on the status of the competitors in the area will help in the decision processes and plans for this new product. Alternatively, the firm may review how

[10] Beverland Michael and Lindgreen Adam: Relationship Use and Market Dynamism-A Model of Relationship Evolution, *Journal of Marketing Management*, 20 (7-8), August 2004, 825-858.
[11] Meissner, Daniel J: The Business of Survival- Competition and Cooperation in the Shenghai Flour Milling Industry, Enterprise and Society, 6(3), September,2005, 364-394.

the industry will develop in the future towards market leadership, potential merger, and acquisition or business partnership. The information requirements for each of these business decisions will be completely different and so the information that should be sought will also be different. Thus before starting to search for information, the competitor analyst needs to sit back and define what the firm is looking for and why. It is important to identify the key areas of concern for the business decision makers requesting the information, and aim to satisfy these. The supplementary information may be interesting, but unless it helps the decision process it should be viewed as superfluous, and should be stored for use at another time or even ignored if it is unlikely to ever have value. Hence, a firm may streamline its search needs towards better planned and focused strategies which would help in answering various intelligence requirements of the business.

The Asian product and services industry has posed a major competitive threat to the western countries. The principal concern for many firms is the impact of low-cost Chinese manufacturing and Indian services on global pricing. Focusing on this concern alone represents a profound misunderstanding of the nature of the competitive threat. Emerging markets might seem an implausible wellspring of innovation. Certainly, most of the companies must overcome significant obstacles to threaten those in developed ones. Yet the challenge remains of serving the harder-to-reach and more cost-conscious consumers of developing countries who are also typically less loyal to established brands. Such challenge may force companies to design and deliver products comparable to the offerings of developed nations for as little as one-fifth the price in order to stand competitive in the price sensitive markets. Doing so requires big changes to the design of products and processes, and these changes may soon affect developed markets dramatically to reconcile their competitive strategies. The spread of Chinese products as low priced mass market drivers may be described as the case of extreme competition wherein, an oversupply of labor, infrastructure, production, and capital has weakened the performance of whole industry while helping upstarts to challenge their established positions in global markets.

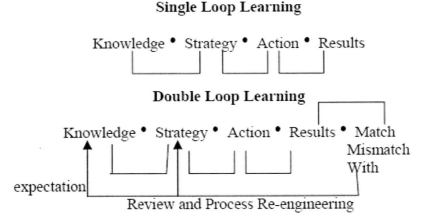

Figure 7.2. Competitor Learning Models.

Many multinational companies are now advertising their services and some specialize in offering information that can be used for competitor research. Some of them include *Dun & Bradstreet* (D&B) with a database of over 30 million companies world wide. The information on patents can be obtained from companies such as *Derwent Information* or from local patent offices. And global press information is available from databases made available by companies such as *Dialog, Lexis-Nexis and Factiva*. There are numerous other web-sources which include discussion forums, web-logs (blogs), protest groups, customer and governmental sites and so on.

COMPETITOR LEARNING MODELS

It is essential that any company planning for competitive strategies should possess high learning skills in order to collect right information, analyze and interpret the results. The organization's knowledge about a competitor and his moves broadly consists of perceptions, beliefs, assumptions and projections. Learning as the detection and correction process has varied implications for outwitting, outmaneuvering and outperforming competitors. Figure 7.2 exhibits the single and double loop learning methods. The single loop learning may occur when the organization detects and corrects the knowledge base without changing thrust on its strategies and actions. This is a closed and confined learning method that does not allow reviewing or re-engineering the information spool. On the contrary, in the double loop learning process the organizational knowledge, information base and strategies in addition to its action plans are open for review and re-engineering in the long-term interest of the company.

There are three levels of competitor analysis —a system, an individual competitor and specific components of the competitor. The framework of competitor analysis includes the infrastructure and culture of an organization and value chain, networks and relationships representing the environment of the company. The entire analysis must focus on the current strategy of the competitor firm and its future steps. Besides the assumptions in business risks and prospects, it is also important to analyze the assets, capabilities, competence levels and technology usage of the competing firm. In all these exercises, the data must be reliable and comprehensive to make the competitor learning process stronger. Signals are perhaps the most important core concept in competitor learning. A signal is an inference drawn by an individual in some specific context from the data and information about a competitor pertaining to the past, current and future strategies. The core components of the signal are indicators of the data and information. The inferences on signals received from the competitors on the basis of data need to be drawn to derive strategies for implementation.

A competitor signal is difficult to interpret and assess if there is no proper database and the indicators are not relevant. The ambiguity about indicators may occur by words, actions, unclear strategies of the organization and biased information. The signals from the competitor may be direct or indirect. The analyst needs logical aptitude and strong reasoning to use the indirect signals appropriately for building strategies. The competitors send signals in the market about all the vital indicators of business like product, services, advertisement, prices, channels etc. in a distorted fashion to weaken the business rivals. It is thus necessary to capture the signals well in time and draw inferences. Late attention to the signal may lead to detection lag, caused by the extended length of time between the availability of the information and its capture by the analyst. The competitors' signaling is very volatile and needs to be attended immediately to avoid any time lag or delay in drawing the inferences out of the available information. Knowledge is an important component in the process of competitor learning. Knowledge in the business activities is an outcome of intellectual efforts performed by the individuals with an objective of providing vital information on the move of the rivals in the market. There are some companies who provide information services as consultancy. However, the large companies, which have the narrow objective of only production, have realized the importance of building a knowledge base for sustaining competition and heading towards continuous growth. The business players of product and services need to replenish their knowledge continuously on consumer behavior, competitor moves, technology development and future market dynamics. The linkages outside the company in the form of alliances, informal business partnership, and networking also are contemporary sources to the knowledge on the competitor learning. It may be observed on the present business platforms that the large corporations and MNCs have been acting with ever greater ingenuity by crafting linkages with rivals, channels, customers, suppliers and technology sources. The competing television channels may be one of the examples of such strategies, which develop variety of contacts for getting information from the customers and the reaction of the rivals in the market. The customer behavior towards the products and services of any company is analyzed on the basis of the perceptual dimensions on the qualitative parameters. The perceptual indicators may broadly include brand loyalty, corporate image, competitive standing and the extent of business credibility earned by the company in the market.

Analysis of the information for learning the competitor movements should be aimed at knowing who is winning and loosing the business game in each arena, who is controlling the majority of business stakes in the market and which company is redefining its business strategies in a modified way convenient to its customers and suppliers on the win-win platform. Theorists have highlighted the issue of 'market driving' wherein, in contrast to focusing on being close and listening to the market/customer (market driven), the firm 'leads the customer' or reshapes the markets to their own requirements. This study aims to present an empirical study of market driving that generates insights into not only what factors lead a firm into a market driving approach but also how market driving occurs in practice. A review of existing literature reveals that while a range of contributions have considerably advanced our understanding of both market driven and more recently, of market driving organizations, few empirical studies have been presented. An exploratory discussion has been presented in the case study of De Beers in China as a potentially valuable source of insights, complemented by a propositional inventory. The case of De Beers proposes that two factors lead to the adoption of a market driving approach, namely customer familiarity and preconceptions of product characteristics, and the extent of market control. This study also contributes insights into the nature and dynamics of market driving. In particular, four tenets of market driving are identified which include market sensing, changing customer preferences, channel control through relationship formation, and local sensitivity[12].

The *competitive intelligence* also contributes to the learning process of a growing firm. Competitive intelligence is the information available to the competitors for free access on the public resources, which is periodically updated to present the current contents and potential strategic information. The information acquired by the competitors through public sources

[12] Harris L C and Cai K Y: Exploring Market Driving-A Case Study of DeBeers in China, Journal of Market-Focused Management, 5 (3), September, 2002, 171.196.

serves as an important input in formulating marketing strategy. A firm must be aware of the perspectives of its competitors before deciding which competitive moves to make. The competitive intelligence includes information beyond industry statistics and trade gossip. It involves close observation of competitors to learn what they do best and why and where they are weak. There exist three types of competitive intelligence—defensive, passive, and offensive. The defensive intelligence is the information gathered, analyzed and used to avoid being caught off-balance. In this process a deliberate attempt is made by the competing firm to gather information on the prevailing competition in a structured fashion and to keep track of moves of the rivals that are relevant to the firm's business. The passive intelligence is the temporary information gathered for a specific decision. A company may, for example, seek information on a competitor's sales compensation plan when devising its own compensation plan. An offensive intelligence is the information gathered by the firms to identify new opportunities and from a strategic perspective; such intelligence is most relevant for a growing firm amidst competition.

PLAYING IN THE COMPETITION

The organizations that seek to win the market by modeling their strategy in a suitable way should build their energy on two platforms. First, they need to endeavor to model the competitive game in view of the various entities involved such as organizational players, market arenas, information builders and scorers. Second, the company should get acquainted to the market place rules as how the customers, channels, factors and institutions are attracted, won and retained in the business. The competitors strive to attract, obtain, and retain the support, commitment, and involvement of end customers, channel members, factor suppliers, and institutions within the context or conditions of strategy games. Such elements include the structure of the game combatants, the arenas, and the nature of the stakes they hold and the entire composition of the business domain. The marketplace rules pertaining to how best to package and distribute products, create image and reputation, deliver service, build relationships emerge over time are the basic challenge for the firms. Many firms may intend to redefine or rescale the customer satisfaction from narrow product functionality to include all aspects of interactions with customers, for example, the Japanese automobile manufacturers redefined *quality* for many consumers to distinguish their quality, services and customer values against the competing overseas brands. In the competitive marketplace some firms may look for introducing frequently the product upgrades to keep up with pace of market competition. Besides, some firms may initiate major efforts to develop new capabilities and competency and monitor their progress in doing so against specific competitors as one element in their scorecard to determine who will reserve their plans to win in the future marketplace.

The companies try to alter the number of players by creating situation for deposing them from the market or change their own position relative to other players. The strategies such as alliances, mergers and acquisitions are the direct means of reducing the competition or deposing the existing rivals from the market. The Hindustan Lever Ltd., the giant in the FMCG segment in India, through a series of acquisitions largely reduced the number of players in the consumer goods segment. The development of networks, linking suppliers, manufacturers and consumers is another popular strategy to discourage competition in the particular segment of goods and services. The quick implementation of research and development, new products development and brand extensions indirectly break the existing competition in the market and allow the new company to re-deploy its marketing strategies. The pace of rivalry is such that no firm can now afford to take its resources for granted. Some firms may be recognized as being in the low-tech business segment such as textiles, shoes etc. Furniture, paint, and books, are feverishly pursuing new knowledge that might radically reshape established products or traditional ways of manufacturing and distributing them. In high-tech businesses such as electronics, firms that include IBM, Apple, Motorola, Intel, and Microsoft have formed multiple alliances with entities all across the activity/value chain and share innovative knowledge, skills and capabilities. Several modes of competition can be employed within the end-customer and channel arenas to get and keep customers. Although rivals compete in many distinct ways, firms can make eight key choices to distinguish and differentiate themselves in the eyes of customers and channels which may be described as product-mix, product features, functionality, service, distribution or availability, image and reputation, selling and relationships, and price[13].

The examination of the policy determinants of economic growth by exploiting a new firm level database for ten OECD countries shows that the contribution to productivity growth from firm level dynamic processes should not be overlooked, most notably in high-tech industries where new firms tend to boost overall productivity. There is evidence that burdensome regulations on entrepreneurial activity as well as high costs of adjusting the workforce negatively affect the entry of new small firms. Overall, there are a number of different features of entrant and exiting firms across countries. In particular, in the United States entrant firms tend to be smaller and with lower than average productivity, but those surviving the initial years expand rapidly. By contrast, in Europe firms tend to enter with a relatively higher size and productivity, but subsequently do not expand significantly. These findings tend to support the hypothesis of greater market experimentation in the United States, compared to many continental European countries, which is likely to be the result of differences in regulatory settings across the Atlantic[14]. As the world economy becomes increasingly integrated and globalized, U.S. companies face an unprecedented opportunity and challenge. In the global marketplace, China has made great strides in economic and commercial developments. China is becoming a manufacturing base for the world in providing quality products at low prices. As more businesspeople turn their attention to China's progress, they also need to review the business trends in its neighboring country, India. In spite of its problems, the Indian government and people are determined to increase India's contribution to the world economy[15].

The companies also maneuver the arena of customers, channels, institutions and the geographical coverage in order to reconfigure their competitive strategy. The software companies like Intel, Microsoft and 3M always keep extending the product line implementing the R&D results and never let the competition stagnate in the end-customer arena. The

---

[13] For detailed discussion on the corporate key choices to withstand competition, see Peter Senge: *The Fifth Discipline*, New York, Doubleday/Currency, 1990.

[14] OECD: Sources of Economic Growth in OECD Countries, Firm Dynamics, Productivity and Policy Settings, *The Sources of Economic Growth in OECD Countries*, OECD, pp. 210-262 (53).

[15] Anshu Saran and Guo Chiquan: Competing in Global Marketplace: The case of India and China, *Business Horizon*, March 2005.

healthy companies feel that the greater the competition, the higher will be the challenge to establish the brand in the market. The Suzuki collaboration with Maruti Udyog Limited in India has changed the dominance of the popular brand holder Premier Automobiles Ltd. and created a new competitive context of small city cars. The channels of supply for any company are always vulnerable to the competition. The common practice followed by the competitors is breaking the supply chain by offering more perks and margins than the leading brand. However, if the channels are favorably treated with long-term advantages, the endeavor to build the linkages with them would withstand any competitive rivalry. The collaboration between Proctor and Gamble and Wal-Mart involving strong integration of product ordering, inventory control and logistics may be a classic example in this context[16]. The factor advantage in the competition may be defined as the relationship of the manufacturing or marketing company with the service providers who develop loyalty towards them. The service providers may be the suppliers of raw materials, packaging services, machine rentals and the like. Many companies use the legal support, government patronage etc. to shape the competitive conditions to their advantage while building the institutional arena in the business.

The premium automobiles segment has been dominated by two capital and hi-tech giants- BMW and Mercedes. While BMW's plants run at 95% of capacity, Mercedes' German factories operate at around 80%, say analysts. One reason is declining sales of the E-Class and C-Class models, both of which have suffered quality problems. A face-lift for the E-Class in 2006 and a new C-Class expected in late 2007 should help buoy weak sales. But union contracts that make Mercedes workers' work rules less flexible than the rivals' are also to blame for the relatively low output. At BMW, employees work less during periods of slow demand and then bank the unused hours, paying them back during peak periods, thus eliminating a lot of overtime pay. Mercedes recently instituted more flexible schedules and got union agreement to shuttle workers among plants, long a practice at BMW. Improving quality is also vital. The drive to lead in new technologies has resulted in cars packed with different electronic systems, which must all be integrated into a core system that functions harmoniously, a devilishly hard task. By contrast, BMW has sought to install common electronics backbones across many model lines. It also saves money by sharing more components among models. However, some business analysts feel that the Mercedes has been over invested in the wrong things. When the competition figured out that the company does not have to design an entirely new car to offer, Mercedes is still working to offer something new with its cars. Mercedes insists its cars use the same electronic architecture but admits that many components vary across the wide array of models. The crux of the problem lies in designing less complex cars and improving test procedures before a model launches. Redesigning and reengineering all Mercedes models for better quality could take two years. The major issue that remains at the bottom line of the business is whether any brand can hold competition for its projected gains?[17]

The stakes in the business may be understood as the benefits of winning the game and the cost of losing the business in the market. Many companies in the market place intend to escalate the stakes in the business as one of their competitive strategies in various arenas as discussed in the previous sections. The companies also redefine their market place strategies

---

[16] Fahe Liam: *Competitors: Outwitting, Outmaneuvering and Outperforming*, John Wiley and Sons, Canada, 1999.
[17] Gail Edmondson: Mercedes' New Boss Rolls up his Sleeves, *Business Week (online Edition)*, October 17, 2005.

for gaining the win-win situation in the market. Table 7.1 exhibits the parameters that are used for redefining the marketplace rules by many companies in order to keep up with market competition. There are many competitive strategies used by the companies to get and retain the customers and the channels. The companies desiring to strengthen themselves against the competitive threats in the market need to develop different modes of entering into the market. The companies also re-focus their strategies to attract the customers and retain them for the long-term benefits. Table 7.1 discusses the major issues related with redefining market place. Many organizations are driven by one or a few overarching, long-run goals that imbue the organization with a collective challenge, shared vision and sense of mission or purpose. Such goals have been designated by others as a strategic intent or vision and super ordinate goals. Among goals set by many companies, a few may include: reorientation towards R&D to products that are new to the marketplace; extend product lines to attract new segments of customers; use alliances to build a significant marketplace position in leading Asian or European countries; build new manufacturing facilities for new product development and introduction; and develop new marketing capabilities to outmaneuver specific competitors across major customer segments.

The market place strategies also determine the mergers and acquisitions of the companies for competitive advantage. Acquisitions and alliances are two pillars of growth strategy. But most businesses don't treat the two as alternative mechanisms for attaining goals. Consequently, companies take over firms they should have collaborated with, and vice versa, and make a mess of both acquisitions and alliances. It's easy to see why companies don't weigh the relative merits and demerits of acquisitions and alliances before choosing horses for courses. The two strategies differ in many ways: Acquisition deals are competitive, based on market prices, and risky; alliances are cooperative, negotiated, and not so risky. Companies habitually deploy acquisitions to increase scale or cut costs and use partnerships to enter new markets, customer segments, and regions. Moreover, a company's initial experiences often turn into blinders. If the firm pulls off an alliance or two, it tends to enter into alliances even when circumstances demand acquisitions. Organizational barriers also stand in the way. In many companies, the mergers and acquisitions group reports to the finance head and handles acquisitions, whereas a separate business development unit looks after alliances. The two teams work out of different locations, jealously guard turf and, in effect, prevent companies from comparing the advantages and disadvantages of the strategies. But companies could improve their results, the authors argue, if they compared the two strategies to determine which is best suited to the situation at hand[18]. Firms, such as Cisco, which use acquisitions and alliances appropriately, grow faster than rivals do.

Marketplace rules can be changed at three distinct but related levels such as the aggregate marketplace or, more narrowly, a competitive domain; a product-customer segment such as a niche within a competitive domain; and local channel member. The marketplace rules have been discussed in Table 7.1. All rivalry ultimately is acted out at the local or micro level. Each individual customer selects among rivals' offerings. At this level, the game is typically zero-sum: purchasing one rival's offering means lost opportunity for other competitors. The firms generally make the choices which have been experienced in the past by the competitors

---

[18] Dyer Jaffrey H, Kale Prashant and Singh Harpreet: When to Ally and When to Acquire, *Harvard Business Review*, July, 2004.

Table 7.1. Redefining the Marketplace Rules

Redefining Parameters	Attributes of Parameters
Modes of Competition	• Product line and width • Logistics and supply chain aspects • Price, sales and customer relation • Corporate and brand image
Focus	• Attracting, winning, retaining customers and channels
Levels	• Aggregate • Segment • Local
Trends	• Product –service-value differentiation • Customized solutions • Price, communication and delivery of goods and services.

to accomplish three distinct, though related, tasks which include attracting, winning, and retaining customers and channels. Attracting customers is a prelude to winning or acquiring them. The brand name and long standing image of the product influence and attracts customers to try a product.

The Dell Computer Corporation has plans to enter the competition in the Indian market with its subsidiary. Dell is one of the most globally preferred computers among the business class customers. The company finds that India is growing fast in sales of personal computers and there exists room for Dell to become a major player in the market. Its mode of entry will be through direct selling to its clients with total product customization as a global strategy. The company has plans to offer services to its international clients in the country and then follow it up with large corporate units, the Government and potential institutions in the future. This is one of the strategies to select the customer segment and operate safely in the market outwitting the competitors. The company is also having an alliance with a leading brand in the country— Tata InfoTech Ltd. and plans to launch on a joint platform. The customer support is a major thrust of the company and it is setting up a customer call center to redress their needs more efficiently, take orders from the clients as well as provide services to customers. Ever since the incorporation of the company in 1984 by Michael Dell, it has positioned itself in the top five of the computer sales category across the countries in the world and hopes to replicate the same in the Indian market. The company has an idea of offering software solutions instead of boxes and continues the relationship over the long term.[19] The company is looking for local outsourcing for the effective delivery of the products and service and the Indian outfit will be supported by Penang, the Malaysia production base. The company has chosen e-commerce as one of the contemporary strategies to reduce load on the physical channels. The deliveries are promised in a week that may turn to be a major attraction for the clients and a tall task for the service providers. The plans of the company seems to be complex but Dell being a big brand that has proved itself the world over and with a high brand loyalty and image, it has all hopes to succeed in the Indian market penetrating the competition in the computers business. Chip Sunders, the Vice President of the company says, *"Though there are successful players, we will be the winners"*.

---

[19] Reviewed from the Peoples and products, Advertising and Marketing, August 31, 2000, pp 8-12.

Satisfying buyer needs may be a prerequisite for industry profitability. One of the underlying issues in developing the competitive strategy is to address the profitability in reference to the capability of the firm whether it can capture the value in the process for retaining the buyers, or whether this value is competed away to others. The buying power of customers determines the extent to which they retain most of the value created for themselves. The threat of substitutes determines the extent to which some other product can meet the same buyer needs, and thus places a ceiling on the amount a buyer is willing to pay for an industry's product. The power of suppliers determines the extent to which value created for buyers will be appropriated by suppliers rather than by firms in an industry. The intensity of rivalry acts similar to the threat of entry. It determines the extent to which firms already in an industry will compete away the value they create for buyers among themselves, passing it on to buyers in lower prices or dissipating it in higher costs of competing. Some companies engaged in manufacturing automobiles and heavy trucks, create enormous value for their buyers but, on average, capture proportionately less of it for themselves through profits. On the contrary in the services industries such as bond rating services, medical equipment hiring, and oil field services and equipment, firms also create high value for their buyers but have historically captured a good proportion of it. The intensity of rivalry plays a major role in determining whether existing firms will expand capacity aggressively or choose to maintain profitability. Industry structure also determines how rapidly competitors will retire excess supply. Exit barriers keep firms from leaving an industry when there is too much capacity, and prolonged periods of excess capacity.

P&G has a variety of leading brands in the Indian market such as Ariel, Tide, Head and Shoulders, Pantene and Pringle. One more new idea, which is on schedule of the P&G portfolio, is *Febreze*. This product belongs to the P&G Home Products Division which include hair care and fabric care segment. This product has created a niche and holds a monopoly in the fabric odor cleanser category of products across the regions in India. This product was first taken off in the US markets in 1997 and now is available in 20 countries across the world. P&G has launched *Febreze* in Chennai, Coimbatore and Madurai in mid 2000 with a turnover of over Rs 6500 Million. The R&D of the company is confident to attract customers and enjoy the monopoly in the market for a time, as the company does not foresee any competition to come up in the near future. The product attributes are very close to the customer needs, as it is the first cleaning spray that safely and permanently eliminates odours trapped in the household and other fabrics. This product helps in reaching the difficult-to-clean fabrics, upholstery, carpets, and curtains, mattresses and car seats, which are largely unmanageable and remain unattended. This product is an outcome of the research carried out by the company. The target customers for this product are segmented as per the need parameters and largely constitute the car owners, housewives, hotels and airlines. The Febreze is not a perfume and hence does not compete with perfumes of room-deodorant brands in the market. To stand unique in the market the promotional and advertising strategies have been developed on the conclusions drawn on the research. The product has also been advertised on the net, print and electronic media. The strength of the brand, quality, positioning and the promotional formulae blended with the customer needs may open up an entire new segment depending on how its use values are perceived by the customers.

The results of an imbalance between supply and demand for industry profitability also differ widely depending on industry structure. In some industries, a small amount of excess capacity triggers price wars and low profitability. In view of the key role of competitive advantage in superior performance, the centerpiece of a firm's strategic plan should be its generic strategy. The generic strategy specifies the fundamental approach to competitive advantage a firm is pursuing, and provides the context for the actions to be taken in each functional area. In practice, however, many strategic plans are lists of action steps without a clear articulation of what competitive advantage the firm has or seeks to achieve and how. A firm's strategy is the route to competitive advantage that will determine its performance. Build, hold, and harvest are the results of a generic strategy, or recognition of the inability to achieve any generic strategy and hence of the need to harvest. The multinational firms largely practice strategic planning in reference to the market share to describe a competitive position of the firm. Market share *per se* is not important competitively; competitive advantage is. The strategic mandate to business units should be to achieve competitive advantage. Pursuit of leadership for its own sake may guarantee that a firm never achieves a competitive advantage or that it loses the one it has.

Conceptual framework of competitive forces in the marketplace has been provided by Porter as a five-force model for industry analysis is shown in Figure 7.3. These five forces of competition interact to determine the attractiveness of an industry. The strongest forces become the dominant factors in determining industry profitability and the focal points of strategy formulation. The model identifies the key structural features that determine the strength of the competitive forces within an industry in reference to profitability. It may be explained through the model that the degree of rivalry among different firms is a function of the number of competitors, industry growth, asset intensity, product differentiation, and exit barriers. Among these the most influential variables may be identified as the number of competitors and industry growth. The industries with high fixed costs tend to be more competitive because competing firms are forced to cut price to enable them to operate at the economies of scale. However, with the differentiation strategy the rivalry is reduced among the products and services offered by the competitors, in both real and perceived senses. Another significant concept which may be explained through this model is associated difficulty of exit from an industry, which may result into struggle for survival among the firms and intensified competition. Further, there remains the threat of entry into the industry by new firms which may enhance competition. Several barriers, however, make it difficult to enter an industry. Two cost-related entry barriers are economies of scale and absolute cost advantage. In this process of competition the new entrants face an up-hill challenge of scaling at a high level of production or to accept a cost advantage. However, absolute cost advantage remains with the long standing firms in the market which possess technological and brand advantages for their products and services. The substitute products in the market affect the industry potential adversely as well as pose threat to the customer preferences. Bargaining power of buyers refers to the direct or indirect pressure tactics to force the industry to reduce prices or increase product features, in view to optimize the customer value. Buyers gain power when they have choices—when their needs can be met by a substitute product or by the same product offered by another supplier. In addition, high buyer concentration, the threat of backward integration, and low switching costs add to buyer power. Similarly the bargaining power of suppliers refers to their ability to force the industry to accept higher margins or reduced services, in the interest of augmenting or securing their profits. The factors influencing supplier power are the same as that of buyer power. In this case, however, industry members act as buyers.

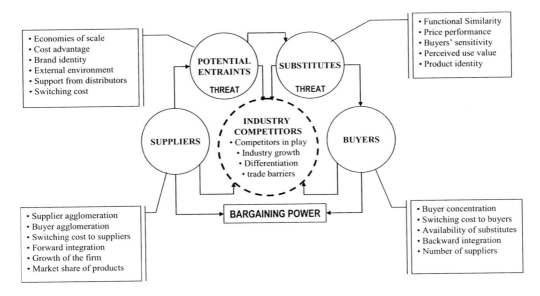

Figure 7.3. Competitive Strategy: Network of Market Forces.

COMPETITOR STRATEGIES

The companies engaged in competitive business should aim at conducting the competitor analysis to build competitive advantage and this cannot be done in isolation from the market and the rest of the industry, because being better than a competitor will not guarantee success if what is offered gives little value to the customer. Hence, it should be understood by the firms that any inferences which might be drawn from competitor analysis must be considered in conjunction with the other environmental factors. Every company has strategic options, although this does not mean that all options are sensible for every company. It may choose to operate within the rules of the industry, without major change to what it offers. The options may include a stronger focus on a niche strategy, seeking to identify and exploit segments where its products would have an advantage, or what might be termed improvement strategies. A competing firm may be attacked in various ways by a new and prospecting business firm in a given territory in order to optimize the market advantage. The most effective way for a firm to attack may be through implementing a creative and entrepreneurial strategy on a sound knowledge analysis in view of the changes in the competitive arena. Alternatively, a firm may attempt to pre-empt a competitor by getting into the market first with a new product, in an area of strategic importance. However, attacking the strategy of a competitor can leave the firm in a weaker position. The prospecting firm may also attack on the competitor's alliance instead of direct attack on the target. An example of this was the acquisition of Rover by BMW. There were undoubtedly many reasons for this acquisition, but one of them was to cause Honda to withdraw from the alliance it had operated for many years with Rover, and its predecessor British Leyland. Similar patterns of alliances changing allegiance have been observed in the airlines industry. The basic rule of any attack strategy is to know the industry, the market, and the competitors being attacked. If the weak points of the competitors are known, and their likely reactions predicted, the attacker is more likely to arrive at a successful strategy. It is this rational analysis which enables a decision to be made about whether the rewards of success outweigh the costs, and whether the chances of success are high enough to justify the move.

In a competitive business arena the competitors as players may be categorized as hard and soft players. The hard competitive players in business single-mindedly pursue competitive advantage and the benefits it includes— a leading market share, great margins, and rapid growth. They pick their shots, seek out competitive encounters, set the pace of innovation, and test the edges of the possible success of their products and services in the market. Soft players, by contrast, may look good, but they are not intensely serious about winning. They do not accept that you must sometimes hurt your rivals, and risk being hurt, to get what you want. The commonly employed methods in taking up the hard competitor strategies in bursts of ruthless intensity may include devastating rivals' profit sanctuaries, deceive the competition, unleash massive and overwhelming force, and raise competitors' costs[20]. The soft players do not play to win; they just participate in the business and try to survive. This approach envelops the issues such as leadership, corporate culture, knowledge management, talent management, and employee empowerment for analysis to the soft players. Every firm is risk averse in facing the business competition as it is a fact of business life, but many companies fail to manage it well. Good risk management not only protects companies from adverse risk but also confers a competitive advantage, enabling them to be more entrepreneurial and, in the end, to make bigger profits. Companies should clearly articulate their risk strategies, understand the risks they are taking, and build an effective risk-management organization that helps foster a responsible risk culture.

Changing aircraft technology, big capital investments and the shifting priorities of governments have repeatedly forced airline operators to scramble to stay air borne. Consequently, a swing of new low-cost airlines is attacking big incumbent network carriers, some of whom will probably not survive. Such aviation companies sparked meteoric growth by exploiting latent demand for cheap travel, but they can't create profitable markets indefinitely. Major sources of traffic in Northern and Central Europe will soon be saturated. However, interestingly, the differences go deeper as America's budget airlines are starting to move up-market in service quality, whereas Europe's give every impression of moving relentlessly down-market. They emphasize dirt-cheap tickets, yet they are also expanding as they try to fend off start-up competitors. The competition from low-cost carriers has increased the customer's price sensitivity, undermining the ability of the incumbents to charge a premium not only on routes where they compete with these carriers. In order to cope, scheduled carriers must choose their battles carefully and revise their business designs. The adaptation might be subtle for stronger players; for others, it might resemble the radical transformation *Aer Lingus* has begun. Most of the expansion in America has come from *JetBlue, Frontier and AirTran; Southwest*, which accounts for nearly half the sector, has been obliged by the wider air-travel recession to check its expansion, although it is now returning to its former growth path of 10% a year. While in Europe after the liberalization of Europe's domestic airline market was completed in 1997, *Ryanair and EasyJet*, the pioneers, explicitly and expertly mimicked American budget airlines such as Southwest and ValuJet (now *AirTran*). The Indian skies are also experiencing the boom of low-cost airlines like *Air Deccan*. The low-cost carriers find success by stimulating and exploiting pent-up demand for

---

[20] For detailed discussion on the hard and soft core competitor strategies see Stalk George Jr. and Lachenauer Rob: Hardball-Five Killer Strategies for Trouncing the Competition, *Harvard Business Review*, April, 2004.

cheap travel. Their entry into a market brings out people who would otherwise travel by train or car, if at all. In 2002, low-cost carriers and network carriers went head-to-head on 80 routes in Europe and America; since then, the former have increased their capacity on those routes by 15 percent, while the incumbents' capacity has shrunk by 4 percent. The biggest difference between low-cost carriers in America and Europe is that they have existed in Europe for less than ten years. In many markets, growth has stagnated after an initial spurt in demand. On these more established routes, growth for low-cost carriers (as for incumbents) now ranges from 4 to 6 percent. However, as they move up-market in America to fill the void left by big network carriers, and as they move to more expensive airports in Europe, the risk is that low-cost carriers everywhere will start to acquire the very same high costs that made their network competitors so vulnerable[21].

Markets involve many competitors, are compromised of *active terrain* in the way of customers and offer the opportunity of access to alternative resources by means of supply market mechanisms. Perhaps this is why IBM has been attempting to change the warfare metaphor they have been using to one of gardening, where customers are to be cultivated.

There are four major competitor attack strategies which are implemented by the companies at international, national and regional levels. These strategies include the frontal attack, flanking attack, encirclement and guerilla attack. The following fundamental principles are involved in planning and implementation of competitor attacks:

- The competing company needs to assess the strength of the target competitor and consider the amount of support that the target might congregate from allies. It would be appropriate to choose only one target at a time.
- The competing company should explore weaknesses in the target's position and launch attack on the core of weakness.
- It is necessary to work out the time-span as how long it will take for the target to realign their resources so as to reinforce this weak spot.
- The competitor may then launch the attack on as narrow a front (frame of weaknesses) as possible. Whereas a defender must defend all their borders, an attacker has the advantage of being able to concentrate their strategic and tactical tools at one place.

The *frontal attack* implies a head-on confrontation where the defense is at its strongest. Some such attacks mirror the defendant's marketing strategy, and hope to achieve results through sheer perseverance. Others have only one point of difference on price. By cutting price for what is otherwise a matched offering, the attacker hopes to be able to persuade customers to switch. Only in markets where there are many niches is it possible to use the full-frontal attack selectively. In markets where the products are nearer each other, an attack on one competitor is really an attack on all of them. In full-frontal attacks, the victory usually goes to the strongest. However, a dominant competitor is less likely to make a full-frontal attack on a competitor, unless it is a niche operator where the effects of the warfare can be isolated. The main consideration in the frontal attack is the strength of the leader's position and a company entering into such warfare may find a weakness in the leader's strength and

---

[21] For details see Urs Binggeli and Lucio Pompeo: The battle for Europe's Low-fare Flyers, *McKinsey Quarterly* (On-line edition), August 2005. Also refer *The Economist*: Turbulent Skies, July 08, 2004.

attack at that point. The company may launch the attack on as narrow a front as possible. The frontal attacks may be strategically fit and lead to an advantage in the business situations as described below:

- The market is relatively homogeneous
- Brand equity is low
- Customer loyalty is low
- Products are poorly differentiated
- The target competitor has relatively limited resources
- The attacker has relatively strong resources

Frontal attacks have appeal in industries where very large cost reductions can be gained from increases in volume, and where price reductions may stimulate growth in the market as well as stealing share from competitors. However, frontal attacks are often unsuccessful. If defenders are able to re-deploy their resources in time, the attacker's strategic advantage is lost. The frontal attacks are very expensive and risky for the companies of any status.

On the contrary to the frontal attacks, where company goes for attacking at the strongest zone, the *flanking attack* goes for areas of weakness. This may be to find geographical areas where the competitor is not performing as well as elsewhere, or to identify segments of the market which have not been spotted by the competitor. If the product has been specifically designed for the segment, it may be some time before the defender can respond. A good flanking move must be made into an uncontested area and the tactical surprise ought to be considered as an important element of the plan. The disadvantage with a flanking attack is that it can draw resources away from your center defense, making you vulnerable to a head-on attack. In business terms, a flanking attack involves competing in a market segment that the target competitor does not consider mission critical. The target competitor will not show his concern about activities of other firm if they occur in market niches. It usually involves subtle advertising campaigns and other discrete promotional measures, like personal selling and public relations. It often entails customizing a product for that particular niche. Rather than finding uncontested market niches, the attacker could also look for uncontested geographical areas. The strategy is suitable when:

- the market is segmented
- there are some segments that are not well served by the existing competitors
- the target competitor has relatively strong resources and is well able to withstand a head-on attack
- the attacker has moderately strong resources, enough to successfully defend several niches

The geographical flanking attacks may be described in reference to the strategy of the retail supermarket which erects its new store in an area where its rivals are weakest. Another is First Direct which established a telephone retail banking operation, which not only avoided the need for branch offices but also enabled the company to accept only the business it wanted, thus cherry picking the more profitable ones. Product flanking is a competitive marketing strategy in which a company produces its brands in a variety of sizes and styles to gain shelf space and inhibit competitors. The defender companies may need to add extensions to an existing product line by introducing new products in the same product category in order to give customers greater choice and help to protect the company from a flanking attack by a competitor.

> The U.S. market leader, Marlboro has been hitting all-time highs this year. Despite the sharp advertising restrictions agreed to by cigarette marketers in 1998 and a dramatic rise in state excise taxes since 2002, Marlboro is galloping ahead of the competition. The brand, which commands an average $3.28 per pack, now owns more than 40% of the market. That surge has driven a broader gain for Philip Morris overall, which also makes Virginia Slims, Parliament, and other brands, and added significantly to the company's profits, possibly more than $200 million a year. Marlboro became one of the world's most valuable brands capturing the traditional mass marketing through the strong impact of advertising in print media and billboards. In 2003, more than $15 billion was spent on marketing cigarettes in the U.S., according to the most recent data from the Federal Trade Commission, a 21% jump over 2002. The company has passed through setback during the past and later has become a more deft and efficient marketer as a result of the legal settlement that sought to hobble the cigarette makers. Back in 1998 the Master Settlement Agreement (MSA) with the state attorneys general ended tobacco advertising in most of its traditional forms. But by forcing Marlboro to go viral, be aggressive in retail stores, and be more creative in its media plan, it put the company on a successful path now being followed by every marketer from General Motors and Audi to AXE deodorant. Today, all kinds of companies are pursuing similar viral marketing campaigns that draw consumers into brand communities. Contests and rewards keep smokers loyal, but to add new followers, marketing experts are of view that some low-tech means of persuasion are also important such as in-store promotions, price cuts, and other deals. The rivals are unhappy and complain that the advertising restrictions leave them with little chance of closing Marlboro's lead. One hot spot in Marlboro's marketing is a growing database of 26 million smokers to whom it sends everything from birthday coupons to the chance to attend events like November's birthday concerts. Indeed, Marlboro isn't just a brand; it is an exclusive club of loyalists[22].

The companies which attack the competitors in several ways such as branding, pricing, advertising and promotions, value additions, sales in up-markets, product featuring and the like in a given time may be described as *encirclement attack*. The successful encirclement strategies usually attempt to identify and exploit new niches, and to beat the offer made to the customer by competitors. The encirclement strategy is a much broader but subtle offensive strategy and is commonly planned in two ways. A company could introduce a range of products that are similar to product-mix of the target competitor. Each product will liberate some market share from the target competitor's product, leaving it weakened, demoralized, and in a state of siege. Alternatively, the encirclement can be based on market niches rather than products. The attacker expands the market niches that surround and encroach on the target competitor's market. This encroachment liberates market share from the target. The encirclement strategy can be implemented successfully under the following conditions:

- The market is loosely segmented
- Some segments are relatively free of well endowed competitors

---

[22] For details on the competitive edge of Marlboro's marketing strategies see *Business Week* (Online edition): Leader of the Packs, October 31, 2005.

- The attacker has strong product development resources
- The attacker has enough resources to operate in multiple segments simultaneously
- The attacker has a decentralized organizational structure

An example of *Sears Roebuck,* a chain retail store in the US, may be used to explain the encirclement strategy. The attempt by US retailers Sears Roebuck to change the financial services industry in the USA was an encirclement attack on competitors from several different industries at the same time. The in-store credit card was converted to Discovery, a full credit card by the company. All state Insurance had been part of the Sears Roebuck group for many years. The new niche the company hoped to conquer was the private consumer who wanted one-stop shopping: to buy a house, furnish it, obtain all necessary loan facilities, and insure everything in any Sears' store. The strategy failed, because the niche was not large enough. The acquisitions therefore did not upset the competitive situation in their industries, and the Discovery credit card became a frontal attack on existing credit card competitors. At one time Sears were reported to have secured the record for signing up the largest number of defaulting clients in the shortest time[23]. The electronics industry has been transformed due largely to the personal computer segment. For decades, the electronics industry's primary objective for personal computer products was to offer the maximum power and functionality for the lowest possible price. This focus resulted in tremendous innovation and a proliferation of products at prices that virtually everyone could afford. It also began to erode profit margins for electronics companies. Led by the personal computer segment, the electronics industry built a model supply chain that is tightly linked and highly competitive. Vertically integrated companies became outmoded, replaced by companies which specialized in standardized components and software and did business with each other companies. Though swift at capturing and extending cost reductions and efficiencies, this evolved supply chain model led to product commoditization and standardization. Any innovation that a company produced could be copied quickly and usually at a lower cost. Therefore, competitive advantage was fleeting. Rapid technology change and short product lifecycles contributed to the further erosion of profit margins[24].

Table 7.2. Core Elements of Market Place Strategy

Scope	Competitive Posture	Goals	Moves and Directions
Customer and product segments	Product line Features Functionality Services Brand and sales CRM*	Type of Strategy	Influence Positioning Marketing-mix Vision

* Customer Relationship Management.

---

[23] Hussey David and Jenster Per: *Competitor Intelligence-Turning Analysis into Success,* John Wiley, West Sussex, 1999

[24] Brody Paul, Wenzek Hagen and Osterday Tom: *Product Styling-The New Competitive Differentiator in Electronics,* IBM Institute for Business Value, February, 2004.

The *guerrilla marketing* warfare strategies are a type of marketing warfare strategy designed to wear-down the enemy by a long series of minor attacks rather than engage in major battles. A guerrilla task force of a competitor firm is divided into small groups that selectively attack the target at its weak points. To be effective, guerrilla teams of the competitor set themselves underground between the strikes. The guerrilla marketing strategies of competitors involve targeted legal attacks on the competition, product comparison advertising, short-term alliances, selective price cuts and orchestrating negative publicity for a competitor.

MARKET PLACE STRATEGY

The market place strategy includes elements of product and customer segments, competitive posture, goals and moves and directions of the firm. The products and customers are categorized in different ways. The products and services may be classified as per the product line matrix—length and width (type and items). The core elements of market place strategy are exhibited in Table 7.2. The customers are segmented on the basis of the products and services they use at any point of time. The customer demographics are also considered to a large extent in segmenting the customers. The needs of customers relate more directly than any of the demographic profiles. The distributing channels better know the competitor's position and direction of the competitor than any other external agency. The tapping of right information taking the distribution channels into confidence would be more appropriate than any other means to the company. Rival business firms often choose distinctly different channels to reach the end users. The competitive posture reveals how a competitor competes in the market place to attract the customers win and retain them. The customer is the kingpin in determining the competitive posture. The competitive posture of the company consists of product line, attributes of the product, functionality, service, availability, image, sales relationship and pricing pattern. The product line broadly refers to the range of products available with the competitor. The distributors and retailers are more concerned with the width (item under product range). Some companies focus on narrow range of products and build high image among the customers. The product attributes vary in terms of shape, design, style, color and added advantages. Further, the customers may view the functionality of the product as the satisfaction derived from the products. The dimensions of the functionality are highly product specific.

In the competitive markets, the efficiency of the services discharged and extended to the buyers also contributes in building or breaking the market place strategy. Products, in the same market or competitive domain, largely vary in their availability may be due to weak or faulty supply chain management. The competing firms must study this situation and develop strategies accordingly. Beside all, the price game played by the mercantile and service sector companies is very sensitive and may carry enough strength to destroy the rival's business. Such market tactics among the companies dealing with fast moving consumer goods (FMCGs) and services have been observed time and again. The example of price war may be cited appropriately of the airlines— Jet Airways, Sahara India and Indian Airlines for attracting more passengers on the domestic trunk routs by slashing the prices. The position and direction of the market place may be assessed by measuring the coverage of product-customer segments and changes that are taking place thereof. The types of strategies that can be adopted in the market place are exhibited in Figure 7.4.

A niche domain involves a narrow product line and customer segment. A competing company must take a note that the rival is always expert in terms of product and customers. The spread domain entails a narrow products range targeted at a large segment of customers. Such firms invest more time and resources in building brand and securing the customer segments (eg., Bata Ltd. has a narrow product-mix but has a wide customer segment). The proliferated domain involves a wide range of products aimed at narrow customer segments (Say class market buyers). Many companies offer a wide range of products in the restricted region. A blanket domain is attained when the competitor has positioned the products and services in all the available segments (*e.g.,* Bajaj Scooters Ltd. in the automobile sector). In general, if the entry into an industry is relatively easy, many firms, including some marginal ones, are attracted to it. The long-standing, committed members of the industry, however, do not want new entrants to break into their territory. Therefore existing firms discourage potential entrants by adopting strategies that enhance competition. However, if the products offered by different competitors are perceived by the customer to be more or less similar, firms are forced into price and, to a lesser degree, service competition. Such competition can be really severe. The marketplace rules may sometimes lay the exit barriers on the rationale of the cost-benefit adjustment. The exit barriers implant deterrence and such strategy may be described as to:

- Persuade new entrants that the market is not worth entering, because of the way you will react, or
- Try to stop encroachments into a segment of the market which is important to you, or
- Attempt to keep a competitor from increasing its market share.

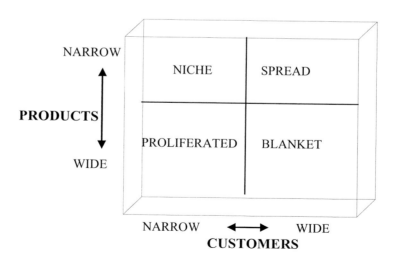

Figure 7.4. Types of Market Place Strategy.

The best deterrence is a strong position, which makes it difficult for an attacker to gain a foothold in an economic way. This is not achieved just by having the largest market share. Indeed sheer size and past success often breeds complacency, despite the achievements of the past. For a variety of reasons, it may be difficult for a firm to get out of a particular business. Some of the possible reasons include the relationship of the business to other businesses of the firm, high investment in assets for which there may not be a beneficial alternative use, high cost that may incur towards discharging commitments, etc. Successful companies like Wal-Mart and Intel have devised innovative responses to these threats and have outperformed their competition. A strong competitive position for a firm has market share as a component, and this may be most important when the learning curve effect means that high volumes give lower costs, which in turn allow prices to be set which other competitors find difficult to meet. But it is also about technological foresight, adequate levels of research and development, and giving customers value in all respects so that they have little incentive to change.

Many organizations feel that in growing competition establishing strategic alliances would better check the competitor's penetration in the market. They recognize that alliances and relationships with other companies of repute are fundamental to outwit, outmaneuver and outperform the competitors by ways of better branding, better service and tagging global brands for assuring the quality of goods and services. Alliances and relationships thus transform the concept of competitor. The strategic alliances may be in various forms like branding, logistics, research and development, productions and operations management, packaging, services, sales and customers. The tie-up relationship of any computer firm with Compaq drives the customer demand for both the brands —the mother brand and the aligned brand. The business alliances have to be identified by doing an exercise scientifically. The company has to list all alliances that it is planning to have to outperform the competitor, categorize all available alliances by activity, value chain and resources and identify the key alliances as which alliance will have the cutting edge on the market place strategy of the competitor. It is essential to identify the alliance partner and know about their marketplace strategies. The purpose of the alliance has to be made transparent at the very beginning of the deal. The type of alliance and context of alliance are the relevant competitive conditions, leadership and motivations for the partners. The company has to draft the terms of alliance clearly for striking the final deal. The terms of alliance must delineate the resources contribution of each partner, roles and responsibilities of either of the alliance partners, duration of alliance and the benchmarks. The company proposing to have alliances must assess the evolution date of the alliance, alliance attributes, signals of the market place and consequences for the competitor in terms of changes in the market places strategy. The company should also identify the indicators to monitor the terms of alliance with a view to reorient the business needs, mutual interest and commitment. Marketing environment for a competitive environment is a combination of factors that the customers use as tools for pursuing its marketing objectives in the identified markets for achieving targets. These factors have to be strategically mixed in marketing planning for offering quality services and optimizing customer value. It is an integrated approach for promoting the services with a view to expand the area under services market. The traditional components of marketing-mix including product, pricing, place and promotion are further supplemented by another set of 5Ps consisting of participants, people, pace, process and physical evidence in marketing of services

A company trying to outwit, outmaneuver and outperform the competitors must also keep a constant watch on its future movements and should draw valuable projection for building the counter strategies to check or defuse its moves. The company must assess the market place strategy alternatives being considered by the competitor firm. The analysis of strategy plots need to be examined carefully. The options of some of the following alternatives of the competitor firm may be examined:

- Aggressive penetration of high-price market
- Low price market entry
- Maintaining the present strategy

Multiple signals typically emerge out of the projected strategy of the competitor and have to be interpreted appropriately. The signals must be assessed in reference to the supporting logics, competitive consequences and the implications thereof.

COMPETITOR ANALYSIS: CAPABILITIES AND COMPETENCY

The degree of competition in a market is largely affected by the moves and countermoves of various firms' activity participating in the market. Generally, it begins with a firm trying to achieve a favorable position by pursuing appropriate strategies as what is advantageous for this firm may be harmful to rival firms and in response the rival firms may move counter strategies to protect their interests. The competition attracts the firms seeking to capitalize on an available business opportunity. As the number of firms get involved in the process of sharing the pie, the degree of competition increases. When the entire market represents one large homogeneous unit, the intensity of competition is much greater than segmented market However, if a market is not appropriate for segmentation, firms may compete to serve it homogeneously, thus intensifying competition. Hence, in either of the market situations the intensity of competition is unavoidable for the participating firms. Understanding the capabilities and competency (C&C) of the rival and developing the company's own are the most important tasks in sailing through the marketing competition. This is essential for winning the market place in the future, to sustain and get the circumstantial leverage. The capabilities in general address as how well an organization performs or executes some of the vital activities like, customer relationship management, services, supply chain management, etc. The competency may be stated as what an organization does well across the region and subsidiary units or customer segments. In all, the C&C involve action, the focus and emphasis on what the competitor does in the market to outperform his business rival. The common competence that can be judged in reference to the competitor are as follows:

- Quick movement of the products to the marketplace from R&D unit
- Faster response to the market opportunities
- Providing convincing and unique solutions to the customer problems
- Hire, train and retain best personnel
- Develop, nurture and extend the best relationship with customers and alliance partners.

There are four key tasks in the management of core competency which include selecting core competency, building core competency, deploying core competency, and protecting core competency. Companies are likely to differ in terms of their abilities to select, build, deploy and protect core competency. These differences are, in turn, likely to yield differences in corporate performance. Building core competency requires the accumulation and integration of knowledge, residing both within the firm and without. For example the core competence of a telecom company may reflect in managing billing systems, an insurance company's core competence in claims processing, and Sony's core competence in miniaturization are each a tapestry of many individual technologies and skills. The core competencies of the companies are those that push down the competitors' products in all the business domains. These strategies are central to the customers, channels and alliance advantage. There are many attributes of C&C, however, the following may be defined as the key attributes of the C&C:

- Dynamism
- Span
- Robustness
- Security against imitations
- Ability to expand.

The dynamism of the C&C refers to continuous change for the betterment of the policies and execution of the strategies. The organization must be able to identify the new markets continuously and never be static at any point of time. An organization must have a wide span to discharge their competency without specifying the boundaries of time and area. It is essential for a company to retain its C&C for a longer duration and unrestricted to any areas of change. C&C also vary in their acceptability to the current and future business domains. A competitor cannot always leverage a competence for the new products or services development in changing business domains. The companies must secure that their C&C strategies are not replicated by other firms or used in any distorted manner. Indeed, any C&C of any company should be able to enhance continuously so that it adds to the sustainable advantages. In practice, today's global competition is more dynamic and multidimensional than those models suggest. The mature industry paradox is that leadership demands differentiation, yet differences are quickly copied. Single-factor innovations tap one competency, and capable competitors can usually match it. Multiple competency strengthen several dimensions and in effect redefine the basis of competition. The "shadow strategy task force" is offered as a method to force managers to relinquish the comfort of the firm's accepted view of itself. This approach begins with the objective of identifying the strategies and competency that, in the hands of competitors, might be used to attack the firm's competitive position successfully. Especially critical of the task force are individuals with insight into how customers, suppliers, and competitors view the firm's products and services. Developing new competency requires constant experimentation. The innovation-imitation-equilibrium cycle suggests that industry leaders teach customers what to demand by defining the current state of the art in performance, price, service, and other dimensions; customers learn to judge competitive offerings against these standards, and the learning effect is cumulative[25].

---

[25] Werther William B and Kerr Jaffrey L: The Shifting Sands of Competitive Advantage, *Business Horizons*, May, 1995.

The LG Electronics India and Samsung in India have entered the electronics market as rivals and are getting along in the business with the same spirit and surviving the market competition. Both the companies are of Korean origin and are into almost identical product segments in the market. Their pricing strategies are similar and they follow largely identical business models to compete with each other in the Indian market. In the marketplace these companies are the most spirited rivals and use throwing punches figuratively on each other's performance to prove their capabilities and build customer loyalty. These two companies fight for each piece of consumer electronic goods in the market. In early July 2000 Samsung came-up with an advertisement proclaiming itself the leader on the 310-litre and above frost-free refrigerators segment, LG responded by challenging both the Samsung and ORG-GFK, which provided the market share data to the advertiser for making it a public claim[26]. Growth in an adjacent market is tougher than it looks; three-quarters of the time, the effort fails. But companies can change those odds dramatically. Results from a five-year study of corporate growth conducted by Bain & Co. reveal that adjacency expansion succeeds only when built around strong core businesses that have the potential to become market leaders. And the best place to look for adjacency opportunities is inside a company's strongest customers. A research study revealed that the most successful companies were able to outgrow their rivals consistently and profitably by developing a formula for pushing out the boundaries of their core businesses in predictable, repeatable ways. Companies use their repeatability formulas to expand into any number of adjacencies. Some companies make repeated geographic moves, whereas others apply a superior business model to new segments. In other cases, companies develop hybrid approaches. The successful repeaters in the study had two common characteristics: they were extraordinarily disciplined, applying rigorous screens before they made an adjacency move, and in almost all cases, they developed their repeatable formulas by carefully studying their customers and their customers' economics[27]. The strategies of Japanese firms have often emphasized its conflicting nature, at least in international markets. It is certainly clear that Japanese firms have more systematic and formal procedures for identifying competitors and analyzing their behavior. It is tempting to conclude that their success is the success of conflict-based strategies. In practice it is almost impossible to come to such judgments. While they are aware of competitors and their weaknesses, they are also keen students of both markets and technology. It is certain that a combination of factors, many of them subtle and difficult to comprehend, leads to the success, in some markets, of Japanese companies. Such success cannot be attributed solely, if at all, to a policy of competitor elimination[28].

There are many ways to categorize core competency. However, broadly these may be distinguished as market-access competency, integrity related competency and functionality related competency. The market access competency includes management of brand development, sales and marketing, distribution and logistics, technical support, etc. All these skills help to put a firm in close proximity to its customers. The attributes associated with competency like quality, cycle time management, just-in-time inventory management and so on which allow a company to do things more quickly, flexibly or with a higher degree of reliability than competitors constitute the integrity-related competency of a firm. The functionality-related competency lead to the skills which enable the company to invest its services or products with unique functionality, which invest the product with distinctive

[26] Business Today, September 21, 2000 p 22.
[27] Zook Chirs and Allen James: Growth Outside the Core, *Harvard Business Review*, December, 2003.
[28] For details on the competitive behavior of Japanese companies see Easton G *et.al.*, *Managers and Competition*, Blackwell, Oxford, UK, 1993, 246-281

customer benefits, rather than merely making it incrementally better. The functionality-related competency is becoming more important as a source of competitive differentiation, relative to the other two competence types. In the growing competitive phenomenon, the companies are converging around universally high standards for product and service integrity, and are moving through alliances, acquisitions and industry consolidation to build broadly matching global brand and distribution capabilities. Interestingly, the Japanese concept of quality has shifted from an idea centered on integrity ('zero defects') to one focused on functionality ('quality that surprises' in that the product yields a unique functionality benefit to the customer). Comparative analysis examines the specific advantages of competitors within a given market and offers structural and response advantages. Structural advantages are those built into the business, e.g., a manufacturing plant in Mexico may, because of low labor costs, have a built-in advantage over another firm. Responsive advantages refer to positions of comparative advantage that have accrued to a business over time as a result of certain decisions. This type of advantage is based on leveraging the strategic phenomena at work in the business. Besides, the examination of the business system operating in an industry is useful in analyzing competitors and in searching out innovative options for gaining a sustainable competitive advantage. The business-system framework enables a firm to discover the sources of greatest economic leverage, that is, stages in the system where it may build cost or investment barriers against competitors[29]. The framework may also be used to analyze a competitor's costs and to gain insights into the sources of a competitor's current advantage in either cost or economic value to the customer.

In the developed markets both the brands are perceived as low profile and are paying high cost for changing such perception. However, the Indian market has opened up the opportunity for these brands to position at a premium scale at relatively low costs. Both the companies play as high profile rivals in the Indian market as their business strategies closely cut across each other to achieve their business goals. Most companies focus on matching and beating their rivals. As a result, their strategies tend to take on similar dimensions. What ensues is head-to-head competition based largely on incremental improvements in cost, quality, or both. The multinational companies which are dynamic in strategy experimentation and innovative companies break free from the competitive pack by staking out fundamentally new market space by creating products or services for which there are no direct competitors. This path to value innovation requires a different competitive mind-set and a systematic way of looking for opportunities. Instead of looking within the conventional boundaries that define how an industry competes, managers can look methodically across them. By doing so, they can find unoccupied territory that represents real value innovation. Rather than looking at competitors within their own industry, for example, managers can ask why customers make the trade-off between substitute products or services. For example, *Home Depot*— a US chain retail store on construction materials and services—looked across the substitutes serving home improvement needs. Intuit looked across the substitutes available to individuals managing their personal finances. In both cases, powerful insights were derived from looking at familiar data from a new perspective[30].

---

[29] Normann Richard and Ramirez Rafael: From Value Chain to Value Constellation-Designing Interactive Strategy, *Harvard Business Review*, July-August, 1993

[30] Chan Kim W and Mauborgne Renee A: Creating New Market Space, *Harvard Business Review*, January 1999.

ANALYZING A COMPETITOR'S SIGNALS

The signals coming out of the business moves of the competitor are an important source of data and information in the market place. As stated in the pretext that the behavior, statements and the organizational information are the major sources of learning the competitors' moves, the signals emerging from the competitor show the magnitude and direction of the information flow. The market place indicators are the principal sources of information for analyzing the signals in reference to the behavioral patterns, statements and the organizational culture of the competitor.

The indicators of organizational change include market place strategies, customer value chain, alliances, relationships, networks, assumptions, assets, capabilities and competency, technology, infrastructure of the company and the like. The business credentials, credit worthiness of the company in the market and its financial status also provide important indications to the competitors for learning their respective moves in the market. It may be understood that an increase in the competitors' credit intakes with any financial institution may generate a signal of its intent to implement a major strategic initiative to expand its business such as an acquisition or planning for capital investment for augmenting its production or marketing activities. The change in the values, beliefs and behavior of the customers, suppliers and business facilitators also indicates the intensity of signals of the competitors. The signals, which indicate the history of the company, current moves and future strategy, may be broadly categorized as below:

- Prospective signals
- Retrospective signals
- Current signals, and
- Anticipated signals
- Alerting signals
- Refuting signals

The prospective signals indicate the future change in the competitor's strategy while retrospective signals indicate significant competitor change that has been resulting in his strategies for some time and such information may give a strong base to the competing firms to outwit the competitors from the roots. The concurrent signals of the competitor indicate the ongoing moves thereof in the market place and sometimes indicate the probable future action of the competitor. Such signals are anticipatory and show a way to the future business moves of the competitor. The alerting signals need to be studied carefully and should not be ignored at any level, as these may become fatal for the competing firms at times. The alerting signals reflect the product line shifts, alliances, customer relationships, pricing and promotional strategies of goods and services and new product launch in the market. It is also possible that in the process of analyzing the signals of the competitor some signals may be contradictory to each other and may refute. The analyst should carefully examine such signals and look at their re-conformity.

In 1995, Lakmé Limited, a Tata group company and Hindustan Lever Limited formed a 50:50 venture as Lakmé Lever to market and distribute Lakme's cosmetic products and in

1998, Lakmé sold its brands to HLL, renamed itself Trent and entered into the retail business. The HLL has entered into the cosmetics market when there is gatecrash of MNCs like Revlon, Maybelline and others and has to build strong market place strategies to outwit the competitors. The corporate statement of HLL after acquisition of Lakmé delineates that by taking on the fashion and glamour platform, the company is not just leading the market over other competitors but has also got a virtual ownership of this plank[31]. It will be very difficult for any other brand to adopt a similar approach. This statement gives a strong prospective signal of its strategies to the new entrants. Lakmé is at the forefront of product innovation and the most preferred brand in cosmetics. The positioning of the Lakmé products for the HLL seemed a bit complex but a clear strategy was drawn for the same. Lakmé cosmetic products have been positioned as its *aspiration colour cosmetics brand* to cater to the upper-mass customer segment of the company which desires both colours, glamour and skin care. The HLL played safe to protect its primary brand Ponds in the exclusive skincare segment of the customer. The value addition of colors has made the Lakme position itself into a broader spectrum of customer needs and competes with the MNC brands in the product segment. The new-designed aspiration led strategy of HLL for Lakme products has made a dent in the move by the competitors, more prominently Revlon and Maybelline, which have also targeted the same consumer segment. The HLL has a strong product strategy and market intelligence to build suitable strategies to be the market leader. Some of the strategies in reference to Lakme cosmetics is synchronized as below:

- The non-transfer lipstick colors have a long range
- The above product has been launched in wake of the similar range from Maybelline company
- Lakme's nail enamel colours have been launched soon after the launch of Maybelline and Revlon launched their nail-enamel range

The company (HLL) has currently three brands in the cosmetics segment. Firstly, Lakmé itself which is positioned as a fashion brand, Secondly, *Elle 18* which has enjoyed as a teen brand and has captured the largest market share among the female consumers of the age group among 15-25. The third brand of HLL is *Orchid,* a super premium that has not seen really much excitement since its re-launch in 1999 in the upper consumer segment. The company also plans at aiming the rural markets after exploring the potential carefully. However, by appropriating the fashion platform Lakmé has positioned itself at the glamour end.

It may be necessary for a firm to determine the business cluster for its operations as they foster high levels of productivity, innovation and lay out the implications for competitive strategy. The territorial surroundings of business of a firm also contribute to the competitor vision and analytical dimensions though conventionally, economic geography towards global competition poses a paradox. Conceptually, location should no longer be a source of competitive advantage. Open global markets, rapid transportation, and high-speed communications should allow any company to source any thing from any place at any time. But in applied business sense, location remains core to competition[32]. The contemporary global business paradigm is characterized by distinctive clusters which may be described as critical masses in one place of linked industries and institutions varying from suppliers to

---

[31] Business Today, September 21, 2000, p 48
[32] Porter Michael E: Cluster and the New Economics of Competition, *Harvard Business Review*, November-December, 1998

universities to government agencies, which enjoy unusual competitive success in a particular field. The business clusters affect competition in three broad ways of:

- Increasing the productivity of companies based in the area
- Driving the direction and pace of innovation, and
- Stimulating the formation of new businesses within the cluster

However, the territorial, cultural, and institutional proximity provides companies with special access, closer relationships, better information, powerful incentives, and other advantages that are difficult to tap from a distance. The competitive advantage lies increasingly in micro resources which include knowledge, relationships, and motivation that distant rivals cannot replicate. For example, as the economy of China is under transition which is growing manifold and opening further, the opportunity it presents to multinationals is changing. Foreign companies are moving to country development and new strategic choices. Now, foreign firms can actually go after the Chinese domestic market, and it's worth going after. Improvements in China's infrastructure, workforce, and regulatory environment are making it possible for companies to lower their costs to reap new competitive advantages. However, in order to optimize the benefits and sustain the international competition in the Chinese playground of business, the multinational companies must properly nest their effort into overall organization, show "one face to China" at the national level but also tailor local strategies, be wary of joint ventures, and mitigate risk, in particular the theft of intellectual property[33].

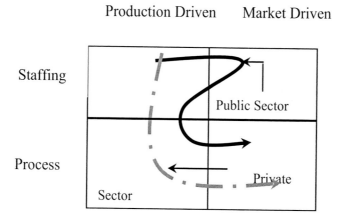

Figure 7.5. Re-engineering Typology in Business.

RE-ENGINEERING INTERNATIONAL BUSINESS

Business performance of a company matters a lot for a customer to orient himself towards its brand, product or services. A company providing aviation or health services to the customer is rated by its efficiency in delivery and recognized by the certification that the company carries to testify its quality of services. Similarly the companies manufacturing and

---

[33] Lieberthal Kenneth and Lieberthal Geoffrey: The Great Transition, *Harvard Business Review*, October 2003

marketing the fast moving consumer goods (FMCG) also get an advantage in gaining large customer response over their rivals on achieving the certification from an international organization for their process, quality and services. The companies operating on the competitive edge should periodically re-engineer their business strategies by adopting various measures. The companies in the developing countries which are open to global trade have started realizing the importance of re-engineering for process improvement in order to acquire competitive strength. The public sector undertakings (PSU) in India have also realized the need for process re-engineering in business while the private sector companies had thought of such change long back. The process-orientated production has been leveraging corporate expertise in the market place for over a decade. The business re-engineering typology in Indian context may be seen as exhibited in Figure 7.5. Initially the PSUs attempted re-engineering by way of restructuring production and marketing functions and lately some of the PSUs like Bharat Heavy Engineering Corporation, National Thermal Power Corporation, Public Sector Banks, Power Grid, etc., are thriving on process oriented re-engineering to make their stand more competitive in the market.

The private sector has re-engineered its business process for a long time on the line of process change for implementing better product and market-driven strategies. The process-driven dynamics has been proved to be effective to build the competitive strategies and sustain amidst market competition. Conventional wisdom says that companies from the periphery of the global market can't compete against established global giants from Europe, Japan, and the United States. Companies from developing countries have entered the game too late and have a paucity of resources. Some of the examples of corporate business moves may be cited in reference to such countries that are considered as emerging markets like Brazil which is relatively more prosperous. These companies now enjoy global success because they treated global competition as an opportunity to build capabilities and move into more profitable segments of their industry. The path to globalization is not easy, but the authors show that it is possible. The multinational companies in the emerging market broke out of the mind-set that they were unable to compete successfully on the global stage. Later, these companies adopted strategies that made being a late mover a source of competitive advantage and developed a culture of continual cross-border learning[34].

CUSTOMER VALUE AND REENGINEERING PROCESS

In the era of global competition, regardless of whether the company operates in FMCG, industrial goods or services, leading organizations around the world are being driven to rethink their business strategies and reorient them towards process change for reaching higher efficiency levels. In order to engineer their process change it is essential to consider the customer value criteria based on the attributes of four major business determinants - quality, service, cost and time. The customer value metrics is detailed in Table 7.3 among various attributes of quality the companies must look for continuous improvement in the products deliverables and minimize the variances. The customer support in terms of product and price should be prioritized for achieving competitive excellence. The cost factors may need very

---

[34] Bartlett C A and Ghoshal S (2000), Going Global: Lessons from Late Movers, *Harvard Business Review*, 78 (2), 132-142

important consideration in the processes re-engineering as the quality improvement efforts would lead to price rise due to design improvement, quality assurance, restructuring the distribution and logistics strategies, inventory and staffing. The customer value largely depends on the cost of time involved in the change process. Doing re-engineering forces the companies to quantify the business efforts by way of quality, service and cycle time reducing the cost to the customer at the same time increasing the speed of innovation and new-product development. The time required for market preparation includes the concept selling, pre-positioning advertising and information for market initialization. The lead time is the time taken for stabilizing the sales and customer response to the changes engineered in order to outwit, out maneuver and out perform the competitors in the market. In the process of re-engineering the business strategies it is essential for the companies to analyze the customer response to the innovation and modify the entire the process accordingly before finally setting the changes in the market. In all, reengineering the customer value may be expressed in simple notation as:

$$\text{Customer Value} = \frac{\text{Quality} * \text{Service}}{\text{Cost} * \text{Time}}$$

The process reengineering concept broadly include the philosophies of *just-in-time* (JIT), *total quality management* (TQM), *break-even point analysis* and most recently introduced application of *enterprise resource planning* (ERP). These applications and strategies generate pull and push effects in the market releasing signals to the competitors.

Table 7.3. Re-engineering Customer Value

Quality	Service	Cost	Cycle Time
• Customer relationship • Useful applications • Minimum variance • Process integrity • Minimizing waste • Regular improvement	• Customer support • Flexibility in meeting customer demands • Delivery and service • Information flow • Value assessment	• Innovation • Quality assurance • Logistics • Staffing • Materials management	• Market preparation • Lead time • Ordering and delivery • Response analysis

CORPORATE CONCEPTS OF REENGINEERING BUSINESS

Reengineering business strategies for competitive advantage necessarily makes a company redefine its corporate objectives and bring some differentiation in terms of quality of the products, services offered and the customer governance in the process. A company has to define the following corporate objectives while doing the process of production and marketing reengineered:

- Customer satisfaction and service
- Business safety from the new entrants and existing competitors

- Production efficiency, quality assurance and innovation
- Financial performance and growth
- Customer relationship management and grievances solving
- Creativity in marketing
- Organizational development and human resources

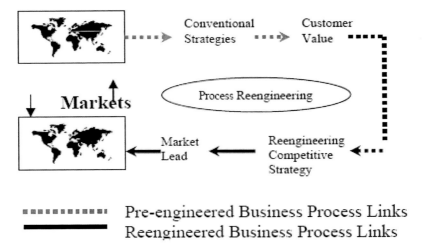

Figure 7.6. Engineering Market Interplay.

It is possible for a company to take advantage of implementing the process improvements either to enhance its lead in the existing market or to enter new markets, once the company successfully implements the reengineered process along with the value chain elements. The enablers in the process change in a company are people, management, leadership skills, organizational culture, expertise, market place stimuli and the performance measurements. The companies getting prepared to reengineer the business process and keep up with the competition have to give away the bureaucratic way of thinking and must put efforts to shift to the new market driven paradigms. Figure 7.6 exhibits the market interplay engineering path for the companies looking to adopt process change strategy for regaining the competitive strength. In this process it is necessary for a company to reorient its team leaders with new paradigm elements and process-oriented operations to stand ahead in the competition and outperform the business rivals. Such reorientation must be towards creating vision, articulating and sharing values, transparency in the team work, and relationship management at all levels —customers and channel managers. The company has to develop a corporate core team for building functional expertise among the managers implementing the competitive strategies. The company has to establish direct contacts between the market place and customers to have direct control over the flow of goods and services and customer reactions.

The companies open to global trading must accept the challenge of competition. The competitive pressures drive the companies to look at their process and determine that they can become competitive or even leapfrog the competition by focusing on the process, lead attribute and quality. For example, the *Baskin Robbins* Ice Cream Company in its logo writes *31*, the number indicates their distinguished 31 flavors (one flavor a day) which adds to its performance and lead in the market. The Hewlett Packard computers in the early 90's thoroughly redesigned its printers and reengineered by simplifying the process and are now leading in Indian markets. In many instances, competition goes hand in hand with the customer service as the competition is also related to the customer needs. Hence the companies need to redefine their process to connect to the customers and subsequently reengineer them. Reengineering business process for a company is a systematic approach for gaining strength in three basic areas comprising optimization of cost, handling renewed competitiveness and building competitive dominance in the market. Of many competitive dimensions the product performance, market reach, rate of new product development and innovation, resource leverage and customer loyalty are major ones which need to be emphasized by the company for achieving competitive advantage. The reengineering strategy gives an opportunity to the company to reduce their cost to the optimal level by process improvement and provided competitive focus in achieving best in the market or to be a class brand. The process improvement is fundamentally an approach to clean-up the redundant activities in the business and set up swift process to reach the market.

COMPETITIVE FOCUS

The company planning to take the lead in the market should develop a strategic vision for dominance in the market place. It should also plan to achieve the output by implementing the strategy successfully. This phase may be viewed as *discovering* the competitive strength of the company. Later, on the basis of results of discovery, the business process needs to be *reengineered* and *executed*. These are the three important phases in reengineering the business function with competitive focus, a company has to be prepared for planning to outwit, outmaneuver and outperform the competitor. There are various factors associated with these phases of change in business strategy for a company to be one of the best companies surviving in the market. Table 7.4 exhibits the factors associated with the business reengineering phases of dominance, redesign, and realize.

A company making efforts to become the market leader has to put substantial energy and resources in learning the competitor's move and later unlearn the same among the core team responsible for building strategies. In this process it is necessary to generate new ideas and assess their suitability to administer in the market and adaptability in the work environment of the company. Once the appropriate strategy is selected the core team has to take all steps to apply the same against the move of the competitors. These steps will help the company to play its dominance in the market against the competing forces. The dominance will also help the company to redefine the engineered strategy to its suitability in the market and commitment to apply the same against the competitors. The time taken for realizing the reengineered strategy results against competitors varies according to the intensity of business penetration and customer relationship. However, to get a quick realization to the reengineered business efforts, a company has to build teams, plan execution of strategy in detail, confirm investment (if any), assess and recognize the impact. The company, during such market intervention operations has to handle the communications very carefully among the staff members and channel managers to avert any fowl interpretations and actions thereby. Communications to the staff members and channels should be comprehensive in the context of strategy reengineering, the vision of work has to be made known to the concerned, explain rationale and assess the impact. The core team has to be trained to execute the task, control strategic points of the plan and to provide continuous inflow of the impact information to the top management of the company. Any business strategy implemented in the market should have strict measures against the task, time and target. Nevertheless, the cost-benefit assessment is important to evaluate the success of the interventions moved against competitors and redefine the next moves. The on-going management reviews and key indicators analysis are essential for a company to count its sustainability amidst competition in the market. The company must prepare a checklist of strength, weakness, opportunities and threats in reference to the moves of the competitor. The company has to prepare for the opportunities and build strategies to overcome the threats from the competitors. There are some factors like advertising and communication where equal opportunities exist for both the potential and rival business companies. This is an innovative sector where the higher the creativity and reach the larger is the impact on the market.

Table 7.4. Framework of Reengineering Business Process

Dominance	Redesign	Realize
<ul><li>Learn and unlearn new ideas</li><li>Assess suitability</li><li>Make appropriate selection</li><li>Apply against competitors</li></ul>	<ul><li>Learn and unlearn new ideas</li><li>Analyze suitability</li><li>Redefine and engineer strategy</li><li>Commit</li></ul>	<ul><li>Mobilize people/ staff</li><li>Communicate and PR</li><li>Execute redesigned packages</li><li>Measure performance</li><li>Sustain</li></ul>

A company should acquire the strategies of outwitting, outmaneuvering and outperforming the competitors to win the race. It is necessary for the successful business companies to look for such a place of business that provides them more location advantage and hold the customers for their goods and services. A broad set of process standards will soon make it easy to determine whether a business capability can be improved by outsourcing it. Such standards will also help businesses compare service providers and evaluate the costs vs. the benefits of outsourcing. Eventually these costs and benefits will be so visible to buyers that outsourced processes will become a commodity, and prices will drop significantly. The low costs and low risk of outsourcing will accelerate the flow of jobs offshore, force companies to reassess their strategies, and change the basis of competition. The speed with which some businesses have already adopted process standards suggests that many previously non-scrutinized areas are ripe for change[35].

The driving forces of competing firms, their organization and micro-economic environment need to be studied carefully by the company planning to overtake competitors in the business. Further in the process of winning the battle of rivals it would be helpful for a company to understand the changing stakes of the competitors and forces after such developments. It is necessary to build-up strong, comprehensive and reliable database for capturing the activities of any business rival or competitor. Data is thus the basic input for competitor learning. In the competitive markets, the efficiency of the services discharged and extended to the buyers also contributes in building or breaking the market place strategy.

---

[35] Davenport T H (2005), The Coming Commoditization of Processes, *Harvard Business Review*, 83 (6), 100-108

Products, in the same market or competitive domain, largely vary in their availability may be due to weak or faulty supply chain management. An increase in the competitors' credit intakes with any financial institution may generate a signal of its intent to implement a major strategic initiative to expand its business such as an acquisition or planning for capital investment for augmenting its production or marketing activities. Hence strategy building against the competitor is a very careful exercise that needs to be done by the practicing managers.

REFERENCES

Evans, Philip.B; Wurster, Thomas S.: Strategy and the New Economics of Information, *Harvard Business Review,* Sept.-Oct. 1997, pp.71-82.

Williamson, Peter J.: Asia's New Competitive Game, *Harvard Business Review,* Sept.-Oct. 1997, pp. 55-67.

Drucker, Peter F.: Looking Ahead: Implications of the Present, *Harvard Business Review*, Sept.-Oct. 1997, pp.18-32.

Kenny David and Marshall John F: Contextual Marketing, *Harvard Business Review*, November-December, 2000, pp 119-125.

Leong, G. Keong.; Ward, Peter T.: The Six Ps of Manufacturing Strategy, *International Journal of Operations & Production Management,* Vol.15, No.12, 1995, pp. 32-45.

Belohlav, James A.: Quality, Strategy, and Competitiveness, *California Management Review*, Vol. 35, No. 3, Spring 1993, pp. 55-67.

Fahe Liam: *Competitors: Outwitting, Outmaneuvering and Outperforming*, John Wiley and Sons, Canada, 1999.

Peter Singe : *The Fifth Discipline*, Doubleday/Currency, New York, 1990.

John J McGonagle *et.al.*: *A New Archetype for Competitive Intelligence*, Quorum Books, Westport, CT, 1996.

Porter. Michael E: *Competitive Strategy: Techniques for Analyzing Industry and Competitors*, The Free Press, New York, 1980.

Rajagopal: *Marketing: Strategy, Implementation and Control*, Rawat, New Delhi, 2004.

Warren Kim : *Competitive Strategy Dynamics*, Wiley, New York, 2002.

Boyatzis, R: *The Competent Manager: A Mode for Effective Performance*, John Wiley & Sons: New York, 1982.

Chapter 8

GLOBALIZATION AND CORPORATE VENTURING

Born-globals or international new venture firms, which are positioned in contrast to the more established international firms, are the subject of growing debate emerging from pro-globalization and developing nations. The decision for a new venture to internationalize at an infant stage is influenced by the size of its home market and by its production capacity, as well as by cultural and economic forces that also influence other more traditional firms that stage their entry into international markets[1]. However, a majority of small firms lack the resources and competences required to implement advanced international strategies and to engage in global business activities. These firms also face considerable barriers while attempting to engage in international partnerships, joint ventures and foreign direct investments. Unlike, *born-globals*, international joint ventures (IJV) are an important organizational mode for expanding and sustaining global business and have been of special relevance for the emerging Chinese market for decades. While these joint ventures offer specific economic advantages they also present serious management problems that lead to high failure rates, especially in developing countries. Because of the strategic relevance of international joint ventures and corresponding management challenges, research on success factors for managing IJVs in China has received broad attention, resulting in a variety of studies[2].

The corporate venturing strategy has regained its strength with the booming concept of globalization, virtual business and rising demand for high value products. The concept of corporate venturing has become a significant method for business development[3]. The principle reason behind the popularity of this strategy may be the presumed ability of corporate venturing to facilitate continuous growth by embracing high-level innovation and accessing cutting-edge technological development. Some companies have conceived the corporate venturing as a core concept in their strategic planning[4]. Firms become multinational companies (MNCs)s by setting up manufacturing or marketing subsidiaries overseas. Some researchers argue that internationalization is a process of transferring an MNC's knowledge,

[1] Fan, T and Phan, P (2007), International new ventures: revisiting the influences behind the `born-global' firm, *Journal of International Business Studies*, 38 (7), 1113-1131.

[2] Nippa M, Beechler S and Klossek A (2007), Success Factors for Managing International Joint Ventures: A Review and an Integrative Framework, *Management and Organization Review*, 3 (2), 277-310.

[3] Gompers Paul A and Lerner J (2001), The Venture Capital Revolution, *Journal of Economic Perspectives*, 15(2), pp 145-169.

[4] Burgelman R A (1983): A Process Model of Internal Corporate Venturing in the Diversified major Firm, *Administrative Science Quarterly*, 28, pp 223-244.

which embodies its advantage, from one country to another. That is, knowledge flows from headquarters to overseas subsidiaries. Venturing is serious business, requiring skill, patience, and entrepreneurial flair. Most new ventures involve entering unfamiliar markets, employing unfamiliar technology, and implementing an unfamiliar organizational structure[5]. An approach of particular promise is the new-style joint venture, in which a small company with vigor, flexibility, and advanced technology joins forces with a large company with capital, marketing strength, and distribution channels. The most intensive corporate involvement occurs in the internal venture, in which a company sets up a separate entity within itself in order to enter new markets or to develop entirely new products[6].

The discussion on the issues of corporate venturing has received considerable attention in academic literature in the recent past with focus on the later stages of the venturing process, such as the organizational designs for carrying out the corporate venture activity, the criteria for developing a portfolio of ventures into a winning entity, the development and growth of a venture, and possible exit strategies[7]. It has been found that the research studies also laid strong applied focus on the later stages of the venture process. The process of globalization resulting in the free trade and business development opportunities for multinational companies has further strengthened the corporate venturing as a strategy for international business development. It involves investment in high-risk activities that generate new businesses within or closely related to the activities of the parent corporation. Hence, this may be described as a business development strategy, which seeks to generate new businesses for the corporation in which it resides[8]. Corporate venturing is used strategically to encourage corporate renewal in the parent organization, as a growth driver by investing in ventures with high growth potential, or to diversify the core business of the parent by investing in ventures in diverse industries. The ideas for new businesses can originate either inside the organization or externally. Activities hosted by the corporate venturing unit will often be new to the organization and require the parent company to extend their resources by acquiring new equipment, people or knowledge. The corporate venturing activities possess significantly higher risk or failure rate and greater uncertainty (Block & MacMillan, 1993). Such attributes of corporate venturing appear to distinguish this strategy from other business development strategies such as takeovers, corporate R&D, traditional venture capital financing, and joint ventures[9].

GE is one of the prominent companies engaged in fabrication of jet airplane engines and Honda is primarily known for automobiles. These companies together are exploring ways to build engines for small jets airplanes. Their new joint venture, GE Honda Aero Engines is equally owned by GE Aircraft Engines and Honda Aero (50:50) and was formed in 2004 to produce engines for 4-8 seat business jets. In particular, the company began producing Honda's HF118 engine for the light business jet market in 2005. Going forward, GE Honda Aero Engines will produce turbofan engines in the 1,000 pound to 3,500 pound thrust range

---

[5] Kogut B and Zander U (1993), Knowledge of the Firm and the Evolutionary Theory of the Multinational Corporations, *Journal of International Business Studies*, 24(4), pp 625-645.

[6] Robert Edward B (1980), New Ventures for Corporate Growth, *Harvard Business Review*, July, 58 (4), 134-142.

[7] Gompers Paul A (2002), Corporations and the Financing of Innovation: The Corporate Venturing Experience, *Economic Review*, 4, pp 1-17.

[8] Von Hippel E (1977), Successful and Failing Internal Corporate Ventures: An Empirical Analysis, *Industrial Marketing Management*, 6, pp 163-174.

[9] Albrinck J, Hornery J, Kletter D and Neilson G (2001), Adventures in Corporate Venturing, *Strategy and Business*, 22, pp 119-129.

by way of comparison, GE's most powerful jet engine can produce more than 125,000 pounds of thrust. Similarly, a joint venture between General Electric's GE Industrial unit and Japan-based Fanuc, manufactures automation and control products such as servo units, motors, motion controls, nano-to-high-end controllers, switches, and amplifiers, as well as related software needed for operation. Other products of this joint venture company include controls and Ethernet ports used for computer networking, embedded computer systems, and operator interfaces. GE Fanuc serves global customers in a variety of industries, including aerospace, communications, medical, electronics, and government[10].

The knowledge may also flow in the opposite direction in the process of establishing and running its overseas operations. An MNC learns, intentionally or unintentionally, from the process the multinational firms build new capabilities to adapt to changing environments through the corporate venturing as a core of strategic business management. However, contemporary research has addressed this question only recently. How do the firms develop a capability to create and develop ventures through corporate venture capital, alliances, and acquisitions has been addressed in an integrated model[11]. The model is based on two longitudinal case studies of large corporations operating in the information and communication technology sector in Europe. The model envisages learning processes, which enable the firm to build up an external corporate venturing capability, by utilizing learning strategies both within and outside venturing relationships. The study finds that the firms engage in acquisitive learning, in order to build this new capability and adapt to the firm specific context through experiential learning mechanisms. Corporate venture firms often rely heavily on their ability to develop firms around "winning" ideas and too little on how they can promote the development of a continuous flow of high quality ideas.

INTERNAL AND EXTERNAL FIT

Firms with growth aspirations have several ways of reaching their goals. Mergers, acquisitions, and joint ventures are a few of the better-known approaches to firm growth. Another route, which is of interest to both managers and researchers, is corporate venturing-growing a business from the inside out. The motives for launching a corporate venture include improving corporate profitability, generating strategic renewal, fostering innovation and gaining knowledge that may be parlayed into future revenue streams[12]. The corporate venturing has been identified as a vehicle for firm growth and has addressed several issues unique to this growth mechanism. The relationship between a corporate parent and its corporate venture has also been studied, however, to empirically test whether the connection, or fit, between parent and venture influences performance of corporate venture, not substantial literature is available. Although arguments have been laid as high levels of relatedness between corporate parent and corporate ventures are desirable while other

---

[10] General Electric Inc.: Corporate profile www.ge.com

[11] Keil Thomas (2004), Building External Corporate Venturing Capability, *Journal of Management Studies*, 41(5), 799-205.

[12] Zahra S A (1996), Governance, Ownership and Corporate Entrepreneurship: The Moderating Impact of Industry's Technological Opportunities, *Academy of Management Journal*, 39(6), 1713-1735.

researchers have contended that tight coupling is negating to venture success[13]. However numerous studies have argued that corporate venturing is a dynamic process, that is, one in which the relationship between parent and venture evolves as the venture matures. The debate revolves around which point on this spectrum is optimal for corporate venture performance.

It is generally agreed that corporate venturing has a positive effect on firm performance, although such benefits are not guaranteed and ventures may take several years to become profitable. The corporate ventures go through a series of stages as they mature[14]. However, there is general agreement that the nature of corporate ventures is dynamic, not static. Effective corporate venturing has been described as a balancing act with needs for creativity and change on one side and demands for cohesiveness and complementarities on the other. The profitability of individual companies depends on technical expertise and the ability to accurately price long-term contracts. Large companies enjoy economies of scale in design, manufacturing, and purchasing. Small companies can compete effectively by concentrating on selected components and parts manufacturing for particular prime contractors. Increasingly, small companies are developing system integration capabilities as large firms outsource more aspects of contracts.

FINANCIAL AND INVESTMENT VENTURING

On the financial upfront corporate venturing induces the prospecting entrepreneur to exert an effort that is higher than within the corporation, but lower than the traditional venture capital financing framework. The competition from venture capitalists increases corporate venturing activity, the salaries of potential entrepreneurs, and total economic output. Factors affecting corporate venture success may be broadly classified as intrinsic and extrinsic. Intrinsic factors are those inherent to the venture itself, and are subdivided into two categories: product related and managerial. Extrinsic or environmental factors are those determined by the characteristics of the investment sponsor, *e.g.*, corporation or venture capital fund. Extrinsic factors are also subdivided into two categories —structural, which are determined by the organizational and functional relationship to the investment sponsor and procedural, related to managerial processes to be imposed by the investment sponsor[15]. Large companies have long sensed the potential value of investing in external start-ups, but more often than not, they fail to get it right. Remember the dash to invest in new ventures in the post- 1990s globalization drive and the hasty retreat when the economy turned? The framework describes four types of capital investments for the corporate venture, each defined by its primary goal-strategic and financial, and by the degree of operational linkage between the start-up and the investing company. Driving investments are characterized by a strong strategic rationale and tight operational links. Enabling investments are also made primarily for strategic reasons, but the operational links are loose. Emergent investments, which are characterized by tight operational links, have little current-but significant potential-strategic

[13] Dougherty D (1995), Managing Your Core Incompetence for Corporate Venturing, *Entrepreneurship-Theory and Practice*, 19(3), pp 113-135.

[14] Schrader RC and Simon M (1997), Corporate verses Independent New Ventures: Resource, Strategy and Performance Differences, *Journal of Business Venturing*, 12(1), 47-66.

[15] Skyes Hollister B (1986), The Anatomy of a Corporate Venturing Program: Factors Influencing Success, *Journal of Business Venturing*, 1(3), Autumn, 274-293.

value. Passive investments, offering few potential strategic benefits and only loose operational links, are made primarily for financial reasons. The passive investments in corporate venture capital dry up in a recessional economy, but may enable gains and drive investments, usually for those which are sustainable in the market. The trend of venture investment in USA is exhibited in Table 8.1.

It has been observed that the focus on investments in the global area are not necessarily being driven by venture firms identifying opportunities in far-away lands and then acting alone in making the investment. Rather, networks of relationships among venture firms around the world are beginning to develop identifying the best opportunities wherever they may be by creating an investor group with partners on the ground that can help the local company succeed in a global marketplace. Such venture concept has shown a broad-based rebound in primary and secondary capital markets around the globe. The resurgence of initial public offerings in places like Germany, London, and India is further evidence of this trend. The future investor pool seemed to go to the ventures in Western Europe, followed by the United Kingdom and Canada[16]. However, China and India have interestingly accounted for seven and four percent of the global venture investments during 2006. The key to successful international investing is to develop strategic alliances with foreign-based firms or local enterprises in the destination markets. However, relocating partners or relocating portfolio companies are not favorable strategies towards increasing the global presence of venture firms. In the case of India, barriers to entry were fewer than those identified in China.

Greater trade openness in Latin America would help to improve institutions. The opening up of markets can play an important role in weakening vested interests and reducing economic rents associated with long standing economic and institutional arrangements. Trade can thus spur improvement in domestic institutions that otherwise would not have been possible. In addition, international agreements can be an important external anchor and catalyst for institutional change by breaking through domestic impediments to reforms. Chile and Mexico provide important role models for the region. Institutional strengthening in both countries has allowed them to establish a successful inflation targeting framework, lower public debt, open the trading regime, and build a strong regulatory and oversight framework for the banking system. Both countries also provide important lessons of targeted social spending. Chile's example, in particular, of institutional changes that limit the room for inconsistent fiscal behavior by the regional governance, provides an especially valuable lesson to other countries that have frequently witnessed high fiscal volatility.

Table 8.1. Venture Capital Investment in USA (2003-06)
(Amount in US $ Millions)

Company Disbursement Year	Number of Deals	Average Investment per Deal	Total Investment
2003	2911	6.78	19731.35
2004	3072	7.32	22485.69
2005	3128	7.37	23048.64
2006	3560	7.39	26295.62

Source: PricewaterhouseCoopers/National Venture Capital Association. http://www.nvca.org/ffax.html

---

[16] Deloitte and Touche: Global trends in venture capital survey 2006, Deloitte and Touche, USA LLP.

TECHNOLOGY AND INNOVATION

In view of globalization the media and academics have frequently maligned corporate investments in venture capital and have highlighted visible failures. The best ideas have languished in many corporations, either because of internal resistance or an inability to execute on the initial insight. In other cases, more nimble companies, often venture-backed start-ups, have turned innovative ideas of corporations into commercial successes[17]. The origin of Unilever's home pregnancy test "Clearblue", which was launched in 1985, has been used as a case study to examine the viability of one version of this strategy. Unilever was able to translate its extensive knowledge base in immunology into a successful branded product in medical diagnostics by creating a separate corporate entity as *Unipath* with a distinctive culture, shielded from the mainstream of the organization. However, this product could be able to make impact on marketing and financial resources through its corporate abilities. However, the very distinctiveness of *Unipath* orphaned it within Unilever, and the business was divested in 2001[18]. Such downsides emerge in high technology business ventures as large established corporations face many challenges to develop and sustain dynamic capabilities in innovation and the creation of new businesses because of constraints arising from technological and resource lock-ins, and routine and cultural rigidities. The number of firms using alliances as part of their corporate venturing or market entry strategies has surged over the past decade. Three common reasons found for pursuing alliances are technology convergence, market access and alliance partners' complementary resources[19]. Theoretical and empirical evidences suggest that highly related ventures benefit from existing resources, exploiting corporate know-how, and sharing experience effects. High-relatedness implies high levels of resource sharing that should decrease the incremental costs needed to launch the venture. Thus high-related ventures have greater amounts of resources to be used for aggressive entry strategies than low-related ventures. However, the top management cannot decide a priority whether or not a new corporate venture should be highly related to the parent firm; high image firms should only venture in highly related businesses. Building image at the corporate level pays if various high-related ventures are present[20].

The rise in consumer health awareness is driving innovation in the global cosmetics and toiletries industry over the last five years, consumer health awareness has increased significantly around the world due to a growing focus on health issues in the media and an increasing investment in health initiatives on the part of governments, according to the research from Euromonitor International. While it is clear that increasing consumer concerns for health and wellness have obvious repercussions for markets such as packaged food and Over-The-Counter (OTC) healthcare, the study has also found that it has become an increasingly influential factor in the cosmetics and toiletries market. Things went a step further last year when L'Oréal and Procter & Gamble forged joint ventures with Nestlé and

---

[17] Gompers Paul A and Lerner J (2001), The Venture Capital Revolution, *Journal of Economic Perspectives*, 15(2), pp 145-169.

[18] Jones Geoffrey and Kraft Alison (2004), Corporate Venturing: The Origins of Unilever's Pregnancy Test, *Business History*, 46(1), 100-122.

[19] Ghandour A Fares, Swartz Paulina, Grenek Heidi M and Roberts Edwards B (2004), E-Business Transformation vial Alliance Clusters, *Technology Analysis and Strategic Management*, 16(4), December, pp 435-455.

[20] Sorrentino Mario and Williams May L (1995), Relatedness and Corporate Venturing: Does it Really Matter? *Journal of Business Venturing*, 10(1), January, pp 59-73.

Pharmavite respectively to expand into OTC dietary supplements, encouraged by trends indicating that consumers are increasingly keen to co-ordinate health regimens with beauty practices. The Nestlé/L'Oréal joint venture heralded the launch of Innéov Fermeté (an anti-ageing formula), while Procter & Gamble and Pharmavite jointly launched Olay Vitamins. More recently roles were reversed somewhat as Healthspan, a Guernsey-based mail order vitamin supplier for the UK market, launched a dedicated range of make-up and skin care products which target women aged between 45 and 60. The research shows that the trend is widespread in the US market, as US consumers are becoming increasingly convinced that beauty starts with "wellness". Retailers are increasingly linking their beauty lines to non-beauty products, positioning health products, like vitamins, in close proximity to cosmetics. Manufacturers for their part are introducing cosmetic lines that tout claims often found in OTC products, like Sally Hansen's Healing Beauty Fast and Flawless make-up line, with products featuring anti-wrinkling and acne-fighting ingredients. The market is clearly strong for cosmetics and toiletries products that associate themselves with wellness, with many lines now routinely infused with vitamins and increasingly with natural and herbal extracts[21].

Corporate venturing can be an important source of technological innovation for corporations by providing a window on emerging technologies, market opportunities, new business models, and distribution channels,. However, effective implementation requires a clear view of the objectives, dedication to understanding the process, and discipline. There are two major tactics for external investing: invest in a venture capital fund, or invest directly in a start-up company, and the strategy a company chooses should be tied to its objectives[22]. One of the most challenging aspects of corporate venturing is finding the right people, and corporations must be willing to devote significant time and resources to working closely with their portfolio companies if they wish to gain satisfactory value from their external investments. A study examines the variety of corporate venturing activities in the pharmaceutical and life sciences sectors, identifies the range of initiators, motives and structures, and evaluates the potential opportunities for professional venture capital firms[23]. It is discussed in the study that on one hand, pharmaceutical companies need to maintain the new product pipeline that has increased the demand for technology acquisition and on the other, mergers and rationalization within the sector have resulted in a significant growth in technology divestment. Both trends have boosted corporate venturing activity. The study finds that while there is a wide range of venturing options, there is considerable confusion in the industry over ends and means. Specifically, many firms have failed to differentiate sufficiently between strategic, financial and operational goals, and have therefore created inappropriate forms of corporate venture.

Another study conducted with a small number of corporate executives having line experience in corporate venturing showed that joint ventures appear to be a highly useful way of starting off in venturing activity at the same time reducing the initial risk[24]. The study indicated that experience of executives at venturing resulted in improvement in venturing

---

[21] Leonie Tait: Increasing interest in health and wellness drives innovation in cosmetics and toiletries, Euromonitor International, 11 January 2005. Web site: www.euromonitor.com

[22] Markham S K, Gentry S T, Hume D, Ramachandran R and Kingon A I (2005): Strategies and Tactics for External Corporate Venturing, *Technology Management*, March, 48(2), pp 49-59.

[23] Tidd J and Barnes S (2000), Spin-in or Spin-out? Corporate Venturing in Life Sciences, *The International Journal of Entrepreneurship and Innovation*, 1(2), pp 109-116.

[24] Macmillan I C, Block Z and Narasimha S P N (1986), Corporate Venturing Alternatives, Obstacles Encountered and Experience Effect, *Journal of Business Venturing*, 1(2), Spring, 171-191.

performance, but only after several venture attempts. It has been observed that many executives take for granted that the first company in a new product category gets an unbeatable head start and reaps long-lasting benefits. However, much depends on the pace at which the category's technology is changing and the speed at which the market is evolving. By analyzing these two factors, companies can improve their odds of succeeding as first movers with the resources they possess. Gradual evolution in both the technology and market provides a first mover with the best conditions for creating a dominant position that is long lasting (Hoover in the vacuum cleaner industry is a good example). In such calm waters, a company can defend its advantages even without exceptional skills or extensive financial resources. When the market is changing rapidly and the product is not, the first entrant with extensive resources can obtain a long-lasting advantage (as Sony did with its Walkman); a company with only limited resources probably must settle for a short-term benefit[25].

INTERNATIONAL ORGANIZATION DESIGNS

In the *international business division structure*, the firm's activities are separated into two units comprising domestic and international operations. The main function of such an international division is to draw a distinction between its domestic and international business. A worldwide *geographic organization* can overcome the problems associated with the international division structure. In this structure, foreign and domestic operations are not isolated, but are integrated as if foreign boundaries did not exist Worldwide markets are segregated into geographic areas. Operational responsibility goes to area line managers, whereas corporate headquarters maintains responsibility for wide planning and control. Major attributes of the geographic organizational design of multinational companies are as below:

- Product lines are less diverse
- Products are sold to end users
- Marketing is a critical variable
- Similar channel is used for marketing of all products
- Products are based on the local consumer needs

This organizational design has various advantages markedly delegation of line of authority and explicit responsibility. Specifically, the merits of this system include:

- Responsibility and delegation of line of authority
- Manufacturing and product sales coordination
- Large number of executives
- Conflicts of roles and responsibilities
- Lack of specialists in the product sales line

---

[25] Suarez F F and Lanzolla G (2005), The Half Truth of First Mover Advantage, *Harvard Business Review*, 83 (4), 121-127.

An important disadvantage in geographic organizational design may be seen as a large number of top level executives involved in operational tasks which lead to the conflict in power play and command execution in the organization. Besides the agglomeration of top management personnel, the individual products may suffer, as responsibilities can not be fixed easily on the operational executives. A product organization design is different than geographic design wherein a worldwide responsibility to product group executives at the line management level is assigned and emphasis is placed on the product line rather than on geographic differences. The coordination of activities in a geographic area is handled through specialists at the corporate staff level, but in the product organizations, focus is laid on the performance of product-mix in a given area. Multinational companies which operation within this structure have a variety of end users, handle diversified product lines with high technological capability and logistics cost are diverted to the local manufacturers. This type of organizational design has several benefits including:

- Decentralization of authority
- High motivation of the divisional heads
- Adding or dropping new products have marginal impact on operations Control of product through the product life cycle.

In this organizational structure, a firm is segregated along product lines considering each division as a separate profit center with the division head directly accountable for profitability. Decentralization of operations is critical in this structure and more decisions are likely to be left to the local manager, who is then usually more highly motivated. Decentralization of authority is a prime advantage of this structure where division heads are highly motivated. This structure allows the product managers to add new products and product lines and withdraw old ones with only marginal effect on overall operations. Another advantage of this structure is that the control of a product through the product life cycle can be managed more readily and securely. However, firms following this organization structure often face the problem of coordination among product and territory managers. In addition, it is felt that executives quickly get biased towards the regional and corporate staff in managing any product process.

In recent years, a synergy of all the above organizational structures has emerged among the multi national companies which are defined as *matrix structure*. The matrix structure offers greater flexibility than the single line of-command structures already discussed and reconciles this flexibility with coordination and economies of scale to keep the strength of large organizations. The attributes and advantages of matrix organization include:

- Multiple command line
- Product and geographic coordination
- Product lines in a national setting
- Organization design reacts quickly to the local environment demand

For the multinational firm, the matrix organization is a solution to the problem responding to both economic and political environments. General Electrics Company in Asia operates with matrix structure and has been successful. A matrix organization can encompass geographic and product-management components. However, some of the disadvantages in following this organizational design are power struggles among the supervisory personnel and parallel decision making.

CORPORATE VENTURE CONTROL MANAGEMENT

A control feedback system is one of the core components of international marketing management and it serves to assess performance. Monitoring is one of the tools to measure the degree of the success of international marketing and needs to be incorporated in the plan itself. The marketing plans need to specify the periodicity of the control exercises and its prime objective. The monitoring calendar for international marketing firms may be designed keeping the following checks in mind:

- Budgetary control
- Plan implementation
- Performance of marketing functions (11Ps) which include product, price, place, promotion, packaging, pace, people, performance, psychodynamics, posture and proliferation
- Periodical appraisals of marketing information
- Social, cultural and political changes

The overall objective of these checks and controls is to determine the achievement of targeted results on time. These points need to be administered from the corporate office of the business firm in a centralized manner in order to enable effective planning and execution process. The standardization of marketing-mix is usually centralized to ensure the quality of all the components of the mix across the markets in the operational region. Besides, it is important to provide a common business language across markets which would help in understanding local markets more analytically. The checks need to be exercised at different levels of the marketing plan execution and to build-up a strong communication and information system. A consolidated document of the target group index (TGI) may be an appropriate tool for information processing and analysis. The variables which need to be covered in the TGI include consumer goods, industrial goods, services, spatial and temporal trend of demand and price, distribution patterns, marketing budgets, response to advertising, communication services and the like. International marketing research needs to be conducted on specific issues of interest and inferences may be tagged along with the Monitoring and Evaluation (M&E) process. Nevertheless, M&E should be conducted periodically as a tool of control.

There is a close relation between types of activities undertaken in different countries and their institutional structures. A distinguishing characteristic of the financing of high technology firms is their evolving pattern of control by different investor groups. While stock markets are an important component of the development of the most successful firms, they are not the most common. Regulation is a significant influence on institutional structure. The degree of risk taking by financial institutions and the diversity of their investments are affected by trade-offs between competition and stability and the emphasis placed on minority investor protection[26].

Profit Impact on Marketing Strategy

In developing strategy, both corporate and business unit management need to be able to realistically appraise the level of performance that should be expected for a given business, and to be clear as to what factors explain variations in performance between businesses, and within a business over time. Important guidelines that help address these questions have been developed from the Profit Impact of Market Strategy (PIMS) program[27]. At the heart of the PIMS program is a business unit research database that captures the real-life experiences of over 3,000 businesses. Each business is a division, product line, or profit centre within its parent company, selling a distinct set of products and/or services to an identifiable group of customers, in competition with a well defined set of competitors, for which meaningful separation can be made of revenue, operating costs, investment, and strategic plans. The business's served market is defined as the segment of the total potential market that it is seriously targeting by offering suitable products and/or services and toward which it is making specific marketing efforts. On this basis each business reports, in standardized format, over 300 items of data, much of it for at least four years of operations. ROI is defined as follows: pre-tax after deduction of corporate expenses but prior to interest charges divided by average investment where this is equivalent to the historic net book value of plant and equipment plus working capital (i.e., total assets less current liabilities). Note that four-year averages are used for all figures. The information collected covers, *inter alia*, the market environment, competitive situation, internal cost and asset structure, and profit performance of the business. A full listing of the information captured by the PIMS database is given by The Strategic Planning, Institute's PIMS data manual[28].

The businesses in the database have been drawn from some 500 corporations, spanning a wide variety of industry settings. These corporations are based for the most part in North America and Europe. An understanding of why one business should be loss making while another achieves premium returns lies at the heart of strategy formulation. To explain this variance, cross-sectional analysis is carried out on the database to uncover the general patterns or relationships that account for these profit differentials. The fundamental proposition that underpins this approach is that the name of a business has no bearing on its level of performance. Research on the database has identified some 30 factors that are statistically significant at the 95 percent probability level or better in explaining the variance in profitability across businesses. These factors, which operate in a highly interactive way, collectively explain nearly 80 percent of the variance in ROI across the database. The more powerful factors are listed in Table 8.2 under four categories: marketplace standing, market environment, and differentiation production structure. It should be noted at the outset that part of the explanation of variance is definitional. This comes about because some of the

---

[26] Mayer C (2002), Financing the New Economy: financial institutions and corporate governance, *Information Economics and Policy*, 14 (2), 311-326.

[27] Schoeffier S, Buzzell, R D and Heany D F (1974), Impact of strategic planning on profit performance, *Harvard Business Review*, 52 (2), 137-45.

[28] Buzzell R D and Gale B T (1987), *The PIMS principles*, New York, The Free Press.

Table 8.2. Key- determinants of ROL in the PIMS database

Category of factor	Impact on ROI as factor increases
Marketplace standing	+
Market share	+
Relative market share	+
Served market concentration	
Market environment	+
Real market growth	+
Selling price inflation	+
Market differentiation	-
Purchase amount immediate customers	-
Importance of purchase to end user	
Differentiation from competitors	+
Relative product quality	+
Relative price	-
Relative direct cost	-
% Sales new products	-
Marketing/sales revenueb	-
R&D/sales revenue	
Capital and production structure	-
Investment/ sales revenue	-
Investment/ value added	-
Receivables/ investment	+
Fixed capital /investment	-
Capacity utilization	+
Unionization	-
Labor effectiveness*	+

profit-explaining variables, such as investment/sales revenue, contain elements, which are also present in the construction of the dependent variable, ROL. However; the emphasis is on behavioral relationships. Definitional elements are included in the independent variables only when it is impossible to separate out the behavioral and definitional effects of a particular factor.

COMPETITION VS. COOPERATION

The global competition is observed on both aggressive and defensive dimensions in the market. The companies that are capable of managing appropriate diffusion of technology and adaptation process among the customer segments are found to be highly successful. Competition among multinationals these days is likely to be a three-dimensional strategic game wherein the moves of an organization in one market are designed to achieve goals in another market in ways that aren't immediately apparent to rivals[29]. There is growing consensus among international trade negotiators and policymakers that a prime area for future multilateral discussion is competition policy. Competition policy includes antitrust policy (including merger regulation and control) but is often extended to include international trade measures and other policies that affect the structure, conduct, and performance of individual industries. The leading alliances between the major multinational enterprises may be seen in reference to production, finance, and technology and supply chain along with other complementary activities. To compete in the major global markets the multinational companies manage with substantial financial resources. Logistics and the supply chain management is an art of management of flow of materials and products from the source of production to the end user. This system with the multinational companies includes the total flow of material right from the stage of acquisition of raw materials to the delivery of finished products to the customers. The function of distribution is the combination of activities associated with advertising, sales and physical transfer of the goods and services to the retail and wholesale delivery points as is being observed by the global companies in order to establish their competitive strength in the market. The logistics management is an important function handled by such business companies in the marketing process and effective logistics management improve both cost and customer service performance of the company. Globalization of distribution is particularly important for companies using internet for e-commerce as they can operate on economies of scale with wider reach of customers.

It has become a common belief in view of growing competition that cooperative strategy is the new form of competition facing the recent development in the world economy, technology, and corporate strategy. Companies use inter-firm coordination to acquire new technologies and expand their product/market reach, which is the crux of corporate entrepreneurship. Inter-firm linkages expand information and resource access by widening the sweep of environmental scanning for a firm and by linking with complementary assets in other corporations. And corporate entrepreneurialism through the pursuit of innovative capabilities or administrative structures is at the nexus of joint venturing among domestic or cross-border partners[30]. Many East Asian economies have grown briskly in the past few years. However, future development will depend on the quality and timeliness of regional and national policy actions. The policy agenda must address the problems that buffeted the region in the late 1990s associated with the weakness of domestic institutions and policies in the context of globalization. These problems include financial shocks, rapid shifts in the competitiveness of major exports, changes in international production networking, and significant reconfiguration in the geographical composition of production systems that had provided the foundation for growth. Sustaining dynamism in East Asia requires policy initiatives that contain the risks from shocks and manage the ongoing shifts and changes in ways that enhance both the competitiveness of firms and the stability of the economies[31].

It is argued that the propensity to cooperate may be negatively affected by competition. Experimental evidence supports this hypothesis. In a set of three experiments in which

---

[29] Ian C. MacMillan, Alexander B. van Putten and Rita Gunther McGrath: Global Competition- What is the First Move, HBS Working Knowledge, Harvard Business School, June 23, 2003.

[30] Park S H and Kim D (1997), Market valuation of joint ventures: joint venture characteristics and wealth gains, *Journal of Business Venturing*, 12 (2), 83-108.

[31] Yusuf S, Nabeshima K and Altaf M A (2004), *Global Change and East Asian Policy Initiatives*, World Bank, July, 1-468.

different degrees of competition characterize the markets participants reduce their contributions to a public project as the degree of competition increases However, the cooperation and partnerships are justified only if they stand to yield substantially better results than the firms could achieve on their own. And even if they are warranted, they can fail if the partners enter them with mismatched expectations. In matters of the heart, it may be better to have loved and lost, but in business relationships, it's better to have headed off the resource sink and lingering resentments a failed partnership can cause. However, when regulation is cut back in order to bring more competition to the marketplace, we again witness the true consequences of this competition: its advantages often prove illusory or short-lived or selective which has been viewed controversial by many corporate analysts[32].

The contemporary ideology on the competition emphasizes largely on the competitive environment which contribute to various dimensions of rivalries. It has been observed that the low-end competitor indulging a company in offering much lower prices for a seemingly similar product, has been the common fear of each industry leader managing his business among competitors. The vast majority of such low-end companies fall into one of the four broad categories which include strippers, predators, reformers, or transformers[33]. The global companies often try to promote competition among their salespeople by offering incentives to the best performer and marketing planners develop strategies to defeat their competitors as a way to ensure their company's success. Hence it may be stated that in the corporate business management practices competition is largely accepted as a desirable and effective way to improve performance[34]. Certainly one would expect competition to be more effective under some circumstances. It is surprising to learn how difficult it was to find empirical evidence about situations in which competition proved superior, especially when one may look at the range of evidence examined by Kohn. However, he emphasizes that the competition leads to produce a less positive regard for people of different ethnic backgrounds. Many organizations feel that in growing competition establishing strategic alliances would better check the competitor's penetration than the own brand or technology driven company. They recognize that alliances and relationships with other companies of repute are fundamental to outwit, outmaneuver and outperform the competitors by ways of better branding, better service and tagging global brands for assuring the quality of goods and services. Alliances and relationships thus transform the concept of competitor. The process of competition and cooperation is exhibited in Figure 8.1 which delineates the path of strategy development among global firms.

A competing firm intends to push the aggregate sales in short run by leveraging the marketing mix components particularly those related to price and promotion to get short run market advantages. However, such efforts may lead to higher risk and uncertainty to sustain with its competitive strategies in a given market causing variability in the market share of the firm. It is necessary for the managers to look into cause and effect chain while adapting the competitive marketing strategies as sometimes it may induce irreversible results. Alternatively, if a firm chooses to develop its business through cooperation with the existing firms in a given market, the firm may derive value centered goals with focus on strategic

---

[32] Kohn Alfie (1986), *No Contest: The Case Against Competition*, Boston: Houghton Mifflin.
[33] Potter Don (2004), Confronting Low-end Competition, *Harvard Business Review*, 45 (4), 73-78.
[34] Armstrong Scott J (1988), Review on Alfie Kohn's Book, *Journal of Marketing*, 52, October, 131-132.

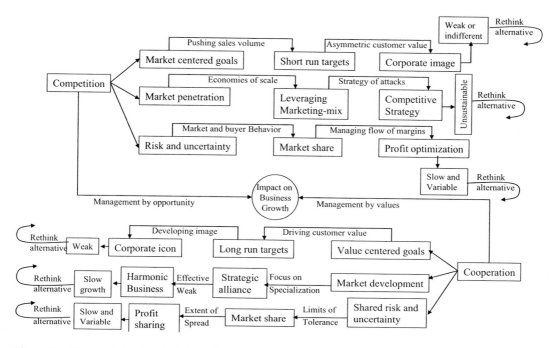

Figure 8.1. Process Mapping in Adaptation of Competition or Cooperation Practices as Growth Drivers in a Firm.

given alliance. The alliance firms would have advantage to share risk, uncertainty and profit in a given market over a specified time. The managers of a firm may opt for leaning to cooperation as a safe and mutual growth driver to go international or expand their business in the domestic market with long-run business equilibrium. However, proper choice of strategy is situation and firm specific and a more effective approach for managers may be to act on the particular circumstances in which they find themselves[35].

The competition among firms is increasingly shifting from company *vs.* company to supply chain *vs.* supply chain. Benefits can be grouped as customer-oriented benefits, productivity benefits, and innovation-related benefits. Factors supporting collaboration are observed as trust, common goals for cooperation, and existence of cooperation mechanisms, while barriers are related to three factors such as lack of trust, risk-benefit evaluation, and lack of common goals for cooperation[36]. The collaboration in the business strategy may be considered analogous with the cooperation in the reference to prevailing concerns of the globalization. On the contrary, heavy competition in India in almost all product categories has been experienced due to diversification by large and medium companies and increased entry of multinationals which has restricted the growth of domestic companies. Previously, large companies enjoyed high profit margins by targeting premium priced products in the upper strata of Indian society. High levels of competition from equally reputed brands have not only decreased the companies' market share but also created price wars, reducing profit margins

[35] Krubasik Edward G (1988), Customize your Product Development, *Harvard Business Review*, 66 (6), 46-52.
[36] Cetindamar D, Catay B and Basmaci O S (2005), Competition through Collaboration-Insights from an Initiative in the Turkish Textile Supply Chain, Supply *Chain Management -An International Journal*, 10 (4), April, 238-240.

and limiting market growth. This has motivated companies to consider the lower classes and the rural segments, which they had previously ignored[37]. In reference to the above two dissimilarities in the business development process, it may be stated that in practice, Kohn's ideology of cooperation as a tool to replace competition, thus can not be generalized.

Achievement and Competition

Knowledge-based competition has magnified the importance of learning alliances as a fast and effective mechanism of capability development. The parameters of success and effective knowledge transfer are used interchangeably to indicate a relatively high level of achievement of intended as well as the unintended benefits to a firm[38]. However the cooperation is more effective when the size of the organization is smaller and the degree of interdependence is higher among its units. He strongly phrases his idea on cooperation as a rider over the negativity of competition. In his view competition works just as any other extrinsic motivator does. The movement of public services into direct competition with their private enterprise counterparts is a common feature of public sector policy throughout the developed world. The publicly funded provision of school education has not been exempt from this trend. The creation of a competitive climate is placing public school leaders and teachers under pressure to improve performance in an environment where parents-as-consumers choose the schools to which they send their children[39]. However, Kohn disagrees with the fact of involving increasing competitive efforts for augmenting the extent of achievements and argues that so far from making us more productive, then, a structure that pits us against one another tends to inhibit our performance. Children simply do not learn better when education is transformed into competitive struggle. Many teachers conclude that competition holds attention better even though they have never worked with cooperative alternatives (Kohn, 1986, p 50).

Relationships among competition, athletic skill, and social relationships among children have received considerable attention from social psychologists and have also sparked considerable public debate. Most studies of these relationships have concentrated on sports programs involving upper elementary or older boys. Competitive environments heightened the tendency for athletic skill to function as a generalized status element in peer networks. After-school sports programs contributed to the reproduction of athletic skill as a basis of peer status, even for young children[40]. A passive argument has also emerged on pushing children to competition though at times his arguments seem to be pro competition. It has also been observed that forcing children to compete is something defended precisely on these grounds— that early experience with competition will lead to more effective competition in later life. Competition works just as any other extrinsic motivator does. The distinction between trying to do well and trying to beat others is not the only explanation we can come up with for the

---

[37] Dubey Jayshree and Patel Rajani P (2004), Small Wonders of the Indian Market, *Journal of Consumer Behaviour*, 4 (2), December, 145-151.

[38] Daghfous A (2004), Organizational Learning, Knowledge and Technology Transfer-A Case Study, *The Learning Organization: An International Journal*, 11 (1), January, 67-83.

[39] Dempster N, Freakley M. and Parry L (2001), The Ethical Climate of Public Schooling under New Public Management, *International Journal of Leadership in Education*, 4 (1), January, 1-12.

[40] Landers-Potts M and Grant L (1997), Competitive Climates, Athletic Skill, and Children's Status in After-School Recreational Sports Programs, *Social Psychology of Education*, 2 (3-4), 297-313.

competitions failure. Competition also precludes the more effective use of resources that cooperation allows. The dynamics of cooperative effort make this arrangement far more efficient, while competitors hardly are predisposed to like and trust each other enough to benefit from it.

Some studies have shown that cooperation is a better tool for growth and achievement as compared to the competition. While analyzing the behavioral attributes of children it has been observed that combining co-operation with other behaviors has been observed as a successful strategy for competing for resources. The children quickly learn to co-operate, however, viewing times varied significantly between them, suggesting that they were competing against each other even while co-operating. The inequitable outcomes appear due to individual differences in the ability to combine helping others with more competitive behaviors[41]. It has been evident from Kohn's debate for and against competition, that when we compete we do so out of primary concern for our own welfare. Working together as a group would not be a strategy for maximizing individual gain but a logical consequence of thinking in terms of what benefits all of us. Sometimes such a tradeoff will occur, but it will not be seen as catastrophic. More to the point, this question will not occur to someone whose worldview is different from our own. It would seem as odd as your feet asking whether the body as a whole benefits from jogging at their expense (Kohn, 1986, p 66).

Economic Competition

The contemporary concepts of economic advancement are largely based on the concepts of collaboration; cooperation and competition for developed countries include an entire range of governmental functions, including sectoral policy reform, economic integration, privatization, public sector enhancement, labor market competitiveness, investment climate enhancement, E-government, soft infrastructures for developing a knowledge economy, macroeconomic management and effective long-range planning. The weight of the public sector constitutes a serious impediment to more rapid growth for many countries. Importantly, the large expenditure burden it requires does not always translate into an efficient and equitable distribution of services. Such performance is reflected by the public sector efficiency and governance in promoting the economic advancement of a country[42]. Competition is a pivot of economic development which allows cooperation to lead the competition many times. The inadequate functioning of some product markets and lack of competition has undermined the dynamism of the economy, in particular productivity growth. While discussing economic environment Kohn seems to be pro-competition and states that despite the enormous discrepancy between perfect competition and the actual state of our economic system, competition is still the stated ideal. Businesspeople and public officials use the term as an honorific, discussing ways in which they can make their companies and countries *more competitive* and never pausing to ask whether a competitive system really is the best possible arrangement.

---

[41] Charlesworth W R (1996), Co-operation and Competition: Contributions to an Evolutionary and Developmental Model, *International Journal of Behavioral Development*, 19 (1), March 1996, 25-38.

[42] Rajagopal (2007), Competition vs. Cooperation: Analyzing Strategy Dilemma in Business Growth under Changing Social Paradigms, *International Journal of Business Environment*, 1 (4), 476-487.

The competitive drivers support the companies for matching their strategies appropriately with their moves in the market. The existence of many global competitors indicates that an industry is mature for international business operations. The global competitors operate on cost advantages over the local competitors. The emergence of strong global competitors has served to develop the market infrastructure for the local companies and also help in transfer of technological skills enabling the domestic company to explore the scope of expansion. The competitive efforts put pressure on companies to globalize their marketing activities to derive optimum performance by interpreting appropriately the competitor signals. When Kodak backed out from sponsoring the 1984 Los Angeles Olympics, Fuji Film entered into the sponsorship issue immediately at the prescribed price and was one of the official sponsors of the Olympics. By the time Kodak reconsidered to participate in this international event, the time had run out. However, for the Olympics of 1988 and ABC-TV, Kodak became the sports program sponsor[43].

The need for economic as well as market competition has been endorsed by many applied studies conducted to evidence the driving factors in the economic growth. Market competition is essential for any economy to be efficient. In order to develop competition in a transition economy, it is conventionally thought that privatization should take place first. This wisdom has been challenged by the Chinese reform experience of the last two decades, which modified the incentive structure of state enterprises and created markets and market competition in the absence of large-scale privatization. China's experience, however, raises the question of whether its chosen type of reform is sufficient to promote competition in a market dominated by public firms. It has been observed in the Kohn's readings that though he delineates competition as a driver of growth but at the same time argues that is not a healthy psychological attribute to nurture growth of either an individual or an organization. He discusses that the distinction between trying to do well and trying to beat others is not the only explanation we can come up with for competitions failure. Competition also precludes the more effective use of resources that cooperation allows. The dynamics of cooperative effort make this arrangement far more efficient, while competitors hardly are predisposed to like and trust each other enough to benefit from it.

However, the contemporary economists favor competition as an important tool for economic growth. They discuss whether standard procedures and widely accepted insights of competition policy remain valid when one deals with potentially anti-competitive conduct in innovative industries. The question of appropriateness arises because competition in these industries displays features that are radically different from those encountered in traditional sectors of the economy. Competition is for the market rather than in the market, dynamic aspects of competition matter more in knowledge-based industries[44]. In reference to international economic development the competitiveness among nations in exploiting resources has certainly proved to be a major attribute. It has also been noticed that global competitiveness is the key element to survive in business and it is a task that the business sector along with governments has to confront. Since the latter half of the eighties and all

---

[43] Thomas C Finnerty: Kodak Vs. Fuji – The Battle for Global Market Share, Institute of Global Business Strategy, Lubin School of Business, Pace University, New York, 2000, pp 1-23.

[44] Encaoua David and Hollander Abraham (2002), Competition Policy and Innovation, *Oxford Review of Economic Policy*, 18 (1), Spring, 63-79.

through the decade of the 90's, issues of reforms have swept the economies of Latin America and Caribbean countries[45].

Managers of corporate parents and their ventures have a longstanding and pertinent question of how closely to tie the parent and venture for achieving growth and success. Though the technological capabilities with the MNCs in Mexico tend to facilitate lowering cognitive inertia of managers, the dependency relational factors seems to be increasing, affecting the internal fit of the ventures. Hence the parent ventures may provide higher autonomy in a phased manner to other ventures in reference to their growth and age. However, effective implementation of autonomy requires a clear view of the objectives, dedication to understanding the process, and discipline in the venture. The venture success is associated with high levels of awareness, commitment, and connection with the parent. It may be necessary for the Latin American corporate ventures also to engage in acquisitive learning through the convergence of best management practices in order to develop appropriate strategic internal and external fit. Hence the parent companies need to take responsibility for knowledge sharing in ventures. An effective win-win situation may be acquired between the parent and venture by sharing value potentials and offering equity in the venture. This would allow the venture managers to focus fully on the commissioning and ongoing sustainable operation of the new facilities to ensure productivity, cash flow and profitability of the business. It would be appropriate for the venture to have greater financial independence accompanied with higher accountability. And, as a venture gains in independence and accountability, the relational dimensions would develop stronger ties with venture and offer improved internal as well as external strategic fit[46].

Competition has been identified by some researchers as an aggressive tool to achieve market power while cooperation is determined as a management instrument for defensive positioning against competition. Though both forms of organizational tools lead to growth and development, cooperation is considered to be more balanced and welfare oriented. Hence there has been major emphasis on cooperation in international trade among the nations who have joined the stream of globalization. Collaboration across the supply chain has become a crucial element in the creation of business value in such a complex manufacturing environment. The collaborative planning, forecasting and replenishment (CPFR) process is a powerful tool to enhance the cooperation between partners from upstream to the vendor/suppliers and downstream to the customer.

In fact in varied business situations both competition and cooperation are used to build the organizational and customer value. The optimal portfolio demand for products under competition varies strongly with the values associated with the brand, industry attractiveness, knowledge management and ethical issues of the organization. The extent of business values determines the relative risk aversion in terms of functional and logistical efficiency between the organization and supplier while the switching attitude may influence the customers if the organizational values are not strong and sustainable in the given competitive environment[47]. The success of a firm largely emerges from the three different management practices that

---

[45] Rajagopal (2005), Institutional Reforms and Trade Competitiveness in Latin America, *Journal of Applied Econometrics and International Development*, 5 (1), April, 45-64.

[46] Rajagopal (2006), Innovation and Business Growth through Corporate Venturing in Latin America: Analysis of Strategic Fit, *Management Decision*, 44 (5), 703-718.

[47] Rajagopal and Sanchez Romulo (2005), Analysis of Customer Portfolio and Relationship Management Models: Bridging Managerial Gaps, *Journal of Business and Industrial Marketing*, Vol. 20, No.6, June, 307-316.

refer to the use of information on customer value, competition, and costs respectively[48]. It is argued in a study that the success of these practices is contingent on relative product advantage and competitive intensity, which reveals that there are no general "best" or "bad" practices, but that a contingency approach is appropriate. This may be competition, collaboration and strategic cooperation[49].

Some arguments are contradictory with expressions such as, competition will lower achievement markedly for such individuals which seriously affects the performance of the whole group (class, corporation, society). One way a competitive culture deals with those who find competition unpleasant, of course, is to accuse them of being afraid of losing. It has been argued that across many fields the assumption that competition promotes excellence has become increasingly doubtful. Such competitive pressures ultimately benefit no one, least of all the public. Working against, rather than with, colleagues tends to be more destructive than productive. This corroborates the bulk of evidence on the topic— evidence that requires us to reconsider our assumptions about the usefulness of competition. However, competition is an essential constituent of development and has been evidenced by a large number of research studies in reference to animal and human behavior, social, national and international growth. The more competition there is the more likely are firms to be efficient and prices to be low. Economists have identified several different sorts of competition. Perfect competition is the most competitive market imaginable in which everybody is a price taker.

Global Local Marketing

The global growth products of multinational companies are mostly centralized in the country of origin and the products that emerge tend to have features, advantages and benefits specified by the central marketing system of the company. Hence, key technologies and major product introductions cater primarily to customers in that geographical region. Marketing and customers in other regions are relegated to acceptance of custom modifications; or they have the choice to buy from other local suppliers. The product targeting goes beyond the perceived use values of the customers, local preferences and local language. Expectations regarding size, shape, customized items, price and availability vary widely. Hence regional markets tend to be dominated by local companies. Often the companies offer locally engineered or customized products at a differential price to win market share. For growth and success in the new global economy, the guiding principle must be: *Go Global – think Local!* Automation suppliers must become truly global by allowing local development of products for local markets. The best approach is to develop technology (hardware & software) through global alliances – preferably with relatively small, fast-moving local companies. In a global market, there are 3 keys that constitute the winning difference:

- Marketing abilities that assess correctly the local needs in a global arena.
- Proprietary technology and products targeted specifically for local markets.
- High-value-added services offered through effective local service providers.

---

[48] Rajagopal (2006[b]), Measuring Customer Value Gaps: An Empirical Study in Mexican Retail Markets, *Economic Issues*, 11(1), March, 19-40.

[49] Ingenbleek Paul, Debruyne Marion, Frambach Ruud T and Verhallen Theo (2003), Successful New Product Pricing Practices: A Contingency Approach, *Marketing letters*, 14(4), December, pp 289-305.

In the global village of the new economy, automation companies have little choice – they must find more ways and means to expand globally. To do this they need to minimize domination of the central corporate culture, and maximize responsiveness to local customer needs.

Ever since Fujifilm began actively exporting its products throughout the world in the early 1960s, it has been one of Japan's leading companies regarding overseas operations. Besides establishing a world-spanning network of local marketing bases, we were among the first Japanese companies to initiate overseas manufacturing, starting with the 1974 construction of a color photographic paper processing plant in Brazil. Since the 1980s, Fujifilm has arranged for Japanese and local technical staff to cooperatively design and construct overseas manufacturing facilities that make appropriate use of the Company's unique technologies in harmony with local conditions. These efforts have enabled the steady expansion and strengthening of Fujifilm's global production, marketing, and service networks. Having consistently placed strong emphasis on understanding regional characteristics and on respecting and adapting to local cultures, Fujifilm has been highly praised for its localization efforts and contributions to the communities in which it operates. The Company views globalization and localization as two equally crucial elements of its overall business strategy. The localization has been done by the companies to serve the markets in the Americas, Europe and Asia-Pacific.

As continued growth in the digitization of diagnostic imaging has also supported rising demand for dry medical imaging film in North America, Fuji Photo Film, Inc., based in Greenwood, South Carolina, in the United States, has been proceeding with the expansion of its medical-use film factory. In March 2003, the company completed that facility and began operating an integrated manufacturing system that performs a full range of manufacturing processes, from coating to processing. Because the range of products manufactured at the facility has been expanded to include dry medical imaging film, Fujifilm has significantly upgraded its systems for efficiently supplying customers throughout North America with our high-quality medical imaging products and related services. Fujifilm's headquarters in Europe, Fuji Photo Film (Europe) GmbH, recently established marketing companies in Poland, the Czech Republic, Slovakia, and Italy. In view of the huge changes under way in Europe —such as the monetary integration in 2002 and the forthcoming enlargement of the European Union in 2004—Fuji Photo Film (Europe) has been seeking to expand and strengthen its marketing systems so that it can accurately respond to local needs and expeditiously supply products and services. Fujifilm began marketing the DocuCentre Color series of digital color multifunction machines in the Asia-Oceania region during the current fiscal year 2004. The Company also proactively proceeded with measures to expand its manufacturing and marketing systems in the region, particularly in China, which has markets that are expected to grow greatly. Consolidated revenue in this region rose 13.4%, to ¥279.1 billion[50].

The world's most recognized companies and brands, Coca-Cola continues to prosper by innovating and adapting to the local needs of its customers and consumers throughout the world. Despite ferocious competition, significant currency devaluations in key markets, and major acquisition-related write-downs, the company reported first quarter 2002 sales of US$4.08 billion and has predicted long term growth approaching six percent. Global Marketing helps set global marketing strategies and product positioning, which is then implemented locally and adapted to local marketing needs.

---

[50] Fujifilm Corporte Home page: http://home.fujifilm.com/info/profile/operation.html 27 May 2004.

CULTURAL IMPLICATIONS OF GLOBAL VENTURES

Corporate venturing process encompasses people from different cultures and thus every business activity in another country is subject to cultural challenges. The extent of cultural influence varies in accordance with the nature of industrial and consumer products and services. Consumer Products, by virtue of their marketing process such as mass advertising, sales promotion and personal selling tend to require a strong degree of cultural awareness since this knowledge relates to the human communication in the selling process. On the contrary, industrial products may have lesser requirements for cultural awareness, as sometimes the negotiation in business to business or industrial marketing segment is based on a situation and does not depend on the cultural adaptation process. For example, the technical specifications for an industrial ceramic automotive component might be the same in New York as they are in Tokyo or Moscow. Under such circumstances what is important, to make this sale, is the price of the component and how it fits the specifications required by the component.

Corporate venturing is an important source of technological innovation for corporations by providing a window on emerging technologies, market opportunities, new business models, and distribution channels,. However, effective implementation requires a clear view of the objectives, dedication to understanding the process, and discipline. The success in corporate venturing is associated with high levels of commitment, trust, group dynamics and skills in functional management of the venture. In the study the variables of economic and relational dimensions of external and internal fit have shown greater association with venture success. It has also been found that ventures opt for greater autonomy and less economic dependency on their parent ventures for leading success and this finding makes an intuitive sense. It was observed during the study that the parent-venture relationship does not differ between the high and low performers. It appears from the analysis that though economic dependency on parent decreases with the ageing of the venture, managerial accountability increases in the organization. The level of economic change across the phases of venture maturity has not been significantly different between high and low performers. Mexican managers view authority balance as a positive contributor to alliance performance, while authority advantage to the benefit of the Mexican partner at the expense of the U.S. partner is viewed as having a negative impact on performance of the corporate ventures. The best ideas have languished in many corporations, either because of internal resistance or an inability to execute on the initial insight. This study is based on observations made by the previous contributors in the area of trust in corporate relationships; there still exists the need for more longitudinal research studies in the area of corporate venturing with focus on parent-venture, strategic fit between external and internal factors and analytical frameworks of venture performance indices in reference to the developing countries.

Corporate ventures allow consumers to buy goods from all over the world in their local marketplace. While local businesses must compete with these foreign goods on their home turf, they also have new opportunities to develop their export markets by selling in a multitude of other countries. Cultural goods and services are no exception to these new patterns of production, consumption and trade. Cultural markets are increasingly going global as may be observed by the trends in cultural goods trade in the post 1980 period across the countries in different regions. As consumption of cultural goods and services spreads all over the world, production itself tends to concentrate. This results in an oligopolistic market with a highly asymmetric structure. The effects of this market profile are as yet unknown: while we are aware that a large share of the cultural products circulating in most countries are produced elsewhere, we know very little about the impact of this global cultural market on citizens, audiences, businesses and governments. The past few years have seen the emergence of a powerful interest in culture resulting from a combination of diverse phenomena such as globalization, regional integration processes and cultures claiming their right to express themselves — all this in a context where cultural industries are progressively taking over traditional forms of creation and dissemination and bringing about changes in cultural practices. The issue of "culture and trade" has now acquired prime strategic significance.

Cultural goods and services convey and construct cultural values, produce and reproduce cultural identity and contribute to social cohesion; at the same time they constitute a key free factor of production in the new knowledge economy. Culture is an essential dimension of business development. The business solutions should be tailored to locally relevant traditions and institutions and these activities should make use of local expertise and knowledge. The international company entering the host country should ensure that people, their cultures and society, and their organizations and institutions are taken into account in formulating the business goals and operational strategies. Such development coordination with local culture improves the lives of people, especially the poor, and builds the social capital for a company to sustain long in the host country.

Chapter 9

GLOBALIZATION: CHALLENGES AHEAD

It is important to understand that the global political environment has a greater role to play in all business and economic matters today, however, it remains in a constant flux. The political system of a country is shaped after passing through major processes of growth, decay, breakdown and a ceaseless ferment of adaptation and adjustment. The magnitude and variety of the changes that occurred in the world's political systems between the 20's and 80's of the 20th century describe the complex dimensions of the problem. It may be observed that during the last century, great empires disintegrated; nation-states emerged, flourished briefly, and then vanished. The two consecutive world wars transformed the international system and seeded new ideologies that swept the world and shook established groups from power-grid nations. However, many developing countries experienced civil and political revolutions during the post-world-war period in order to determine the most effective governing system and domestic politics in every system was contorted by social strife and economic crisis. In the middle of the 20th century the nature of political life was changed everywhere by novel forms of political activity as the new means of mass communication, increase of popular participation in politics and the rise of new political issues offered better understanding towards international politics and popular governance in reference to global integration. Besides, the extension of the scope of governmental activity and other innumerable social, economic, and technical developments in the developing countries urged for stability in the government for effective implementation of the international development programs and the trade policies have been one among the international priorities.

There are many factors that influence the ideological transition, development and change in the world's political systems. In the recent past, industrialization, population growth, the "revolution of rising expectations" in the less developed countries, and international tensions have affected the political thinking to a large extent. However, the political instability generally occurs when the distribution of wealth fails to correspond with the distribution of political power. This situation may be described in reference to the classical school of political thought as the political stability in a country is largely based on a large middle class in a country. On the contrary the Marxist theories of economic determinism view all political changes as the result of changes in the mode of production. However, the neo-classical political thinkers discuss that the prime cause of revolutions and other forms of violent political changes are due to power polarization and alienation with the capitalistic economic countries. The majority of the world's political systems have experienced one form or another of internal warfare leading to violent collapse of the governments in power and certain crisis situations seem to increase the likelihood of breakdown in the governing politics of a region or a country.

In the politico-economic scenario the economic crisis are another common stimulus to the political setbacks as may be witnessed in the recent Argentinean crisis. The Brazilian economy was also at the cliff in the late 90's due to internal economic instability. The political situation of a country may be explained in terms of economic growth as reflected in gross domestic product and also towards the social scarcity. However, the political environment of a country also contributes in building the social position of individuals. A sense of insecurity and uncertainty for the future, and an aggravation of the relationships among social classes also results in the politico-economic conflicts in a country. A severe national economic crisis develops distrust in the political system of the country and triggers outbreak of revolutions in the political systems. The political unrest in a country triggers the test conditions for the stability of political systems in extremely revealing ways, which often demand either for the change in the political leadership or the structure and process of governance in the system. Since the quality of the political leadership is often decisive, those systems that provide methods of selecting able leaders and replacing them possess important advantages towards internal and global political concerns. Unstable political systems are those that prove vulnerable to crisis pressures and that break down into various forms of internal warfare. The fundamental causes of such failures appear to be the lack of a widespread sense of the legitimacy of state authority and the absence of some general agreement on appropriate forms of political action.

The political sovereignty may be referred to as a country's desire to assert its authority over foreign business through various sanctions. Political sovereignty is the assertion of self, determination of its citizens, and the manifestation of their freedom. It is in and through the determination of its sovereignty that the order of the nation is constituted and maintained. Such sanctions are regular and evolutionary, and therefore predictable. An example is increase in taxes over foreign operations. Many of the developing countries impose restrictions on foreign business to protect their independence. These countries are jealous of their political freedom and want to protect it at all costs, even if it means a slow economic pace without the help of MNCs. Thus, the political sovereignty problem exists mainly in developing countries.

DETERMINING POLITICAL ENVIRONMENT

The political philosophy and the legal environment of a nation largely influence the practice of international marketing. The political environment of a country comprises the international environment, host-country environment and the home-country environment. Many studies have shown that dealing with problems in the political arena is the principal challenge facing international managers in developing pro political strategies to run the business successfully in the host country. It is observed that each country has its own set of national goals; most countries also share many common objectives. Nationalism and patriotism refer to citizens' feelings about their country and its interests. Such feelings exist in every country and the multinational firms, individually or collectively, may be perceived as a threat to that sovereignty. The foreign firms perceive greater threats if they are larger in size and more in number in a country. At the time of any political turmoil, the foreign firms may be targets for attack. Many countries seek "national solutions" to help troubled companies to retain what are perceived to be national champions. International firms need to be sensitive to these issues and to be careful not to be too "foreign." This includes advertising and branding policies as well as ownership and staffing. Establishing local R&D would be perceived favorably in this context.

The international political environment involves political relations among the countries of common ideologies. The foreign firm needs to make all adjustments with the host country's international relations, no matter how non-aligned it may try to be. Such strategic adjustments in tune to the international environment of the host country are required as its operations are frequently related also to the neighboring countries, either on the supply or demand side or both. Another critical factor affecting the political environment is the diplomatic relations of the host countries with others in the region or beyond. If a country is a member of a regional group, such as the EU, NAFTA, ASEAN, its political identity influences the firm's operational and expansion opportunities. If a nation has particular friends or enemies among other nations, the firm must modify its international logistics to comply with how that market is supplied and to whom it can sell. For example, the United States limits trade with various countries and Arabian countries do not entertain any business activities with Israel. The participation of the host country in the regional trade agreements or with the international trade organizations may affect patents, communication, transportation, and other items of interest to the international marketer. As a rule, the more international organizations a country belongs to, the more regulations it accepts, and the more dependable is its economic, political and legal environment. The political environment at home-country is also an important indicator for a firm to decide its entry to the host country. However, an adverse environment therein may constrain its international operations as well as its domestic operations. The best-known example of the home-country political environment affecting international operations used to be South Africa. Home-country political pressures induced more than 200 American firms to leave that country altogether. In the private sector, the bottom line is shareholder value. In government, the objectives can be harder to pinpoint due to being clouded by political agendas, turf battles, special interests and economics. Some of the key issues in reference to measuring the performance of the government in the given political environment of the home country may be considered by the firm as described below:

- *Measuring performance:* Governments need to continue to focus on gauging performance by what is achieved. Leaders should strive to understand the real results that are being delivered, and how much real progress is being made.
- *Improving through competition:* Government's position is often perceived in a fix by the social pressures. The issues of trade protection, allowing foreign companies to participate in the host country, repatriation of profits and other economic issues are subject to the prevailing political ideology in the host country.
- *Streamlining operations*: It is necessary for a foreign firm to examine the conduct of government activities in the home country. Many government operations can be performed by third parties often at lower cost and with equal or higher quality.

- *Promoting efficiency:* Most government employees are smart, industrious people. But like any workforce, their behavior is largely driven by the organization's rewards and incentives.

Many multinational companies face uncertainty in political environment due to instability of political leadership, coalitions and external pressures. Even if the home country and the host country give them no problems, they can face threats in the neighboring markets. Firms that do not have problems with their home government or the host government may be bothered or boycotted in neighboring countries. Escalation of political conflict in many developing countries and their impact on economic development has been a topical issue in recent development literature. The overwhelming emphasis on 'ethnic conflicts' in this literature has, however, precluded looking at political conflict in the wider context of the development process, going beyond the ethnic dimension. In particular, because of the preoccupation with the ethnic roots as the prime source of these conflicts, reverse causation running from economic policy to political conflict has been virtually ignored in the debate[1]. The effectiveness of the political systems in a country may be analyzed by the foreign firms in reference to the following indicators:

- Democratic effectiveness: capable of deepening democracy and democratic citizenship;
- Policy effectiveness: capable of tackling fundamental developmental problems of poverty and social equality
- Conflict-management effectiveness: capable of channeling conflicts and rendering them less destructive.

Political conflict in general could be defined as dynamic and manifest conflict processes consisting of certain phases. In this case the term conflict is used in a more specific meaning: a political process (dynamic situation) in which engaged political parties have incompatible attitudes and behaviors. Internal as well as international conflicts have three interrelated components:

- Conflict situation, manifested in expressing various political aims or conflict of interest that cannot be simultaneously achieved and for that reason can be qualified as mutually exclusive;
- Conflict behavior (in the first place aimed at achieving the aforementioned political aims); and
- Conflicting attitudes and perceptions having an emotional dimension (feeling of anger, mistrust, fear, scorn, hatred, etc.) as well as a cognitive dimension.

Many countries in different parts of the world undergo political conflict of various natures like turmoil, internal war, and conspiracy that can be irregular, revolutionary, and/or sporadic. Turmoil refers to instant upheaval on a massive scale against an established political regime. The internal unrest in a country refers to large-scale, organized violence against a

---

[1] Sirimal Abeyratne: Economic Roots of Political Conflicts- A Case of Sri Lanka, Australian National University, Australia South Asia Research Centre, Working Paper #03, 2002.

government, such as guerrilla warfare. The example may be cited of Vietnam's actions in Cambodia and internal violence by the self proclaimed people's groups like in north-eastern states in India.

Political change in a country sometimes leads to a more favorable economic and business climate. For example, Sukarno's departure from the Indonesian scene improved the business climate there. The political ideology in India after the governance of Late Rajiv Gandhi, the Indian Prime Minister in 1991, became highly favorable for international business as the policy of globalization was adopted and U.S. multinationals found India an attractive place to do business. The political conflict in a country may lead to unstable conditions, but those conditions may or may not affect business. Therefore, political risk may or may not result from political unrest. The international businesses houses must analyze chronologically the occurrence of political conflicts and assess the likelihood of its impact on the business environment.

South Korean agriculture is highly inefficient, and rice farmers feel particularly vulnerable as quotas on imports are gradually lifted. In early 2004 the national assembly approved the trade agreement with Chile after months of delays as thousands of farmers battled riot police outside. The South Korean government signed the free trade agreement with Chile a year ago. The deal was finally ratified in February 2004 after months of bitter argument and a series of violent clashes with farmers. Under the agreement, Chile will lift tariffs on South Korean cars, mobile phones, and electronic goods. In return, South Korea will open its markets to Chilean copper and agricultural goods, including wheat, wool, tomatoes and fish. The farmers have been offered a generous package of subsidies and debt relief, but they say it won't be enough[2].

Many times the political unrest is temporary focused on the international policies of the government. There have been anti-globalization protests in many countries during the international political movements on pursuing the developing countries to join the World Trade Organization. It is important to understand the nature of political conflict in foreign countries and the motivation behind government actions. If a change in government policy is only symbolic without any indications of the change in implementation process, it represents less risk to foreign firms.

GLOBAL FINANCIAL TRENDS AND BANKING SYSTEM

One of the apparent movements noted in the late 1990s that is still in vogue in global finance is the unstable performance financial institutions of the countries as well as the open markets. There were longer-run trends that have set the backdrop for much of the work of central banks in international forums dealing with financial efficiency and stability. Financial instability, connotes the presence of market imperfections or externalities in the financial system that are substantial enough to create significant risks for real aggregate economic performance. Over the past few decades, economic research has identified a variety of imperfections inherent in markets, such as moral hazard, asymmetric information, and externalities. On occasion, these imperfections can become so widespread and significant as to result in outcomes that threaten the functioning of the financial system and adversely affect

---

[2] Charles Scanlon: South Korea Shrug's off Farmers Trade Protest, BBC News, February 16, 2004 http://news. bbc.co.uk/go/pr/fr/-/1/hi/business/3492809.stm

real economic variables. History suggests that these imperfections reach this advanced and disruptive stage when they are exacerbated by large external shocks. Such outcomes include panics, bank runs, severe market illiquidity, and excessive risk aversion. These outcomes are highly undesirable for society because they can be accompanied by a variety of economic distortions: Financial prices can diverge sharply and for prolonged periods from fundamentals, and their correction is likely to impose great cost on society; the availability and pricing of credit may be too lax at times and at other times too restrictive relative to underlying macroeconomic conditions. It has been observed that many nations are trying to overcome the structural defects in financial markets that left their economies prone to boom-and-bust cycles. In some cases, central banks were seen as part of the solution in addressing the results of such market imperfections[3]. The Federal Reserve, for example, owes its existence in large measure to the financial panics in the late nineteenth and early twentieth centuries in the United States that increased public recognition of the need for a lender of last resort, for more-effective bank supervision, and for greater efficiency in the payment system.

The finance function has two principal aspects to provide the monetary resources to do business and to ensure an adequate financial return on the assets of the firm commensurate with its objectives. Even in a strictly domestic business, the able management of funds and investment aims at solving all sorts of problems related to issues including the adequacy of the financial returns, sources and availability of funds, raising supplementary resources and strategies for effective utilization thereof. In the international arena, the problems multiply and so the finance management must not only deal with different currencies and their fluctuating rates, but should also allow for the vagaries of the economic and political environments of nations with varying perspectives. Asset-based financing has become a more commonly accepted tool in the capitalization structure than it was in the past. There has been a transition in the marketplace with respect to traditional money center banks and some companies keep hedging their financing bets by securing both asset-based and cash-flow-based financing. In many organizations, finding sources of capital that are flexible has become a top priority, and asset-based arrangements can help achieve this goal. In general, asset-based financing offers more flexible liquidity than bank financing because it is driven more by collateral and less by covenants. In most cases, asset-based financing involves fewer and more flexible covenants than cash flow loans. In many cases, the only covenant focuses on the borrower's liquidity level. A company's access to asset-based financing often increases as its working capital needs increase because that's when assets are growing. There are some disadvantages of asset based financing strategy as in general, borrowers must provide monthly or quarterly reports to show that they are meeting loan covenants. Strong performance and high liquidity enable companies to negotiate more flexible reporting rules. The asset-based arrangements cost more than cash flow loans, but pricing depends on the borrower's creditworthiness. In recent years, interest rate spreads between asset-based and cash flow-based loans have remained steady, but fees on collateralized loans have increased in some cases.

The market concentration in the banking sector and in other sectors of the financial services industry has been increased in the recent past. The trend also marks towards steady

---

[3] Roger W Ferguson Jr.: The Role of Central Banks in Fostering Efficiency and Stability in the Global Financial System, National Bank of Belgium Conference on Efficiency and Stability in an Evolving Financial System, Brussels, Belgium, May 17, 2004.

increasing share of total credit provided directly through markets rather than through intermediaries like banks. Another important trend has been the expanding scope and availability of financial instruments. The global financial system is still well short of the theoretical ideal of complete financial markets, but clearly it is moving in that direction. The financial system dominated by market-based finance has likely reinforced the status of the market for financial assets as the most important channel of monetary policy transmission. The market dynamic suggests that gauging the overall effect of monetary policy requires an assessment of broad financial conditions, including policy rates, long-term interest rates and foreign exchange rates.

Management of Finance by the Multinational Companies

The financial objectives of the multinational companies are aimed at measuring the performance on the capital employed. Capital employed is the sum of all assets along with the accumulated reserves for depreciation. The multinational companies, in their financial goals, may recognize that not all operations are directly comparable and state that targets for area profit centers and operations will take into account the nature of the operations and performance plans thereof. Emphasis on asset management by the multinational company at all levels is laid in reference to annual targets for cash generation, capital expenditures, and balance sheet items, including inventory and receivables management. The finance managers of the company draw special attention to the differences between actual cash generating capacity and book results. Each production group and profit center both of product categories and territorial develop net cash-generating capacity for its own requirements and also pools-up sufficient funds for the company to meet its high-priority investment commitments and opportunities. Financial objectives constitute the foundation for making financial decisions for a company. The companies should be able to integrate the financial objectives for both domestic and international business. Financial objectives also constitute the foundation for making financial decisions for a company. For example, in order to protect it against exchange rate fluctuations, it might require managers in overseas subsidiaries to forecast regularly the exchange rates month-by-month for the upcoming six months. On the basis of those forecasts, corporate funds in a currency likely to be substantially depreciated would be utilized before funds in stronger currencies.

In most of the multinational companies the cash management is a centrally organized process. The major goal in this process is to concentrate overall group liquidity as much as possible and to a reasonable extent. Ideally this pooling is done across banks and borders. In a broader sense, cash management comprises the organization of the process of all incoming and outgoing payments in the most efficient way. To achieve this, multinational companies depend on the instruments like bank policy and cash pooling software intelligence. In reality the right mix of organizational and software intelligence probably leads to the best result. The quality of cash pooling can be measured by the gap between the forecasted and the realized cash position of a company. It is observed that the smaller the difference between expectations and reality, the higher the efficiency of cash management. Cash pooling is the standard instrument for efficient cash management. There are two basic concepts available: the notional pooling is organized as interest compensation across the participating bank accounts; alternatively the zero balancing approach requires physical concentration of all cash flows on one concentration account. The latter approach is the most used concept today. A logical further step in cash management is the organization of the payments in a centralized way. Such concepts are expressed as *payment factory* whereby all payments for all connected subsidiaries of a multinational corporate can be managed at a single place or a centralized station. This includes single payments as well as mass payments.

The goal of an international money manager may be to obtain finances for foreign project towards expansion, subsidiaries or strategic alliances with the companies of the host country in a way to maximize the resources availability and lower the after-tax interest costs and foreign exchange losses. The exchange rate parity theory suggests that international differentials in interest costs are offset by changes in foreign exchange rates; that is, the expected value for net financing costs will be equal for all currencies over any given time period, provided foreign exchange markets are efficient. However, the multinational companies are susceptible to the following risks related to money management[4]:

- The political risk of assets being taken over by the host country
- The exchange risk whereby the value of the US dollar changes with reference to the host country currency; and
- The translation risk whereby the corporate financial statements are required by the country specific regulations to be based on historical costs rather than current value.

In some countries, gains and losses from long-term exchange transactions are subject to preferential capital gains tax rates or reserves treatment. Conversely, many countries—Australia, Indonesia, South Africa, and Germany— have no taxes on gains or losses arising from most long-term exchange transactions. Traditionally, foreign investors foresee low opportunity for raising capital locally in the developing countries. However, there may be any inadequacy of the local capital in these countries. It has been experienced in India that often the initial public offers of multinational companies fetched an encouraging response. The Honda Motor Company's issue was oversubscribed 165 times within a span of 72 hours. Similarly, Burroughs Corporation's stock and debenture issue was oversubscribed 30 times.

The financial management also involves significantly the matters of repatriation of funds and profits of a multinational organization. Repatriation may be explained as the return from abroad of the financial assets of an organization or individual. A multinational firm needs to formulate a strategy on remission of dividends from overseas affiliates to headquarters. The international dividend policy is determined by the following factors[5]:

- Tax implications.
- Political risk.
- Foreign exchange risk.
- Age and size of affiliate.
- Availability of funds.

---

[4] Kwang C L and Cluik C Y K: Multinational corporation vs. domestic corporations: International environment factors and determinants of capital structure, Journal of International Business Studies, Summer, 1988, pp 195-218.
[5] Eitemann D, Stonehill A J and Moffett M M: Multinational Business Finance, 7th ed. Addison Wesley, New York, 1995, chapter 19.

- Presence of joint venture partners.

The policy of the Government of India is liberal with regard to the remittance of profits, dividends, royalties etc., but the Government is cautious of excessive remittance while approving foreign investment proposals and collaboration agreements. Thus foreign enterprises have complete freedom for the remittance of profit and repatriation of capital subject to exchange considerations. Remittance falling due under the collaboration agreements will however be subject to the approval of the Reserve Bank of India (RBI)[6]. On the contrary, many multinationals operating in China have started to turn in profits, and, as they become more profitable, they are being frustrated by complex arrangements currently in place to deter repatriation. The strict regulations discourage transfer of funds out of China. Multinational companies operating in China are also restricted from lending intra-company[7].

The United States-Argentina Bilateral Investment Treaty (BIT) came into force in 1994. Under the treaty, U.S. investors enjoy national treatment in all sectors except shipbuilding, fishing, and nuclear power generation. An amendment to the treaty removed mining, except uranium production, from the list of exceptions. The treaty allows arbitration of disputes by the International Center for the Settlement of Investment Disputes (ICSID) or any other arbitration institution mutually agreed by the parties. Several U.S. firms have invoked the provisions of the treaty in on-going disputes with Argentine national or provincial authorities. Under the Convertibility Law of 1991, the exchange rate of the Argentine peso is fixed to the dollar at the rate of one to one, under a currency board type of arrangement called "convertibility." This rate is expected to remain unchanged in the medium term. Argentina has no exchange controls. Foreign investment receives national treatment under Argentine law. Firms need not obtain permission to invest in Argentina. Foreign investors may wholly own a local company and investment in firms whose shares trade on the local stock exchange requires no government approval. There are no restrictions on repatriation of funds[8].

In the countries where political risk may not be an important factor, the repatriation policy will be based on availability and use of funds. For example, if funds are needed in the United Kingdom, headquarters might decide to transfer its retained earnings from a German subsidiary to the United Kingdom rather than transferring funds from the United States. An alternative to this action would be the investment of funds in Euro. In reference to the risk factors discussed above On the basis of the six factors just listed and discussed, a multinational firm may follow either a pooled strategy or a flexible strategy for distribution of earnings generated by foreign affiliates. The pooled strategy refers to a stated policy of remittance of profits to the parent on a regular basis. The flexible strategy leaves the decision on dividends to factors   operating at the time. The flexible strategy permits the parent to make the most viable use of funds *vis-à-vis* its long-term global corporate objectives.

---

[6] Government of India: Ministry of Finance, Foreign investment policy, 2001
[7] Asia Today Online: Corporate dilemma: Profits idle in China, 01 December 2003 www.asiatoday.com.au
[8] Bureau of Economic and Business Affairs: Country Reports on Economic Policies and Trade Practices of Argentina-2001, US Department of State, February 2002

Focus on International Investments

Multinational enterprises are an important part of the international economy. Through international direct investment, they bring substantial benefits to home and host countries in the form of productive capital, managerial and technological know-how, job creation and tax revenues. The investment objectives of a multinational company should reflect the following issues:

- Ensure that the operations of enterprises are in harmony with government policies;
- Strengthen the basis of mutual confidence between enterprises and the societies in which they operate;
- Improve the foreign investment climate; and,
- Enhance contribution of the enterprise to sustainable development.

An investment proposal is a type of business plan, but is designed specifically to meet the information needs of potential investors. It is abridged and focuses on those management, marketing and financial aspects of the company that would make it an attractive investment. There are two stages of an investment proposal that include the selling of the proposal and its review. The process of selling and reviewing should go through a variety of formal and informal procedural follow-up and negotiation. Successful international companies continue to be interested in growth prospects, evaluating a variety of proposals from different sources that potentially could lead to investments abroad. These sources include company employees, unknown host country firms, licensees, distributors, and joint venture partners. The following care need to be taken by the multinational company while drafting and pursuing the investment proposals with the governments or organizations of the host countries:

- Focus the investment proposal specific to the requirements of the country or region
- Develop necessary convergence with the macro policies of the country
- Delineate the approval points and schedules
- Check with all the people whose approval is needed
- Define alternative goals and approaches and keep advised accordingly
- Determine the key contacts for all the aspects of the proposal
- Prospect for selling the proposal at the reasonable bid to optimize long-term gains
- Establish priorities and develop activity schedule accordingly
- It is necessary to be on the competitive edge along with participating bidders and draw defense for the project in terms of project execution and achievements
- Identify any potential competitors of the project and any points of potential resistance, and then establish strategies, or at least mental contingency plans, for dealing with them.
- Measure the proposal against all stated corporate policy objectives
- Write the proposal on the prescribed format with the required information only
- Prepare strong defense for all possible objections on the investment project
- Try to keep the project moving forward at a deliberate speed. Don't let it get stalled with excessive reviewing.

The systematic appraisal and professional management of all capital projects help to ensure that the best choices are made and the best value for money is obtained. It is not enough to be satisfied that investment is justified; it is also necessary to ensure that it produces its planned benefits at minimum costs. This cost includes the ongoing current costs generated by the use of capital asset, as well as the initial capital cost. The appraisal stage involves two separate tasks, preliminary and detailed appraisal. The preliminary appraisal aims to establish whether a sufficiently good prima facie case exists for considering a project in depth. It leads to a recommendation, whether to proceed to the detailed appraisal stage. A detailed appraisal should only be carried out if justified by the outcome of the preliminary appraisal and this leads to a recommendation on whether to proceed further with the project in principle. However, it is necessary for the multinational companies to carefully review their investment proposals before the appraisal at the government or sponsor's level takes place. The review of the investment proposal may be undertaken on considering the following issues:

- Review and describe the financial sector. Append the basic statistics for each, including assets, deposits and borrowings, capital and reserves and profits.
- Describe the expected growth of internal rate of returns and its management criteria.
- Describe the money and capital markets. What are the different instruments, their terms and conditions, etc. Estimate the total market value of each type.
- Describe the foreign exchange regime. Which institutions are authorized to deal in foreign exchange rates during the last five years?
- Is credit allocated or directed by the government or regulatory authorities to particular market segments? Are any subsidized credit schemes in operation?
- Describe how the project fits within government's development objectives and policies for the sector.
- Describe the market for the products and services. Provide historical data and forecasts.
- List the main competitors, both domestic and foreign. Give indications of their volumes and market shares. Are any of them planning expansions? What will be the likely reaction of competitors to this project?
- Review the marketing strategy selected and its justification. Describe preparations for market research, product planning, pricing strategies, distribution, promotional programs, advertising, selling and so forth.
- Describe the structure of the Board and management, including organization charts and CVs for key managerial personnel.
- Describe planned human resources management for the project, including availability of personnel. Also describe relevant laws, regulations and practices. Indicate the cost of staff at all levels.
- Describe proposed training programs and programs for localization, if relevant.
- Provide detailed plans for raising the required capital. Provide assumptions and details of pre-operating expenses and how they will be funded and accounted for.
- Provide projected balance sheet, profit and loss account and cash flow projections for the first three years of operation, stating detailed assumptions, especially rate and spread assumptions.

- Compute various measures of performance as appropriate, such as risk assets to capital, operating ratios, return on assets and return on equity.
- Compute sensitivity analyses at various levels of business relative to the base assumption, and
- Discuss realistically the risks involved in carrying out the project, including market, government regulations, management, labor, competition, system failures and so forth. Then review how these risks will be guarded against.

The review process of a investment proposal is shaped according to the perspectives of the management board of a company. Often the process and philosophy of the review of investment opportunities is leader concentric and it changes dramatically with a new person at the helm. In any event, most companies have a comprehensive system for reviewing investment proposals and all strive to determine whether the investment will provide long-term, lasting benefits for the owners. A framework for evaluation can be laid out considering the variables suggested for review of investment proposal. In the final analysis, the evaluation should provide the cost/benefit effects of the project for the host country, Parent Corporation, and foreign subsidiary.

GLOBALIZATION EFFECTS

Globalization and constituting "Europe of regions" have whittled away many restrictions that international borders have previously placed on mobility. The European Union's internal borders have been opened up both physically and symbolically, and cross-border regions have become places for communication and interaction. This new regionalization process has opened up alternative possibilities and new challenges for tourism development, especially in the northern peripheries of Europe, which often consist of national borderlands[9]. Emerging forms of global governance have produced significant challenges to conventional conceptions of international relations. Educational multilateralism is an area that has been significantly affected by such challenges, but to date there have not been many efforts by education scholars to sum up the relative impact and total effect of the various clusters of change affecting educational multilateralism[10].

Rural non-farm employment (RNFE) has become a topic of major importance in rural development, as by the mid-decade of 2000, RNFE constituted 35 percent of rural incomes in Africa and 50 percent in both Asia and Latin America. The traditional view of RNFE was a sleepy hinterland activity cut off from changes in the national, let alone the global economy. That view was assailed by sweeping changes in rural areas starting with the Green Revolution, then rural urbanization, and lately, by globalization intervening via both trade and modernization of the national economy including the rise of modern retail and processing. Surprisingly, the trade effects are least and the domestic market transformation effects are the

---

[9] Prokkola, Eeva-Kaisa (2007), Cross-border Regionalization and Tourism Development at the Swedish-Finnish Border: "Destination Arctic Circle", *Scandinavian Journal of Hospitality and Tourism*, 7 (2), 120-138
[10] Mundy, Karen (2007), Global governance, educational change, *Comparative Education*, 43 (3), 339-357

strongest as most challenges are posed for zones that are rural and urbanized dense zone RNFE with low-moderate local growth drivers[11].

CHANGING CORPORATE CULTURE

Global enterprises are increasingly concerned about the effects of international expansion on their corporate culture. The multinational companies nurture a set of enterprise-wide mindsets which can maintain a unity of purpose while at the same time successfully adapt practices to diverse local economic and cultural conditions[12]. It is observed that if adequately balanced; individualism-collectivism may be a good source of intercultural fit while building shared leadership protecting mutual values. Such managerial outlook would help in reconfiguring individual and cultural orientations and styles of persons of different origin in the design of management teams to build high levels of social effectiveness in the work environment[13]. However, managing the cross-cultural challenges in the workplace may be made easy by developing a strategic fit of values in the organization with flexibility in individual values and shared personality traits. In the low trust cultures the interpersonal relationship remains obscure and business dealings are largely bureaucratized and tagged with evidences. Such negotiation approaches slow down the process of getting the work done and also may cause retrenchment from the business scenario over time. Thus, it is necessary to identify the right and responsive people who could be relied upon as well as qualify on organizational parameters to build future relationship continuum[14].

Wal-Mart China announced in November 2004 a US$1 million commitment to establish the China Retail Research Center at the Tsinghua University School of Economics and Management[15]. The China Retail Research Center is the first academic institution in China dedicated to research of this country's fast growing retail industry. China's rapidly growing economy continues to create unprecedented opportunities for retail corporations like Wal-Mart. Wal-Mart hopes to contribute to China's economic development. The US$ 1 million donation for establishing China Retail Research Center is an example of Wal-Mart's long term commitment to China. Tsinghua University is a world renowned university with strong academic staff and advanced research capability. Wal-Mart's support for the Center will facilitate China's participation and cooperation in the international retail field and drive the healthy development of the country's retail sector. Tsinghua University is a world renowned university with strong academic staff and advanced research capability. Wal-Mart's support for the Center will facilitate China's participation and cooperation in the international retail field and drive the healthy development of the country's retail sector.

---

[11] Reardon T, Stamoulis K and Pingali P (2007), Rural non-farm employment in developing countries in an era of globalization, *Agricultural Economics*, 37 (1), 173-183

[12] Bellin J B and Pham C T (2007), Global expansion: balancing a uniform performance culture with local conditions, *Strategy and Leadership*, 35 (6), 44-50

[13] Carlos M Rodríguez (2005), Emergence of a third culture- Shared leadership in international strategic alliance, *International Marketing Review*, 22 (1), January, 67-95

[14] Bridgewater Sue et.al (2004), The internationalization process and the role of learning in small service firms, in (Eds)McDonald Frank, Mayer Michael and Buck Trevor, *The process of internalization-Strategic, cultural and policy perspectives*, New cork, NY, Palgrave Macmillan, 2004, 211-231

[15] Wal-Mart China Home Page: http://www.wal-martchina.com/english/news

Depending on the context, cultural industries[16] may also be referred to as "creative industries", "sunrise" or "future oriented industries" in the economic jargon, or content industries in the technological jargon. The notion of cultural industries generally includes printing, publishing and multimedia, audio-visual, phonographic and cinematographic productions, as well as crafts and design. For some countries, this concept also embraces architecture, visual and performing arts, sports, manufacturing of musical instruments, advertising and cultural tourism. Cultural industries add value to contents and generate values for individuals and societies. They are knowledge and labor-intensive, create employment and wealth, nurture creativity — the "raw material" they are made from —, and foster innovation in production and commercialization processes. At the same time, cultural industries are central in promoting and maintaining cultural diversity and in ensuring democratic access to culture. This twofold nature –both cultural and economic – builds up a distinctive profile for cultural industries.

> The corporate philosophy of Canon is *kyosei*. A concise definition of this word would be "Living and working together for the common good," but our definition is broader: "All people, regardless of race, religion or culture, harmoniously living and working together into the future." Unfortunately, the presence of imbalance in our world —in areas such as trade, income levels and the environment— hinders the achievement of *kyosei*. Addressing these imbalances is an ongoing mission, and Canon is doing its part by actively pursuing *kyosei*. True global companies must foster good relations, not only with their customers and the communities in which they operate, but also with nations and the environment. They must also bear the responsibility for the impact of their activities on society. For this reason, Canon's goal is to contribute to the prosperity of the world and the happiness of humanity, which will lead to continuing growth and bring the world closer to achieving *kyosei*. To help attaining sustainable, recycling-oriented societies and fulfill its responsibilities as a good corporate citizen, Canon is realizing the concept of environmentally conscious management. The corporate philosophy of *kyosei* remains as the guiding tool for the employees of the company in their quest to build a group of companies which is appreciated and respected around the world. Canon has pursued diversification and laid a solid base for growth well into the future through one of the world's most comprehensive corporate research and development efforts and with a global network of such facilities capitalizing on expertise in each region, Canon is building the future.

Social institutions play a significant role in nurturing the cultural heritage, which is reflected in the individual behavior. Such institutions include family, education, political structures, and the media affects the ways in which people relate to one another, organize their activities to live in harmony with one another, teach acceptable behavior to succeeding generations, and govern themselves. The status of gender in society, the family, social classes, group behavior, age groups, and how societies define decency and civility are interpreted differently within every culture. Social institutions are a system of regulatory norms and rules of governing actions in pursuit of immediate ends in terms of their conformity with the ultimate common value system of a community. They constitute underlying norms and values making up the common value system of a society. Institutions are intimately related to and derived from the value attitudes common to members of a community. This establishes institutions as primarily moral phenomena, which leads to enforce individual decisions on all

---

[16] Lourdes Arizpe: The Cultural Dimensions of Global Change, UNESCO, Paris, 1996

human needs including economic and business related issues. The primary means for enforcement of norms is moral authority whereby an individual obeys the norm because that individual believes that the norm is good for its own sake.

Long before children enter school, most have already been socialized into play, social values, behaviors, attitudes and linguistic repertoires shaped by the videogames, television (TV) programs and spin-off toys which constitute childhood experience. Childhood culture is an imaginary universe which connects TV programs to movies, videogames, toys, T-shirts, shoes, games, crayons, coloring books, bed linens and towels, pencil cases, lunch boxes, and even wallpaper. Beyond the merchandise transformations of movie or TV program characters, media icons extend to fast food chain or cereal box-top contests and special give-away deals, shopping mall entertainments featuring the recent cartoons Lion King, Ice Age or Spirit from Walt Disney productions and contests such a prize trip to Disney Land to meet the characters create a business platform for the target group though cultural penetrations. TV shapes the child's early age into narrative and consumption styles by being located in the centre of family life (however families may be constituted), and by cross referencing to other narrative forms such as movies, stories, comic books, videogames, music videos (often movie soundtracks), of which toys and teens' popular culture are an integral extension. In that regard TV serves as a kind of clearing house for both the verbal communication and artifacts of consumption. For children, the jump from narrative to commodities from Transformer cartoons to Transformer toys; from Disney cartoons to McDonald's give-aways of characters forms the background cultural tapestry that childhood is experiencing in western countries inculcating the consumption behavior. Besides, parents also show interest in taking their children to a fast-food corner and purchase the latest collectibles, and buy the TV advertised cereal or peanut butter that children insist on to avoid embarrassing conflicts in the supermarket. These everyday consumer and social practices constitute social and material relations between parents and children[17].

Social interactions establish the roles that people play in a society and their authority/responsibility patterns. These roles and patterns are supported by society's institutional framework, which includes, for example, education and marriage. Consider the traditional marriage of an Indian woman which is largely arranged by the parents. The social role assigned to the women is to abide by the norms of the society and culture therein and yield to the social pressures. Social roles are extensively established by culture. For example, a woman can be a wife, a mother, a community leader, and/or an employee. However, what role is preferred in different situations is culture-bound. Most Swiss women consider household work as their primary role that makes them resent modern gadgets and machines. The recent concern of the society about organic products has prompted a new thought process on green consumerism. The research into recent buyers of green products and empirical evidence suggests that consumers most receptive to environmentally oriented marketing appeals are educated women, 30-44, with $30,000-plus household incomes in the United States. It has been observed that women consumers are in the forefront of green purchasing and contribute a considerable share in consumption of green products. They do most of the shopping and although it sounds sexist, they may naturally exhibit a maternal consideration for the health and welfare of the next generation. In conventional marketing, demographics

---

[17] Sonia Livingstone and Ellen Helsper: Advertising Foods to Children: Understanding Promotion In The Context Of Children's Daily Lives, Department of Media and Communications, London School of Economics and Political Science, London, May, 2004

are often a key determinant of intent to buy specific products. But in green marketing, what seem to determine willingness to purchase environmentally conscious products — more than demographics or even levels of concern for a specific environmental issue — are consumers' feelings of being able to act on these issues, or empowerment[18].

The urban and ethnic marketing strategy requires an understanding of in-culture nuances and lifestyle of the marketing segment that a business is trying to reach. While urban marketing is employed to reach Hispanic, Latino, Asian American, and African American markets because of demographic clustering of these subcultures in metropolitan areas, it is also used to reach certain niche markets best found in urban environments. Urban and ethnic marketing strategies integrate consumer marketing solutions including internet and technology aspects within the cultural environment of the host country. An international marketer should evaluate the psychographic and demographic profiles that indicate the target market of urban and ethnic groups. The firm may choose to provide the marketing communication to the target segments close to their lifestyle. The General Motors (GM) Company has made significant contributions to the cultural event on "America on the Move" to exhibit at the Smithsonian's National Museum of American History. GM has appeared to be the largest single donor that ever contributed to a cultural group. This promotional strategy has won the car company naming rights and a prominent place in all promotions[19]. However, museum curators insisted that the car company had no influence on content; there had been accusations that the exhibit was a commercial for GM.

STRENGTHENING SALES SYSTEM FOR EFFECTIVE GLOBALIZATION

Effects of sales drivers, which include territory design, compensation, task performance pattern and cultural interface, need to be optimized at managerial level to inculcate higher perceived values on task management among the salespeople. Higher perceived values on the drivers among salespeople help maximizing the outcome performance in multinational companies. Managers need to focus on removing implied status barriers between sales and a strategic direction to help salespeople to build stronger values to overcome cultural diversities and optimize results. It is also important for the managers to train salespeople towards managing customer emotions, collective competence and ethical complexities[20].

The multinational pharmaceutical companies generally assign weights to different performance objectives and incorporate territory data when establishing these objectives while most salesperson performance evaluations are conducted by the field sales manager who supervises the salesperson. However, some firms involve the manager above the field sales manager in the performance appraisal of salespeople. The behavior control is a consistent predictor of salespeople's performance and effectiveness of the sales units in both the countries. This indicates the importance of proactive monitoring, directing, and evaluating salespeople by the managers. The sales managers may implement such controls effectively by

---

[18] James A. Roberts: Green Consumers in the 1990s: Profile and Implications for Advertising, *Journal of Business Research*, 36(3), 1996, p. 217-231.

[19] Martha Hostetter: The Marketing Of Culture, Gotham Gazette, Internet Edition, October 2003, http://www.gothamgazette.com/article/20031023/1/580

[20] Rajagopal (2007), Sales Management in Developing Countries: A Comparison of Managerial Control Perspectives, Journal of Asia Pacific Business, Vol. 8, No. 3, 2007, 37-61.

establishing coordination, training, and feedback process rather than imposing command and control policy. The training of salesmen should be directed at making them aware of the advantages of adopting relational behaviors and at boosting their capabilities and skills preparatory to an effective implementation of such behaviors.

The systems for controlling and appraising the sales force may be designed for the long term and provide incentives for relational behaviors, if behavior-based control systems are used, and utilize relational performance indicators[21]. The high-performance salespeople have greater commitment to their organizations and their sales managers are more satisfied with their units' sales territory designs. The mangers may need to re-conceptualize the fact that the salespeople should shift from a "hard selling" to a "smart selling" approach. The increasing adoption of a relational approach to customers is therefore fostering a deep-going change in the individual skills set and capabilities of the sales force and, farther upstream, a substantial rethinking of company strategies and policies of selection, training, motivation and control of the sales force.

BUSINESS PARTNERING PROSPECTS

The business partnership strategies should be developed keeping in view the heterogeneity in economic development, culture and institutional modalities that exist in both regions, while seeking globally balanced relations. The relationship should be based on fundamental shared principles and values, which in turn can be translated into clear political messages and a general sustained process of dialogue and cooperation. Relationships can be deepened at the bi-regional, regional or bilateral levels, taking advantages of the special circumstances of country groupings. Building relationships should proceed at different levels and speeds among the countries of the region. Considering the multiplicity of forums it is necessary to focus the trade partnering negotiations at bilateral and multilateral levels and avoid overlap between distinct dialogues and similar initiatives taken at other forums. Bilateral negotiations should be strategically pursued in removing/ reducing the non-tariff and investment barriers. The trade related negotiations among the Latin America-East Asian countries should also focus on the technical norms and standards; rules of origin, anti-dumping, subsidies, countervailing measures; other liberalization and deregulation measures (privatization); sub-regional, regional and hemispheric integration processes; and convergence and divergence between regional integration and multilateral trade regimes. The negotiations should also be dealt on simplifying the customs rules and procedures, including non-transparent and inefficient infrastructures; differing customs; improper application of rules of origin, customs valuation, pre-shipment inspection and import licensing. Customs problems can be especially difficult for small and medium enterprises that have less experience and fewer resources for handling these problems.

The trade integration between most of the largest Central and Eastern European countries and the Euro area is already relatively advanced, while the Baltic countries as well as the South Eastern European countries still have significant scope for integration. The necessity of

---

[21] Shultz R J and Good D J (2000), Impact of Consideration of Future Sales Consequences and Customer Oriented Selling on Long Term Buyer-Seller Relationship, *Journal of Business and Industrial Marketing*, 15 (4), 200-215.

foreign investments in the transition countries is the result of industrial restructuring in post-socialist Eastern Europe and the Baltic countries. New markets, lower production costs and higher profit rates have been the main motivators in investing to the transition countries. Bi-regional multilateral trade need to be encouraged among the Latin America and East Asian countries which would enable them to promote liberalization which is conducive to increasing the traditional trade flows among the participating countries. The bi-regional diplomatic negotiations should be evolved towards developing an action plan aiming at reducing non-tariff barriers and transaction costs, as well as promoting trade and investment opportunities between the two regions. Such a plan could provide concrete goals to be achieved in identified priority areas such as customs procedures, standards, testing, certification and accreditation, public procurement, intellectual property rights and mobility of business people[22].

There is a fast change observed in the world markets resulting in the new emerging markets across the countries. In this century China, India and Latin America and the emerging market-based economies in Eastern Europe promise new opportunities for global trade. The European Union provided an outlet, initially for unskilled-labor intensive products of Central and Eastern European countries and more recently for skilled-labor intensive and technology-based products. Knowledge-intensive imports from the European Union have also contributed to industrial realignment in the Central European countries. The trade liberalization between Eastern and Western European countries has lead to gradual normalization of trade relations, and liberalization within CEFTA has reversed the fall in trade intensity among Central European countries. The emerging markets in the developing countries have shown a strong potential for change in preferences during the late 20th century. In most of the advanced countries the birth rate is declining while it is increasing in the developing countries. The growing trade agreements in the countries indicate some likelihood of success because when the level of tariff and non-tariff barriers is already low, a preferential agreement is more likely to have an adverse impact than a beneficial one. However, the reduction in the tariff barriers, duties and liberalization process worldwide has further given a stimulus to the international marketing across the regional boundaries.

REGIONAL TRADE COOPERATION

Trade alliances among the countries have been stronger as globalization received wider acceptance over the years. The impact of increased global economic integration on national and regional environmental standards has been studied in general by a large number of researchers. International trade alliances are formed among the countries by developing the preferential trade agreements among the trade partners to gain the advantages over tariffs, transfer of factors of production and technology. Tariffs have the effect of attracting foreign direct investment to the benefit of consumers in the host country. As transport costs fall, the incentive to impose tariffs falls and the benefits to cooperation rise. Thus, in a repeated game in which cooperation is limited by a self-enforcement constraint, a reduction in transport costs facilitates free trade.

---

[22] Rajagopal (2007), Dynamics of Growth in Foreign Trade in Transitional Economies: Analysis of European, Latin American and Asian Countries, *Journal of East-West Business*, 13 (4), 37-64.

The Thai threat to the Indian auto component industry is felt as serious by the auto parts manufactures as a result of free trade agreement between India and Thailand. That is the conclusion of consulting agency ICRA Advisory Services, which studied the possible impact of the Indo-Thailand free trade agreement (FTA) on the auto component industry. ICRA, in its report presented to the Automotive Component Manufacturers' Association (ACMA) in January 2004, reveals that there is a significant threat of imports from Thailand and cites three reasons to support its conclusion. Firstly, Thailand enjoys a significant manufacturing cost advantage in relation to India. Secondly, there is surplus capacity available in Thailand that can be used to produce exports. And finally, vehicle manufacturers with a presence in both countries may decide to source specific components from Thailand under the FTA for assembly in India. The study reveals that Indian companies suffer a cost disadvantage of 15-20 percent of the total cost over their Thai counterparts mainly due to the adverse tax structure and higher infrastructure costs. Indian companies have limited opportunities for exports to Thailand, as the purchase strategies of Thai vehicle manufacturers will be dictated by their strong links to Japanese majors. Japanese companies such as Toyota, Honda, Suzuki and Isuzu dominate the Thai auto market[23].

It is to be expected that trading partners and neighbors will try to advance liberalization through regional and bilateral trade agreements. There is an array of such initiatives in progress or contemplated at the present time. A total of 162 regional trade agreements notified under the GATT and the WTO are in force across the countries and about 200 new regional trade formations are anticipated by the end of 2005. Regional or bilateral agreements may bring faster results than the multilateral process, may enable parties to conclude levels of liberalization beyond the multilateral consensus, and may be able to address specific issues that do not register on the multilateral menu. The resulting achievements in trade liberalization can be substantial complements to the WTO system, and they can be important building blocks for future multilateral liberalization. The most powerful economic arguments against regional and bilateral trade agreements are that they can cause trade diversion and trade distortions and ultimately undermine the multilateral system because of their discriminatory nature. In some cases, preferential rules of origin have proven to stifle technological developments, networks and joint manufacturing, and to unduly restrict third-country sourcing, leading to trade diversion. Moreover, they can create obstacles to trade facilitation by increasing administrative complexity at customs. One specific example is the proliferation of different preferential rules of origin a prominent source of trade costs and complexity in today's global marketplace in which companies depend on the rapid delivery of products and components from multiple overseas sources. Such effects are costly to business and detrimental to the regional trading areas. Harmonization and simplification of preferential rules of origin and the accumulation of origin could alleviate some of these obstacles to trade facilitation[24].

---

[23] Raghuvir S: Indo-Thai free trade pact – Thai imports may hit auto components companies, *Business Line*, February 04, 2004.
[24] International Chamber of Commerce: Regional Trade Agreements and the Multilateral Trading System, Document # 103, 2002

NEW DIMENSIONS OF COMPETITIVE GROWTH

In view of the economic development of the countries involved and in their political, social, legal and administrative systems, and with equal respect for the views of all participating countries, future business partnering and economic cooperation between Latin America and East Asian countries may be guided by the following strategies:

General Trade Negotiations

- The countries of each region should exhibit multidimensionality by giving priority to strengthening their relations with one another, through efforts that carry forward on the political, economic and social dimensions, particularly in areas of trade, investment, social development, science and technology, education, culture and institutional development.
- The business partnership strategies should be developed keeping in view the heterogeneity in economic development, culture and institutional modalities that exist in both regions, while seeking globally balanced relations. The relationship should be based on fundamental shared principles and values, which in turn can be translated into clear political messages and a general sustained process of dialogue and cooperation. Relationships can be deepened at the bi-regional level, regional or bilateral levels, taking advantages of the special circumstances of country groupings. Building relationships should proceed at different levels and speeds among the countries of the region.
- Considering the multiplicity of forums, it is necessary to focus the trade partnering negotiations at bilateral and multilateral levels and avoid overlap between distinct dialogues and similar initiatives taken at other forums.
- In order to promote the private and public sectors in both regions to take advantage of trade and investment opportunities, Asia and Pacific and Latin American countries should have a framework for discussing and harmonizing common trade and investment interests.
- Economic issues should be a key part of the cooperation process between the two regions in view of the current low levels of economic exchange and the great potential for expansion. Close and growing economic ties are an important element for recovery and sustained growth in both regions. Both regions should work together to develop priorities, policies and measures in economic cooperation and thus maximize interregional synergy, based on the following principles: (i) closer cooperation and dialogue between government and the private sector, with the latter as the engine of growth; (ii) non-discriminatory liberalization, transparency and open regionalism; and (iii) consistency and compliance with applicable international rules, particularly those of the WTO.
- Increased trade and investment based on open markets and firm adherence to applicable international rules would contribute to early restoration of broad-based economic growth in both regions. The policies should be framed to remove the

existing bottlenecks such as information exchange and knowledge sharing to intensify the bi-regional/ bilateral trade and investment flows

Operational Issues in Business Partnering Model

Bilateral negotiations should be strategically pursued in removing/ reducing the non-tariff and investment barriers. The trade related negotiations among the Latin America-East Asian countries should also focus on the technical norms and standards; rules of origin, anti-dumping, subsidies, countervailing measures; other liberalization and deregulation measures (privatization); sub-regional, regional and hemispheric integration processes; and convergence and divergence between regional integration and multilateral trade regimes. The negotiations should also be dealt on simplifying the customs rules and procedures, including non-transparent and inefficient infrastructures; differing customs; improper application of rules of origin, customs valuation, pre-shipment inspection and import licensing. Customs problems can be especially difficult for small and medium enterprises that have less experience and fewer resources for handling these problems.

Bi-regional multilateral trade need to be encouraged among the Latin America and East Asian countries which would enable them to promote liberalization which is conducive to increasing the traditional trade flows among the participating countries. The bi-regional diplomatic negotiations should be evolved towards developing an action plan aiming at reducing NTBs and transaction costs, as well as promoting trade and investment opportunities between the two regions. Such a plan could provide concrete goals to be achieved in identified priority areas such as: (a) customs procedures, standards, testing, certification and accreditation; (b) public procurement; (c) quarantine and SPS procedures; (d) intellectual property rights; and (e) mobility of business people. The detailed descriptions on the above issues are discussed below:

Customs Procedures

- Accelerated alignment and harmonization of tariff nomenclatures with the World Customs Organization(WCO) standards;
- Accelerated implementation of obligations under the WTO Customs Valuation Agreement;
- Endeavor to start negotiations on customs co-operation and mutual administrative assistance agreements between the Latin American and Asian business partners;
- Promotion of transparency through mutual access to existing databases such as customs duties and nomenclature, tariff quotas, import and export procedures and formalities, rules of origin, customs legislation, etc.;
- Improvement of predictability for the business community through publication, and clarification upon request, of customs regulations and procedures in force taking into account, where appropriate, the relevant international customs Conventions, such as the Kyoto Convention;

- Promotion of standardized and simplified documentation taking into account the existing international standards and the ongoing discussions in various international fora.

Standards, Testing, Certification, Accreditation and Technical Regulations

In supporting and enhancing the bi-regional trade related cooperation in the areas of standards, testing, certification, and accreditation bodies, the deliverables which may need to be considered during evolving the trade policies or tenure agreements are discussed as below:

- Close consultation, where appropriate, in relation to the work of international bodies dealing with standards such as the International Organization for Standards (ISO) and the International Electrotechnical Commission (IEC) and to the WTO –Technical Barriers to Trade(TBT) discussions;
- Work towards the improvement of mutual understanding of each other's systems of testing, accreditation and certification of conformity, and the development and dissemination of information materials on national standards, certification and accreditation procedures in SME friendly format;
- Accelerated alignment of national standards to international standards, ensuring that national standards thus aligned are embodied in national laws and regulations, and periodic reporting thereon;
- Identification of sectors of priority interest with a view to the consideration of entering into Mutual Recognition Arrangements (MARS); and
- Establishing cooperation in the promotion of technical and institutional capacity-building in relation to standards, testing, certification, accreditation and technical regulations, including the exchange of information on existing programs, the identification of possible gaps, and the enhancement of cooperation programs as appropriate.

Public Procurement

The governments of Latin America-East Asian countries may develop a Trade Facilitation Action Plan (TFAP) with a focus providing transparency in public procurement, in particular through exchanging information on public procurement procedures, statistics, and opportunities. The plan may include exchange of information on central government procurement procedures and making them available in a format suitable to the business community; sharing inventory of existing database and promoting mutual cooperation on exploring the technical support on public procurement projects.

Quarantine and Sanitary and Phytosanitary (SPS) Measures

The bi-regional trade agreements should also discuss the issues related to promotion of simplification and rationalization in procedures and documentation considering international best practice, and enhancement of transparency on electronic media. This would help enhancing the trade among the partnering countries in plant genetic engineering and value added trade of flora based products. Such negations would facilitate enhancement of transparency in key quarantine and SPS areas including inspection and approval procedures, quarantine requirements and normal inspection processing time.

Intellectual Property Rights (IPR)

The TFAP should also focus on cooperation in technical, institutional and human capacity-building in relation to IPR awareness and enforcement including exchange of information on existing programs, the identification of possible gaps in these programs, and their enhancement as appropriate.

Mobility of Business People

With a view to facilitating direct business-to-business contacts between the two regions, the negotiating countries should draw administrative measures to examine and report on concerns identified by the business community with respect to formalities for business travel and temporary stay.

Trade in Private Sector

The role of private sector organizations and chambers of commerce can be assumed in the creation of a private sector network linking Asian and Latin American companies. The integration process also involves mutual perceptions that are cultural, with an aim to replace the conventional agreements with contacts among actual business people and the possibility of creating common policies and benefits.

NEW VISIONS OF EMERGING MARKETS

There are many new hybrid business cultures emerging across the countries. Of these, the regional ones are re-emerging through international partnering under the aegis of globalization. The evolution of trade partnerships with the companies of the other countries is a phenomenon that often reflects deep structural changes in the whole economic system of a country. It usually takes a long time to unfold since comparative advantages in international business partnering have long-term gains. Globalization has increased the access to the markets as the remote markets have been reduced following the political and economic changes world-wide. The structural reforms in Latin American countries have broadly focused in five major areas comprising international trade, financial markets, labor markets, and the generation and use of public resources. Consequently the financial development has improved, especially the depth of financial intermediation, private sector participation in banking, and the size and activity of stock markets. The economic integration and structural reforms in Latin America considered that import substitution in manufacturing sector would be synonymous with industrialization, which in turn was seen as the key to development.

The market access has also been improved by growing trade blocks at the regional level. Such accessibility to the markets is further reinforced by reducing the trade barriers through far-reaching business communication strategies, product and market development programs, and customer relations. This situation has given a boost in determining the market opportunities as narrowing the trade barriers helped in deregulating certain sectors of trade such as financial services. However, there may be some exceptions to this common pattern. The global market place equipped with the application of global communications has become the focus of the global business arena that makes the world markets remain open and involve in the fair competitive practices. At the same time the anti-globalization moves also exist in the process of development that protest against the hazards of suppressive strategies of the global companies affecting the regional trade entities. The globalization moves have opened up high comparative advantages in many manufactured goods through partnership deals to explore the business in the emerging economies. They generally display an increasing specialization trend and high consumer values. The leading alliances between the major multinational enterprises may be seen in reference to production, finance, and technology and supply chain along with other complementary activities.

Production sharing is the contemporary global economic trend based on the concepts of comparative advantages that offers economic advantages by stages of the production process. The strategy of production sharing has emerged as a solution to an economic problem in developing countries where the absorption of the surplus manpower in industry is a national economic issue. Consequently, the developing countries turn to the developed countries as major cost effective labor market in order to share production of labor oriented products. Investment in production sharing operations has become an integral part of global efforts to reduce manufacturing costs and has contributed to the accelerated pace of cross-border integration of manufacturing in North America and the Caribbean Basin. Currently, production sharing seems to be a growing practice that helps in building and strengthening the international partnerships with global firms like Volvo, a Swedish automobile company having its manufacturing partners for heavy duty engines in India and Mexico. This practice offers both the developed and developing countries a scope to share their resources and strengths for the mutual benefits of international partnering.

The markets today not only provide the multiple goods and services to the customers but also expose their behavior to the cross-cultural differences and innovations. The specialization of the production process has also brought such cultural changes by business penetrations in the low production skills regions across the countries. The apparel from Asian countries like Indonesia, Korea and all types of consumer goods from China, electronics from Japan and perfumery from France may be some good examples to explain the specialization and cross-cultural sharing of consumer behavior. Conducting business is a creative enterprise and doing it out of one's own country is more demanding. The industry structure varies dramatically across the countries in the world and a global enterprise to strive against odds requires strong adaptation behavior. In the international business, a company needs to best prepare itself to achieve competitive advantage in the marketplace. The international partnering in reference to production technology, co-branding, distribution and retailing may bring a high success to the companies of home country in increasing the market share in the region as well as augmenting the customer value for mutual benefit.

The emergence of virtual shopping and liberalization of economic policies in the developing countries all over the world competition has become like a traditional derby in which many companies participate for neck to neck race. In this business game the rules are subject to change without notice, the prize money may change in short notice, the route and finish line is also likely to change after the race begins, new entrants may join at any time during the race, the racers may form strong alliances, all creative strategies are allowed in the game and the state legislation may change without notice and sometimes with retrospective effect. Hence, to win the race any company should acquire the strategies of outwitting, outmaneuvering and outperforming the competitors. In this process, a company must understand thoroughly all the moves of the rival firms from various sources. The locales of the business rivalry have to be spotted to assess their strengths. Under the given situation it may be necessary for a firm to hold the shoulder of a strong brand to swim across the competition safely enhancing the reach to the markets. To do so, international partnering may prove to be one of the most popular and low risk strategies. The companies of the Latin American region may look into this concept not only for growing their market share in the region, also to acquire long-term sustainability in the international business.

Economic globalization is a new worldwide economic order, in which a majority of nations prescribe to the free enterprise system. The triad market refers to the United States and Canada, Japan and Western European countries. This group of countries accounts for approximately 14 percent of the global population and represents about 70 percent of world gross product and absorbs the major proportion of capital and consumer products. However this may not be uniform for all the companies of the triad region and there may be some exceptions. For many European companies like Volkswagen, Latin America may be a more attractive market than Africa and for a British Chocolate company like Cadbury's; India, Australia, Africa and part of Canada may be a more attractive market than others. Some American companies heavily depend on the Middle-east markets. The relative strengths of Triad partner countries also reflect on their resources allocation and corporate spending on the research and development and strategic alliances in terms of capital tie-ups, joint ventures and technical tie-ups with the multinational companies of the partnering countries. General Motors (GM) has increased its equity stake in Japanese automaker Suzuki to 20 percent in 2000 but has sized down in 2003 as GM reduces its total equity in Isuzu to 12 percent but acquires majority ownership of Isuzu's diesel engine businesses and technologies thereof. The Chevrolet Cruze is launched in Japan in 2001 that has been designed and developed by GM and its alliance partner Suzuki. The Cruze is the first GM vehicle to be built in Japan since the 1930s.

Some of the examples of successful partnering globally and in the Latin American countries may be discussed to emphasize the mutual advantage. In 1997 Telmex, a premier telecommunication company of Mexico and Sprint of USA entered into the joint venture to market long distance service to the growing U.S. Hispanic market. This alliance has aimed at catering to the special needs of this large and influential population by offering conveniently packaged calling plans and products. CIFRA Mexico is a holding company operating in the retail sector through 229 outlets that includes a good number of units under a joint venture agreement with Wal-Mart, a USA retail mammoth, in the fields of goods and services. The association with Wal-Mart helps CIFRA to project global image of its services to the Mexican consumers and sustain the local competition. In another venture one of the largest branded food companies, ConAgra of Canada, entered into business partnering with Sigma Alimentos (Sigma), a leading Mexican refrigerated and frozen food marketer in creation of a frozen foods joint venture. ConAgra Foods has acquired 50 percent of Sigma's frozen processed foods subsidiary, Sigma Alimentos Congelados, S.A. de C.V., as part of the joint venture. Sigma Alimentos retains ownership of the other 50 percent. The frozen processed foods joint venture manufactures markets and distributes Sigma's Mexican frozen brands such as El Cazo Mexicano, Menu del Sol and Sugerencias del Chef products. El Cazo Mexicano is a market leading variety of authentic Mexican frozen prepared food in distribution throughout Mexico. Menu del Sol is a line of authentic Mexican food intended primarily for the American retail market. Sugerencias del Chef consists of pizzas and chicken nuggets, among other products, sold in Mexico's retail and foodservice channels. In addition to Sigma's existing Mexican brands, the new joint venture company will market and distribute ConAgra Foods' Banquet, Healthy Choice and Kid Cuisine products, as well as other ConAgra Foods' frozen products, throughout Mexico and Central America[25].

The international partnering also plays a significant role in research and development in manufacturing sector in Latin America. CamBioTec (the Canada–Latin America Initiative on Biotechnology, Environment and Sustainable Development) was launched in January 1995 by the International Development Research Centre (IDRC) of Canada. The objective of the Initiative is to promote the introduction of biotechnology-based products and applications to respond to critical needs in the agrifood and environmental management sectors of selected Latin American countries. The initiative has targeted four Latin American countries for the initial phase of its work: Argentina, Colombia, Cuba, and Mexico. Together, these countries possess a vibrant biotechnology sector and offer a range of opportunities for the application of biotechnology and for the development of partnerships with Canadian firms and institutions. Besides, Latin American countries have been strengthening development partnerships in Asia since the free trade agreements between Chile and Korea and between Mexico and Japan established in 2003. There also have been enhanced cross-investment and increased trade relations between China and several countries in the region. Latin America offers Japanese investors access to resources and markets that can support the growing needs of the Japanese economy.

The opening up of markets can play an important role in weakening vested interests and reducing economic rents associated with longstanding economic and institutional arrangements. Trade can thus spur improvement in domestic institutions that otherwise would not have been possible. In addition, international agreements can be an important external anchor and catalyst for institutional change by breaking through domestic impediments to reforms. Chile and Mexico provide important role models for the region. Institutional strengthening in both countries has allowed them to establish a successful inflation targeting framework, lower public debt, open the trading regime, and build a strong regulatory and oversight framework for the banking system. The native companies of Latin America to explore the partnerships with the global companies towards developing research and development, co-branding, technology, distribution, production sharing activities, retailing and business consultancy services. Such partnership would prove beneficial not only in

---

[25] ConAgra Foods Inc. Home page http://www.conagrafoods.com/

augmenting the corporate image of the Latin American countries but also capturing higher market share for the products and services in the Latin American markets. The retail partnering with foreign retailing companies would also be a profit worthy proposition for the fast moving consumer goods like dairy products, processed meet, Latin carbonated beverages and the like. The retail size is represented by the pull effect on consumer shopping based on the unique sales proposition of the company, like Wal-Mart's retail philosophy of *every day low prices*. There may also be possibility of engaging the strategic international relationship with two or more companies to cooperate out of mutual need and to share the risk in achieving common objectives. The star alliance in aviation industry and multiple alliances in e-commerce *e.g.* Microsoft, Telmex-Podigy in Mexico as internet service provider company, may be described as the success agents of multiple international partnering strategy. Such alliances would offer opportunities for rapid expansion into new markets, access to new technology and the scope of profit optimization. However, it is advisable that the Latin American companies may do a strategic introspection of their organization before developing the partnership proposals in reference to clarity of partnering value proposition to the customer, its relevance to the end customer and the way the value proposition differentiates the company from its main competitors. However, the challenge for retail management is to generate value for the customer that is distinctive and, at the same time, profitable.

WINDOW ON THE WORLD BUSINESS

There is a fast change observed in the world markets resulting in the new emerging markets across the countries. In this century China, India and Latin America and the emerging marketbased economies in Eastern Europe promise new opportunities for global trade. The Pacific region had shown a time-bending leap in the past four decades as the significant Asian population participated in the rapid transition in response to the global movement of trade and services. Asia may be portrayed as the fastest growing market for the top brands of western companies and at the same time, the Asian companies began penetrating into the western markets at low price-high quality strategy. While the luxury and fashion goods are dominating the Asian and Far-East markets, the specialized products like electronics and automobiles from Asian Markets are trying to capture considerable market share in Europe and North American countries. The emerging markets in the developing countries have shown a strong potential for change in preferences during the late 20th century. In most of the advanced countries, the birth rate is declining while it is increasing in the developing countries. It has been observed that the technology has homogenized the world markets for a variety of customer and industrial needs. The reduction in the tariff barriers, duties and liberalization process worldwide has further given a stimulus to the international marketing across the regional boundaries.

International companies, in order to be better among the competition, get significantly in assessing, monitoring and responding to the global competition by offering competitive values, developing superior brand image and positioning the product appropriately, keeping a broader product line, adjustable price and keeping the quality of the products relatively high. Thus, it may be stated in brief that for competing globally the international companies should configure their marketing operation as discussed above, coordinate effectively with the domestic and neighboring markets and establish linkage of various marketing activities in different regions in order to sustain growing competition. Networks have made integration systems an essential aspect of doing business. Businesses rely on significant integration of servers to address the business needs of division, partners, distributors, and other affiliated groups to achieve efficient information access, enterprise-wide communication, and business process systems automation. Changing composition of world trade has been accompanied by a shift in production structures and the composition of domestic output. In industrial countries, growth in the information technology sector is rapidly changing with technology and services while developing countries are specializing in areas like apparel, metal products and electronics.

The Pacific Rim offers a variety of opportunities for American and European companies for the products and services that range from telecommunication instruments to aircraft seats and banking services and a host of other products. Although it is a competitive market, the region is growing economically cohesive that attracts production sharing possibilities with the industrial countries. The Asian producers outside Japan have gained more than one fourth of the global market share for personal computers. Japan and the Pacific emerging triad comprising Singapore, Taiwan and South Korea provide most of the capital and expertise for the rest of the countries of the region that have enormous labor and natural resources. Hong Kong also contributes significantly for the development of international trade in the Pacific region. The long-term trend in Japan is toward a growing demand for cost-competitive and innovative imports, which represents a significant market opportunity for Canadian exporters. The Asia-Pacific region has been the fastest growing trade block over the past three decades though it had experienced a downturn in 1998 and extended aftershocks. East Asia is the principal export market for American goods. The transpacific trade has grown over 50 percent of its transatlantic trade by the end of the 20th century[26].

SHIFTS IN GLOBAL BUSINESS

There are many new hybrid business cultures emerging across the countries. Of these, the regional ones are re-emerging through international partnering under the aegis of globalization. The evolution of trade partnerships with the companies of the other countries is a phenomenon that often reflects deep structural changes in the whole economic system of a country. It usually takes a long time to unfold since comparative advantages in international business partnering have long-term gains. Globalization has increased the access to the markets as the remote markets have been reduced following the political and economic changes world-wide. The structural reforms in developing countries have broadly focused in five major areas comprising international trade, financial markets, labor markets, and the generation and use of public resources. Consequently the financial development has improved, especially the depth of financial intermediation, private sector participation in banking, and the size and activity of stock markets. The economic integration and structural

---

[26] Government of Canada: Report on Canada's International Market Access Priorities- 2004, Department of Foreign Affairs and International Trade, Opening doors to the world, Chapter 6, 2004.

reforms in Latin America considered that import substitution in manufacturing sector would be synonymous with industrialization, which in turn was seen as the key to development[27].

The market access has also been improved by growing trade blocks at the regional level. Such accessibility to the markets is further reinforced by reducing the trade barriers through far-reaching business communication strategies, product and market development programs, and customer relations. This situation has given a boost in determining the market opportunities as narrowing the trade barriers helped in deregulating certain sectors of trade such as financial services. However, there may be some exceptions to this common pattern. The global market place equipped with the application of global communications has become the focus of the global business arena that makes the world markets remain open and involve in the fair competitive practices. At the same time the anti-globalization moves also exist in the process of development that protest against the hazards of suppressive strategies of the global companies affecting the regional trade entities. The globalization moves have opened up high comparative advantages in many manufactured goods through partnership deals to explore the business in the emerging economies. They generally display an increasing specialization trend and high consumer values. The leading alliances between the major multinational enterprises may be seen in reference to production, finance, and technology and supply chain along with other complementary activities.

Production sharing is the contemporary global economic trend based on the concepts of comparative advantages that offers economic advantages by stages of the production process. The strategy of production sharing has emerged as a solution to an economic problem in developing countries where the absorption of the surplus manpower in industry is a national economic issue. Consequently the developing countries turn to the developed countries as major cost effective labor market in order to share production of labor oriented products. Investment in production sharing operations has become an integral part of global efforts to reduce manufacturing costs and has contributed to the accelerated pace of cross-border integration of manufacturing in North America and the Caribbean Basin. Currently, production sharing seems to be a growing practice that helps in building and strengthening the international partnerships with global firms like Volvo, a Swedish automobile company having its manufacturing partners for heavy duty engines in India and Mexico. This practice offers both the developed and developing countries a scope to share their resources and strengths for the mutual benefits of international partnering.

The markets today not only provide the multiple goods and services to the customers but also expose their behavior to the cross-cultural differences and innovations. The specialization of the production process has also brought such cultural changes by business penetrations in the low production skills regions across the countries. The apparel from Asian countries like Indonesia, Korea and all types of consumer goods from China, electronics from Japan and perfumery from France may be some good examples to explain the specialization and cross-cultural sharing of consumer behavior. Conducting business is a creative enterprise and doing it out of one's own country is more demanding. The industry structure varies dramatically across the countries in the world and a global enterprise to strive against odds requires strong adaptation behavior. In the international business a company needs to best prepare itself to achieve competitive advantage in the marketplace. The international

---

[27] Rajagopal (2005), Pasos clave para hacer crecer nuestros negocios a través de asociaciones con empresas de países desarrollados, *Management Herald*, Argentina, February, 22-23.

partnering in reference to production technology, co-branding, distribution and retailing may bring a high success to the companies of home country in increasing the market share in the region as well as augmenting the customer value for mutual benefit.

The emergence of virtual shopping and liberalization of economic policies in the developing countries all over the world competition has become like a traditional derby in which many companies participate for neck to neck race. In this business game the rules are subject to change without notice, the prize money may change in short notice, the route and finish line is also likely to change after the race begins, new entrants may join at any time during the race, the racers may form strong alliances, all creative strategies are allowed in the game and the state legislation may change without notice and sometimes with retrospective effect. Hence to win the race any company should acquire the strategies of outwitting, outmaneuvering and outperforming the competitors. In this process a company must understand thoroughly all the moves of the rival firms from various sources. The locales of the business rivalry have to be spotted to assess their strengths. Under the given situation it may be necessary for a firm to hold the shoulder of a strong brand to swim across the competitive safely enhancing the reach to the markets. To do so, international partnering may prove to be one of the most popular and low risk strategies. The companies of Latin American region may look into this concept not only for growing their market share in the region but also to acquire long-term sustainability in the international business.

Chapter 10

SHORT CASES ON GLOBALIZATION EFFECT

CASE 1.
RETAIL EXPANSION IN GLOBAL ARENA:
STRATEGIES OF WAL-MART TO SUSTAIN COMPETITION

"We're all working together; that's the secret. And we'll lower the cost of living for everyone, not just in America, but we'll give the world an opportunity to see what it's like to save and have a better lifestyle, a better life for all. We're proud of what we've accomplished; we've just begun."

Sam Walton (1918-1992)

Though once a small-town outfit itself, created by home-spun, Arkansas entrepreneur Sam Walton who never lost the opportunity to extol small-town "values", the "super-store" Wal-Mart has succeeded in transforming the face of small towns around the world. At one time welcomed, whole-heartedly, by towns that considered the coming of Wal-Mart to be a sign of revitalization and modernization, more and more communities these days are very skeptical or downright hostile toward the prospect of the arrival of Wal-Mart. Over the past few years the retail titan has suffered through an avalanche of negative publicity — pertaining to a wide variety of issues—and Wal-Mart has become one of the leading symbols of urban sprawl and small-town downtown decay. The world's largest retailer, with 3,562 Wal-Mart stores and another 500-odd Sam's Club stores in 7 countries racked up over $137 billion in sales in fiscal 1998. The corporation is presently positioning itself so aggressively that a new Wal-Mart or Sam's Club opens every 3 days!

The corporation employed 910,000 employees at the start of 1999. Wal-Mart store sizes continue to increase, with emphasis on the regional "superstore", 150,000 square-feet or larger with a full-fledged retail grocery store an integral part. (For comparison, 150,000 sq. ft. is equivalent to 3-1/3 football fields). The corporation typically seeks market areas where there is a customer base of at least 40,000 and targets small to medium-sized towns in particular. Historically, the corporation avoids big city markets where land prices may be too high and competition from other large retailers much stiffer. Instead, Wal-Mart's strategy has been to locate in peripheral, semi-rural areas or city outskirts where it may draw from a regional clientele.

Sam Walton's dream was simple to be stated as giving people high value at low prices and a warm welcome. Today, Wal-Mart Stores, Inc., employs more than 1.2 million associates worldwide. The company has more than 3,000 stores and offices across the United States and more than 1,000 stores internationally. It has also expanded online with Walmart.com, which is dedicated to bringing Sam Walton's dream to the Internet. Low prices have been the retail culture of the company that kept the consumers loyal to the retail brand. It's also because of the Wal-Mart staff starting with the friendly greeters at the front of every store. Prompt, friendly service is a serious matter at Wal-Mart. Sam Walton said "The secret of successful retailing is to give your customers what they want. And really, if you think about it from your point of view as a customer, you want everything: a wide assortment of good quality merchandise; the lowest possible prices; guaranteed satisfaction with what you buy; friendly, knowledgeable service; convenient hours; free parking; a pleasant shopping experience."

"As Wal-Mart continues to grow into new areas and new mediums our success will always be attributed to our culture. Whether you walk into a Wal-Mart store in your hometown or one across the country while you're on vacation, you can always be assured you're getting low prices and that genuine customer service you've come to expect from us. You'll feel at home in any department of any store..." Sam Walton built Wal-Mart on the revolutionary philosophies of excellence in the workplace, customer service and always having the lowest prices. They have always stayed true to the Three Basic Beliefs Mr. Sam established in 1962:

- Respect for the Individual
- Service to Customers
- Strive for Excellence.

But Wal-Mart has another problem: its image. In America, its giant stores are symbols of "big retail", blamed for the destruction of an entire community. To avoid future growth being constrained by political barriers, Wal-Mart may have to raise its head from Bentonville and worry more about how it is perceived. Unpopularity is hard for Wal-Mart executives to understand. After all, everyday low prices have been good for consumers. And a recent study by McKinsey, a consultancy, credited efficiencies in retailing (mainly Wal-Mart's) to more of America's recent productivity spurt than technology investment. Ultimately, few doubt that Wal-Mart has both the patience and the resources to stay on top. Most of Wal-Mart's overseas problems were avoidable. In the 1990s it made the mistake of taking out its organizational culture across the countries, rather than adapting to local markets. When it moved into Indonesia, it shipped in an entire warehouse on a barge. In Germany, its biggest headache, Wal-Mart was ready neither for the entrenched position of such discounters as Aldi, nor for the inflexibility of suppliers and the strength of trade unions. It had little feel for German shoppers, who care more about price than having their bags packed, or German staff, who hid in the toilets to escape the morning Wal-Mart cheer.

The strategy could be difficult to pull off, since the stronger, lower-price retailers are expanding in a long-term effort to take a bigger share of the retail pie. Having less inventory can certainly help profits, but it's no sure bet. While too much can hurt gross margins, due to added markdowns, too little can limit selection and hurt overall sales. Because expenses are being spread over less revenue, retailers risk hurting operating margins. Of course, the discount retailers that are expanding aggressively could easily overplay their hand. But retailing is much like a zero-sum game, with one player taking share at the expense of another. With consumers running out of steam, they're more likely to choose lower-price formats, to save money. That could translate into a sluggish second half for all but a few retailers.

NEIGHBORHOOD MARKET

Walmart.com is a mostly like Wal-Mart store. It features a great selection, high-quality merchandise, friendly service and, of course, Every Day Low Prices. Their goal is striving to bring to the customers the best shopping experience on the Internet Their office is located near California's Silicon Valley, their heart and spirit are still in Bentonville, Ark., the corporate home of Wal-Mart Stores, Inc., and the town where Sam Walton opened Walton's Five and Dime in 1950. From humble beginnings in northwestern Arkansas, Wal-Mart has grown to become a familiar name in households all over the world. At the heart of Wal-Mart's growth is the unique culture that "Mr. Sam" has built. His business philosophy was based on the simple idea of making the customer No. 1. He believed that by serving the customer's needs first, his business would also serve its associates, shareholders, communities and other stakeholders. The goal of Walmart.com is to bring Mr. Sam's culture and philosophy from Wal-Mart stores to the Internet. Neighborhood Markets offer a convenient shopping experience for customers who need groceries, pharmaceuticals and general merchandise. The neighborhood markets offer a convenient shopping experience for customers who need groceries, pharmaceuticals and general merchandise. Generally, they are located in markets with Wal-Mart Super centers, supplementing a strong food distribution network and providing added convenience while maintaining Wal-Mart's Every Day Low Prices. First opened in 1998, Neighborhood Markets range from 42,000 to 55,000 square feet and feature a wide variety of products, including fresh produce, processed foods, fresh meat and dairy items, health and beauty aids, one-hour photo and traditional photo developing services, drive-through pharmacies, stationery and paper goods, pet supplies, and household chemicals. Neighborhood Markets employ 80-100 associates and offer about 28,000 items

CASE 2.
CANON: STRIVING WITH COMPETITION IN GLOBAL IMAGING MARKET[1]

"The reverberations of technological innovation, exemplified by the IT revolution, continue to be felt around the world. As part of our efforts to assume a No.1 position in all our major

---

[1] This case has been written as the basis for class discussion rather than to illustrate either effective or ineffective handling of an administrative situation of the company.

Author acknowledges the academic contribution of Ms. Olga Garcia (ITESM-CCM 00372979) student of the course on Advanced Selling System and marketing executive of Canon Mexico; Maria Carmen Vega and Eduardo Tamson of the above course in conducting the investigation and presenting the case as a part fulfilment of the course in the January-April 2003 trimester of Graduate Program of ITESM-CCM.

businesses worldwide, we are bolstering our capabilities to swiftly bring products with powerful appeal to our customers. To this end, we are refining our fundamental strengths in networking and imaging technologies, and reinforcing our ability to develop original key components that provide new functions and set new levels of performance... ."

Fujio Mitarai, President and CEO, Canon Inc.

Canon started out as a company with a handful of employees and a burning passion. That company soon became a world-renowned camera maker and is now a global multimedia corporation. However, the origin of their success remains unchanged: the passion of the early years of the company and technological expertise amassed over more than 60 years. Canon pioneered the world's first digital full-color copying machine, and the company has continued to introduce the latest innovations in true color reproduction and high-speed output. Small-diameter toner particles and the four-drum system are just two revolutionary advances in this arena. To stay competitive in today's fast-paced, borderless business world, the company is now stressing compatibility with the newest Windows operating systems and localization around the world for all printing conveniences. Canon has also deployed its strengths in optical and precision technologies to create leading-edge systems and components for the broadcasting, medical, semiconductor production and related industries. Products incorporating key Canon components and technologies are leading the way for industries in the digital era.

Canon's global business development is aimed at benefiting homes, offices and industries throughout the world. The company is implementing its global diversification strategy by establishing a Three Regional Headquarters System, cantering on the Americas, Europe and Japan and Asia. Canon Group consolidated net sales were approximately ¥2,940.1 billion (US$24,501 million) in 2002, of which about 75% was generated outside of Japan. The Canon group has 195 associate companies, with a total of approximately 97,800 employees, are pursuing R&D, production and sales and marketing activities around the world. The company continues targeting initiatives consistent with its goal of becoming a truly excellent global corporation.

The impact of the economic slowdown in the United States and Asian markets was felt during the mid-2001 onwards. While the copier market is mature, particularly the low end, it was affected by Xerox's departure from the SoHo market. It has been estimated that the total monochrome and colour copier market for 2001 has declined by 11% to 1.331 million units, compared to the previous year 2000 for total Western Europe. The study states that the total market for copiers, including analogue and digital, black & white, and colour copiers, declined by 7.5% from 1,501,000 units in 2000 to 1,388,000 units in 2001[2]. Several factors affected growth rates, including poor economic conditions, a change in market strategy by leading vendors, the rapid decline in analogue devices, and the continued displacement of copier units to other segments. Placement decline continues due to an increase in other printer and fax-based MFPs, with platens displacing units from the copier market.

- The digital copier market grew 3% over 2000 as a consequence of vendors shifting from analogue and developing their portfolios with digital introductions.

---

[2] CAP, 15 October 2002 CAP Ventures Estimates for 2001, quoated in Tekrati: Analyst Research News, www.tekrati.com

- 2001 saw a further drop in analogue placements, with an estimated year-over-year decline of 24%.
- 2001 saw growth in multifunction placements, with a rise of 18% over 2000.
- Canon leads the market with a 31% market share in the Western European copier market. Despite losing market share, Xerox holds on to second position with 9%, and Ricoh rose to third with 8%.

The market was impacted by the change in strategy from most vendors. Not only did it create a shift in the product portfolio with more colour and digital introductions, but it also created challenges for the channel as they embraced the digitization of the marketplace and developed the "solutions" side of the business to align with the needs of end users. Colour was the star feature of the year for the copier market, with strong growth in the high end of the workgroup exceeding the forecasts for 2001. The 2001 Western Europe Copier Market Estimate and Summary is the first in a series of reports examining the peripherals markets. The principal competing companies in office equipments segment have re-evaluated their information-technology spending priorities. This has resulted in a greater allocation of financial resources to data storage, particularly disaster recovery, and other security-related products. One consequence of this shift: Spending on office-electronics products, which had already been de-emphasized due to the economic slowdown, became even less of a priority for Corporate America[3]. It may be said that this environment will be less challenging for those companies that can emphasize the service and repair portion of their revenue base. As customers attempt to stretch IT budgets by extending the life of office equipment, the likelihood of breakdowns or malfunctions will increase. However, the office-equipment outfits' service revenues would post a modest growth, even in the absence of any significant economic improvement. Consequently, the profitable companies in this segment will have to balance the dual objectives of maximizing operational efficiencies and maintaining a level of R&D spending sufficient to allow successful product launches. Companies that can pull that off should be able to take additional market share from their less resourceful competitors. In reference to the global economic recovery in 2002, some segments of the software and office equipment industry may outperform in the market. Specific categories such as security, entertainment and customer relationship management (CRM) software are all positioned to do well during a rebound. Within these particular groups, the companies that have leading market share, strong balance sheets, and high profitability could sustain the recession and grow stronger in positioning their brands globally.

The digital cameras got into the close competition in the decade beginning in 2001 with continuous improvement in the technology. The consumers have to use a home printer or upload them to a photo Web site, and wait for prints in the mail, or find a specialty photo shop to send them out for processing at premium prices. Retailers are rushing to outfit their one-hour photo labs with equipment to read the images from your digital camera's memory card. Some are installing stand-alone kiosks with a dedicated printer that churns out prints instantly while stores have also self-service kiosks. In the fray of technology Canon has launched the PowerShot S50 that combines user friendly operations, excellent picture quality, a 5-megapixel image sensor, and a great selection of features into a handy, point-and-shoot-style model.

---

[3] Sam Stovall: Office Equipment - The Time to Pull the Plug, Business Week On line, February 25, 2003.

It would probably be hard to find anyone these days to argue against the idea that all activities of a business should be responsive to customer needs. Successful players need to be market-driven, a concept that broadens customer orientation to other key market actors (distributors, competitors and prescribers) and which implies that superior customer value creation is the responsibility of all individuals across all functions of the organization. Within any reference, market environmental turbulence – technological, economic, ecological and political – will influence future development. These external factors can provide specific opportunities for, or severely limit exploitation of, the company's products. The market oriented firm must therefore develop an environment monitoring system in order to anticipate such changes or to facilitate and accelerate the adoption of corrective actions. When the reference market's technological environment is fast changing, market oriented firms tend to be more technology oriented and are inclined to adopt a proactive behaviour in acquiring new technologies. Similarly, if in the market the driving forces for ecological management are powerful, firms are induced to find cost-effective solutions to environmental ills and to develop green product concepts. Thus, turbulence in the external environment can moderate – enhance or undermine – the strength of the link between market orientation and business performance. Competitors, be they direct and/or substitute competitors, are key market participants and a company's attitude towards them is central to its strategy formulation and understanding of competitive advantage. Competitor orientation includes all the activities involved in acquiring and disseminating information about competitors in the target market. In low-growth or stagnant markets competition tends to be fiercer and a key objective will be to counter rivals' actions. In this competitive climate, the destruction of the adversary can become the primary preoccupation. However, the risk of a strategy based only on warfare marketing is that too much energy is spent on driving rivals away and not enough on satisfying customers' needs. A proper balance between customer and competitor orientations is therefore an essential part of the market orientation concept.

CASE 3.
NESTLÉ : EXPERIENCING GLOBALIZATION BENEFITS[4]

The key factor which drove the early history of the enterprise that would become The Nestlé Company was Henri Nestlé's search for a healthy, economical alternative to breastfeeding for mothers who could not feed their infants at the breast.

After heading towards globalization, Nestlé fairly decentralized its country specific business activities to provide better magnitude and direction to the regional planning and management experts of the company for yielding prolific sale and marketing results. The Swiss headquarters of the company offered the brand names and most of the product concepts and process information prescribed the high quality standards for local managers and maintained a large energetic and business influencing staff. Simultaneously, the individual country organizations of the company took the responsibility and autonomy for optimizing

---

[4] Rajagopal: Serving Auto-stores through Mirror Strategy – A Case of Sales Force Management by Nestlé Mexico, Technological University of Monterrey, ITESM, Mexico City Campus, Discussion Paper, 04-02, pp 1-12, 2002 (extracted text from the full paper).

the sales in the local markets. The company has reviewed its business policies to know how the marketing and sales activities could be managed for higher yields and the strategies that were implemented already had resulted in augmenting the growth in these sectors. The sales force structure of the company has one of the largest treasures of human resources and shoulders greater responsibility of moving the products to the market. The case examines the influential role of the sales force of Nestlé in Mexico from the point of view of responsive retail sales management.

The Company formed by the 1905 merger was called the Nestlé and Anglo-Swiss Milk Company. By the early 1900s, the Company was operating factories in the United States, Britain, Germany and Spain. In 1904, Nestlé added chocolate to its range of food products after reaching an agreement with the Swiss General Chocolate Company. Condensed-milk exports increased rapidly as the Company replaced sales agents with local subsidiary companies. In 1907, the Company began full-scale manufacturing in Australia, its second-largest export market. Warehouses were built in Singapore, Hong Kong, and Bombay to supply to the rapidly growing Asian markets. Most production facilities remained in Europe, however, and the onset of World War I brought severe disruptions. Acquiring raw materials and distributing products became increasingly difficult. Fresh-milk shortages throughout Europe forced factories to sell almost all their supplies to meet the needs of local towns. Nevertheless, the war created tremendous new demand for dairy products, largely in the form of government contracts. To keep up, Nestlé purchased several existing factories in the United States. By war's end, the Company had 40 factories, and its world production had more than doubled since 1914.

Finally, Nestlé management reached the decision to diversify for the first time outside the food industry. In 1974, the Company became a major shareholder in L'Oréal, one of the world's leading makers of cosmetics. After the agreement with L'Oréal in 1974, Nestlé's overall position changed rapidly. Nestlé's rapid growth in the developing world partially offset a slowdown in the Company's traditional markets, but it also carried with it the risks associated with unstable political and economic conditions. To maintain a balance, Nestlé made its second venture outside the food industry by acquiring Alcon Laboratories, Inc., a U.S. manufacturer of pharmaceutical and ophthalmic products. Such diversification of the activities of the company was felt in various ways.

> "Today we find ourselves with a very wide range of activities, all of which have one thing in common: they all contribute to satisfying the requirements of the human body in various ways."
>
> Group Chairman Pierre Liotard-Vogt

Taking such a step in a time of increased competition and shrinking profit margins required boldness and vision. Even more waters for Nestlé. The strategy of Nestlé in 80's was twofold: improve its financial situation through internal adjustments and divestments, and continue its policy of strategic acquisitions. Thus, between 1980 and 1984, the Company divested a number of non-strategic or unprofitable businesses. At the same time, Nestlé managed to put an end to a serious controversy over its marketing of infant formula in the Third World. In 1984, Nestlé's improved bottom line allowed the Company to launch a new round of acquisitions, including a public offer of $3 billion for the American food giant

Carnation. At the time, the takeover, sealed in 1985, was one of the largest in the history of the food industry.

The first half of the 1990s proved to be a favorable time for Nestlé: trade barriers crumbled and world economic markets developed into a series of more or less integrated trading areas. The opening of Central and Eastern Europe, as well as China, and a general trend towards liberalization of direct foreign investment was good news for a company with interests as far-flung and diverse as Nestlé. While progress since then has not been as encouraging, the overall trends remain positive. Consolidation since 1996 has been demonstrated by the acquisition outright of the Italian mineral water concern San Pellegrino (1997), the acquisition of Spillers Pet foods of the UK (1998), and also with the decision to divest the Findus brand in order to concentrate on high added-value frozen food products (1999). Since then, Ralston Purina was acquired (2002) and the pet care business is now joint world leader and known as Nestlé Purina Pet Care. In the same year, the former Perrier Vittel water business was re-named Nestlé Waters, recognizing the fact that the dynamic bottled water business accounts for a growing share of Group sales. In the new millennium, Nestlé is the undisputed leader in the food industry, with more than 470 factories around the world and sales of more than CHF 81 billion. In July 2000, Nestlé launched a Group-wide initiative called GLOBE (Global Business Excellence), aimed at harmonizing and simplifying business process architecture; enabling Nestlé to realize the advantages of a global leader while minimizing the drawbacks of size. There have also been two major acquisitions in North America, both in 2002: in July, Nestlé announced that the U.S. ice cream business was to be merged into Dreyer's, and in August, a USD 2.6bn acquisition was announced of Chef America, Inc., a leading U.S.-based hand-held frozen food product business.

In 2001 Nestlé enhanced its business platform for achieving healthy and sustainable growth and performance by moving forward with its worldwide GLOBE project successfully concluding its MH97 program with an additional saving of CHF 900 million in 2001, bringing the total savings to CHF 4 billion launching three new initiatives in the area of production, trade spend and white collar productivity, and continuing its program of divesting non-core or under-performing businesses. Furthermore, major efforts were undertaken to strengthen the market position of Nestlé's strategic brands and product lines and to extend the availability of Nestlé products to consumers everywhere. Strategically important acquisitions like Ralston Purina, sole ownership of Ice Cream Partners USA and the purchase of Schoeller Holding, as well as several key acquisitions in purified water production demonstrate the Nestlé Group's determination and capacity to broaden its activities in key areas.

In this context, Nestlé announces the purchase of Brazilian chocolate and confectionery manufacturer Garoto S/A in Vila Velha in the State of Espirito Santo. The company operates two plants with a staff of over 2500 people and generates yearly sales of slightly more than CHF 310 million. This acquisition strengthens Nestlé's position on the chocolate market in northern Brazil and gives it access to a complementary range of products. Barring major unforeseen events, Nestlé expects the current year to deliver a continued positive trend for its business. Economic indicators point to an overall acceleration in North America as well as in parts of Europe. Latin America, some isolated areas excepted, appears to be making progress, whilst the economic situation in most of Asia is satisfactory. The Company therefore expects to progress both in sales and profits during 2002.

CASE 4.
ROYAL PHILIPS ELECTRONICS OF
NETHERLANDS – MANAGING THE GLOBAL HOME[5]

The Industry Ambience

Globalization has become an instrument for a whole series of dramatic changes in the international economy. The hyperbole in the media and popular novels that suggests a whirling era of giant companies, shifting money, and hapless governments, often hides the distinctive features of changing markets. One of the most internationalized sectors of the consumer electronics industry is the audio-visual equipments displays one of the highest degrees of concentration across the countries for multinational companies. The consumer electronics have also spread considerably in telecommunication products pushing the entry market economy to the toughest ends. The oligopoly in the market for consumer electronics led the challenge to the multinational companies for evolving strong competitive strategies that help in their survival. In this battle the company began to develop cooperative and alliance strategies for mutual sustenance. Two losing teams in mobile telecommunications entered into loose talks in the summer of 2000 to join forces – for Ericsson to cut its dreadful losses and for Sony to re-enter the global arena in mobile handsets. Serious discussions followed by the end of the year, although real planning for a full-scale joint venture started only after a Memorandum of Understanding had been signed in April 2001. The two companies brought together complementary resources in October 2001and made bold statements at the start[6]. However, in the European market, the electronic companies line, Philips is trying to maintain its brand value over the years despite the global concern for the changing customer preferences. Philips has emerged as one of the popular brands in consumer electronics though it had faced a downside growth in the early 90's.

Time Line of Philips

The foundation of the company was laid in 1891 with an objective of making it as one of the world's biggest electronics companies when Gerard Philips established a production and marketing unit in Eindhoven, the Netherlands, to manufacture incandescent lamps and other electrical products. The company initially focused on making carbon-filament lamps and over the period the developments in new lighting technologies encouraged a steady program of expansion. Accordingly, in 1914 Philips established a research laboratory to study physical and chemical phenomena, so as to further stimulate product innovation. Marketing companies had already been established in the US and France before the First World War, and in Belgium in 1919, and the 1920s saw an explosion in their number. It was at this time that Philips began to protect its innovations with patents, for areas taking in X-ray radiation and

---

[5] Case is based on the information provided in the homepage of Royal Philips Electronics of Netherlands with permission to reproduce/quote for non-commercial purpose. Authored by Rajagopal, Professor of Marketing, ITESM, Mexico City Campus.
[6] Sigurdson Jon: The Sony-Ericsson endeavor, The European Institute of Japanese Study, Working Paper # 190, April 2004, pp 1-45.

radio reception. This marked the beginning of the diversification of its product range. Having introduced a medical X-ray tube in 1918, Philips then became involved in the first experiments in television in 1925. It began producing radios in 1927 and had sold one million by 1932. The first electric shaver was launched in 1939, at which time the Company employed 45,000 people worldwide and had sales of 152 million guilders. The company introduced the Compact Audio Cassette in 1963 and produced its first integrated circuits in 1965. Major contributions in the development of the recording, transmission and reproduction of television pictures, its research work leading to the development of the Plumbicon TV camera tube, and improved phosphors for better picture quality were also among the major milestones of the company. Philips established PolyGram in 1972, and acquired Magnavox (1974) and Signetics (1975) in the United States. Acquisitions in the 1980s included the television business of GTE Sylvania (1981) and the lamps business of Westinghouse (1983). The Compact Disc was launched in 1983, while other landmarks were the production of Philips' 100-millionth TV set in 1984 and 300-millionth Philishave electric shaver in 1995. Despite remarkable achievements, the 1990s was a decade of significant change for Philips as the company carried out a major restructuring program.

> "...Now that our company is back on a more stable footing, it's time to turn our attention to growing our business while maintaining the financial discipline we've instilled in our organization...[7]"
>
> Gerard Kleisterlee
> President and Chief Executive Officer, Royal Philips Electronics

Royal Philips Electronics of the Netherlands (NYSE: PHG, AEX: PHI) is one of the world's biggest electronics companies and Europe's largest, with sales of EUR 29 billion in 2003. It is a global leader in color television sets, lighting, electric shavers, medical diagnostic imaging and patient monitoring, and one-chip TV products. Its 165,300 employees in more than 60 countries are active in the areas of lighting, consumer electronics, domestic appliances, semiconductors, and medical systems. Royal Philips Electronics (NYSE: PHG, AEX: PHI), Sony Corporation(NYSE: SNE) and E Ink Corporation announced in early 2004 the world's first consumer application of an electronic paper display module in Sony's new e-Book reader, LIBRIé, scheduled to go on sale in Japan in late April, 2004. This "first ever" Philips' display utilizes E Ink's revolutionary electronic ink technology which offers a truly paper-like reading experience with contrast that is the same as newsprint[8]. The commercialization of this revolutionary display technology is a result of a strategic collaboration started in 2001 among E Ink Corporation, Toppan Printing and Philips together with Sony. Philips works with Sony to co-develop and customize display solutions for innovative mobile devices. The longstanding partnership has resulted in more than 100 patents between all of the companies in a wide range of innovations including chemistry, electronics and manufacturing processes.

---

[7] Philips News Centre: Philips CEO Updates Market at Credit Suisse First Boston Conference, Press Information, May 05, 2004 www.newscenter.philips.com

[8] Philips New Center: First-Generation Electronic Paper Display from Philips, Sony and E Ink to Be Used in New Electronic Reading Device, Press Information, March 24, 2004.

Current Phase of Growth

The European consumer electronics industry has experienced a dramatic centralization and concentration. The main features of this development are the establishment of a mixed membership design which allows multinational enterprises to become direct members of the European association, a significant shift of competences and resources form national associations to the European organization and the integration of Japanese and Korean firms into the European association[9]. The company manufactures over 2.4 billion incandescent lamps every year, and about 30 million picture tubes. The high technology X-ray equipment is manufactured by the company that helps in conducting 2.5 clinical operations each year across the countries. Philips analyzes the behavioral attributes of customers and psychodynamics in different countries and always focuses on their preferences. For example a customer at the Darty electronics store near Place des Ternes in Paris may be a picky bunch as he picks-up Philips and responds "I'm no specialist, but I trust Philips, it's European." Philips seems to be getting back on track stronger. Brand-name products will always capture their share of affluent consumers. But in the low end of emerging markets, companies should take their cues from local competitors: keep local managers in place, adhere to local standards of quality, and maintain the autonomy—and the cost efficiency—of local operations.

US and European consumer goods companies have hit a wall in their home markets; competition is fierce and growth minimal. But as these companies enter the fast-growing emerging markets of Africa, Asia, and Latin America, they face an equally harsh reality. Philips nearly collapsed in the early 1990s; revenues are barely above where they were 10 years ago. Although profitability has been restored, analysts forecast slow overall growth in the next few years. The effective cost cutting, more efficient manufacturing, and solid sales of chips and flat-panel displays have helped the company to achieve net earnings of $872 million in 2003, on revenues of $36.5 billion. Among the highlights: sales in China soared 34%, and the troubled U.S. consumer electronics unit ended the year with its first quarterly profit in a decade. It has been a long, tough climb for Kleisterlee. Revenues have fallen 23% in the past three years, and the company racked up $5.6 billion in losses in 2001 and 2002. Some 55,000 employees — a quarter of the total when Kleisterlee took over — have been shown the door. And Europe's No. 1 electronics maker still faces questions about its place in an industry dominated by Asian giants such as Sony Corp. and Samsung Electronics[10].

Philips' Consumer Electronics division is playing a key role in the realization of the Connected Planet: a vision that allows consumers to access and enjoy entertainment and information services wherever they are, whenever they want, in an intuitive, spontaneous and instant way. Connected Planet is more than just a concept: already, the first Connected Planet products have been launched, including broadband Internet-connected devices such as the Streamium audio and video entertainment systems, the iPronto digital home 'dashboard' and the DesXcape multifunctional smart display device. These products put consumers in control, and give them maximum freedom of choice in terms of content, time and place. This offers consumers wireless access to their music, video and digital pictures, making it seamlessly accessible at any time and place, in home and on the move. Cooperation with world leaders in

---

[9] Knill C and Lehmkuhi D: The globalization of European interest representation: The case of consumer electronics industry, European University, Division of Political and Social Sciences, Working Paper, San Dominico, Italy, 1997.
[10] Andy Rinehardt: Philips-Back on the Beam, Business Week Online, May 03, 2004.

their specific businesses enables Philips to rapidly expand its portfolio of appealing consumer products and services. For example, through a partnership with Nike, a new category of products has been developed. The companies are combining their athletic and digital technology expertise to develop innovative product solutions, specifically designed for physical activity and training. Furthermore, Philips has formed a number of partnerships with leading telecommunications providers in Europe to help deliver the Connected Planet vision. For example, Philips and their Telecom partners developed a joint approach to consumers for offering consumers a combination of Philips products, such as wireless and broadband Internet appliances, along with the broadband service and installation offered by the Telecom operators. With the combination of seven European Telco partners in total - Telefonica, KPN, British Telecom, Belgacom, France Telecom, Telecom Italia and T-Com - Philips will be able to target a growing base of over seven million consumers in some of the largest European markets with a compelling out of the box broadband entertainment experience.

In this move DDB has been appointed sole global advertising agency of the company. By appointing one advertising agency worldwide, Philips hope to ensure complete consistency for brand positioning and to make the best use of synergies across the five product divisions. Since 1995 the company has made huge investments in brand building across the countries with a common idea linked to its long consumer product's line. In conjunction with DDB and with global media strategy advisers Carat International, we have dedicated our branding efforts to covering the full spectrum of all our products. Whether it be shavers or semiconductors, televisions or toasters, light bulbs or laser modules, *Let's Make Things Better* provides a strong, instantly recognizable campaign platform for all our Philips' products. The tools and approaches determined by the company focus in the business excellence through speed and teamwork (BEST) initiative all are based on these two focal areas and all fit in the improvement cycle- *"Plan - Do - Check - Act"*. Building sustainable development into the business processes is the ultimate opportunity for the company in the industry. Philips aims at delivering true value by focusing on the corporate strengths that include lifestyle, healthcare and enabling technologies.

Case Exhibit 1 - Philips: Corporate ranking by products in world markets

Products	World	Europe
Lighting	1	1
Consumer Electronics (audio/video)	3	1
Monitors (units)	4	3
Shavers	1	1
Steam irons	2	2
Semiconductors	9	4
Color picture tubes	3	1
DVD recorders	1	1
Medical imaging equipment	2	1
Dental care (electric toothbrushes)	2	2

Source: *www.philips.com* 28 April 2004.

Financial Achievements and New Global Thinking

Philips recorded a net income of EUR 550 million (a profit of EUR 0.43 per share) in the first quarter of 2004 versus a loss of EUR 69 million (a loss of EUR 0.05 per share) in the same period previous year. Nominal sales amounted to EUR 6,631 million and increased by 2% over the same period last year. Weaker US dollar and dollar-related currencies had a downward effect of 7%, while various consolidations had a 1% upward effect. Comparable sales increased by 8%, predominantly driven by strong sales growth at Semiconductors and Consumer Electronics. Sales growth at Medical Systems was also solid. Income from operations was a profit of EUR 218 million, an increase compared to first quarter of 2003 of EUR 186 million. The main increase came from improved performance at Semiconductors, supported by higher sales, improved margins, and the benefits of earlier restructurings[11].

Philips has laid new propositions to reap better competitive gains and strengthen their marketing base by building new strategies that help increasing the pace of innovation in the face of stepped up competition by commodity players and breaks down the current organizational structure of customer electronics companies from one focused on product development and manufacturing to a more flexible model that emphasizes sales, marketing and a spirit of cooperative competition allowing for open standards and shared development of new technologies. However, the company relies on alliances and partnerships to expand the customer electronics market beyond its boundaries into new categories that address the changing lifestyle needs of consumers. Philips need to establish the pace of innovation in order to maximize the profit potential inherent in new products, while focusing less energy on products that are quickly becoming commodities. It may be observed that innovative new products like DVD enjoyed record-setting market penetration and yet because of "me too" producers, prices and margins plummeted leaving this technology breakthrough on the commodity floor. At the same time it is necessary to understand that in the process of growing global increased collaboration with competitors is key to maximizing the value of technology investments.

Consumers, in general do not express their deep concern about how the technology works but they intend to buy solutions that enrich their lives. The new plasma-gas technologies are bringing big-screen TVs to small rooms. And smaller LCD screens are popping up in grocery stores, gas stations, minivans, on buses—and just about anywhere else that advertisers and content providers have a captive audience. No matter how fast, or what technologies take off, display screens will muscle their way into every public and private space in the coming years, that the consumer electronic companies are confident about. The relationship between microprocessors and dazzling displays has been gaining importance in recent years.

CASE 5. TANZANIAN TEXTILE INDUSTRY: WEAVING THROUGH THE TURBULENT ECONOMY[12]

Tanzania[13] is one of the most indebted nations in the world and falls into the category of least-developed country. It is situated on the east coast of Africa; the United Republic of Tanzania is one of the world's least developed countries. Tanzania, which includes the islands

---

[11] Philips Information Centre: First quarter results for 2004 www.newscenter.philips.com/ extracted on 29 May 2004.

[12] This case has been written as the basis for class discussion rather than to illustrate either effective or ineffective handling of an administrative situation of the country.

[13] Country information in the cases is based on the report of World Trade Organization: Tanzania-February 2000, Trade Policy Review, Press Release (PRESS/TPRB/128, 21 February 2000).

of Zanzibar and Pemba, became independent in 1961. The Constitution of the United Republic of Tanzania was adopted in 1977 with amendments passed in 1984 and 1992. The Constitution calls for a parliamentary form of government with a separation of powers among the executive, legislative, and judicial branches of government. The economy of country is essentially dependent on agriculture and has a per capita GNP of US$210. Tanzania's GDP has grown over 3% over the past few years and is forecast to grow at even higher rates through 2001. The country has a large debt burden which may be an obstacle to economic development as costs associated with debt servicing prevent the allocation of resources to activities that could serve to improve economic capacity, competitiveness, and increased investment. Because of Tanzania's program of structural reforms and fiscal restraint, it is in line to receive debt relief under the IMF and World Bank's Heavily Indebted Poor Countries (HIPC) program.

The main trading partners of Tanzania are the European Union, Japan, India and Kenya. Its exports are primarily agricultural commodities with coffee, cashew nuts, tobacco and cotton constituting the largest sectors. Tanzania imports mainly machinery, transportation equipment, industrial raw materials, and consumer goods. After the decrease in agricultural production during the past few years, attributable to adverse climatic conditions, food and foodstuffs imports have increased sharply. However, the country is actively pursuing a regional integration strategy. It is a signatory of the Common Market for Eastern and Southern Africa (COMESA) - although it has announced its intention to withdraw - and it is a member of the Southern African Development Community (SADC). Tanzania also aims to strengthen the East African Cooperation (EAC) agreement with neighboring Kenya and Uganda. Under the Lomé Convention, Tanzania receives the full range of aide made available to ACP countries by the European Union, the report notes. As a result, many Tanzanian exports to the EU are exempted from import duties. Likewise, Tanzania's goods enjoy non-reciprocal preferential access to the markets of other developed countries through the Generalized System of Preferences. However, due to Tanzania's limited export capacity, the benefits that the country can reap from these preferential arrangements are minimal. Tanzania has been pursuing an aggressive policy of privatization in conjunction with the support it receives from international financial institutions. The intention of the Government is for all *parastatal* entities to be either privatized or liquidated, although no target date for the completion of this process has been announced. Major privatizations are currently under way in the telecommunications and utility sectors as well as in financial services. Tanzania's lack of enforcement mechanisms for intellectual property infringement is currently being addressed and the Government has indicated that enforcement procedures will be strengthened.

Tanzania faces many challenges and obstacles to its trade and economic development. A statutory body of the country governs imports, customs duties, foreign investment, business licensing, intellectual property, export control, competition policy, and other related matters. The Investment Act of 1997 was enacted to help create an attractive commercial environment, and to provide incentives for inward investment. With a few exceptions, 100% foreign ownership is permitted in most economic activities. A separate statute focuses on investment opportunities in the mineral sector. The Mining Act of 1998 similarly liberalizes opportunities for foreign investment and provides special incentives to investors. The country is a founding Member of the WTO, having signed the Final Act of the Uruguay Round and the Marrakesh Agreement on 15 April 1994. Tanzania grants at least most favored nations (MFN) treatment to all its trading partners. As with other WTO Members, Tanzania has adopted in their entirety the results of the Uruguay Round. As a least developed country, Tanzania benefits from the special and differential treatment provided to the developing countries in the form of exemptions or delayed implementation of certain provisions. Tanzania is not currently involved in any dispute settlement proceeding under the WTO.

Tanzania has been making a concerted effort to create an environment that is conducive both to domestic and foreign investment. In keeping with the Government's desire to promote Tanzanian exports, particularly agricultural products, it has placed emphasis on open markets abroad. Nevertheless, its severely limited export capacity has hindered any significant export-led growth. The recent reform of Tanzania's customs duties has resulted in a simplified five-tier structure with tariff rates of 0%, 5%, 10%, 20%, and 25%. This tariff structure is somewhat escalatory with many processed products facing a higher effective rate of protection (ERP) along the processing chain. Such a tariff structure provides substantial import protection to higher-level processing activities, causing resource misallocation and inflicting higher costs to Tanzanian consumers. The simple average of applied import duties is 16.2%. In addition to import duties, Tanzania introduced a 20% VAT in 1997. Excise taxes are also levied on petroleum, alcoholic and non-alcoholic beverages, and tobacco products. The Government of Tanzania relies heavily on revenues from tariffs and VAT; consequently, there is pressure to maintain revenues through high tariff levels.

At independence in 1961, no large textile factories were operating. Between 1961 and 1968 four mills namely Friendship Textile Mills (1966), Mwanza Textile Mills (1966), Kilimanjaro Textile Corporation (1967) and Tanganyika Dyeing and Weaving Mills (1967) were founded. The textile merchants and traders have also set up small textile factories such as Calico Textile, Moshi Textile and Tanganyika Textile Industries. By 1980 there were over 35 textile manufacturing units both in the public and the private sector. It was government with an intention to use locally produced cotton to launch its industrialization campaign by processing mot of the local produce. The aim was to enhance the value added cotton-based exports, reduce dependency on imported clothing, save foreign exchange and create employment. The textile sector was the third contributor to the government revenue through various taxes and as the largest exporter of manufactured goods in the country. However, various problems experienced by textile industries in the late 1980's led to the collapse of the sector to the extent that in 1996 only two industries were operating out of 35 textile mills. These were Friendship Textile Mills and Sunflag Tanzania Limited. The root causes that have been attributed to the collapse of the textile industry include:

- Poor management and financial mismanagement
- High operating costs, high power tariffs, as well as unfavorable taxation policies.
- High level of foreign debts and currency devaluation
- Poor and outdated technology
- Unfair competition from substandard imports as well as high degree of tax evasion by importers.
- Negative export incentives.
- Combined effect of the results of both prolonged and poor production on financial performance
- Management problems resulted towards massive labor redundancies and

- unprecedented idle capacities

Tanzania produces raw cotton and textiles. Cotton is the fifth largest agricultural export commodity contributing 3% of total exports in 2000 after coffee (15%), raw cashew nut (9%), tobacco (7%) and tea (6%). However, the textile industry that was vibrant in the 1970's has lagged behind after market liberalization. This situation forced the government to sell ginneries and textile industries that were previously under public ownership and management in order to revamp the sector. As a result, Urafiki, Ubungo, Mwanza and Musoma textile industries are all under new ownership. Production of textiles was 74,000 sq. metres in 2000 compared with 50,000 sq. metres. in 1999; an increase of 48%. Private textile industries such as Sunflag and A-T Textiles located in Arusha as well as KTM of Dar Es Salaam have been operating efficiently and currently are the largest contributor to the growth of the textile sector. Two of the companies have since been able to take advantage of the African Growth Opportunity Act (AGOA) and have started shipping textile products to USA this year. The opportunities available in the textile sector are related to the AGOA and the capitalization process that will be undertaken by the private owners.

The textile industry in the country is primarily engaged in production and procurement of natural raw materials, i.e., cotton, silk, wool etc. The manufacturing activity is oriented towards primary utilization/processing industries, spinning of yarns, weaving of fabrics, knitting of fabrics, dyeing and finishing of fabrics and manufacture of apparel and other textile end products. During its peak in the 1970's to early 80's the textile industry provided employment to over 35,000 people. The total investment was in excess of US$ 500 million. Currently, the Government has undertaken measures to revive the textile sector through improved government policies including macroeconomic policies. Consequently, most of the public sector textile mills have been privatized and some of the privatized mills are in operation now after new owners (investors) had undertaken rehabilitation and modernization of the industries *viz.* Tanzania – China Textile Mills, Ubungo Spinning Mill, Blanket and Textile Manufacturer, Morogoro Canvas Mills, etc. High production in the textile sector has been witnessed since the first quarter of 1999. The growth of production has increased from 31 million square meters in 1995 to 84 million square meters in 2001.

The principal markets for Tanzania textile exports are European (E.EC) Union, USA, India, Japan, China and Switzerland. The major barriers in the export market is the quality as well as supply constraints. The free export to USA market through AGOA (African Growth and Opportunity Act) have provided a unique opportunity to the Tanzania textile sector but the problem is to reach a requisite standard and quality because maintaining the standard of cotton is a big barrier. Among various constraints, low production of cotton and high costs of operation such as power tariff, transport, etc., may result in supply constraints which will have a negative impact toward achievement of the country's goals. Such problems have boosted the imports of woven and knitted fabrics, second-hand clothes, machinery yarn (synthetic and cotton) from China, India, Europe and USA. Since the domestic industry was performing below capacity, the demand gap has been covered by imports. However, the industry has been experiencing a negative impact due to unfair competition caused by import of substandard clothing materials from Asia.

Case 6.
ING Commercial America:
Global Expansion Moves

ING is one of the largest financial services companies among the prominent global firms, offering banking, insurance and asset management in over 50 countries. It has spread its business to 60 million private, corporate and institutional clients in 60 countries with a workforce of over 115,000 people as in 2003. ING was founded in 1991 by a merger between *Nationale-Nederlanden* and *NMB Postbank Group* to become the first *bancassurer* of the Netherlands. During the past 15 years ING has become multinational with very diverse international activities. The company holds insurance operations and asset-management activities in the Americas. It is well-established in the United States with retirement services, annuities and life insurances and has leading positions in non-life insurance in Canada and Mexico. Furthermore, the company is active in Chile, Brazil and Peru. The operating profits for the company in the Americas have been increasing in €1310 million in 2003 to €1669 in 2004 before tax. In 2004, ING successfully repositioned itself in the wholesale banking market. The insurance business of the company in the Netherlands introduced a far-reaching plan to improve its customer service, with positive results so far. The business lines of the company further sharpened their focus on profitable top line growth, managing costs managing risks and showing good bottom-line results. These four pillars are all equally important to generate above-average returns for shareholders.

The good financial results of ING Group in 2004 underline the efforts of the business lines undertaken in these areas during 2003. Operating net profit went up by 33.0%, revenue growth was 4.7% as compared to a growth in operating expenditure of 2.6%. ING Group renewed its overall strategic direction in 2004 with an objective to create value, which means outperforming peers when it comes to shareholder return. In order to achieve this, the company focused on good execution skills in its core businesses and actively managed the business portfolio. Implementing these priorities allowed the company to lay the foundations for profitable growth. In Mexico, ING Global Pensions looked at broadening the distribution of life insurance via tied agents. Furthermore, ING and its joint-venture partner *SulAmerica* began offering pensions and life products in Brazil in the wake of the reform of the pension system.

Global Operational Expansions

ING has diversified business activities in developing markets which offer a broad range of services in the fields of banking, insurance and asset management and has made its identity obvious in Asia/Pacific, Latin America and Central Europe amidst the competing local and multinational companies. In Latin America, ING is the largest insurer in Mexico and has important businesses in Chile and Brazil. ING has a two-tier board structure consisting of the Executive Board and the Supervisory Board. The company has considered implementing a two-tier board as the best way to create the proper checks and balances in the company. The Executive Board is responsible for day-to-day management of the business and long-term strategy. The Supervisory Board is responsible for controlling management performance and advising the Executive Board. The Supervisory Board is made exclusively of outside directors. In 2004 ING introduced a new structure of six business lines as illustrated in Figure 1. The focus of these business liens is customer oriented which is performed through consultative sales. The operational areas of business lines of the company are discussed in the following section.

- *Insurance Europe*
  Operates the insurance activities in the Netherlands, Belgium, Spain, Greece and Central Europe and asset-management activities in Europe. In these countries we offer life insurance with special attention for pensions. In the Netherlands and Belgium we also offer non-life insurance.

- *Insurance Americas*
  This business line of the company holds insurance operations and asset-management activities in the Americas. It is well established in the US with retirement services, annuities and life insurances and has leading positions in non-life insurance in Canada and Mexico. Furthermore, we are active in Chile, Brazil and Peru.

- *Insurance Asia/Pacific*
  The company undertakes the life insurance operations and asset/wealth management activities in Asia/Pacific through this line of business. It has well established positions in Australia, Hong Kong, Japan, Korea, Malaysia and Taiwan. The activities in China, India, and Thailand are future growth engines for ING.

- *Wholesale Banking*
  The global wholesale banking operations are the core activity performed by the company under this business line. It has five divisions including clients, network, products, corporate finance and equity markets, and financial markets. It offers a full range of products large accounts and individual in the home markets of Benelux countries and elsewhere it operates a more selective and focused client and product approach.

- *Retail Banking*
  ING also performs the retail banking activities in the Netherlands, Belgium, Poland, Romania and India and offers private banking in selected markets, for instance in the Netherlands, Belgium, Switzerland, Luxembourg and several countries in Asia.

- *ING Direct*
  ING Direct operates direct retail-banking activities for individual clients in Australia, Canada, France, Germany, Austria, Italy, Spain, United Kingdom and the United States. Main products offered are savings and mortgages. A separate activity performed by this business line is ING Card, which manages a credit-card portfolio within the Benelux countries.

A clear client focus and strong business logic are the key elements in this structure. ING has a management structure based on the principles of transparency, accountability and client focus. The activities of the company are organized along major functional business lines which include direct banking, risk, management, developing markets and retirement fund management. These business lines are performed through managing for value, customer satisfaction, managing cost, managing risk and adherence to performance driven culture. The functional streams of the company with direct reporting lines enable quick decision-making and foster personal empowerment and strong accountability. Customer satisfaction is at the core of corporate strategy, which is reflected in the mission statement of the company as *setting the standard in helping our customers manage their financial future.* The customer satisfaction is continuously measured by the client services department of the company and revises performance targets periodically. This is done by the company in order to establish the credibility in managing the investments made by the customers, by way of gaining mutual trust.

CASE 7. DAIMLER CHRYSLER:
COMPETING WITH GLOBAL AUTOMOTIVE INDUSTRY

In recent years, the number of car makes and models has grown in every product segment. At the same time, the once vast gaps in quality, performance, safety, fuel efficiency, and amenities have all closed significantly. Although variations in quality and performance persist, the remaining possibilities for differentiating products, and thus achieving competitive advantage, revolve around styling and other intangibles and the emotional benefits they confer on the customer. Marketers have long understood that consumers are influenced by the emotional connections they form with products— and with manufacturers, dealers, and other owners. The consumers attach significantly greater importance to relationship and emotional benefits than to a car's functional attributes at least when they meet minimum standards or don't fall far short of the competition. Nevertheless, those intangible benefits are the weakest links in the automakers' performance ratings[14]. Customers view tends to reflect the conventional wisdom in product design. The perceived value is created when companies use customers as a sounding board for their own ideas. As the auto critiques have opined that few customers would have been able to articulate the minivan concept beyond vague musings and now as the case may be with the PT Cruiser of Chrysler which appends the idea of vintage look and modern comforts together with the car.

An automotive company must understand the factors that affect the performance of a network to restructure it effectively. Of these the first and foremost is geographic distribution: outlets must be close to customers but not too close to one another. In reality, neither condition is met. The once robust networks of the Big Three—GM, Ford, and DaimlerChrysler—were built largely in the 1920s, 1930s, and 1950s, for example, and haven't been adapted to demographic shifts: these networks are too tightly clustered in urban areas and too sparse in the suburbs. The second factor is the skill of the dealers, for some are much better at running their businesses than others are. Indeed, the experience of one major manufacturer suggests that, adjusting for market size and location, dealers in the top quartile sell three to four times as many vehicles as dealers in the bottom quartile. The power and profit in the supply chain is still maintained by the major automobile manufacturers like the U.S. "Big Three" (Ford, GM, DaimlerChrysler), as well as foreign competition like Honda, Toyota, and Nissan, to name a few. Even smaller manufacturing companies, which control very little of the global market share of car manufacturers, still dominate their own supply chains.

---

[14] Anjan Chatterjee, Matthew E. Jauchius, Hans-Werner Kaas, and Aurobind Satpathy: Revving-up Auto Branding, *The McKinsey Quarterly*, Number 1, 2002.

Movement in the car manufacturing industry is taking place on various levels. Consolidation, supply chain integration and globalization are reconfiguring the automotive landscape, while mobility problems are pushing the car industry into rethinking the very existence of the business and the concept of transport. Numerous trends on various levels are currently reshaping the automotive industry. Some trends will have a lasting impact. Other trends will be short lived. The source of many of these trends is the changing environment in which the car is operating. Changing world demographics, newly emerging economies, increasing environmental legislation, diminishing protectionism and shifting subsidies are at the origin of many trends as the car manufacturers are forced to adapt to the profoundly changing surroundings. Challenges within the car companies themselves, such as declining profitability and mounting over-capacity are also a contributory factor.

The Time Ahead

The worldwide upswing that had been hoped for in the middle of 2003 did not materialize. In the euro zone, economic expectations were further dampened by the very significant appreciation of the euro against the US dollar. Sales of automobiles in the United States in the second quarter were lower than in the second quarter of 2002. Even lower unit sales were only avoided by offering customers higher incentives. Demand also declined in the automotive markets of Western Europe.

However, in the beginning weeks of the next quarter, important leading indicators indicated a potential towards an improvement in economic prospects. On this basis we expected a gradual stabilization in demand for passenger cars and light trucks in the United States during the second half of the year. In Western Europe, however, we expected demand for passenger cars to remain at a low level for some time. Also, in the market for medium and heavy trucks no signs were seen of a sustainable upturn. Mercedes Car Group expected to attain in 2003 similar high levels of the previous year in terms of unit sales, revenues and earnings, despite the continuation of difficult market conditions. Chrysler Group had taken further steps to improve and stabilize its earnings in the second half of the year, particularly in the areas of marketing and sales, and had implemented substantial additional cost savings. For the year as a whole, Chrysler Group is still strove to achieve a slightly positive operating profit on an ongoing basis. However, there were substantial risks due to the potential development of the competitive environment in the United States.

The Commercial Vehicles division expected to achieve a significant improvement in its operating profit compared with 2002, as a result of new attractive models and the effects of the ongoing efficiency-improving activities. The Services division had planned that the operating profit from its ongoing business for the full year would be higher than in 2002, partly due to more favorable refinancing conditions. With difficult market conditions particularly in Japan and the United States, the same contribution was not expected from MMC to our results as in the last year. MMC will continue to implement its turnaround and will push forward with new initiatives to improve sales. The DaimlerChrysler Group had been looking ahead to generate revenues of approximately EUR 135 billion in full-year 2003, lower than the previous year (2002: EUR 149.6 billion), primarily due to the appreciation of the Euro against the US dollar but also as a result of lower unit sales.

BIOGRAPHY OF THE AUTHOR

Dr. Rajagopal is Professor of Marketing at Monterrey Institute of Technology and Higher Education (ITESM), Mexico City Campus and Fellow of the Royal Society for Encouragement of Arts, Manufacture and Commerce, London. He has been listed with biography in Who's Who in the World, 2008. He teaches Competitor Analysis, Marketing Strategy, Advance Selling Systems, International Marketing, Services Marketing, New Product Development and other subjects of contemporary interest to the students of undergraduate, graduate and doctoral programs. Dr. Rajagopal holds masters and doctoral degrees in Economics and Marketing respectively from Ravishankar University in India. His specialization is in the fields of Marketing Management, Rural Economic Linkages and Development Economics. He has to his credit 27 books on marketing and rural development themes and over 300 research contributions that include published research papers in national and international refereed journals. He has imparted training to senior executives and has conducted 55 management development programs. His research contributions have been recognized by the Government of Mexico and he has been awarded the status of National Researcher (SNI-level II) since 2004

INDEX

B

C

D

E

H

M

N

O

S

X

Y

Z

3 5282 00668 8678